The Story of Zen

Richard Bryan McDaniel

Foreword by Genjo Marinello Roshi

Afterword by Dosho Port Roshi

THE STORY OF ZEN
Richard Bryan McDaniel

Text © Richard Bryan McDaniel, 2019
All rights reserved

Cover photo: Shannon Starkey
    Mountain Gate-Sanmonji zendo, Ojo Sarco, New Mexico
Author photo: Chelsea Stevens
Editing & Design: John H. Negru

Published by
The Sumeru Press Inc.
Ottawa, ON
Canada

ISBN 978-1-896559-51-3 (pbk.).
ISBN 978-1-896559-52-0 (epub)

LIBRARY AND ARCHIVES CANADA CATALOGUING IN PUBLICATION

Title: The story of Zen / Richard Bryan McDaniel ; foreword by Genjo
   Marinello Roshi ; afterword by Dosho Port Roshi.
Names: McDaniel, Richard Bryan, author.
Description: Includes bibliographical references.
Identifiers: Canadiana (print) 20190160845 | Canadiana (ebook)
   20190160896 | ISBN 9781896559513 (softcover) | ISBN 9781896559520
   (HTML)
Subjects: LCSH: Zen Buddhism—History.
Classification: LCC BQ9262.3 .M33 2019 | DDC 294.3/92709—dc23

For more information about The Sumeru Press
visit us at *www.sumeru-books.com*

Contents

5   Foreword
13 Preface

Part One
21 The Buddha
55 What He Taught
85 The Mahayana
105 Daoism

Part Two
131 Chan
167 Zen
199 Encounter
229 Out of Asia

Part Three
263 The Zen Boom
311 Things Fall Apart
343 Revisioning
377 Contemporary Voices

423 Epilogue at Springwater
439 Afterword

445 Acknowledgments
449 Bibliography
455 Glossary
463 About the Author

Foreword

Genjo Marinello Roshi
Chobo-Ji, Seattle, WA

Rick McDaniel has done something extraordinary by writing a book that traverses the evolution of Zen Buddhism from the historical Buddha to the present. Relating moving traditional and mythological stories and compelling personal accounts, and without sugarcoating pitfalls and shortcomings, he brings the whole scope of the tradition alive for the reader. As *The Story of Zen* chronicles the flowering of Buddhism from India through Asia to North America, you can immerse yourself in myths surrounding the previous lives and birth of the Buddha, his core teachings and career, his struggles, insights, the lore around his death, and how his *sangha* (community) struggled to survive without him. Reading further you will find a succinct account of the beginning of both the Theravada and Mahayana branches of this world religion, and watch how Mahayana blends with Daoism and some elements of Confucianism to become the foundation of the Zen tradition known as Chan in 5th century China. Within a few centuries, Chan explodes in a manifestation of human genius as great as the much later European Renaissance. Reading on you will learn how Chan leaps to other countries in Asia and is called Zen in Japan. In the 12th century, two principle branches of Chan Buddhism take root in Japan as the Soto and Rinzai schools. Early in the 20th century Zen makes its way to North America and Europe, and the very first seeds of American sangha begin to take root with the works of D.T. Suzuki and Nyogen Senzaki. Arriving at post-war America, *The Story of Zen* explores how Beat Zen and Alan Watts begin to popularize the tradition. Then the major Japanese emissaries such as Shunryu Suzuki, Eido Shimano, Taizan Maezumi, and Joshu Sasaki start Zen centers in San Francisco, New York City and Los Angeles. What follows is an unhealthy idealization of Zen masters who, in turn, abuse their roles and tragically end up harming the very students whom they are meant to nurture and serve. Today, after much consternation and major breakups, a healthy revisioning and reseeding is taking place, and the book concludes with a look at the next generation of American Zen teachers.

When I read *The Story of Zen*, it is like reviewing my forty-four years of Zen practice. I began my study of Buddhism in 1972 when I first read the Buddha's *Sermon at Benares* in my college freshman English class. I took my first course in Buddhism at UCLA in 1975, and read *What the Buddha Taught* by Walpola Rahula. I must have underlined at least half the lines in this book, and I was hooked. *The Story of Zen* recaptures all the fundamental points of Rahula's book and then takes the story much father.

I had my first encounter with Zen when I met Brian Daizen Victoria, a Soto Zen priest who was at that time a UCLA graduate student in East Asian studies. He turned me on to meditation, and I soon devoured the following books: *Zen Flesh Zen Bones* by Paul Reps and Nyogen Senzaki; *Three Pillars of Zen* by Philip Kapleau; *Zen Mind, Beginner's Mind* by Shunryu Suzuki; and *Zen and Japanese Culture* by D.T. Suzuki. As Rick reports, these authors were of seminal importance to my generation. After I graduated, I moved to Seattle and hooked up with the Seattle Zen Center. I did my first Zen sesshin with Dr. Glenn Kangan Webb and the Soto Zen Master Hirano Katsufumi Osho-san in the summer of 1977. After three days of intense hardship, I had my first breakthrough realizing that my limited idea of self was really only a transparent phantom, seamless with all of reality. *The Story of Zen* explores how these breakthrough experiences (*kensho*) can both aid and fool our egos about enlightenment. For one thing, "enlightenment" is not a static condition: sometimes we are clear, other times we are not; sometimes we feel like a nut and other times we don't. Moreover, seeking an emotional catharsis or a breakthrough experience can get in our way of awakening, and we must remember that awakening is a process of natural unfolding; we never arrive.

After our small Zen center hosted the Dalai Lama in October 1979, I petitioned to be a Zen *unsui* (Zen priest in training) and did my *tokudo* (ordination ceremony) the following October. My ordination teacher was the recently-arrived Rinzai Osho, Genki Takabayashi. I traveled to Ryutaku-Ji in1981 where I trained with Sochu Suzuki Roshi and met both Soen Nakagawa Roshi and Eido Shimano. Noticing that *The Story of Zen* refers to Ryutaku-Ji many times, I realize that this Japanese temple has been one of the most important stepping-stones for bringing Zen to America. Besides my apprenticeship with Genki Takabayashi, I trained briefly with Joshu Sasaki and completed my koan study with Eido Shimano, who named me as one of his Dharma Heirs in 2008.

As Rick describes in the chapter "Things Fall Apart," these two Zen teachers of mine, Joshu Sasaki and Eido Shimano, abused their authority and repeatedly harmed their own sanghas more than any other first-generation founders. In 2010, it became clear to the whole world that Eido Shimano had not stopped his abuse of his position of authority with students, as many others and I had foolishly supposed for some years. Upon hearing these new revelations, I was the first member of the Zen Studies Society (ZSS) Board to ask him to resign. I also asked him to get treatment for his sexual addiction, which he declined. In December of 2010, I asked members of the American Zen Teachers Association to write letters to Eido Shimano and ZSS asking that he permanently desist from all teaching roles. When it was clear to me that Eido was trying to teach again after his official retirement and I thought the ZSS board was not putting enough restrictions on him, I resigned from the ZSS board in early 2011.

Two of my most significant teachers were responsible for the worst kinds of transgressions one could make with their own sangha, and my beloved ordination teacher also had problems. Sickened and discouraged I persevered and began work with the late Roshi Bernie Glassman. The "Revisioning" chapter of *The Story of Zen* covers Bernie's Three Tenets and his Zen Peacemaker Bearing Witness retreats. So far, I have done five of these retreats: three in Poland; one in Rwanda; and one in South Dakota. In Seattle I have worked to establish a Zen residential practice center, Chobo-Ji, with appropriate and workable checks and balances, and community service and social justice outreach. Here the only thing separating ordained from lay followers of the way is the robes they wear and the degree of commitment they have made to Zen training with the intention of perpetuating this slowly evolving form for future generations.

I consider myself a teacher of Zen form, but not a teacher of Zen; the practice is the teacher. I have no disciples, and want nothing to do with being a Zen guru. On the other hand, as a senior, and hopefully a relatively mature follower of the way, I've dedicated my life to propagating this form for future generations. The greatest gratification I've had as a Zen teacher is to serve as a catalyst for fellow followers of the way to see deeply into their original nature and more fully live our Great Vow to care for all beings great and small, animate and inanimate.

Most of the books, teachers, and all of the most significant experiences in my life related to Zen are covered in *The Story of Zen*. Now if someone asks me for just one reference book on Zen, this is the one I will recommend. Rick has taken themes he has examined in his previous books – *Zen Masters of China*, *Zen Masters of Japan*, *The Third Step East*, and *Cypress Trees in the Garden* – and synthesized them into one volume that gets to the heart of the transmission of this tradition from East to West. I've only met Rick once, when he traveled through Seattle and visited Chobo-Ji, but I can tell you that he has a better grasp of the ups and downs of this stream of Buddhism than anyone else I have met. He has interviewed more than a hundred Zen teachers trying to understand and convey the richness of this tradition with which he long has been associated and practiced. In my over forty years of training there is almost nothing here that I haven't been previously exposed to, but I was constantly amazed with how he wove it into one seamless tapestry, filling in gaps in my own exploration and understanding. Therefore, I'm delighted by and grateful for his efforts.

After reading the chapter "Things Fall Apart," one may feel tempted to close the book, abandoning any hope that organizational Zen can move forward in a positive way. Every form of human development individually or collectively will have bumps and falls. The last two chapters, "Revisioning" and "Contemporary Voices," will, I hope, restore confidence that this tradition may yet healthfully root here in the West. I don't think this will be possible if we don't move further away from what I call "Guru Zen." There is nothing intrinsically wrong with authority or hierarchy. I think any sort of rigorous skilled discipline or practice requires reliance on authority that has done advanced training. Moreover, Zen *sesshins* (weeklong meditation marathons) require a hierarchical form to contain the potential breakdowns and breakthroughs that often accompany intense retreats. However, the idealization that is often projected on the person leading a sesshin or Zen center is a poison. If swallowed by the "Zen Master," it becomes Guru Zen. Certainly, this happened in a major way with some of my teachers, including Genki Takabayashi, though much less so with others. I haven't met anyone entirely immune to the poison of idealization, including myself. In my view, deflecting student idealization and vilification is one of a Zen teacher's major responsibilities.

Buddhist doctrine tells us our apparent self (*atman*) is not real (*anatman*); yet, anyone without a strong sense of self is liable to be unstable. Anyone who takes himself or herself too seriously, or his or her role as a Zen teacher too seriously, will end up being arrogant or much worse. Without confidence based on long experience, leadership is impossible. Without a great deal of self-awareness and deep open heartedness, healthy leadership is unachievable. However, to have confidence, self-awareness, open heartedness and some measure of humility does not make one immune to our most basic instincts for survival, that include primitive physical and psychological needs for nurture and love. If a Zen teacher's needs are not being adequately met outside the sangha, leaders blasted with idealization and not sufficiently mature may end up feeding on their own sangha. It would be helpful if everyone doing Zen training were aware of these primitive tendencies so that we became less likely be possessed by our own hungry ghosts. This is much more easily said than done. Anyone who thinks that multiple breakthroughs into one's deep infinite nature constitute psychological maturity is setting themselves up for a big fall. We never arrive at maturity or mastery; wherever we are we are just beginning.

The chapter "Revisioning" starts off with a quote from Zen Master Dogen, who when asked to tell something of his life replied, "Just one mistake after another." Maturity and mastery are possible only if we are deeply mindful and willing to learn from our endless mistakes. Any teacher who thinks they are enlightened, knows the truth, and has attained something to teach others is already sunk. In my view, koans should be used only to help knock at the door of our own deep nature and not as a means of propping up the teacher's mastery. When the gateless gate swings open, the artificial barriers between host (questioner) and guest (responder) fall away, and there will usually be a good laugh. I think that most teachers in "Contemporary Voices," the last chapter of *The Story of Zen*, would agree that, at best, senior followers of the way can be companions and guides to practices that have worked for them. Then all that remains is to point at the moon saying, "look, look!"

If you're going to have a story,
have a big story, or none at all.

Joseph Campbell

Preface

WHEN D.T. SUZUKI – who was largely responsible for introducing Zen to the west – first visited a Zen monastery as a young man at the end of the 19th century, he was shown into a private room where he was told to practice *zazen* (seated meditation) until the teacher was able to see him. As it happened, the master was absent from the temple for several days. When Suzuki finally met him and tried to pose a question that had arisen from his reading, the teacher responded that the question was stupid and sent him back to his room to continue meditating. No further direction was provided.

Suzuki's story is not unique. Often the initial instruction received by western students who traveled to Japan in the 1950s and '60s amounted to, "You sit there." Suzuki had the advantage, at least, that he had been raised in a culture permeated by Buddhism. In the same way that non-Christian Americans in the mid-20th century would have been familiar with the fundamentals of Christian teaching even though they didn't accept them, the Japanese who visited a monastery and were told no more than to "sit there" had an inkling of what was expected.

Circumstances have changed since the first pioneers began the process of adapting Zen to the west. Today, not only would someone coming to a Zen Center for the first time expect more detailed instruction in meditation, they would doubtless respond poorly to having their questions, no matter how naïve, dismissed.

The Zen Masters who had refused to countenance theoretical questions had not done so arbitrarily but because they wanted new students to realize that such questions were beside the point. Zen is not a matter of gaining information; it's not studied by accumulating more knowledge. Rather it is a practice by means of which one acquires direct personal insight. Today, however, it's generally recognized that Westerners investigating meditation traditions are naturally and legitimately curious about things such as who Buddha was or why certain Zen teachers had such glaring personal weaknesses. Having these questions answered brings them no closer to achieving insight, but it does keep the door open for further involvement.

In both Asia and North America, it's a challenging time for institutional Zen. It is fading in Japan, where scores of temples are either being closed or remain open essentially for the benefit of tourists. In North America, religious and spiritual institutions are generally on the wane except – oddly – for the most conservative. At the same time, meditation and mindfulness are growing in popularity as secular therapeutic practices. At one time, Zen had been almost the sole source of information about these techniques. Now there are options, with multiple alternative forms of meditative instruction available: various forms of yoga, competing schools of Buddhism and Hinduism, distinctly Christian meditative techniques, mindfulness seminars. Recorded guided meditations can be downloaded, "For Dummies" books on the subject abound, and there are even meditation apps for smart phones. In this environment, then, what is the purpose of Zen?

When one asks this question or others – whether Zen differs in any significant way from other meditative techniques, whether one has to be a Buddhist to practice Zen, or even what Buddhism is – often the answer one receives is given in the form of a story, and many of the details of those stories would have made up the information that the young Suzuki had assimilated before he made his first visit to a Zen temple.

The term "story," with all its connotations, is deliberately chosen. All human institutions – be they faith traditions, nations, or soccer clubs – have stories they tell about themselves, and these stories are usually equal parts fact and fable. Although they may feign to be history, they are, at best, partisan renderings of historical data. They're not necessarily deliberate distortions of the truth; rather they are an expression of the way the members of that institution see themselves and wish others to see them. It is precisely because these stories reveal how the members of a particular group view themselves that they are valuable. Stories, by their very nature however, are interpretations, and one of the fundamental teachings of Buddhism insists on the importance of viewing ourselves, the world around us, and things in general not as we imagine them to be, not in terms of the stories we tell about them, but as they actually are, "empty" of the modifiers we usually attach to them. This book attempts to take a critical look at the stories that Zen – principally North American Zen – tells about itself and, in doing so, to see beyond the interpretations, the modifiers, and come to an understanding of the "why" of Zen. What is there about Zen that makes it unique and worth preserving?

Part One examines the preliminaries, the Buddhist and Daoist roots of the Zen tradition. Part Two looks at the development of Chan Buddhism in China and its evolution into Japanese Zen and eventual spread beyond Asia. Part Three, then, looks at the way North Americans have sought – and continue to seek – to transfer this Asian tradition to a new environment and to people with very different cultural heritages.

My earlier books are, to some extent, preliminary studies for the present one. The sources for the material in the chapters on Chan and Zen are the same as those I used for *Zen Masters of China* and *Zen Masters of Japan* (Tuttle Publishing, 2012 and 2013), and the chapters on American Zen make use of interview material I collected in 2013 and 2014 for *Cypress Trees in the Garden* (Sumeru, 2015) in addition to interviews conducted specifically for this project. There is some inevitable repetition, although hopefully it's supplemented by a deeper analysis and treatment.

A Note on Terms and Names

There are two main streams of Buddhist scriptures: the Theravada, recorded in the Pali language, and the Mahayana, originally preserved in Sanskrit. Consequently, there are Pali and Sanskrit variants of most Buddhist terms. Zen descends from the Mahayana line so, for the sake of consistency, I have used the Sanskrit terms throughout this book even when (as in the chapter on "What He Taught") it might have been expected that I would use the Pali.

A similar problem exists with Chinese and Japanese terms and proper names. In the 5th century CE, the Japanese adapted Chinese ideograms for their first written language, but they did not pronounce them as the Chinese did. So, while a particular character has the same meaning in both languages, the word it represents – the sound – is often entirely different, thus 禅 is pronounced Chan in Chinese and Zen in Japan.

To complicate things further, in current usage Chinese pronunciations are rendered into the Roman alphabet using the Pinyin system developed in China in the 1950s. This replaced the 19th century Wade-Giles system which remained in common use in the West until about 1979. Books written before 1980 and several after that date use Wade-Giles variants. Consequently, the name of the individual who originated the koan most frequently assigned to Zen students is written 肇州聪申. When receiving this koan, it's probable that the student will be told that individual's name is Joshu Jushin, the Japanese rendering. In older books on Zen, he may also be referred to as Chao-chou Ts'ing-shen, the Wade-Giles form. The preferred current Pinyin rendering is Zhaozhou Congshen. For Chinese names, I've used the Pinyin form. For terminology, except in the chapter on "Chan," I have chosen to use the Japanese forms (thus "Zen" instead of "Chan," "koan" instead of "gongan") not only for the sake of consistency but also because the Japanese variants are more familiar in the West.

Part One

Part One

An inquirer asked Yanguan Qian, "Who was the Buddha?" Yanguan replied by requesting of his visitor, "Would you please pass me that water pitcher."

The inquirer looked around, saw the pitcher, and passed it to the master. Yanguan poured himself a cup of water and then asked the visitor to replace the pitcher. The visitor did so, then, thinking that perhaps Yanguan had not heard his original question, put it again:

"About the Buddha – who was he?"

"Oh, yes," Yanguan said. "Well, you know, he's been dead a long time now."[1]

---

1. Uncited passages are my renderings of existing translations of traditional Buddhist documents.

The Buddha

Background

Philip Kapleau, the founder of the Rochester Zen Center, first formally investigated Zen while he was in Japan as a court reporter for the War Crimes trials after the Second World War. He and a friend visited Ryutaku-ji Temple where they were given a tour by the young abbot, Soen Nakagawa. Kapleau had read a little about Zen and understood it to be free of superstition and religious cant, so he was surprised by the amount of ritual activity taking place. As they came upon the various altars with their statues of the Buddha, sundry Bodhisattvas (roughly equivalent to saints), and historical figures, Nakagawa lit incense and bowed before them. Kapleau objected, "I thought Zen masters were famous for burning Buddha statues and spitting on them. Why do you bow before them?"

"If you want to spit," Nakagawa said, "spit. I prefer to bow."

Despite its reputation for iconoclasm, Zen is a Buddhist sect, and – like all sects of Buddhism – its story begins with the account of the Buddha's life.

The supposed date of the Buddha's birth has been set at anywhere between 620 and 400 years before the birth of Christ, the consensus being around the year 550 BCE; however, the earliest extant Buddhist writings date from about 100 BCE. The tale is that the earliest sermons given by the Buddha were memorized verbatim by his attendant, Ananda, and then passed on orally to other eidetic minds over the course of 400 years before being written down. The total number of texts supposedly transmitted in this manner is enormous; the earliest English translation of the *Tripitaka* – the scriptures accepted as valid by Theravadan Buddhism – is 57 volumes long.

The fact is that we cannot be certain that we know anything at all about the life of the Buddha or what he originally taught. Inevitably, as the oral tradition progressed, stories were added, deleted, embellished, and reinterpreted. As I noted in *Zen Masters of China*, religious traditions begin with myth, pass through legend, and only slowly come to verifiable historical reporting. The account of the Buddha's life is a carefully crafted fiction composed over a period of centuries. The story, so central to the Zen tradition, of the flower sermon – in which the Buddha is said to have transmitted the Dharma (the teaching) to the monk Mahakasyapa – doesn't appear in any Indian source at all; it's a Chinese invention first recorded thirteen centuries after the Buddha's death. Further, the interpretation of the events of the biography varies from sect to sect; the way in which the Zen tradition understands the Buddha's enlightenment is very different from the way earlier Buddhists appear to have understood it.

There's no need to doubt that an individual known as Siddhartha Gautama lived and taught in the region that is now Nepal some 2500 years ago, but there is also no need to assume that the stories told about him are literal renderings of events.

Accordingly, then, 500 years before the birth of Jesus of Nazareth, a child named Siddhartha was born in the foothills of the Himalaya Mountains. He was the son and heir-apparent of the leader, traditionally portrayed as a king, of the Shakya clan. It was the end of what is known as the Vedic Period, the period during which the oldest Hindu scriptures – the *Vedas* – were composed.

The culture in which this young prince was raised was very different from those with which we, who live in pluralistic societies, are now familiar, and, although Siddhartha would come to challenge many of the beliefs and structures of Vedic culture, he was also very much a product of them. Actually, the concept of a "culture" as we understand it would have been foreign to the people of that time and region. There was simply the community in which they lived and the assumptions that community made about the way the world worked. Many of these beliefs were recorded both in the *Vedas* and the later *Upanishads*. During Siddhartha's lifetime, there were already differing schools of interpretation regarding these beliefs, but there was general agreement about certain fundamental issues which can seem peculiar to contemporary Western readers.

One of the structures taken for granted was the caste system. It established that one's social standing was determined not by one's actions or talents but by the family into which one was born. Siddhartha was born into the military class known as the Kshatriya, the class with the highest social standing. Next in status was the priestly caste, the Brahmin. Following them was the Vaisya, originally a caste of artisans that evolved over time into the mercantile class. The lowest caste – the Sudra – was made up of laborers, servants, and slaves.

In this period, the Brahmin hadn't yet established themselves as the premier caste, but the route by which they would do so was already established; they were responsible for carrying out the rites and sacrifices which were an integral part of the culture. In an age when people didn't have much scientific information about the universe, it was common to assume that certain events, which couldn't otherwise be explained, were the result of the actions of supernatural beings such as gods, demons, and spirits. The movement of the sun, moon, and stars, weather conditions, fire, and natural formations such as rivers were associated with specific gods who – it was believed – controlled them.

People also hoped, and the Brahmin taught, that these gods could be influenced by human activity such as rites and sacrifices. The Brahmin were the keepers of these rituals and, for a fee, performed them, earning themselves significant stature and power within the community. There were rites for almost every aspect of life, from the coronation of a king to rites intended to help one acquire a sexual partner. These rituals made up a large part of what someone looking at the culture from without would consider its religious activity. The community, on the other hand, would have seen these as practical, almost mechanical, means for achieving particular ends.

In addition to their ritual responsibilities, some Brahmins were drawn to ponder those basic philosophical questions which have intrigued humankind since the capacity for reflection developed: questions about the origin of the world and the purpose of human existence. Several competing schools attempted to plumb these issues. The approach that the society as a whole developed to these mysteries, however, was very different from traditional western thought on the same subjects.

The *Upanishads* don't picture a God external to the universe who created and maintains it. Rather, they conceived of an original single being who, in some fashion, became the universe of multiplicity and the range of beings within it, including the soil, rivers, animals, humankind, spirits, demons, and gods. There were several explanations of the way in which the division of the original being into the world of multiplicity took place. In one, all of creation is merely the dream of this being, and it will pass away when he wakes.

Another explanation, given in the *Brihadaranyaka Upanishad*, describes a primordial rape. In the beginning, it states, the world was a single body shaped like a man which divided itself into two, giving rise to male and female. Finding the female attractive, the male mated with her and from their union the human race came forth. The female, seeking to avoid him, hid herself as a cow, but he became a bull and pursued her again. From that union cattle came forth. Once more she sought to hide from him in the form of a mare, but he became a stallion, and so on through all the creatures which now populate the planet, "down to the very ants." When all was completed, he declared: "'I alone am the creation, for I created all of this.' From this 'creation' came into being."[2]

In yet a third explanation, the world of multiplicity came about when the primordial being underwent self-sacrifice and dismemberment. In this version, the Kshatriya were formed from the arms (the strength) of the primal being; the Brahmin from its head; the Vaisya from the loins; and the Sudra from its feet.

The common thread linking these stories is the perception that each individual entity in creation is a manifestation and part of this original being which is called Brahman[3] and can be thought of as loosely equivalent to God. Therefore, at the core of each individual human there is a spark of divinity, the atman. This spark can, with proper training and effort, be brought to awareness. Through this process, one can then experience one's essential unity both with the rest of creation and with the Godhead itself.

A summary of this belief with which many of the early Zen advocates in North America were familiar is found in Aldous Huxley's introduction to Swami Prabhavananda and Christopher Isherwood's translation of the *Bhagavad Gita*. At its core, Huxley wrote, there are four fundamental doctrines:

1. The phenomenal world of matter and of individualized consciousness – the world of things and animals and men and even gods – is the manifestation of a Divine Ground within which all partial realities have their being, and apart from which they would be nonexistent.
2. Human beings are capable not merely of knowing about the Divine Ground by inference; they can also realize its existence by direct intuition, superior to discursive reasoning. This immediate knowledge unites the knower with that which is known.
3. Man possesses a double nature, a phenomenal ego and an eternal Self [Atman], which is the inner man, the spirit, the spark of the divinity within the soul. It is possible for a man, if he so desires, to identify himself with the spirit and therefore with the Divine Ground [Brahman], which is of the same or like nature with the spirit.

---

2. Patrick Olivelle (trans.), *Upanishads* (Oxford World's Classics, 2008.)
3. When encountered for the first time, the terms Brahman, Brahma, and Brahmin can be easily confused. "Brahman" refers to the underlying reality of the Universe. "Brahma," the Creator, is one of the trinity of primary gods in Hinduism, along with Vishnu, the Preserver, and Shiva, the Destroyer. "Brahmin" refers to the priestly caste.

4. Man's life on earth has only one end and purpose: to identify himself with his eternal Self and so to come to unitive knowledge of the Divine Ground.[4]

The fact that there was more than one explanation of how the primal being became the world of multiplicity didn't pose the same philosophical problems to Vedic culture that, for example, attempting to reconcile the Genesis story of creation with the perspective of contemporary science presents to certain schools of Christianity. The essential thing to understand about this teaching is that it was not a theory; rather, it was an attempt to express an insight, an experience of reality which certain religious practitioners had achieved, the experience of *moksha*, illumination or enlightenment.

It was also accepted that the experience of illumination was one which those who sought it were capable of attaining through the various practices known as yoga. These may have included the physical exercises with which we associate the term today, but primarily the term referred to a range of activities that included meditation, devotional practices, and often severe austerities.

The inevitable corollary of this understanding of existence was the belief that the world of multiplicity is ultimately *Maya* – or illusion. It is illusion because instead of seeing the unified whole of Brahman, we see only the world of separate entities. On a more philosophical level, it is illusion because even that world of multiplicity which we perceive is only one "interpretation" of reality and an interpretation which has been culturally determined. The culture in which Siddhartha lived, for example, viewed the world through one set of conventions, whereas contemporary North Americans and Europeans view that same world in a very different manner. Both cultures take certain things for granted which the other would find incomprehensible.

The idea that the purpose of human life is for the individual to "identify himself with his eternal Self and so to come to unitive knowledge of the Divine Ground" is an elitist one. Clearly most people fail to achieve this goal. Farmers, mothers, and warriors, for example, all had other priorities, and other gods – the Hindu pantheon – to pray to for assistance in their lives. A culture cannot survive if food isn't raised, children nurtured, and the land protected from invaders. The Brahmin explained this seeming discrepancy by positing that individuals required a long spiritual

---

4. Aldous Huxley, Introduction to Prabhavananda and Isherwood (trans.) *The Song of God: Bhagavad-gita* (New York: New American Library, 1951).

evolution through several lifetimes before reaching that stage in which they could focus on fulfilling their full human potential.

This process of rebirth was driven by *karma*, a term roughly equivalent to the English word *action*. The concept is that all actions have consequences. Good actions have good consequences; bad actions have bad consequences. These consequences may be neither immediate nor apparent; however, the total weight of one's actions during a particular lifetime will determine one's next birth. Good actions would result in a favorable rebirth; bad actions would result in a less favorable birth, perhaps in a lower caste, perhaps in a sub-human state. The obligation of each caste is to carry out the duties appropriate to that class and thus earn merit which could lead to future birth in a "higher" caste.

The doctrines of atman and karma resulted in a number of social situations which, from a contemporary point of view, appear appallingly unjust although they would not necessarily have seemed so to the people of Siddhartha's society. The exploitative treatment of lower castes, for example, would have been defended on the grounds that those individuals were condemned to their current status because of their behavior in previous lives. The path to securing a more favorable birth lay, in part, in meekly accepting their lot in this life.

Previous Lives

The story of the Buddha doesn't begin with his birth. The Future Buddha lived many lives prior to that birth – some in human form, others in animal form, at times male, at times female. According to one tradition, this sequence of births began with his incarnation as a beast of burden in the lowest reaches of Hell. From there he slowly evolved over countless subsequent incarnations.

Stories of the Future Buddha's past lives became popular folk tales that were originally passed down orally. One of these concerns the markings on the moon, which are a good example of the way in which cultural conditioning determines how people see things. In our culture, we see a man's face in the shadows on the moon's surface. Siddhartha's culture saw the outline of a rabbit.

The tale goes that in one of his former lives the Future Buddha was a rabbit with three companions – a monkey, a jackal, and an otter – each of whom gathered food in its own manner. The rabbit was the wisest and daily exhorted the others to live virtuously. One evening, he reminded his companions that the coming day was a time of fast. He also encouraged them to give whatever food they had to the poor and hungry.

The next morning, the four friends all went into the forest to search for food. The monkey found a mango tree laden with ripe fruit that he gathered and took home. Likewise, the jackal looked for the carcasses on which he fed and found a dead iguana, and the otter caught several fish. They carried these back to their lairs without eating them because they remembered it was a day of fast.

Meanwhile the Future Buddha remained in his burrow reflecting that if a person in hunger were to visit him, he would have nothing to offer except the grass on which he fed but which men cannot eat. Because he had nothing else to offer, the Future Buddha vowed that if someone looking for food did come that day he would sacrifice himself and give the supplicant his own flesh to eat.

The god Sakka heard this vow and thought it was mere boastfulness, so he descended to Earth to test the Future Buddha. He took the shape of a *bhikkhu*,[5] a wandering monk. In this form he went first to visit the monkey and begged for food. When the monkey willingly proffered his mangos, the supposed bhikkhu remembered it was a day of fast and, with gratitude, declined them. In the same way, he tested both the jackal and the otter, who also offered what they had.

Finally, he visited the Future Buddha in his incarnation as a rabbit, once again begging for something to eat. The rabbit replied that unfortunately the only food he had to offer was grass; however, he said, were the bhikkhu to build a fire of hot coals, he would jump on it – so that the bhikkhu would not have the responsibility of taking his life – and his flesh would nourish the visitor.

Still doubtful, the bhikkhu built the fire as requested, and the Future Buddha came forward without hesitation – pausing only to shake himself so that any insects in his fur would not also be destroyed in the fire – then leapt onto the coals, but they were as cold as ice. At that point, Sakka revealed himself to the Future Buddha explaining that he had heard the rabbit's vow and thought it boastfulness. Now he bowed in respect, then took up a mountain and squeezed it to make ink. Using this, he drew the outline of the rabbit on the bare surface of the moon to commemorate the Future Buddha's nobility of spirit and generosity.

After numerous rebirths in various animal forms, the Future Buddha at last attained birth as a human of the Brahmin caste named Sumedha. This was during the lifetime of the Dipankara Buddha, many lifetimes before the Future Buddha's birth as Prince Siddhartha. Sumedha lived as a householder, raising a family and accumulating wealth, but, when his children were grown, he gave away all his possessions and adopted the life of a *sannyasi*, a forest hermit. One day, as he was practicing his devotions

---

5. The word "bhikkhu" literally refers to a beggar, one who lives by begging for alms.

in the forest, he heard a commotion and went to learn its cause. He found a group of men clearing a road in the jungle. They explained that the Dipankara Buddha was passing through the region, and they were making a path for him. Sumedha immediately joined their labor, but when the Dipankara Buddha approached there was still one spot in the road which hadn't been properly drained. Sumedha lay down on that spot so the Holy One could walk on his body rather than soil his feet in the mud.

When the Dipankara Buddha saw Sumedha lying on the ground, he gazed countless ages into the future and perceived that Sumedha would eventually become the Buddha Shakyamuni. Sumedha was deeply moved by this prophesy and dedicated the remainder of his life to the study of the Ten Perfections,[6] vowing to practice them in all his future births, not only for his personal benefit but for the benefit of all humankind.

And so the Future Buddha passed from life to life, growing in perfection, until the time came for his final birth. Then, residing temporarily in the Heaven of Delight, he considered what would be the most appropriate time and place and who would be the most appropriate mother for that birth. Having determined these, he took on human form for the final time.

Birth and Childhood

The parents of the Future Buddha, King Suddhodana and Queen Maya, resided in the city of Kapilavastu. The Queen's name referred to the worldly "illusions" from which spiritual aspirants sought liberation. The Mahayana writer, Ashvaghosha, explained that her name demonstrated her freedom from all illusion and deceit; he claimed Queen Maya was Duty itself abandoning its "subtle nature" and taking on visible human form.

In Vedic culture, all things and all actions were seen as deeply interconnected, and, if all beings are ultimately parts of a single primal entity, then it's natural to assume that if it were possible properly to interpret the significance of one set of events this would shed light on other events taking place simultaneously. That is the rationale behind the various forms of soothsaying such as astrology and the interpretation of dreams.

So it was that when Queen Maya had a dream which perplexed her, Brahmin priests were called in to explain its meaning. They informed the royal couple that the dream – of an elephant with six tusks touching the queen's womb – signified that she had conceived a son who, during countless former lives in both animal and human form, had acquired significant merit. Such a being had the ability to choose the time and place of his own rebirth and, doubtless, had chosen Queen Maya to be his mother because of her virtue. The Brahmin predicted that the child would either become

---

6.   Paramitas, cf. p. 75 below.

a powerful emperor or, if he chose to follow the path of religion, a great spiritual leader whose teaching would help the peoples of all the nations of the Earth overcome ignorance and suffering.

As the time for her delivery neared, Queen Maya left Kapilavastu to return, as was the custom, to her parents' home in Devadaha. Along the way, her caravan stopped to rest at the gardens of Lumbini which were renowned for their beautiful flowers and fruit trees. The queen got out of her carriage and walked among the trees to refresh herself until she came upon one which she particularly admired. As she reached up to touch its branches, her labor began. And so, standing and holding onto the flowering branch of the tree, she delivered her child without pain.

Some traditions relate that the newborn stood upright at once and took seven steps, proclaiming, "I alone am the World Honored One! This is my last birth; from this time forward, there will be no further births for me!" After this, he lay down and became as other infants.[7]

The queen and her retinue brought the infant back to Kapilavastu, and King Suddhodana was presented with his son. Eight Brahmin soothsayers were consulted to examine the significance of the time, place, and circumstances of the boy's birth. Seven of these agreed with the prediction given by the dream-interpreters. The newborn was destined to become either a great political or a great spiritual leader. The eighth soothsayer, the Brahmin Kondanna, alone disagreed, predicting that the child was destined to become not just a great spiritual leader but a fully-enlightened being, a Buddha. There had been other Buddhas in the past, but the world had not seen one for many ages.

Five days after the birth, the child was given the name Siddhartha – "one who achieves his goal." His family name was Gautama. Two days later, Queen Maya, having completed her responsibilities for this lifetime, died to be reborn in one of the celestial realms. The baby was given into the care of his mother's sister, Prajapati, another of his father's wives.

When Siddhartha was still only a few days old, Asita Kaladevala, a hermit famed for his holiness, came to the palace to visit him. When the hermit was taken into the nursery to see the child, he started to weep. King Suddhodana was concerned that Kaladevala foresaw some tragedy in the child's future, but the holy man assured the king this was not the case. He explained: "I foresee that this child will become the greatest Spiritual Leader humankind has ever known. I weep because I know I will die before I have the chance to hear him expound the Dharma."[8]

---

7. The Chinese Chan master Yunmen Wenyan's comment on this story was, "Had I been there, I would have cut the precocious brat down with my staff and fed his body to the dogs in order to ensure peace throughout the world."

8. "Dharma" here means "teaching." See p. 56 below.

Suddhodana dismissed the predictions of Asita Kaladevala, confident that his son would become the powerful emperor which the other Brahmin soothsayers, save Kondanna, had foreseen as one of the child's possible futures. It seemed unlikely to the king that the prince would be drawn to religious life.

In the spring of his ninth year, Siddhartha attended the ceremonies associated with the annual first plowing of the fields. In ancient cultures, matters of fertility were treated with great reverence. The well-being of a community depended upon the continued fertility of their fields, their livestock, and their women. The occasion of the first plowing was a time when Brahmins carried out complex rituals intended to ensure a healthy harvest. The king took part as well, solemnly digging the first furrow.

As the seemingly endless religious ritual droned on, the young prince became restless and wandered off. In the heat of the day, he sought shade under a large flowering tree where he naturally assumed a cross-legged posture and fell into a deep reverie in which he thought about the rituals he had been observing. He wondered how the chanting of the Brahmin could affect the coming harvest. He pondered the process of agriculture: tilling the soil, sowing the seed, cultivating the crops, and so on. The process seemed complete in itself. If weather conditions were favorable and the crops properly tended, they would grow; if weather conditions were poor or the crops improperly tended, the harvest would be bad. Siddhartha didn't see any way the Brahaminical rituals would affect things one way or another. And so, seated in this manner, he entered the first degree of contemplation.

After the ceremonial activities had been completed and the banqueting and celebrations begun, King Suddhodana and Queen Prajapati noticed that Siddhartha was missing and searched for him anxiously. When they finally found him, he was still seated with folded legs and lowered eyes, breathing steadily. Seeing his son in the traditional posture of a meditating yogi, Suddhodana was reminded of the prophecies of Kaladevala and Kondanna.

Suddhodana wanted his son to succeed him on the throne and strengthen the land of Shakya. He expected Siddhartha to become a great monarch. After Siddhartha had completed those responsibilities, after he had raised a family and reached old age, he could then retire to the forest and become a spiritual aspirant if he chose.

There were many spiritual aspirants in the land, bhikkhus and sannyasis, who lived as hermits or as homeless wanderers, often practicing austerities and choosing to dwell in poverty. Many – like Sumedha in the distant past – had completed their social responsibilities and now sought, in their final years, to practice a devotional life in order to accumulate merit for their next birth. But there were also those who, while still young, became disillusioned with the secular world either through circumstances in their own lives or because they had come to recognize the inevitable suffering inherent in life.

Finding Siddhartha seated in meditation beneath the flowering tree made Suddhodana worry that the boy might have a predilection for the life of a renunciate. The king decided to take steps to shield his son from the more unpleasant realities of life in order to distract him from morbid speculation. Suddhodana arranged for the prince to be raised in a sumptuous environment, distant from the squalor and turmoil of the lives of his subjects. The Prince knew only luxury and pleasure, waited upon by beautiful, compliant servant girls who catered to all his whims. He was provided the best teachers available and easily mastered both the intellectual and physical training he was given. He was familiar with the *Vedas* and the other literature of his time, with mathematics and history; he was a fine musician and was proficient in archery, swordsmanship, riding, and the other military skills appropriate for a king.

Because of his great physical beauty, generous personality, and his many accomplishments, Siddhartha was generally admired by those who met him. He had, however, a cousin, Devadatta, who was also an accomplished young man. Devadatta was a prince as well, the son of Suddhodana's younger brother, Dronodanaraja, and he realized that under other circumstances he would be the one eliciting the admiration his cousin now received which made Devadatta envious of Siddhartha.

The Four Signs

When the time was appropriate, Siddhartha was married to Yasodhara, the daughter of Suddhodana's sister, Pamita, and King Dandapani of Koliya, and, in due course, Yasodhara became pregnant. Oracles were consulted who predicted that the child would be a son. It was customary that when a king had a grandson ensuring the line of succession, he could choose to retire and leave the throne to his son. So Suddhodana proclaimed that, as soon as his grandson was born, Siddhartha would become King in his stead.

Although he was raised in luxury and coddled by both servants and courtiers, Siddhartha had not become spoiled or self-absorbed. He grew up to be a sensitive, kind, and reflective young man. He was observant and astute and was well aware of the self-serving avarice of many of the court officials. When he spoke to his father about the corruption he saw, Suddhodana explained that a king didn't have absolute authority and power. He had to depend upon members of his court, even some whom he recognized might not be honest but were, nonetheless, influential. Suddhodana expressed the hope that Siddhartha might be a wiser and stronger king than he had been. But Siddhartha recognized in himself the same seeds of selfishness, anxiety, and greed that had influenced certain of his father's ministers for the worse. It seemed unlikely that corruption could be done away with unless a means were found to rid humankind of these tendencies.

As the time for the birth of his child – and thus his own coronation – crept closer, Siddhartha became conscious of how little he knew about the people he was supposed to rule. So accompanied by his chariot-driver, Channa, he set out to tour what was to be his capital city and saw for the first time the people who were to be his subjects. Along their way they came upon an aged and frail man supporting himself on a staff. Having never before seen anyone in this state, Siddhartha asked Channa about the man. Channa explained that he was only one who had grown old and debilitated with the passing of years. Siddhartha asked if perhaps the man alone was subject to this deterioration of age or whether all men were? Channa replied that all men, even the prince, were subject to the weakening of their powers and faculties as they grow older.

This revelation distressed Siddhartha so much that he returned to the palace without going any further that day. But on two future occasions, he ventured again into the city. On the first of those trips, he came upon a man sick with fever, and on the second he encountered a funeral procession. Once again Channa informed him that – like old age – all persons were subject to illness and death as well. Siddhartha lamented, "How can humankind bear the burden of knowing this to be their fate?" And again, he fled to the confines of the palace walls.

He remained committed, however, to learning about the conditions in which his future subjects lived, so once more he set out. This time he and Channa came upon a figure with a shaved head walking with serenity and dignity. He wore a robe which left one shoulder bare and carried a begging bowl. Siddhartha gazed at him in wonder and asked Channa what manner of man this was. "He is a bhikkhu," Channa told him, "one who has left his home and given up all of his possessions. He has learned to control his passions and his ego. He spends his time in meditation and devotional activities."

When he heard these words, Siddhartha felt as if he understood for the first time the purpose of his life and the destiny for which he had come into the world. He rushed back to the palace to see his father and informed the king that he had discovered his true calling. He would give up his royal status and take up the life of a bhikkhu. "Perhaps by my efforts, I will be able to find a means to control selfishness and the other passions which corrupt men; perhaps I will find a path which will liberate all of humankind from the sorrows of old age, sickness, and death."

The king argued that it would be more appropriate for the prince to assume the responsibilities of the office to which he had been born. Siddhartha retorted that as important as those obligations were, they paled beside the opportunity to seek a means to liberate all persons from the sorrows which plague them. The king insisted that concern about such matters was the product of a morbid preoccupation with only certain aspects of life. There was joy and happiness as well as sorrow. Because of the merit Siddhartha had accumulated from previous lives, he had been born into his current state and had been rewarded with the opportunity to taste such pleasures as most other men only dream of. He told his son that whatever his heart desired, he only had to ask for it, and it would be his.

In that case, Siddhartha replied, there were three things he desired. "First, that I shall always remain youthful, vigorous, and of pleasing appearance. Second, that I will never fall ill. Third, that I should not be subject to death and decay."

Suddhodana realized that he had lost the argument, but he decided that it would be in his son's best interest if he were kept from leaving the palace grounds again. So, he ordered soldiers to be posted at the gates of the palace to prevent the prince from leaving and taking up the life of a bhikkhu.

The following morning, Yasodhara gave birth to a male child. Holding his newborn son, Siddhartha didn't feel the satisfaction which most fathers feel but reflected instead that the child would be an impediment to him if he lacked the strength to abandon him and his mother in order to seek, for the benefit of all humankind, a path to liberation. Therefore, he named the boy Rahula – "the fetter."

For the remainder of the day, Siddhartha brooded on the fact that the social responsibilities he was acquiring would only become greater as time passed. If he were to follow the path of religion, he needed to leave the palace before the coronation took place and further bonds were forged to prevent him from pursuing his destiny. So, when evening fell, Siddhartha went to Yasodhara's chamber where he found mother and child sleeping peacefully. He had a great urge to take his son in his arms but feared to wake them. So he stood in the doorway for a while then bid them a silent farewell and vowed to return to present the path to liberation to them once he had found it.

Then he had Channa saddle their horses. Suddhodana had been confident that, with the birth of Rahula, Siddhartha would lose interest in taking on the life of a bhikkhu; therefore, he had relaxed the guards at the palace gates, and so without difficulty Siddhartha and Channa set out. At the first light of morning, they came to the river that marked the border of

Shakya. Siddhartha crossed it, passing outside his father's territory. On the other bank, he used his sword to cut off his long, princely hair. He gave the locks and the jewelry he was wearing to Channa and told him to return them to the king. Then he continued on his way alone and on foot.

He was 29 years old when he renounced his royal status and entered the path of religion.

His Quest

Shortly after departing from Channa, Siddhartha came upon a hunter wearing a monk's robes because he had discovered that if he was disguised in this manner the beasts of the forest didn't fear him. Siddhartha offered to exchange clothes with the hunter, who readily agreed to do so. So Siddhartha continued on his way dressed in the traditional garb of a bhikkhu. From that time, he was no longer known as Prince Siddhartha but rather as the Bhikkhu Gautama.

His immediate task was to find a teacher who could lead him on the path to liberation. He had heard of the meditation master Alara Kalama who dwelt in the city of Vesali. Gautama joined Alara Kalama's community and quickly brought attention to himself by the speed with which he mastered each of the techniques he was presented.

Alara Kalama believed, as was common at the time, in the existence of an eternal soul – the atman – that could, over the course of many lifetimes, attain liberation from the world of Maya. To aid this process of liberation, Kalama taught several degrees of ecstatic meditation. In the first exercises, the practitioner escaped the burdens of life and entered into a state of bliss. Not all of Kalama's students were able to achieve the degree of concentration required to attain this state, and many who did were content to remain at that level. Gautama achieved the state easily but recognized that it didn't actually address the fundamental sufferings associated with life.

Alara Kalama next taught him to pass beyond the state of bliss and non-bliss to an awareness of union with all of creation – an experience equivalent to the unitive knowledge of Brahman that traditional yogis sought. Very few of Alara Kalama's students had been able to attain this state, but, once again, Gautama achieved it easily and was eager to pass beyond it. Finally, Alara Kalama introduced him to the state of "No Materiality" wherein he realized that all the universe with which he had experienced such a deep union was simply a projection of his own mind. Gautama mastered this practice as well.

Alara Kalama was deeply impressed by Gautama's attainment and told the young bhikkhu that he had nothing more to teach him. He invited Gautama to remain with him, and the two of them would share leadership of the community of monks. But Gautama wasn't satisfied with what he'd learned, so, thanking Alara Kalama for all he had taught him, he took his leave.

Gautama journeyed south, crossed the Ganges River, and entered the kingdom of Magadha. Every day he spent time practicing the meditation techniques he had learned, focusing his concentration and awareness inward. He prayed to no gods nor took part in traditional devotional practices during this period because he understood that the means of alleviating suffering must be found in oneself.

Each day he went into the villages and cities he passed in order to beg for food as he had while studying with Alara Kalama. So it was that on one occasion he was begging in the city of Rajagaha. The monarch of Magadha, King Bimbisara, was standing on his terrace at the time. He noticed Gautama in the street below and was impressed with the noble bearing of this monk. Bimbisara arranged to meet Gautama and learned that the he was the son of his ally, Suddhodana. He invited Gautama to stay in his city and share his kingdom for the benefit of the people. Later, he argued, when Gautama had reached the fullness of his years he could resume the life of a bhikkhu. But Gautama declined the offer, pointing out that if he didn't use the vigor and strength he had in youth, old age and sickness would inevitably weaken him, and he would feel deep regret at having failed to pursue his proper goal.

Seeing that Gautama was set in his course, the king requested then that, when he found the path he sought, he return and present it to the people of Rajagaha, which Gautama promised to do.

Near Rajagaha was the ashram of Uddaka Ramaputta, another celebrated teacher of the time. In addition to teaching – as Alara Kalama had – the traditional concept of a reincarnating atman, Uddaka Ramaputta emphasized the working of karma and the necessity of strict moral behavior in order to secure a favorable future birth. When Uddaka Ramaputta discovered that Gautama had already experienced the state of "No Materiality" – which none of his own students had been able to attain – he revealed a further stage of meditation to him. This was the state of "Neither Perception nor Non-Perception," an ecstatic state in which one experiences a deep sense of unity with all of Being. Gautama achieved it after only fifteen days of practice.

Uddaka Ramaputta was overjoyed to have found a worthy successor to himself. So – like Alara Kalama and King Bimbisara – he invited Gautama to remain with him and assume co-leadership of the community. Gautama, however, still wasn't satisfied with his accomplishments. It remained clear to him that ecstatic meditative states provided only temporary relief from the inevitable sorrows of life; once the period of meditation was over, those basic problems remained.

Realizing there was nothing more traditional teachers – however advanced – could show him, Gautama left Uddaka Ramaputta's ashram and set off on his own. He retired to the forest alongside the Niranjara River, now known as Bodh Gaya, where he took up ascetic practices, thinking: "If wood is wet, fire cannot be made. Perhaps – in a similar manner – as long as the body is subject to desire and ambition, one cannot find that enlightenment which alone leads to liberation."

The severity of his self-mortification attracted the attention of five monks who had been disciples of Uddaka Ramaputta. One of these was Kondanna, who had predicted to King Suddhodana that his child would become not a monarch but a fully enlightened Buddha. The five Brahmin monks joined Gautama and together they lived lives of extreme austerity. The story goes that there were days when the Bhikkhu Gautama ate only a single grain of rice. As a result, his body became so gaunt he appeared to be little more than a skeleton covered with dry skin. For six years, Gautama persisted in this lifestyle. Then one day, as he was walking to the river for a mouthful of water, he collapsed in complete exhaustion. His body was so wasted that he couldn't get up.

He reflected that this discipline hadn't led to enlightenment. "It is obvious that a life in which one pursues the gratification of one's physical desires does not lead to enlightenment," he thought. "Now it is also clear to me that neither does a life of extreme self-mortification." There had to be, he decided, a Middle Way which avoided those two extremes.

Gautama feared that his discovery of the Middle Way had come too late and that he would die in his weakened state without having accomplished his goal. Then a young girl named Sujata came by with a bowl of milk which she was taking as an offering to the forest gods. When she saw Gautama lying alongside the path by the river, she supposed he was a corpse until she saw his eyes flicker. She sat beside him, lifted his head onto her lap, and slowly fed him the milk.

The food restored Gautama's strength, and he abandoned asceticism. Once again he ate regular meals and took care of his physical needs. When his five companions learned of this, they assumed Gautama had abandoned the path of religion and left him to continue their own practices in the Deer Park at Isipatana some distance to the west.

Enlightenment

On one level, the Buddha's enlightenment was a simple thing. He saw past the superstitions and – to a large extent – the cultural suppositions of his day and grasped the way things actually were. It was very much a human, rather than a divine, revelation, so although he understood the laws of causality in a new and revolutionary way, he interpreted the mechanics of causality within the context of the limited understanding of social and scientific principles available to his era.

After the departure of his five companions, Gautama retired to a grove of fig trees where he pursued the practice of self-reflection. Observing his body, he realized that it was in a constant state of change. Muscles formed, grew strong, then weakened over time; young limbs grew old. He found nothing in his body that was not subject to change, nothing that remained constant or permanent.

In the same way, he examined his thoughts, emotions, and senses. In none of these did he find anything stable or unaffected by change. From this examination, he came upon the insight of "non-self" or "emptiness" – the realization that all beings are essentially in a constant state of flux, empty of any permanent self or atman. Most people live under the illusion that they are permanent and stable beings. Gautama understood that to seek permanence in that which is fundamentally impermanent must necessarily contribute to human suffering.

He next recognized the essential interdependence of all being. His body, he realized, depended upon the rice and other food he ate. The rice depended upon the paddies – the soil and water in which it grew – as well as upon the sun and rain and the farmers who cultivated it. All things, he understood, are fundamentally empty of permanent self and are mutually interdependent.

He also realized that the six years in which he had tried to rid himself of mind-deluding passions through the practice of asceticism had failed because such effort only sought to suppress the passions. The true path to conquering them was clear awareness – seeing the emotions, understanding their cause, and so becoming free of attachment to them.

As these insights grew, he recognized that he was drawing near to the goal of finding a path of liberation for all humankind. The next day, when Sujata brought him a ball of rice, he wrapped it in a banana leaf and carried it with him to the fig tree which, from that time on, would be known as the Bodhi Tree – the Tree of Enlightenment.

Gautama went to the south side of the tree to sit but felt as if the land on that side were sinking beneath his feet. So, he walked around it, first to its western and then to its northern sides. Each time the land still felt as if it were sinking. Finally, he came to the eastern side of the tree and there the land felt stable. He placed himself on this immovable spot vowing to remain there until he came to full and complete enlightenment.

The story then relates that the tempter – the demon Kama-Mara – heard this vow and grew frightened. This demon's name means "Love-

Death," and he was the personification of all the pleasures, fears, and attachments which enslave people. Kama-Mara rose from his throne in the underworld and sought to divert the Bhikkhu Gautama from his goal.

First, he assumed the appearance of a messenger whose clothing was in disarray and who panted heavily as if he had run a long distance. In this disguise, Kama-Mara presented a message purported to be from the nobility in Shakya claiming that Devadatta had usurped the throne of Suddhodana and had thrown the king into prison. Then Devadatta claimed Suddhodana's wives for himself as well as all the goods and lands which had belonged to the king. The message declared that Devadatta abused the women of the harem in the vilest manner and that he was despoiling the countryside, placing undue burdens of taxation on the people. The nobles, so the false report went, begged Prince Siddhartha to return, take his rightful place on the throne, and restore order to the land.

But Gautama reflected that it was the passion of malice which led Devadatta to usurp the throne; lust provoked him to abuse the women; greed drove him to ruin the people; and cowardice prevented the nobles and citizens from defending their king and themselves. The knowledge that the seeds of these weaknesses and proclivities existed in all persons only made Gautama more firm in his resolve to remain seated until he found the path of liberation.

Kama-Mara then assaulted the Bhikkhu Gautama with natural terrors – a whirlwind, thunderous rain, and darkness that obscured the sun in the middle of the day – but Gautama remained centered and calm in his meditation, undistracted and without fear.

Next Kama-Mara revealed himself to Gautama in his terrifying form, riding a war elephant, bearing weapons in his one thousand arms, and surrounded by an army of ferocious and terrifying demons. In this form, Kama-Mara rode up to the Bhikkhu Gautama and shouted: "You've no right to sit on that spot! It belongs to me! By whose authority do you dare take it?"

Without disturbing his meditation, the Bhikkhu Gautama touched the ground with the fingers of his right hand, and the Earth itself took on the sound of a thousand human voices proclaiming: "I witness to his right to sit here."

Finally, Kama-Mara called upon his three daughters – Pining, Lust, and Desire – along with their one thousand voluptuous attendants to present themselves to the Bhikkhu Gautama in their most provocative forms. At the same time, Kama-Mara reminded Gautama of the predictions which had been made at his birth, that he could become the Emperor of all the World, but the Bhikkhu Gautama had long overcome those temptations, and he remained undisturbed.

So, Kama-Mara was defeated and went off in despair.

Having overcome the tempter, Gautama continued his meditation into the evening. In the first watch of the night, it is said, he was able to see all of his past lives and experienced great compassion for all living creatures who came into being, died, and were reborn endlessly. In the second watch of the night, he was conscious of the universality of human suffering, experiencing the suffering of all living beings as if it were his own. He recognized the way in which suffering was the product of previous action. In the third watch of the night, he attained complete understanding of the chain of causation or Dependent Co-Arising.

Finally, at the break of day, as the sun rose in the east behind him, Gautama saw the Morning Star on the horizon. At that moment, he attained the full and complete enlightenment that is beyond words because it is a direct, unfiltered encounter with and experience of reality. Although not recorded in the Pali scripture, the Zen tradition maintains that at the moment of his awakening, the Bhikkhu Gautama said, "Wonder of wonders, all things, just as they are, are whole and complete. All beings are endowed with Buddha-nature."

Gautama was 35 years old when he attained enlightenment, and the story relates that he remained beneath the Bodhi Tree for a further 49 days after his awakening, deepening his insight. On the forty-ninth day, he reflected that although he had found the Path of Liberation he'd sought so diligently, he was uncertain whether he would be able to communicate it to others.

The next morning, as he went to the river to bathe, he paused to observe the lotus flowers growing in the water. The flowers were at different stages of development. Some were little more than roots buried in the mud; others had stems which still had not risen to the surface of the water; still others had emerged but their leaves remained curled shut; the buds of yet others were just opening; and finally there were flowers in full bloom. In like manner, he reflected, people were at various stages of development, but in each person there existed the seed of enlightenment – their inherent Buddha-nature. With proper cultivation, all persons – regardless of gender or caste – were capable of realization and enlightenment. So, Gautama came to the decision to share the Dharma with others.

Had his former teachers, Alara Kalama and Uddaka Ramaputta, still been living, they would have been the first to whom he presented his teaching, but both had died during the six years he had been engaged in ascetic practice. So, he decided that the first persons with whom to share the Dharma should be his former companions residing in the Deer Park at Isipatana.

As he made the journey to Isipatana, Gautama came upon a caravan. The men of the caravan were greatly impressed by the serenity of the monk they saw before them. Stopping him they asked, in all seriousness, if he were a god or celestial being of some sort. He told them he was not. They asked, then, what he was, and he told them simply, "I am awake!" From that time forward, the Bhikkhu Gautama was known as the Buddha Shakyamuni – the Awakened One, Sage of the Shakya – although he always referred to himself as the Tathagata, "the one who has attained."

Turning the Wheel of the Dharma

When the five ascetics saw the Buddha approaching, their intention was not to acknowledge him, but, as he drew nearer, they were struck by the peace and equanimity he radiated, and spontaneously they showed him the reverence due to a fully enlightened Buddha.

The teaching that the Buddha presented to his former companions is known as the First Turning of the Wheel of Dharma. He began by expounding the Middle Way. "There are two extremes which one seeking to follow the spiritual life must avoid. First, one must avoid a habitual enslavement to the passions and the pleasures of the senses, but so also must one avoid needless self-mortification."

Next, he presented what was to become the core of his teaching – the Four Noble Truths and the Noble Eightfold Path.[9] It is said that as soon as the Bhikkhu Kondanna heard this, he attained enlightenment and became an *arhat*, one who achieves liberation from false perception. Before four days had passed, the other Brahmin companions also attained enlightenment and *arhatta*.

The clarity and simplicity of what the Buddha taught quickly attracted followers, and, within a short time, he had ordained sixty bhikkhus at Isipatana. Once these monks were properly trained and had a clear understanding of the Dharma, the Buddha sent them out to share the teaching with others. These bhikkhus traveled as homeless monks, carrying only their begging bowls with them. As they spread the knowledge of the Four Noble Truths and the Noble Eightfold Path, even more people came to Isipatana seeking to be followers of the Buddha. Soon the numbers asking to join the company of bhikkhus – or *sangha* – was so great that the Buddha announced it would no longer be necessary for him personally to ordain all those who sought entrance.

A simple ceremony evolved by which aspirants became members of the sangha. All that was required was for the individual to declare that he sought refuge in the Three Treasures: "I take refuge in the Buddha – the

---

9. Cf. pp. 59-63 below.

one who shows the way. I take refuge in the Dharma – the path of liberation. I take refuge in the sangha – the community of support that lives in mindfulness and harmony."

Once the community at Isipatana was stable and strong, the Buddha left it under the direction of Kondanna and proceeded to Rajagaha in order to keep his promise to King Bimbisara.

In the course of his journey, the Buddha encountered a community of fire worshippers led by Uruvela Kasyapa, a famous teacher of the day. The fire worshippers led ascetic lives dedicated to Agni, the god of fire. Kasyapa taught that fire was the basic element of creation. That is why all living beings have heat in their bodies, and, when that heat leaves, the living being dies. Fire, he taught, was the sacred element by which sacrifice was offered to the gods who controlled the forces of nature, who determined whether crops would be good or poor, whether a person would prosper or not. Through devotional rites and prayers to Agni, the personification of fire, fire worshippers sought to achieve the traditional goal of Brahmanical religious practice, the union of Atman with Brahman.

The Buddha challenged many of the assumptions basic to the beliefs of the fire worshippers. He taught that events in existence were determined not by super-human forces but rather by the laws of cause and effect. One condition or situation is the result of earlier circumstances, which are themselves the result of prior circumstances. He denied the existence of a stable, permanent self (*atman*). Human beings were, he taught, made up of elements (*skandhas*) which were in a constant state of change.

Uruvela Kasyapa challenged the Buddha, asking: "If there is no permanent Self or Atman, what is the point of entering into the path of spirituality? If there is no Self, who or what will be liberated by entering such a path?"

The Buddha didn't answer Kasyapa directly. Instead he asked the fire worshipper if he acknowledged the existence of suffering. Kasyapa, of course, did. As the Buddha continued to question him, Kasyapa also admitted that he understood suffering to be the result of certain causes, and that if those causes were removed, suffering would come to an end. That, the Buddha told him, was the essence of his teaching: The existence of suffering, the origin of suffering, the cessation of suffering, and the path which leads to the cessation of suffering.

The story says that after listening to the Buddha, Uruvela Kasyapa realized he had wasted more than half his life in activity which wouldn't help him achieve liberation, and so he, with his five hundred followers, all became disciples of the Buddha.

The Sangha Expands

Accompanied by his new followers, the Buddha came to Rajagaha, and the entourage settled in a palm grove near the city. When King Bimbisara heard that the Buddha had returned, he went to him accompanied by his wife and his son, Prince Ajatasattu. As the king approached, he was uncertain about the relationship between the Buddha and Uruvela Kasyapa. The former fire-worshipper was older than the Buddha and was a well-known and respected religious leader. So, the King and his party assumed that the Buddha was the elder monk's disciple. Uruvela Kasyapa sensed the King's confusion and prostrated himself before the Buddha, declaring: "The Blessed Buddha is my master, and I am his disciple."

Learning that Uruvela Kasyapa had become a follower of the Buddha, many others were also drawn to his teaching. King Bimbisara became a lay disciple and a generous patron of the sangha. He presented them with a bamboo grove north of Rajagaha, beside Gijjakuta Mountain, known as Vulture Peak, because its shape was thought to resemble that of the bird.

The Bamboo Grove at Vulture Peak was the first stable residence established for the Buddha's monks. The bhikkhus lived as homeless wanderers for most of each year, but during the rainy season, when travel was difficult and dangerous, they met for a three-month retreat at one of the monastic sites donated to the order.

One day while the order was staying at the Bamboo Grove, Bhikkhu Assaji – who had been one of the five companions at Uruvela – went into the town to beg for his daily meal. Along the way, he was observed by a monk named Sariputta, a student of Sanjana Belatthiputta, whose ashram was nearby. Sariputta was impressed by the dignity with which Assaji went about his rounds, so he approached Assaji and asked if he, too, was a student of Sanjana Belatthiputta. Assaji replied that he was a follower of a teacher from the land of Shakya now recognized as the Buddha for this age. When Sariputta asked what this Buddha taught, Assaji replied in verse:

Whatsoever things are produced by causes,
The Buddha has revealed those causes;
As well, how things cease to be,
This too the Buddha reveals.

It's said that upon hearing this simple verse, Sariputta suddenly and clearly gained insight into the basic Buddhist concept of *anitya*, or the impermanence of all things.

After parting with Assaji, Sariputta went to visit his friend, Moggallana, telling him that he had heard of a new teacher some claimed was a fully enlightened Buddha and suggested they visit him in order to judge for themselves. So they came to the Bamboo Grove and became members of the sangha. In time, they would become the Buddha's chief disciples.

After learning that Sariputta and Moggallana had become followers of the Buddha, many other students of Sanjana Belatthiputta left their teacher to join the sangha. So it was that other teachers came to resent the Buddha and his followers.

Return Home

Fame of the former Shakya prince who had become a fully enlightened Buddha and was now teaching in the kingdom of Magadha spread throughout the region. Soon these stories reached King Suddhodana, who sent messengers to ask the Buddha to visit his family. As the Buddha approached the city of his birth – accompanied by 20,000 bhikkhus and arhats – he was met by his parents and members of the Shakya nobility. Because these were generally older than the Buddha, they thought of him as their social inferior. When the nobles were assembled before him, the Buddha greeted his father and aunt, then he expounded the Four Noble Truths and the Noble Eightfold Path. After hearing this, King Suddhodana prostrated himself before his son, declaring that he was, indeed, a fully-awakened Buddha deserving of all respect. Following the example of their king, the remainder of the Shakya nobility also prostrated themselves – some, no doubt, reluctantly – before the Buddha.

The Buddha met with Yasodhara and learned that since he had entered the religious life, she had emulated him by shunning the luxuries of the court. Like the bhikkhus, she ate only a single meal a day and slept on a mat placed upon the floor. She reminded the Buddha that he had a son who had right of inheritance from him, and the Buddha – who did not always show good judgment – interpreted this to mean Rahula should become a member of the order, and, although the boy was only seven years old, the Buddha had his head shaved and ordained him.

When Suddhodana learned that Rahula had been made a monk, he was deeply grieved and let the Buddha know that he thought the ordination was inappropriate. The Buddha considered his father's objections, then acknowledged that it had been wrong to ordain the boy without speaking to the king and Yasodhara first. He ruled that, from that time forth, children should not be admitted into the sangha without first obtaining the permission of their parents.

While the Buddha and his disciples were staying at Kapilavastu, many Shakya youth joined the order. Among these were the Buddha's cousins,

Ananda and Devadatta. Ananda was renowned for his memory, in particular for his ability to recite, word for word, the sermons he heard the Buddha give.

Mahakasyapa and Ananda

As the rainy season approached, the Buddha and his followers prepared to return to the Bamboo Grove monastery at Magadha. The Buddha took leave of Suddhodana, Prajapati, and Yasodhara, but Rahula – now a member of the order – accompanied his father.

When they arrived at the Bamboo Grove, they found many others waiting there seeking to become bhikkhus, including a monk named Kasyapa who came to be called Mahakasyapa (Great Kasyapa) to distinguish him from Uruvela Kasyapa. Mahakasyapa and Ananda would come to represent two distinct approaches to understanding or experiencing the truth of the Dharma.

Mahakasyapa has special significance for the Zen tradition, which considers him the "Second Patriarch of Zen" – following the Buddha himself. He became Second Patriarch in this fashion: At one of his daily Dharma talks, the Buddha simply sat before the assembled monks and twirled a flower between his fingers. While the other bhikkhus sat, some impatient for the sermon to begin, Mahakasyapa smiled even though he attempted to control his expression. The Buddha noticed that smile and told the assembly: "I have the eye of the true teaching, the heart of nirvana, the true aspect of no-form, the unquestionable Dharma. Today I have passed these onto Mahakasyapa."[10]

The core of the Buddha's teaching wasn't found in his words but rather in the experience of enlightenment which came about not through an intellectual understanding or appreciation of the Dharma but rather through a direct seeing into truth. This is an experience that goes beyond words, that words can only hint at – in the way that language can only hint at sensations such as smell or taste.

Ananda would serve as the Buddha's personal attendant for twenty-five years and would have an exhaustive knowledge of all the Buddha's words, but he didn't attain arhatta during his teacher's lifetime. Consequently, there was a potential crisis at the Council called after the Buddha's death in order to codify his teaching. Because only fully enlightened Arhats were permitted to attend, Ananda – in spite of his scholarship – was excluded. Wounded by not being able to participate, Ananda spent the evening before the Council pacing in frustration and grief. Eventually, exhausted in

---

10. This story is found neither in the Pali canon nor in the Indian Mahayana sutras; it is a Song Dynasty invention of the Chinese Chan school.

both body and spirit, he went to lie down, and at that moment, when thought came to an end, he finally attained awakening: the direct, experiential understanding of the Buddha's Dharma which all of his intellectual knowledge of the teaching had failed to provide.

After the death of Mahakasyapa, Ananda became the Third Patriarch of Zen.

His Career

In the fifth year following the Buddha's enlightenment, a conflict broke out between the kingdom of Shakya and that of Koliya in the north, from which both Queen Maya and Yasodhara had come. The issue was water rights. The Rohini River separated the two kingdoms and was used by both for the irrigation of farmland. But in that year, there had been a drought, and, consequently, the river didn't carry enough water to irrigate fields on both banks.

Each side claimed rights to the river, and tension between the two escalated until they were on the brink of war. Suddhodana was now an old man and had grown feeble. He realized he didn't have the strength needed to prevent a war that inevitably would be costly to both sides, so he asked his son to intervene. The Buddha resolved the conflict by appealing to the vanity of the young nobles who were preparing to go to battle. He asked the leaders of both camps which was more valuable, water or the blood of the nobility. When the leaders assured him that the latter was, he asked if it was then wise to sacrifice what was of high value for the sake of something of lesser value. This argument was sufficient to put an end to hostilities. The opposing leaders declared themselves the Buddha's lay disciples and each chose two hundred and fifty young men to become members of the sangha.

These five hundred, however, had not themselves chosen to become monks; rather, they entered the order at the behest of their elders. As a result of the ordination of these five hundred, dissension began to develop among the members of the sangha. Likewise, the five hundred wives of these young nobles were grieved at the loss of their husbands.

Some months later, King Suddhodana died, and the Buddha's half-brother, Mahanama, became king. Then Queen Prajapati, along with the five hundred wives whose husbands had been compelled to become monks, approached the Buddha requesting to be accepted into the sangha. There was no precedent in the culture for women to enter a religious order, so the Buddha politely but firmly refused their request. Queen Prajapati told the women to be patient, and, when some time had passed, she once again appealed to the Buddha. He told her he was sympathetic but explained it was not the custom to ask women to endure the hardships which bhikkhus routinely endured.

When Prajapati brought this message to the women, they immediately surrendered all the comforts of court life. They shaved their heads and dressed in the traditional robes of wandering monks. They walked barefoot and ate only a single meal a day. After further time had passed, Prajapati visited the Buddha a third time and informed him that all of the women had demonstrated they were fully capable of living the life of homeless wanderers. The Buddha expressed his admiration but told her that he still could not accept them into the sangha for fear of the scandal it would cause.

Prajapati then approached the Bhikkhu Ananda and asked him to intervene with his cousin on their behalf. Ananda agreed to plead their cause and asked the Buddha whether women had the capacity to attain arhatta. The Buddha acknowledged they did. Ananda asked if then, perhaps, Buddhas were born into the world for the benefit of men only. The Buddha denied this. Then, Ananda asked, would he not receive women into the holy order of monks? The Buddha considered the matter carefully before replying, telling Ananda that it was not from doubt that women had the capacity to attain arhatta that he had been reluctant to accept them into the sangha but from fear of the dangers both within the sangha itself and to its reputation in the wider community if women were brought into it. Then Sariputta suggested that if careful regulations were put into place, the dangers would be reduced. The Buddha agreed to these conditions, although he remained concerned about the decision.

Prajapati became the abbess of the women's order, and, not long after, Yasodhara also joined the company of nuns.

By the ninth year after the Buddha's enlightenment, the sangha began to take on a character independent of him. As in any group, there were a wide variety of personality types, opinions, and points of view. There were also various degrees of commitment to the order and its discipline. Those bhikkhus – such as the 500 young men from Koliya and Shakya – who entered not so much by their own choice as at the behest of others had a different degree of commitment than those who had entered on their own; likewise as some bhikkhus gained more authority within the order, others felt overlooked and became resentful.

Until he reached the age of 55, the Buddha accepted no privileges greater than those of the other monks. But as he grew older, his senior advisors insisted he have a personal attendant. His cousin, Ananda, was nominated both because of his devotion to the Buddha and because of the ease with which he was able to commit the Dharma discourses to memory. So, for the remainder of the Buddha's life, Ananda was his constant companion.

Opposition

The popularity of the new sect angered many of the Brahmin caste, especially because the Buddha was not of that caste and openly challenged their teachings and ways. He taught that Brahminical rituals and sacrifices had no efficacy; he denied the existence of the Atman. He flaunted tradition by allowing into the order both women and untouchables (those born outside the four castes and so low in the social order it was believed that even to touch one would result in pollution). Certain members of the sangha found the life too hard and left it. Some of these later slandered the order. There were also rival teachers, such as Sanjana Belatthiputta, who were displeased to have lost disciples to the Buddha. And so, some came to seek a means to discredit the Buddha and his sangha.

One day the King's soldiers came to the Jetavana Grove monastery looking for a woman named Sundari who was missing from her home. They had heard rumors that she had been raped and murdered by the bhikkhus, and they had to determine if the rumors were true. Searching the area, they found the woman buried in a shallow grave near the Buddha's hut. News of the discovery spread throughout the district, and people became suspicious of the monks who still continued their daily begging rounds ignoring the insults and accusations hurled at them. People claimed that it was only because the Buddha was a friend of the king that none of his followers had been arrested for this crime. Some of the newer sangha members found this antagonism too hard to bear and left. The Buddha counseled the remaining monks to have fortitude and to continue their activities as usual. Finally, one evening the two men who had actually murdered Sundari became drunk in a tavern and boasted about what they had done. When soldiers questioned them, they confessed that they had been hired by one of the rival sects to kill the woman and bury her near the Buddha's hut.

The greatest threat to the sangha, however, came not from without but from within – from the Buddha's cousin and childhood rival, Devadatta.

Devadatta had acquired status within the brotherhood both because of his own merits and because of his kinship to the Buddha. Slowly he won the loyalty of many senior bhikkhus as well as the friendship of King Bimbisara's son, Prince Ajatasattu, who was impatient to assume the throne of his father. Devadatta confided to his supporters that he was concerned that the Buddha, now 76 years old, no longer had the physical energy he had once had. Devadatta argued that it would be best for both the Buddha himself and the sangha if he retired from the leadership of the order and allowed someone in better health to take command.

So, with the backing of three hundred monks, Devadatta approached the Buddha and suggested it was time for him to rest from his labors. Devadatta added that, although unworthy, he would be willing to take up direction of the sangha in order to permit his cousin's retirement. The Buddha declined the offer, pointing out that, even if he were to retire, there were Arhats senior to Devadatta more capable of leading the order in his place. As he had not asked them to take his place, it would be unseemly to ask Devadatta to take on a role for which he had neither the insight nor the talent.

At the next assembly of monks, Devadatta and his supporters took another approach. When the Buddha completed his Dharma talk, Devadatta stood and proposed a number of new rules which would help the sangha achieve the Buddha's lofty goals. These would have strictly controlled where bhikkhus dwelt, what they accepted in alms, what they wore, where they slept, and what they ate. The Buddha replied that any bhikkhu who wished to follow those rules was free to do so but that they were not necessary for the attainment of liberation.

Privately, Devadatta told his followers that the Buddha's refusal to accept the new rules demonstrated his growing weakness. Some agreed with him and put themselves under his guidance, keeping the new rules and condemning those who did not for the laxness of their practice. The situation became grave, and finally, at the advice of Sariputta, the Buddha expelled Devadatta from the sangha. He did not leave alone, however; five hundred others chose to depart with him.

Around the same time, King Bimbisara realized that his son, Ajatasattu, was seeking to overthrow him. Rather than provoke a civil war, Bimbisara abdicated the throne. But Ajatasattu was concerned the king might change his mind and raise up supporters in order to regain command, so – on the advice of Devadatta – he had the king placed under arrest. When the coronation of Ajatasattu took place, Devadatta and his followers attended, but the Buddha and his disciples did not.

Even though his father was under house arrest, Ajatasattu still worried that the former king might be able to muster enough support to reclaim the crown. So Ajatasattu forbade the palace servants to bring Bimbisara anything to eat and eventually caused his father's death by starvation. When Bimbisara died, his widow – Queen Khema – returned to the household of her brother, King Pasenadi, in Kosala.

Ajatasattu and Devadatta also plotted to kill the Buddha so that Devadatta's new order of monks would have preeminence in the land. They hired thirty-one notorious criminals to assassinate the Buddha. Notwithstanding that these criminals had readily accepted this commission, once they were in the presence of the Buddha they were so impressed by his virtue and equanimity that all thirty-one gave up their weapons and became members of the sangha.

Sariputta and Moggallana, the Buddha's two chief disciples, were saddened by the division that had arisen in the brotherhood because of Devadatta's treachery and went to Gayasisa where the apostates were residing. When Devadatta gave his daily Dharma talk, he looked out over the assembly and noticed Sariputta and Moggallana among the monks. Overjoyed to see that his cousin's two chief disciples appeared to have joined his order, he invited Sariputta – who was noted for his eloquence – to address the monks. As Sariputta spoke, however, Devadatta fell asleep. Then Sariputta told the bhikkhus gathered there that they were mistaken in following Devadatta; the true path to liberation was only to be found within the Buddha's sangha. He was so persuasive that 380 of the 500 returned to the Bamboo Grove monastery. When Devadatta woke to find the majority of his followers had abandoned him, he was more intent than ever on destroying his cousin.

One evening as the Buddha was making his way down the slope of Vulture Peak, he heard a noise behind him; turning, he saw a boulder the size of a cart coming at him. He was just able to get out of its way. Several monks believed they had seen a man on the peak above running away. They were certain he had pushed the boulder down the slope deliberately. A third and final attempt on the Buddha's life came a few days later. While he and several bhikkhus were going about their daily begging rounds, an elephant charged them. The monks recognized it as an animal known for its ferocious nature and later learned it had been fed inflaming intoxicants at Devadatta's prompting. Even this beast, however, became pacified in the presence of the Buddha and knelt down in the street to allow its head to be scratched.

In the meantime, King Pasenadi, angered by Ajatasattu's behavior, reclaimed territory he had presented to King Bimbisara on the occasion of his wedding to Khema. War broke out, and Ajatasattu and his chief generals were captured. Pasenadi wasn't sure how to deal appropriately with his nephew and so consulted the Buddha. The Buddha explained to Pasenadi that he was a fortunate king because he had a number of wise and competent advisors who helped him govern his realm. Ajatasattu, on the other hand, was the victim of spiteful and incompetent advisors. The Buddha suggested that Pasenadi allow his nephew to return to Magadha but encourage him to replace his current set of advisors – including Devadatta – with men of wisdom and good will.

As a result of this generous behavior, Ajatasattu became remorseful over his past deeds. He remembered how much he had once loved his father and was crushed by guilt. He became unable to rest or to conduct the affairs of his office. Finally, his wife called the physician, Jivaka – Ajatasattu's half-brother and personal physician to the Buddha – who told Ajatasattu that there was no physical cure for what he was suffering. He advised his half-brother to seek out the Buddha, accept the Dharma, and become a lay disciple; only the Noble Eightfold Path could give him ease. Ajatasattu was too ashamed to approach the Buddha on his own, so his mother, Queen Khema, accompanied him. They proceeded to Vulture Peak where, in front of the assembly of monks, the king prostrated himself before the Buddha and proclaimed the three refuges.

By this time, all but six of Devadatta's followers had left to return either to the sangha or to lay life. Then Devadatta became ill and bedridden. When he realized that death was approaching, he asked his remaining disciples to carry him to the Jetavana Grove so he could beg forgiveness from the Buddha for his years of envy and treachery. The six disciples bore him on a litter to Jetavana, and there, in spite of his weakness, he struggled to his feet, stood before the Buddha's hut, and declared: "I take refuge in the Buddha! I take refuge in the Dharma! I take refuge in the Sangha!"

The Buddha came out of his hut, but, before he could speak, Devadatta fell dead to the ground. Tradition says that Devadatta was reborn in a body of flame in Hell, but that, because he had sought refuge in the three gems with his last words, he will eventually be reborn as the future Buddha Sattisara.

Death and Parinirvana

By the time the Buddha had attained his 80th year, many of his friends and companions – including Yasodhara and Rahula – were already dead, and the kingdom of Shakya had been destroyed by war. King Pasenadi was dead as the result of the treachery of his son and generals. Both Sariputta and Moggallana were dead.

During the rainy season that year, the Buddha became ill, and Ananda looked after him with anxiety. When the Buddha recovered, Ananda expressed concern. The Buddha, however, reminded him that all component things are subject to impermanence, adding, "The Tathagata is like an old cart which has been worn out from much use. All things which are born will surely die, Ananda. So, too, will the Tathagata die."

When Ananda claimed that the community still needed the Buddha's guidance, he denied it, saying, "I have turned the wheel of the Dharma for forty-five years. In all that time, never have I made a distinction between exoteric and esoteric doctrine; never have I had the closed fist of a teacher who holds certain things back. You have all that I have to teach; nothing have I concealed."

Ananda then argued that the Buddha had not identified who should be responsible for leading the order of monks after his death, and the Buddha replied that he did not intend to do so. Since he did not believe that the order depended on him, why should he leave instructions concerning how the sangha should be ordered after his death? "Just follow the Noble Eightfold Path," he told Ananda. "Be lamps unto yourselves. Wisdom and enlightenment are found within, not without."

As the weather improved, so too, did the Buddha's health, and he and Ananda proceeded to Kutagara, where they dwelled for three months.

A blacksmith name Cunda was a devout lay disciple of the Buddha and, when he learned the Buddha was residing at the area, asked permission to offer him a meal. The Buddha accepted the invitation. Cunda served a dish made with pork and mountain truffles. That evening, the Buddha was stricken with severe stomach cramps and dysentery. He was unable to sleep and, in the morning, was very weak. He understood that this would be his final illness, but he told Ananda that he wanted to proceed to the village of Kusinara.

Along the way, the Buddha told Ananda that the meal he had been served by the smith, Cunda, would be his last. He insisted that no one was to accuse Cunda of seeking to harm him, and that Cunda himself was not to feel any remorse over the matter.

When they reached the forest of sal trees near Kusinara, the Buddha chose two shade trees to rest beneath. News that he was dying spread throughout the district, and bhikkhus and arhats as well as pious lay people from the region came to be with him. The Buddha looked over the people gathered there and spoke to them one last time: "Remember this: Impermanence is inherent in all component things. Work out your own salvation with diligence."

Then he closed his eyes and passed into Parinirvana – never to be subject to rebirth again.

Whatsoever things are produced by causes
The Buddha has revealed those causes,
As well, how things cease to be,
This too the Buddha reveals.

What He Taught

Early Buddhist thought can appear desolate and pessimistic to those encountering it for the first time. But our current Western standards of living and our expectations about life are very different from those of Siddhartha's contemporaries. 2500 years ago, human beings were much more vulnerable to the vagaries of nature. Rivers, such as the Ganges south of Siddhartha's homeland, were prone to floods that could destroy the crops upon which communities depended. People lived in modest dwellings, sometimes constructed of mud, that were at risk of disintegrating during the yearly rainy season. Diseases we can now control – such as malaria, dysentery, and cholera – were devastating. The tropical jungle surrounding human settlements was the abode of dangerous animals. War was common and brutal. Slavery was practiced. Torture was used routinely. Life expectancy was only a fraction of what it is today. Ordinary citizens led lives of dreary toil and frustration, in many cases barely managing to survive. When the Buddha spoke about the inevitability and pervasiveness of suffering, he wasn't making an abstract philosophical point; he was stating the obvious.

Western religions also recognize that suffering, brutality, and injustice are common. They differ from Buddhism in an absolutely fundamental manner, however, because they also believe that there will be another life – after death – in which there will be peace, joy, and the righting of all wrongs, at least for those who lived worthy lives. From this perspective, the concept of nirvana presented in the Buddha's original teachings can seem unremittingly bleak.

Although his teaching underwent modification and interpretation by subsequent cultures and generations, it is clear that the path of liberation the Buddha offered his followers was liberation from life after death, specifically liberation from rebirth. Nirvana means "blowing out," as a candle flame is snuffed. One attains nirvana by extinguishing the desires or craving that lead to rebirth, and as a result one achieves peace in this life and, even more importantly, is no longer subject to future lives and the inevitable sufferings associated with them.[11] This is not precisely annihilation, because in extinguishing one's "self" one is subsumed into that totality of Being from which all things proceed and to which they inevitably return.

In some Buddhist traditions, heavens and hells (or more properly, purgatories) exist, but such realms are temporary and lead inevitably to further rebirth, suffering, and death. And, of course, rebirth is not always in a human state. As the writings emphasize, "difficult to obtain is the conception of persons." It is more likely one will be reborn in a sub-human state. The earliest Buddhist teachings stress that birth and life necessarily entail suffering, and they conclude that peace is ultimately only to be found in liberation from rebirth.

Although normally considered a religion, Buddhism bears little resemblance to other faith traditions. The Buddha himself is not presented as a supernatural being nor as an intermediary of the Divine. Although belief in gods and other paranormal entities were common in his time and culture, the Buddha gave little attention to them and refused to be drawn into discussions about them. The concept of a God external to and responsible for creation is dismissed. Buddhism does not recognize a "first cause" nor does it acknowledge any sense of human responsibility – either through worship or ethical behavior – to divine beings. To call the tradition "Buddhism" is itself misleading. The idea that it is a faith system is a Western rather than an Asian notion. A better term is "Buddhadharma" or the "teachings of the Buddha."

Unfortunately, we don't know with certainty exactly what those teachings were. The sutras – the sermons attributed to him – were not written down until 400 years after his death. Until then they were transmitted orally, a process during which they would inevitably have been modified, clarified, organized, and expanded. It is clear that new teachings were composed and attributed to the Buddha long after his demise. The Buddhadharma, then, is not the product of a single enlightened mind but the collective reflection of generations of minds over a period of centuries.

The term "Dharma" in pre-Buddhist literature had multiple meanings and connotations: law, custom, nature, quality, correct order. It also referred to the structures operative in nature and the universe. So, the Dharma as preached by the Buddha is the revelation of the structures of the universe, the way things are.

The history of Buddhism has consisted of different cultures and ages reinterpreting the Dharma as they received it and adapting it to their

---

11. The issue is a little more complex than presented here, because although the Buddha accepted the concept of rebirth, he denied the existence of a permanent, stable self or atman.

circumstances; the way the Zen tradition will come to understand the concepts presented in early Buddhist writing will be very different from the way they are viewed in other parts of the Buddhist world. There is no reason to doubt that similar processes have been going on from the time of the First Council called immediately after the Buddha's death. The biography acknowledges that even during the Buddha's lifetime there were quarrels within the sangha; individual bhikkhus emphasized particular aspects of the Dharma and questioned others. The Buddha himself changed his position on issues, notably regarding the inclusion of women in the sangha. All things, the Buddhadharma asserts, are in a constant state of flux, and this is true of Buddhism itself as of anything else.

By the first century CE, two broad streams of Buddhist teaching had been established. One, known as the Theravada or Teachings of the Elders,[12] is today prominent in South East Asia, Sri Lanka, Thailand, Laos, and Myanmar. A second stream, the Mahayana, spread north, through China, Tibet,[13] Korea, and Japan. Theravada scriptures were recorded in the Pali language, while the root documents of the Mahayana tradition were written in Sanskrit and then translated into the languages of the regions where it became established.

Because the Sanskrit texts include those of the Pali Canon as well as a large number of sutras not found there, it was assumed for a long while that the Pali works reflected an earlier – and therefore, ostensibly, more authentic – record of the Buddha's original teachings. But then documents written in a third language, Gandhari, were discovered dating back to the first century BCE, significantly earlier than existing Pali texts. These demonstrated that elements of what had been assumed to be later Mahayana concepts had arisen much earlier than previously supposed.

The total number of individual teachings attributed to the Buddha is enormous, traditionally set at 84,000. The Pali Canon, first committed to writing in the first century BCE, is also known as the *Tripitaka*, or "Three Baskets," because it's divided into three separate collections. The first, the *Vinaya*, deals with rules governing the sangha; the second, the *Sutra Pitaka*, consists of recorded sermons of the Buddha and is divided into five *Nikayas* or volumes. One of these alone, the *Anguttara Nikaya*, contains more than 2,300 sutras. The final basket, the *Abhidharma*, is made up of commentaries on the scriptures dating from the 3rd century BCE. The first English rendition of the Pali Canon came to 57 heavy tomes. In comparison, the Christian Bible seems little more than a pamphlet.

---

12. This stream is also at times called the Hinayana (Lesser Vehicle), a pejorative term used by Mahayana (Great Vehicle) adherents.
13. Tibetan Buddhism posits a third stream, the Vajrayana, that is a development of the Mahayana.

There is general agreement that the First Turning of the Wheel of the Dharma, the presentation the Buddha gave to his former companions in the Deer Park at Isipatana, reflects his most basic concepts and can, with some safety, be assumed to be the foundational premises of his original teaching.

In the Pali texts, the content of the First Turning – the Four Noble Truths and the Eightfold Path – is the expression of the Buddha's enlightenment experience.[14] With his clear unsurpassed enlightenment, Gautama awoke to the understanding of the process of causality that underlies existence and, in doing so, completely quenched the flames of desire that drive that process and thus freed himself from future rebirth. Accordingly, at the time of his enlightenment he was said to have exclaimed:

> Through many births I have passed
> Seeking, in vain, the builder of the house.
> Now the framer of the house has been found,
> And never again shall a house be framed for me.
> The beams are broken,
> The king-post is shattered!
> I have passed into the stillness of Nirvana;
> The ending of desire has been attained at last![15]

The Middle Way

The Buddha began the discourse to his former companions by presenting the concept of a Middle Way, which would become one of the titles by which his teaching is known.

On the one hand, he agreed with Kondanna and the other ascetics about the need to reject the path commonly followed by the "worldly-minded" who remained blindly subject to their appetites and whose activity was devoted to little more than seeking pleasure when possible and vainly trying to avoid suffering. This is the life of the householder. Like the ascetics, the Buddha held that such a way of life could not lead to liberation from suffering; the very premises on which it was based made suffering inevitable.

On the other hand, the asceticism of Kondanna and his companions was equally unprofitable. Gautama determined from personal experience that self-mortification in itself did not lead to liberation either. Instead the Buddha preached a Middle Way between the extremes of the householder and the ascetic, and this he defined in the Four Noble Truths and the Eightfold Path.

---

14. The Zen tradition will interpret the Buddha's enlightenment experience differently.
15. *Dhammapada*, Chapter 11.

The Four Noble Truths

The Noble Truth of Dukkha

The four noble truths are the Buddha's reflection on his own quest to find a way to overcome suffering.

The first Noble Truth states that all life is characterized by *dukkha*, which is often translated as "suffering." The word, however, is more general than that. There is no single English term that captures all of its connotations: unpleasant, awkward, painful, annoying. The etymology of the word refers to a wheel that is off-kilter. Perhaps "unsatisfying" is as close as we can come to an appropriate translation. There is something off-balance about life, something inherently unsatisfying.

The Buddha stated that this sense of dissatisfaction isn't an indication that there's something wrong in one's individual life; dissatisfaction, rather, is the natural condition of life. One's birth involves pain to both mother and child; we fall ill; we grow old and are subject to death and decay. Throughout our lives we encounter unpleasant situations, and pleasant circumstances inevitably pass. We have cravings that remain unfulfilled or, if achieved, bring only transitory satisfaction. All of this is dukkha.

Further, because the culture in which he lived took the concept of reincarnation for granted, it was believed that after death one would be reborn and be subject to further suffering. This is called *samsara* in Sanskrit, the Wheel of Birth and Death. There is birth, suffering, and death followed by rebirth, further suffering and death, and on and on. What the Buddha sought when giving up his princely status was a way to put an end to this cycle.

The Noble Truth of the Origin of Dukkha

The Second Noble Truth states that dukkha is the product of desire or craving.

Life is inherently unsatisfying because we can't accept things as they are; we want our lives and the world we encounter to be different. We want to be free of pain, which is unavoidable. We want to be well, but we get sick. We want to remain young and vital, but we grow old and infirm. We want to live forever, and we die. We crave pleasure and the satisfaction of our appetites, but pleasures are fleeting, and appetites are never satisfied. We want to be able to avoid what is unpleasant and want pleasant circumstances to persist. We want to be loved and admired. We want power and position. We want chocolate ice cream and only vanilla is available.

The Noble Truth of the Cessation of Dukkha

The Third Noble Truth follows from the first two. If dukkha is the product of desire, then it follows that if desire were extinguished suffering would cease to be. Emancipation from craving, the Buddha asserts, alone leads to the cessation of dukkha.

Further, if one were wholly free of desire, then rebirth would come to an end because there would be no desire driving the energy that seeks to be reborn. This is nirvana, the quenching of desire and release from the cycle of samsara.

The Noble Truth of the Path of Liberation

The Fourth Noble Truth outlines the Noble Eightfold Path, which is the Buddhist formula for being able to overcome desire.

The very simple solution the Buddha came to regarding the matter of craving was not to cling to it. Desires arise, as do other emotional states, but they also pass away naturally. It's not so much that craving in itself promotes suffering. Suffering arises when one identifies with the craving, when one – to put it simply – determines that one's happiness is dependent on achieving or acquiring something as opposed to finding satisfaction with what is.

The Noble Eightfold Path

The Eightfold Path consists of three groups of tenets. The first two assert the need to properly understand the human condition; the next four concern behavior; the final two are specific to spiritual practice. The steps of the path are expressed positively rather than negatively. They are not prohibitions but descriptions of what is "right" or "appropriate" in the sense of what is effective.

The concept of sin as understood within the Judeo-Christian tradition is absent from the Buddhadharma, nor are spirituality and morality equated in the same way as they are in the West. Because Buddhism does not recognize a creator external to the Universe, it does not envision a divinely prescribed moral code. The goal of the Eightfold Path and the Buddhist precepts is practical. There are appropriate and inappropriate patterns of behavior. Certain patterns of behavior are discouraged not because they transgress Divine Laws but because they are recognized as perpetuating that desire which is the root of suffering – both one's own and that of others.

From the Zen perspective, the last two steps of the Eightfold Path are the most significant. Right Mindfulness and Right Concentration train the individual to focus on what is occurring at this moment, thus short-circuiting the craving for the present moment to be something other than it is. It's a difficult undertaking, of course, so the earlier elements of the Eightfold Path describe a way of life that makes Right Mindfulness and Right Concentration easier to develop.

(1) Right Understanding

In the texts of the Pali Canon, the Buddha introduces each of the eight steps then provides specific examples of how the step is applied.

> What, then – O Bhikkhus – is Right Understanding? To understand suffering; to understand the origin of suffering; to understand the cessation of suffering; to understand the path which leads to liberation – this is Right Understanding.[16]

The initial step in the path, then, is to recognize the first three Noble Truths.

(2) Right Intention

> What, then, is Right Intention? To resolve to follow the path of liberation with compassion and for the benefit of all humankind – this is Right Intention. Not to use the path as a means of glorifying oneself – this is Right Intention. To be free from the intentions of lust; to be free from the intentions of ill-will; to be free from the intentions of cruelty – this is Right Intention.

Having fully grasped the first three truths, one resolves to follow a way of life that diminishes one's enslavement to desire.

(3) Right Speech

> What, then, is Right Speech? To speak truthfully, reliably, with sensitivity and integrity – this is Right Speech. If one knows something, to say, 'I know this;' if one does not know, to say, 'I do not know' – this is Right Speech. To avoid tale-bearing, harsh language, and boastful talk – this is Right Speech.

(4) Right Behavior

> What, then, is Right Behavior? To avoid killing living beings; to be filled with compassion for all living beings – this is Right Behavior. To avoid taking what does not belong to one whether in the village or in the forest – this is Right Behavior. To avoid improper or exploitive sexual activity – this is Right Behavior.

---

16. The Four Noble Truths and the Eightfold path are presented in several sutras, but the formula given in the *Dhammacakkappavattana Sutra* is the one most frequently referenced.

Right Behavior is further clarified in the Five Precepts – or rules of conduct – that call upon both monastic and lay Buddhists (1) to avoid doing harm (ahimsa), [17] (2) to refrain from stealing, (3) to refrain from sexual misconduct,[18] (4) to refrain from false speech, and (5) to refrain from taking intoxicants. There are a further three precepts – eating only once a day, avoiding frivolous activities, and disciplining one's sleeping habits – that are advised for those who wish to undertake a more arduous practice.

The precepts that monastics – "home-leavers" – agree to abide by are far more demanding. For males there are a total of 227 precepts, while women are required to accept an additional 84 for a total of 311 precepts (including one that prohibits them from eating garlic).

(5) Right Livelihood

> What, then, is Right Livelihood? To avoid a livelihood that is unjust, exploitive, or cruel – this is Right Livelihood.

Monks and nuns pursued no livelihood as such but obtained their food by begging and depending upon the generosity of the general population. For lay people, however, Right Livelihood emphasizes that certain ways of earning a living, while legal, are still inappropriate. Although Zen became the religious tradition of the Samurai warrior class in Japan, early Buddhists would have interpreted this step to forbid any activity that involves violence against other persons or any sentient beings.

(6) Right Effort

> What, then, is Right Effort? To avoid what is unwholesome – this is Right Effort. To seek to overcome negative habits and to develop positive habits – this is Right Effort. To seek to maintain positive habits – this is Right Effort.

Right Effort calls upon the Buddhist to seek to overcome negative states of mind (greed, anger, and delusion) and to cultivate positive states of mind (generosity, loving kindness, and wisdom).

(7) Right Mindfulness

> What, then, is Right Mindfulness? To be attentive to what is occurring in one's body – this is Right Mindfulness. To be attentive to one's feelings as they arise – this is Right Mindfulness. To be

---

17. This precept is usually interpreted as imposing a vegetarian diet on Buddhists, although the biography relates occasions when the Buddha accepted invitations to meals that included meat dishes.

18. That in the case of monks and nuns means any sexual activity.

aware of what is occurring in one's mind – this is Right Mindfulness. To be aware of the way in which one's thoughts and feelings affect one's perception – this is Right Mindfulness. To be aware of what is occurring all about one – this is Right Mindfulness.

Right Mindfulness – attentiveness – calls upon Buddhists to avoid being distracted by the endless chain of thoughts running through the mind and to be conscious of what is actually occurring both internally and externally. Our usual mode of perception is not to see things as they are but rather as we have been conditioned to see them by either cultural pressure or personal habit. We form opinions that we then rehearse in the endless interior monologue taking place in our minds, clouding our ability to perceive things clearly and objectively. Right Mindfulness is the antidote to this distorted view of ourselves, other people, our surroundings, and our circumstances.

(8) Right Concentration

What, then, is Right Concentration? To focus the attention with clarity – this is Right Concentration.

Right Concentration (samadhi) is also, at times, called Right Meditation, although in early Buddhism a distinction is made between meditation (jhana) and concentration. Concentration is the necessary first step in formal meditation practice which can take a number of forms.

In one sense, concentration and meditation are practices that strengthen one's capacity for Right Mindfulness in ordinary activity. As the aspirant becomes more skilled in meditative practice, Right Concentration becomes a formal exercise by which he sees through the illusion of the individual self, extinguishes the flames of desire, and achieves the freedom of Nirvana.

The Fire Sermon

After the sermon to his former companions at the Deer Park, the Buddha's next major presentation was to the fire worshippers led by Uruvela Kasyapa. In that talk, he emphasized that it is not pleasure, as such, that is the primary impediment to liberation but rather desire, craving. In the Middle Way, pleasure is not pursued for its own sake, as householders do, but – although the early Buddhists displayed, at times, a puritanical attitude towards pleasure – neither was it aggressively avoided. The challenge was to remember that both pleasure and beauty are ephemeral, and therefore it's futile to seek satisfaction in them. It's not pleasure itself that leads one away from the path but the fires of desire and attachment which arise from them:

All things, O bhikkhus, are on fire. And what are all those things which are on fire? The eye is on fire; forms are on fire; eye-consciousness is on fire; impressions received by the eye are on fire; and whatever sensations, pleasant, unpleasant, or indifferent, which originate in dependence upon impressions received by the eye, these also are on fire.

And with what are these on fire? With the fire of desire, with the fire of hatred, with the fire of illusion; with birth, old age, death, sorrow, lamentation, misery, grief, and despair are they on fire.

The ear is on fire; sounds are on fire; ear-consciousness is on fire; impressions received by the ear are on fire; and whatever sensations, pleasant, unpleasant, or indifferent, which originate in dependence on impressions received by the ear, these also are on fire. So, too, the nose is on fire; the tongue is on fire; the body is on fire.... The mind, too, is on fire; mind-consciousness is on fire; impressions received by the mind are on fire; and whatever sensations, pleasant, unpleasant, or indifferent, which originate in dependence on impressions received by the mind, these also are on fire.

And with what are these all on fire? With the fire of desire, with the fire of hatred, with the fire of illusion; with birth, old age, death, sorrow, lamentation, misery, grief, and despair are they on fire.

Perceiving this, O bhikkhus, the learned and noble disciple no longer forms attachment to the eye, to eye-consciousness, to impressions received by the eye, to whatever sensation, pleasant, unpleasant, or indifferent which originates in dependence upon impressions received by the eye. Likewise, the learned and noble disciple no longer forms attachment to the ear...to the nose... to the tongue...to the body.... Likewise, the learned and noble disciple no longer forms attachment to the mind, to ideas, to impressions received by the mind, to whatever sensation, pleasant, unpleasant, or indifferent which originates in dependence on impressions received by the mind.

And because he is no longer attached to eye, ear, nose, tongue, body, and mind, the learned and noble disciple is free of desire, of passion, of illusion. In the one free of desire, of passion, of illusion arises the knowledge, "I am delivered; rebirth is at an end; holiness is perfected, and there is no returning to this world." The one who is free knows this.[19]

---

19. *Adittapariyaya Sutta.*

An early Western criticism of Buddhism is that it advocated a stoic and joyless resignation to life. The sutras also acknowledge that some the Buddha's contemporaries found teachings like the Fire Sermon negative and bleak. The story is told of a young man who, having heard the Buddha preach, declared before the assembly, "This is a philosophy for the dead not for the living!" The Buddha, however, believed that his responsibility as a spiritual teacher was similar to that of a physician. Like a physician, he identified the disease, sought to understand the cause of the disease, and then proposed a cure. The disease was the universality of suffering; the cause is "ignorance" or the clutching attachment that results from desire (a form of ignorance); the cure is found in overcoming ignorance and attachment. Only those who were still immersed in their attachments criticized the Dharma for being negative.

In another story, the Buddha was grieved to hear of a group of bhikkhus who, because they misunderstood his teaching, formed such a deep aversion to the body and sensory impressions that they committed suicide. Speaking of those deaths, he emphasized that a bhikkhu's path should avoid both aversion and clinging. "Clinging and aversion are both ropes that bind. A free person transcends both in order to dwell in peace and happiness. These brothers did not understand this."

Impermanence and the Skandhas

When Sariputta asked Assaji what the Buddha taught, Assaji's poetic reply referred specifically to the issue of causality:

Whatsoever things are produced by causes,
The Buddha has revealed those causes;
As well, how things cease to be,
This too the Buddha reveals.

The concept of causation is central to all of the Buddha's teachings. The child Siddhartha was first struck by it when, attending the plowing ceremony, he realized that the Brahmin rituals had nothing to do with the future fertility of the fields. If conditions were right, the crops would flourish; if conditions weren't right, they wouldn't.

This form of reasoning is put this way in the sutras:

When this is, that comes to be;
When this arises, that arises.
When this is not, that does not come to be;

When this ceases, that ceases.[20]

Causes result in effects that in turn become causes of further effects. It's a never-ending process to which all things are subject. Everything is in a continuous state of becoming, and nothing ever reaches a final state of achievement. Things come into being, exist, then pass away subject to conditions over which they have no control. Another way of saying this is that all things are impermanent. One of the causes of dukkha is precisely that people want the world to be stable and static when it is not.

The process of impermanence is easy to observe in one's own life. One is no longer the child one once was nor is one yet whatever one may become in the future. On the other hand, each stage of one's life is determined by the earlier stages; and one's current choices and actions determine what one's future will be.

After extensive and exhaustive self-reflection, the Buddha was unable to discover a stable, solid reality upholding the sense of self. Instead, he posited that what one mistakenly views as a "self" is actually an aggregation of five components calls skandhas – 1) form; 2) feeling; 3) perception; 4) choice; and 5) consciousness – each of which is in a constant state of change.

Form refers to the physical body and the senses associated with it. Feeling is response – pleasant, unpleasant, or indifferent – to sensation, including emotional responses. Perception is the process of identifying a sensation/response and forming an idea or concept about that it – identifying it as something specific. Choice is the conditioned reaction to the identified object of perception, the activity that follows perception.

Consciousness is the process of awareness. There are not only the physical senses in themselves, there is also consciousness of those senses; likewise, there is consciousness of the response to the perception and the choices that follow. Therefore, the Buddhadharma speaks of a particular form of consciousness identified with each of the six senses (the mind is considered a sixth organ of sense in Buddhist analysis).

Anatman

The Buddha emphasized that nowhere in the skandhas can one find a stable and permanent self. Instead there is only a succession of states of being that arise and pass away. This is the doctrine of anatman – no atman or soul – that distinguishes Gautama's teaching from other philosophical perspectives both in his era and culture and down to the present time. It's a challenging concept to grasp because the denial of a permanent soul

---

20. *Paticca-samuppada-vibhanga Sutra*, also a primary source for the Twelvefold Chain of Dependent Co-Arising.

seems, at first, inconsistent with the notion of successive lives that early Buddhism also takes for granted.

It is the idea of an unchanging essence that the Buddha rejects. Obviously, individuals feel themselves as stable, perduring beings, but the Buddha enquired whether there was an actual static entity wherein that sense of self resided or if it were an illusion. It cannot be the body nor the mind, both of which are subject to change – to growth, maturity, and decline.

In most religious traditions, some form of "soul" is considered the enduring essence of an individual, remaining constant regardless of changing circumstances including death. In that sense, it is one's truest self. In the Vedic tradition, this true self is Atman, and it is the Atman that is subject to rebirth. The Buddhadharma denies the existence of an Atman or any form of permanent Self. The self is understood to be a construct, dependent upon a series of components that are always in flux. When these components pass away or change, so does the sense of selfhood.

The term the Buddha used was "void" – the skandhas and the sense of self arising from them are void of any enduring essence that can be identified as a soul. There remains, however, a perpetually transforming energy created by karmic factors that persists beyond the dissolution of a particular mind-body (the Buddhist equivalent of the law of the Conservation of Energy). It is that energy which is driven to seek rebirth.

To put it another way, although the storehouse of memory, habitual activity, and conditioned perception that one identifies as one's self passes away with the dissolution of this body/mind, the energy that produced that body/mind persists and – if still caught up in the cycle of samsara – seeks regeneration in another body/mind in a process that can be compared to passing a flame from one candle to another. Nirvana blows out the flame before it can be passed on.

The Twelvefold Chain of Dependent Co-Arising

The Twelvefold Chain of Dependent Co-Arising is second only to the Four Noble Truths in being the most frequently cited teaching of early Buddhism. Some variation of it is found in 96 different sutras. The biography relates that the Buddha came to be aware of the Chain by clearly observing his own mind and physical processes on the night of his enlightenment. In some versions of the story, it is the realization of this chain that is the central content of that enlightenment. In the first watch of the night before his full and complete awakening, he became conscious of all his previous lives. In the second watch, he recalled the Four Signs and understood that whenever there is birth it will be followed inevitably by old age, sickness, and death. The cycle of rebirth, he determined, was due to attachment. Attachment arose from desire, desire from perception,

perception from the senses. It was clear that the senses are connected to the physical form, that where there is form and senses there is awareness. Where there is awareness, there is thought, and thoughts can either be accurate or inaccurate; so one could argue that ignorance – inaccurate or incomplete awareness – is the consequence of the capacity for thought.

We may no longer accept some of the premises on which this analysis is based; however, the understanding that all things arise because of prior conditions remains valid.

Although it is presented as such, the chain is not sequential. Rather, the elements arise simultaneously and are dependent upon the others for their existence. There is an inevitability in the chain. Once one element arises, the others follow inexorably. Given the interdependence of the links, the analysis could begin with any one of them, but it's traditional to start with Ignorance.

(1) Avidya – Ignorance

Ignorance can take many forms, but the most fundamental error is the belief in a stable and independent existence, the belief that one is an autonomous being, as opposed to recognizing that everything we think of as our "self" is nothing more than the fleeting emanations of the skandhas. It is also the failure to recognize that dukkha is the result of desire and, as a consequence of that misperception, to continue to seek fulfillment where it can't be attained.

(2) Samskara – The Formation of Karma

Because of ignorance, karma is generated.

Karma essentially means action. The law of causality recognizes that actions produce consequences. Positive actions produce positive outcomes; negative actions have negative consequences. When we act from Ignorance, we produce karma that impacts our present life and perpetuates the cycle of the Wheel of Samsara. Within one lifetime, one experiences the impact not only of the karma generated in that lifetime but in previous lifetimes as well, and the karma generated in this lifetime affects both present and future lifetimes.

(3) Vijnana – Consciousness

The next two links in the chain can be difficult to follow. The third link asserts that the karma of previous lives results in consciousness. That is to say, consciousness arises because of prior conditions. Nor is consciousness objective, stable, or continuous; rather it responds to cultural conditioning, is constantly changing, arises and passes away from moment to moment according to circumstances.

(4) Nama-Rupa – Mind and Body

The term "nama" refers to the psychological aspects of an individual (mind) and "rupa" to the physical (form). Consciousness manifests itself in a physical form and in the mind associated with that physical form. Mind and matter, in that sense, come about simultaneously and are co-dependent. Feeling, perception, and volition are functions of consciousness and so can be said to arise from it and have no independent existence separate from it.[21]

(5) Sadayatana – The Six Senses

With the arising of form come the six sense organs – eye, ear, nose, tongue, body, and mind.

(6) Sparsha – Contact

Through the senses, one experiences or makes contact with the physical world.

(7) Vedana – Sensation

From contact, sensation arises, which will be pleasant, unpleasant, or indifferent according to circumstances. Sensation is no more constant than any of the other elements in the chain. What is experienced as pleasant at one time may be perceived as unpleasant or neutral at others.

(8) Trishna – Craving

From contact and sensation comes craving for further contact, which is identified in the Four Noble Truths as the source of dukkha.

(9) Upadana – Clinging

Craving by its nature is unquenchable and can never be satisfied, so it provokes further craving. Upadana is the inevitable clinging that follows from that continued craving. Even though sensual pleasures never bring fulfillment, we cling to them and fall into habitual forms of behavior.

Clinging to ignorance or wrong views prevents us from entering the Noble Eightfold Path which begins with Right Understanding. When

---

21. Nama-rupa can also be translated "name and form." In this understanding, forms arise and are named, but there is nothing substantial to which that name applies. The example of a chariot is used. If the component parts of a chariot – wheels, axel, carriage, shafts – were disassembled there would be nothing left to which the word "chariot" refers. "Chariot" was simply a temporary condition that arose when certain circumstances arose and passed away when those circumstances ceased to be.

people have invested energy in a particular viewpoint, their sense of identity becomes associated with those concepts; consequently, it is often more difficult to give up belief than it is to break habits of behavior or surrender worldly possessions.

(10) Bhava – Becoming

After death, clinging causes the energy generated by one's karmic choices to seek a new life or becoming.

(11) Jati – Birth

Becoming is then manifested in birth (or rebirth).

(12) Jara-Maranam – Aging and Death

Birth leads to aging and eventually to death, at which point the Karma which has been generated once again begets another life grounded in ignorance.

This whole process makes up the Wheel of Samsara. The cycle can, however, be broken. If one adopts Right Understanding or Right View – the first step in the Noble Eightfold Path – and lives accordingly, ignorance is dispelled, and the entire structure of the chain falls apart. By recognizing this, the Buddha achieved his goal of finding a way to overcome the suffering inherent in old age, sickness, and death.

> Through the entire cessation of ignorance, the formation of karma ceases;
> Through the cessation of the formation of karma, consciousness ceases;
> Through the cessation of consciousness, mind and body cease;
> Through the cessation of mind and body, the senses and their objects cease;
> Through the cessation of senses and their objects, contact ceases;
> Through the cessation of contact, sensation ceases;
> Through the cessation of sensation, craving ceases;
> Through the cessation of craving, clinging ceases;
> Through the cessation of clinging, becoming ceases;
> Through the cessation of becoming, birth ceases;
> Through the cessation of birth, aging and death, sorrow, lamentation, pain, grief, and despair cease.
> Thus, the whole mass of suffering ceases.[22]

---

22. *Paticca-samuppada-vibhanga Sutra.*

Gods, Miracles, and the Noble Silence

What the Buddha defined in both the Four Noble Truths and the Twelvefold Chain are processes that require no external power in order to occur. All beings will come into existence when conditions are appropriate and pass away when other conditions arise. The concern of humankind, then, should be directed toward addressing these issues; the more abstract matters about which the Brahmin speculated were, he asserted, irrelevant to spiritual development.

On the other hand, the Pali Canon is as full of miraculous occurrences as is the New Testament. For example, when the future Gautama determined to return to Earthly life for a final time in order to attain Buddhahood, deities representing ten thousand universes assembled to praise his decision. When his conception in the womb of Queen Maya took place, spontaneous cures occurred throughout the world, human beings briefly behaved with kindness and generosity to one another, and lotus flowers fell from the heavens.

The existence of supernatural beings such as gods is not rejected in the canon, and specific deities – such as Sakka who drew the portrait of the rabbit on the moon – are identified, but these are just another order of being and not the creators or governors of humankind. Stories are recounted of the Buddha ascending to the realm of the gods, preaching the Dharma there, and inspiring them to become his disciples.

Heavens and Hells are among the various realms in which one can be reborn,[23] but these are temporary abodes. One may, through merit, be reborn in the Heaven of Delight, but when that merit is exhausted, that existence will come to an end and lead to yet another birth. Likewise, condemnation to Hell is not eternal. Devadatta was said to have been reborn as a body of flame in Hell, but – because he took refuge in the Buddha, Dharma, and Sangha in his last moments – he will eventually be reborn as the Buddha Sattisara.

Even if supernatural beings exist, however, it's futile to seek their intervention in human affairs. This point is made in a conversation between the Buddha and Uruvela Kasyapa, who asked if there were any value at all in devotional rites and sacred prayers.

"Tell me, O Kasyapa," the Buddha replied, "if there was one who sought to cross a river in order to get to the other shore, what

---

23. There is a realm of the gods (Devas), a realm of demons, the human realm, the animal realm, the realm of Hungry Ghosts, and the Hell realm. The human realm is the most auspicious because only in it can one achieve Nirvana and release from the Wheel of Samsara.

should such a one do?"

"If the river is shallow, he could wade across. Otherwise he would need to swim or use a boat."

"And if such a one were not willing to wade, swim, or use a boat – what then? Could such a one stand on one side of the river and call over to the other side asking it to come to him? Even if such a one were to spend the remainder of his life in this effort, would there be any value in it?"

"None at all."

"Exactly so! And in the same manner, one cannot achieve liberation through prayer and devotional rites even if one were to spend the remainder of one's life in the effort. It is only by following the Noble Eightfold Path that one can achieve liberation."

When specifically asked questions about matters such as the existence or non-existence of gods, spirits, or supernatural forces, the Buddha maintained a Noble Silence and refused to speculate about them. The story is told of a monk named Malunkyaputta who complained about the Buddha's failure to answer such questions.

"Lord, it has occurred to me that there are many issues which you have not elucidated for the bhikkhus. Such as: whether the world is eternal or finite, whether the atman and body are one or are separate, whether or not there is an existence after death for those who have attained Nirvana and Parinirvana,[24] and many other issues. I consider these important issues and have decided that if my Lord will not provide me with clear answers to these questions, I will have no choice except to leave the sangha and resume the life of a layman."

"O Malunkyaputta," the Buddha replied, "did the Tathagata ever say to you that if you led the religious life he would answer these questions?"

"No, Lord, you did not."

"Or, Malunkyaputta, did you say to the Tathagata when you entered the sangha, 'I will lead the religious life only if you answer these questions'?"

"No, Lord, I did not."

"That being true, Malunkyaputta, why do you come with these questions at this time? One who would insist that such questions be answered before he lives the religious life is like a man who has

---

24. Parinirvana is the complete entry into nirvana that occurs with death and the freedom from rebirth.

been wounded by a poisoned arrow. Imagine that such a man's relatives rush to obtain the services of a physician, but, when the physician arrives, this man said to him, 'I will not have this poisoned arrow drawn out until I have a physical description of the one who wounded me, his name, caste, and country of origin; I will not have this poisoned arrow drawn out until I know the type of wood used to form the bow from which it was shot and what type of bow-string was used; I will not have this arrow drawn out until I know the name of the fletcher who fashioned it and am told the type of materials he used.' Such a man, O Malunkyaputta, would die before learning the answer to these questions.

"In the same way, one who before agreeing to lead the religious life demands to know whether the world is eternal or finite, whether the atman and body are one or are separate, whether or not there is an existence after Nirvana, and so forth, such a one would die before he had achieved liberation.

"The religious life, O Malunkyaputta, does not depend on these issues. Whether the world is eternal or finite, whether the atman and body are one or separate, whether or not there is an existence after Nirvana – none of these matters are of any importance. Still there remains suffering, the causes of suffering, the cessation of suffering, and the path that leads to the cessation of suffering. These are what the Tathagata teaches.

"And why, O Malunkyaputta, has the Tathagata taught suffering, the causes of suffering, the cessation of suffering, and the path which leads to the cessation of suffering? Because on these the religious life does depend, and because these teachings lead to liberation."[25]

The Style of Teaching

The highly formalized manner in which early Buddhist teachings are presented probably doesn't reflect the actual teaching style of the Buddha himself. The sutras were composed in a manner that allowed them to be easily memorized and recited. As with the presentations of the Four Noble Truths and the Twelvefold Chain of Dependent Co-Arising above, the topic of the talk is broken down into a series of numbered headings that are then elaborated upon in repetitive detail. There are hundreds of such lists in the Buddhist canon and specific elements are repeated in more than one list.

---

25. The story is found in the *Cula-Malunkyovada Sutra*.

The Three Characteristics of Existence are inferred from the Buddha's analysis of the human condition:
- Dukkha (dissatisfaction)
- Annica (impermanence)
- Anatman (void of any permanent self).

The Three Types of Suffering enumerate the major causes of Dukkha:
- Pain
- Change/Impermanence
- Conditionality

The Five Hindrances are the impediments to progress on the Eightfold Path:
- Desire
- Aversion
- Sloth
- Restlessness
- Doubt

Lists approach similar subjects from different perspectives. So in addition to a list of the hindrances on the path, there is a list of the Three Poisons that can draw one away from the Eightfold Path.
- Greed
- Hatred
- Delusion

Lists can also be complimentary. Balancing the Three Poisons, for example, are the Three Wholesome Qualities:
- Generosity
- Loving kindness
- Wisdom

The Ten Fetters are conditions overcome as one progresses along the Eightfold Path:
- Delusion of Self
- Doubt
- Dependence on ritual
- Sensual desire
- Ill-will
- Desire for life in the physical realm
- Desire for life in the spiritual realms
- Pride
- Self-righteousness
- Avidya – Ignorance

Similar to the Five Hindrances and the Ten Fetters, the Ten Kleshas are conditions that defile the mind and hamper progress. These include the Three Poisons and seven other fetters:
- Greed
- Hatred
- Delusion
- Conceit
- Wrong Views
- Doubt
- Sloth
- Restiveness
- Lack of Shame
- Recklessness

The Ten Perfections (or Paramitas) are the qualities of character to be cultivated by the disciples:[26]
- Charity
- Moral Behavior or Discipline
- Renunciation
- Wisdom
- Zeal
- Patience
- Honesty
- Commitment
- Loving-Kindness
- Tranquility

Nirvana

The goal of early Buddhism is release from the Wheel of Samsara – the cycle of birth and death – that is attained by nirvana.

"Nirvana" is the Sanskrit version of the Pali word "nibbana" that is derived from the verb "to blow" and a suffix meaning "out," therefore "to extinguish, as the flame of a candle." In pre-Buddhist writing, nirvana often referred to the state of bliss attained when one achieves moksha or illumination.

In early expressions of the Buddhadharma, one who attains nirvana is termed an arhat, an achiever of perfection, and the term arhatta, then, is synonymous with nirvana. Such a person has freed themselves from the

---

26. In Mahayana Buddhism, this list is reduced to six perfections necessary for the spiritual life: Dana (Charity), Shila (Moral Discipline), Kshanti (Patience/Tolerance), Viraya (Zeal), Dhyana (Meditative Practice), and Prajna (Wisdom).

enslaving passions and by doing so has overcome suffering. It's also claimed that an arhat is one in whom the sense of "self" is no longer present.

Although with nirvana the "will to live" dissipates, the current life continues. The metaphor used is that of a potter's wheel that will keep spinning until the accumulated energy turning it is exhausted. At the end of life, with the final stilling of the wheel, the arhat enters into complete nirvana – or parinirvana – in which name and form are surrendered for the final time.

In later forms of Buddhism, this is not precisely annihilation, because in overcoming the sense of self in awakening one recognizes one's unity with that totality of Being – Huxley's "Divine Ground" – from which all things proceed and to which they inevitably return. A popular Zen analogy uses the example of a doll made of salt that discovers its true identity by allowing itself to be dissolved in the ocean. Early Buddhism, however, refuses to speculate on the nature of parinirvana. When Malunkyaputta asks about the state of the arhat after entering parinirvana, he assumes that the arhat is freed from rebirth but wonders if he continues in some other manner. The Buddha replies that he has not revealed whether the arhat exists after death or does not exist after death. "Neither have I revealed that he both exists and does not exist, nor that he neither exists or does not exist after death." These are matters, he tells Malunkyaputta, that are not edifying, nor do they contribute to the effort to overcome the appetites and the attainment of wisdom. Whether or not the arhat persists in some manner, still there is suffering, the cause of suffering, and the Noble Path to overcome suffering.

The Four Stages

Although the biography relates that many of the Buddha's early followers achieved arhatta merely by hearing him speak, most who entered the brotherhood found attainment more arduous. It was even acknowledged that it could take more than one lifetime to accomplish. A sequence of four stages of progress was identified.

Stream Enterers

Those just beginning the Buddhist life were termed "stream enterers." They gave up the comforts and consolations of the life of a householder and took refuge in the Three Gems – Buddha, Dharma, and Sangha. In this stage, monks and nuns overcome the first three of the Ten Fetters – the delusion of having a self, doubt about the teaching, and engagement in futile ritual behavior. They also strive to overcome envy, dishonesty, hypocrisy, and the desire to dominate others. When Stream Enterers die, they will be reborn in the human realm – the only realm in which it is possible to attain nirvana.

Once Returners

In the second stage, the fetters of sensual desire and ill-will are weakened as well as the tendencies to greed, hatred, and delusion. If Once Returners do not achieve nirvana in their current lifetime, they will do so in their next.

Non-Returners

The Non-Returner completely overcomes the fetters of sensual desire and ill-will. Such a person is on the verge of full release.

Arhats – The Perfected Ones

Arhats are free of all ten fetters: the delusion of self, doubt, ritual behavior, sensual desire, ill-will, as well as desire for continued life in either the physical or spiritual realms, pride, self-righteousness, and ignorance. With the achievement of arhatta – nirvana – they are free from all future rebirth.

It's worth noting that in the earliest Buddhist iconography, the Buddha is never shown; the seated meditating figure with which we're familiar is something that arises from Greek influence much later. Instead, he is either represented by a pair of footprints or is simply missing from a scene although there is room left for him. This was to emphasize that with parinirvana he achieved complete extinction.

The Sangha

The Buddha and his disciples led a highly disciplined and regulated existence. Unlike later Zen monks, they did not live in communities or engage in physical labor, but lived either singly or in small groups as homeless wanderers for much of each year. They owned nothing except their robes, undergarments, a begging bowl, a water filter, a needle (they sewed their own garments), and a razor. During the three months of the rainy season, they gathered together in retreat centers donated by wealthy supporters. At these, it was the Buddha's habit to give regular Dharma talks that evolved into the sutras passed down orally for generations. The memorization and recitation of these sutras became a major sangha activity after the Buddha's death.

Monks were expected to abide by 227 precepts; nuns had to abide by 311. There is an undeniable sexism in early Buddhism bordering on misogyny. Like other traditions that advocated celibacy, women were held culpable for the fact that men found them alluring. The Buddha warned Ananda that by allowing women into the sangha, the teaching would not prevail as long it would have otherwise. On the other hand, Ananda convinced the Buddha to accept women into the order on the grounds that they don't differ from men at all in their ability to adhere to the Eightfold Path or to attain arhatta.[27]

All activity was supposed to be undertaken in mindful awareness, as dictated by the Noble Eightfold Path. Sangha members maintained themselves by daily begging rounds, taking care to display an appropriately dignified comportment as they did so. They ate a single meal a day and refrained from taking food between meals. As time passed, temples and monasteries were established that often became quite lavish, but the individual monks attached to these temples maintained modest lifestyles.

There were no vows. Although becoming a monk or nun was usually a lifelong commitment, no dispensation was needed in order to return to lay life, and those who did find the life too arduous were encouraged to do just that, with the hope that by living a virtuous lay life they would generate adequate merit to be reborn in more favorable conditions.

Respect was shown to the elders in the order, but there was no hierarchy as such, and senior monks did not have authority over the younger or less experienced. What discipline existed was enforced by the community as a whole which – in council – could address matters of conduct. Monks found guilty of serious infringements of the precepts (sexual misconduct, theft, killing, and claiming miraculous powers) could be expelled if the community came to that decision.

The reason why claiming miraculous powers was considered grounds for excommunication is that the effectiveness of such activity was specifically denied in the teachings. In later centuries, monks would chant sutras for the benefit of others and special ceremonies would be conducted, but the early Buddhist sangha dismissed all such pretenses. The monks had no priestly functions.

Because the teachings were preserved orally, it was difficult to establish an orthodox canon of what the Buddha taught during his lifetime. Within a short time after the Buddha's death – although still centuries before the sutras were committed to writing – there were twelve different schools each claiming it preserved the Buddha's original teaching. In a sutra composed long after his death, the Buddha is purported to predict that each of these schools would be a "repository of twelve aspects of my teaching without priority or inferiority, like the twelve sons of one father, all honest and true."

All twelve of these schools were in agreement about the ineffectiveness of non-Buddhist paths. Nirvana was only attainable by those who

---

27. When one of his female students asked Taizan Maezumi of the Zen Center of Los Angles about the Buddha's prediction that the inclusion women in the sangha would lessen the lifetime of the Dharma, Maezumi's response was that the price was worth it.

adhered to the Noble Eightfold Path, and to question that was grounds for expulsion from the community. On the other hand, the order did not seek to impose itself on others. Although the Buddha argued with the Brahmin about their beliefs – and poked fun at them in his famous analogy of blind men trying to describe an elephant – he counseled the community to treat adherents of other creeds with courtesy and respect. The story is told of a former follower of Mahavira (the founder of the Jains) who, after he joined the sangha, was advised by the Buddha to continue supporting his former order financially.

Practice

Because early Buddhist monks did not engage in physical labor, a significant portion of their time was available for contemplative and meditative exercises. Traditionally there were forty subjects of reflection in early Buddhism, including meditating on corpses in various forms of corruption in order to fully understand the transience of life. Less gruesome topics included the Three Gems or various virtues.

For both householders and Stream Enterers, a basic practice was cultivating the Four Immeasurables – Apramana – or Sublime States of mind (Brahma-vihara). These included: Metta (Loving-kindness) – active good will to others and a desire to contribute to the well-being and happiness of others; Karuna (Compassion) – a commitment to relieve the suffering of others; Mudita (Empathetic Joy) – the ability to feel genuine happiness when others are happy; and Upekkha (Equanimity) – the ability to remain objective and serene in the face of the inevitable vicissitudes of life.

Although the Four Immeasurables are inherently positive, the aspirant to arhatta had to transcend them as well, since nirvana is the dying out of all passions, positive as well as negative.

Reflection on the Immeasurables – or on decaying corpses – is a form of contemplation, but it isn't what is identified as "jhana" in Pali or "dhyana" in Sanskrit, the terms that would be approximated in Chinese as "Chan" and pronounced by the Japanese as "Zen." Contemplation or reflection consists of focusing the mind on a concept. Dhyana – or meditation – in its purer form is stilling or quietening the internal vocal and emotional chain of thought that runs through the mind, what Buddhists refer to as the "monkey mind" that jumps from one thought to another without cease.

"Mind cleansing" meditations predate the Buddhadharma, and the techniques employed by early Buddhists are similar to those common in yoga systems of the period. The etymology of the word "yoga" – like the English word "religion" – derives from a root meaning to unite or bind; yoga thus originally referred to devotional practices through which one sought union with the divine. A necessary preliminary to such union is quietening the discursive mind as much as possible.

This is not a rejection of rationality, as some critics have suggested, but rather a recognition that, because the discursive mind rehearses a learned or conditioned point of view, one is unable to perceive things as they actually are. The random thoughts that pour through the mind perpetuate ignorance (avidya) because they prevent one from being able to think outside the parameters of one's conditioned perspective. As Anaïs Nin put it, we don't see things as they are; we see them as we are. While reflection on the Immeasurables and other contemplative activities can generate positive karma, leading to favorable rebirth, they do not lead to the ultimate goal of nirvana. That requires a rigorous emptying of self and a calming of the mental muzak in the mind. A series of practices evolved that cultivate this, beginning by strengthening the capacity for one-pointed attention (samadhi). These teachings are the basis of the later meditation schools in China and Japan.

The easiest focus for meditative attention is the breath, basic instruction for which is given by the Buddha in the *Anapanasati Sutra*. One is instructed to take an erect posture with folded legs and mindfully breathe in and breathe out.

> Taking in a long breath, the monk is aware that he is taking in a long breath. Taking in a short breath, the monk is aware that he is taking in a short breath. As he breathes in, the monk is sensitive to the entire body. As the monk breaths out, he is sensitive to the whole body. The monk trains himself to breathe in calming the bodily processes, and to breathe out calming the bodily processes.

The monk continues in this manner to become conscious of and calm mental activity, and then to steady and eventually release the mind.

> The monk trains himself to breathe in observing impermanence and to breathe out observing impermanence. The monk trains himself to breathe in cultivating dispassion and to breathe out cultivating dispassion. The monk trains himself to breathe in focusing on cessation and to breathe out focusing on cessation. The monk trains himself to breathe in focusing on relinquishment and to breathe out focusing on relinquishment.

By undertaking this practice, the Buddha explains, the monk will naturally put aside greed and distress. Being focused – ardent, alert, and mindful – putting aside greed and stress, mindfulness becomes a factor of awakening, as does persistence. One in whom persistence has been aroused becomes calm in body and mind which, in turn, leads to serenity and concentrated attention, relinquishment, clear knowing, and final release.

Four Foundations of Mindfulness

After one-pointed attention is cultivated through breath meditation, it can be applied to other aspects of one's life, as described in the *Satipatthana Sutra*. In it the Buddha presents the "Four Foundations of Mindfulness" as the most efficient means for overcoming pain and sorrow and realizing nirvana. These are mindfulness of body, mindfulness of sensations or feelings, mindfulness of mental activity, and mindfulness of the teachings (Dharma).

The sutra begins with instructions on breath meditation that are not substantially different from those in the *Anapanasati Sutra*: Assuming a formal seated posture, the monk focuses on his breath, recognizing a long breath as a long breath and a short breath as a short breath. Then, while still focused on the breathing, the monk consciously calms the body. The monk then extends the practice to times when the body is in motion. So, when walking, he is aware of walking, when standing, he is aware of standing. All activity – no matter how trivial – is engaged in consciously. To this point the instructions are unremarkable, but then – with the characteristically rosy perspective of the Theravada tradition – the sutra counsels the monk to develop non-attachment to the body by being conscious of all the elements that make it up, including tendons, bones, internal organs, the intestines, the contents of the stomach, feces, bile, phlegm, pus, and sweat. Like a butcher carving a cow into pieces, the monk is to view his own body as made up of the four elements (water, earth, fire, and air). Or if coming upon a corpse exposed on public charnel grounds, one should reflect that one's own body is likewise subject to death and decay and will return to the elements of which it is composed.

The second foundation focuses on awareness of feelings or sensations. When having a pleasant or unpleasant sensation, the monk is aware he is having a pleasant or unpleasant sensation; when having a sensation that is neither pleasant nor unpleasant, he is aware of that as well. The third foundation considers states of mind, whether or not one is experiencing craving, aversion, or delusion. If one's mind is scattered, jumping from one thought to another, one is aware of that. If one's mind is focused, one is aware of that.

Finally, the monk is aware of the elements of the Dharma as experienced in his own person. He is aware when the five hindrances – sensuality, ill will, sloth and torpor, restlessness and anxiety, and doubt – are present and when they are not present. He also realizes how these arise, and how they can be abandoned. He observes the skandhas and the six senses (including mind). He is aware when the seven factors of awakening are present and when they are not: mindfulness, investigation of mental states, energy, joy, tranquility, concentration, and equanimity. And he is aware of the Four Noble Truths, recognizing this is suffering, this is the arising of suffering, this the cessation of suffering, and this the noble path that leads to the cessation of suffering.

The sutra concludes with assurances that if the Four Foundations of Mindfulness are observed, the monk will either attain arhatta or, if some residual clinging to the physical world remains, the state of Non-Returning in his or her next – and final – birth.

Although there is no prohibition for lay people to undertake this type of meditative discipline, it is understood that they would be unlikely to do so. Early Buddhist teaching is addressed not to the general population but specifically to those who have chosen to be renunciates, to be "home-leavers." Those who remain householders are inevitably still caught up in the Wheel of Samsara, still driven by that desire which is at the root of suffering. All that early Buddhism can offer to the farmers, mothers, and warriors necessary for the maintenance of society is the hope that by acquiring merit in their current lives – through support of the sangha and virtuous activity – they will eventually be reborn as one who chooses to abandon the fetters of family life, as Gautama did, and follow the path of liberation.

"The bhikkhus must not accept the words of the Tathagata out of respect," the Buddha told Ananda. "Nor should they believe the words of the Tathagata solely because others do. The bhikkhus must analyze the teachings of the Tathagata as a goldsmith analyzes gold by cutting, melting, scraping, and rubbing it."

Gandavyuha Sutra

The Mahayana

AFTER THE BUDDHA'S DEATH, a council was called to codify his teaching. Ananda recited the sermons he had memorized, and the assembly assented to their accuracy. The story goes on, however, to note that as the gathering was coming to an end, Bhikkhu Purana arrived late. When he was told of the decisions made by the council, he said that he preferred to abide by the Dharma as he personally remembered the Buddha presenting it.

The Buddha had specifically cautioned his disciples not to accept his teachings on his authority alone but to test them the way a goldsmith tests gold for purity – carefully and thoroughly – in order to determine whether their own understanding validated the teaching. That invitation to trust one's personal insight led to a proliferation of schools after the Buddha's death. Early Buddhism was comfortable with this, as demonstrated by the tradition of the twelve schools that "without priority or inferiority" were to be considered "like the twelve sons of one father, all honest and true." But inevitably there arose interpretations which some members of that early community felt strayed too far from the original Dharma.

The Theravada tradition relates that seventy years after the Buddha's death a Second Council needed to be convened to consider the case of a group of monks who were thought to be transgressing the guidelines laid down in Vinaya. After a careful hearing and discussion, the offending monks were found guilty on ten counts: They stored salt; they ate after mid-day; they sought alms after eating in the same day; they participated collectively in a ceremony that was intended for individual practice; they carried out official business when the assembly was incomplete; they followed certain private practices initiated by their teachers that were not part of the Vinaya; they drank buttermilk (which was considered food rather than a beverage) after noon; they consumed non-fermented strong drink; they used meditation mats of an inappropriate size; and they handled gold and silver. These schismatics refused to change their ways and termed themselves the Mahasanghima, or Greater Sangha, and – according to this version of events – it is from these that Mahayana Buddhism descended.

The story told by the Mahayana, on the other hand, asserts that there were certain teachings privately transmitted by the Buddha to his closest disciples, warning them to keep these secret until such time as the sangha had matured sufficiently to understand them. Whether these included instructions about salt storage or not is moot.

The iconography found today in Zen temples and centers, the chants declaring that "form here is only emptiness, emptiness only form," even the emphasis on the centrality of seated meditation are not found in early Buddhism. They all arise from the Mahayana.

The term Mahayana means "Great Vehicle," a term chosen by the adherents of the school to contrast themselves with the Hinayana or "Lesser Vehicle." The distinction is based on the contention that the Mahayana was able to address the spiritual needs of all persons – lay or ordained – in contrast with the Hinayana which focuses solely on individuals committed to monastic practice. The adherents of early Buddhism naturally reject the term and refer to themselves, instead, as the Theravada, those who follow the Teachings of the Elders.

Regardless of the accuracy of the story about the buttermilk drinkers, the development of Mahayana Buddhism was driven by two opposing tendencies – a desire for a popular devotional cult for the masses and a natural inclination among the educated classes to philosophical speculation.

The earliest Buddhist writings we are aware of are the Rock Edicts of the Emperor Ashoka (reigned 268 - 232 BCE) that describe a popular devotional religion promoting ethical behavior leading to posthumous reward. This indicates that by Third Century BCE, the Mahayana was well established as a devotional religion separate from the austere monastic tradition of the Theravada. It's notable that although Ashoka himself professed Buddhism, his edicts called for tolerance of all religious perspectives, specifically forbidding the practice of disparaging (without specific cause) other points of view.

Whereas the Theravada represents a stark rejection of this world and of all its allures, seeking escape in meditative absorption and ultimately in nirvana, the Mahayana will come to teach that this world – just as it is – is a Buddha Realm and that all one needs to do is recognize that fact. In the Theravada tradition, nirvana is contrasted with the suffering inherent in life. From the Mahayana perspective, to make such a distinction is to continue to be caught up in dualistic thought, and all dualisms are illusory from the perspective of that ultimate reality that they term the Void.

Bodhisattvas

Originally Buddhist teaching was largely addressed to individuals who had – through numerous previous lives it was assumed – amassed sufficient merit so that in their current lifetime they were prepared to become home-leavers and seek release from the Wheel of Samsara. It was also understood that this release could only be attained through their own efforts. There was no more value in calling upon super-human powers for aid in this endeavor – as the Buddha told Uruvela Kasyapa – than there was in calling to the opposite shore of a river for assistance in crossing. As the teaching became more widespread, however, the lay population sought for some means of participating and so, gradually, devotional forms of the Buddhadharma emerged.

Early Buddhism did not deny the existence of super-human realms where gods and demons resided, but these were viewed simply as other orders of beings who were just as in need of the Buddha's teaching as was humankind. Gautama himself, it was stressed, came to awakening – achieved Buddhahood – without miraculous intervention, but there was a sense among some of his followers that his accomplishment was unique. The Mahayana would come to refer to the Buddha's awakening as Anuttara-Samyak-Sambodhi, "full and complete" as compared to lesser accomplishments. Gautama's teaching brought others to arhatta because it was the teaching of a fully attained Buddha capable of leading others to release from suffering and to nirvana.

This uniqueness was implied during the Buddha's own lifetime in the refuge ceremony by which new members entered the sangha. In doing so they expressly sought refuge not only in the teaching (Dharma) and the community (Sangha) but in the Buddha himself. The wording of the vows didn't alter after his death, and the roots of a devotional cult were established.

The quest for realization – as critics of Buddhism have pointed out – is self-centered. One attains wisdom and release for oneself. But the story of the Buddha's life emphasized that it was compassion for others that drove him to seek a means of release for all humankind. It was that impulse that carried him through endless rebirths and specifically motivated his decision to be born for a final time, and – during that last lifetime – to abandon his wife and newborn child in order to seek a means of helping all living beings. Gradually Buddhists began to feel that the energy of that compassionate drive persisted in some way after Gautama's entrance into Parinirvana.

Speculation theorized that in some way the Buddha existed in a variety of manners. Early Buddhism had already accepted the pre-existence of the Buddha in former lives before his incarnation as the son of King Suddhodana and Queen Maya. The step from this towards accepting that various Buddhas had both pre- and post-existences in extra-terrestrial Buddha Realms was a short one. A range of beings was envisioned who deliberately postponed their entrance into the freedom of Parinirvana so that they could continue to work for the benefit of others. These were termed "Bodhisattvas" – Awakened (Bodhi) Beings (Sattva) – and were contrasted with arhats who only sought salvation for themselves.[28] A pantheon of bodhisattvas, capable of being invoked and petitioned in a manner similar to saints in Catholicism, was imagined as existing in a supra-physical manner. These included Buddhas of the past (such as the Dipankara Buddha who had lived during the time of Shakyamuni Buddha's pre-existence as the Brahmin Sumedha), Buddhas who dwelt in other realms (such as Amitabha Buddha who dwells in the Pure Land or Western Paradise), and Buddhas of the future, such as Maitreya who will come to restore the Dharma to the earth when it has died out. Some Bodhisattvas – such as Sariputta and Moggallana – were figures from the Buddha's biography. Others, who didn't appear in the Pali texts, were associated with particular attributes, for example Manjusri with Prajna/Wisdom[29] and Avalokitesvara[30] with Karuna/Compassion. Bodhisattvas, thus, were seen by the devotionally-minded as figures who could be implored for assistance, and by more sophisticated individuals as personifications of specific qualities.

As the mythologies associated with Bodhisattvas evolved, they were associated with specific Buddha realms in which believers could hope to attain rebirth. One of the most popular forms of Mahayana Buddhism is the Pure Land School which teaches that by keeping mindful of the Buddha Amitabha – through persistently reciting his name – devotees could be assured of rebirth in the Paradise-like "Pure Land" where they would have the opportunity to continue studying and practicing the Dharma until they came to full awakening.

The Bodhisattva idea subtly changed the way in which the goal of practice was understood. Enlightenment was no longer sought essentially for one's own sake but for the sake of others. Practitioners in the Mahayana took upon themselves the Four Bodhisattva Vows not only for their present lifetime but for extended lifetimes to come, beginning with the formidable promise to work for the salvation of all sentient beings:

---

28. The term in its Pali version – Bodhisatta – is found in the earlier Buddhist texts where it refers to one who is on the way to realization but has not yet attained it; thus in the portion of the biography describing his search for a way to enlightenment, the future Buddha is referred as the "Bodhisatta Gautama."

29. Prajna is a uniquely Mahayana concept, although it is a development of the earlier Pali Panna, which meant insight into the three characteristics of being (Dukkha, Annica, and Anatman). Prajna in the Mahayana refers to the much broader intuitive insight that arises from awakening.

30. Avalokitesvara – originally a male figure – later became identified with the goddess Guanyin in China known as Kannon in Japan.

I vow to save all sentient beings everywhere.
I vow to cut off all the passions everywhere.
I vow to study all the Buddhist teachings everywhere.
I vow to achieve the unsurpassed Buddha Way.[31]

Upaya

Pure Land practice is an example of the way in which the Mahayana strove to find ways of accommodating the laity. It recognized that the Dharma needed to be presented in manners appropriate to the conditions in which people of all classes found themselves. As the twenty-fifth chapter of the *Lotus Sutra* – referring to the salvific power of the Bodhisattva (Bosatsu) Kannon – puts it:

> If beings are to be saved by his assuming the form of a Provincial chief, the Bosatsu will manifest himself in the form of a provincial chief and preach them the Dharma.
>
> If beings are to be saved by his assuming a householder's form, the Bosatsu will manifest himself in the form of a householder and preach them the Dharma.
>
> If beings are to be saved by his assuming a lay-disciple's form, the Bosatsu will manifest himself in the form of a lay-disciple and preach them the Dharma.
>
> If beings are to be saved by his assuming a state-officer's form, the Bosatsu will manifest himself in the form of a state-officer and preach them the Dharma.[32]

An array of "upaya" – or skillful means – arose by which the Dharma could be presented and practiced, allowing persons to engage in spiritual practices suited to their nature and station in life. These included sutra chanting, visualizations, mantra recitation and devotional activities. These practices were promoted as having miraculous potential. The Lotus Sutra makes a number of incredible claims, even assuring the devotee that if a man facing execution were to focus his thoughts on the Bodhisattva, the executioner's sword would break into pieces before harming him.

Metta and Karuna

Metta or Loving-Kindness is identified as one of the Three Wholesome

---

31. Philip Yampolsky (trans.), *The Platform Sutra of the Sixth Patriarch* (New York: Columbia University Press, 1967), p. 143.

32. Suzuki, D.T., *Manual of Zen Buddhism* (New York: Grove Press, 1960), p. 16.

Qualities in the Pali texts and is one of the Four Immeasurables that stream-enterers were encouraged to contemplate and cultivate, but it was also stressed in that canon that Metta by itself was not sufficient for attaining release.

The concepts of nirvana and release from the Wheel of Samsara, however, remained abstract to many people, whereas ideas such as metta and karuna (compassion) were easily graspable and so became more central in Mahayana teaching than they had been in the Pali Canon. Karuna, in particular, acquired parity with prajna. It is karuna, after all, that moves the Bodhisattva to remain within the Wheel of Samsara for the benefit of others.

With this shift in emphasis came a corresponding adjustment in the way in which karma was understood. It was recognized as having both a personal and a collective aspect. With the awareness of the interdependence of all of being, there arose the understanding that one's actions affect others as well as oneself. So one's personal activity not only influences one's future rebirth, it also has consequences for the rest of Being as well. All persons are the product of both personal and collective karma, and individual and collective behavior generate karma that will impact later generations.

Emptiness

The Mahayana developed in two opposite directions. On the one hand, Buddhist teaching was simplified in popular devotional rites; on the other, the exhaustive analysis of the human condition found in the *Tripitaka* evolved into a philosophic system that became increasingly complex with the passage of time and eventually required a specialized and often obscure vocabulary in order to express.[33] The sutras of the Mahayana – still attributed to the Buddha – were the result of centuries of reflection on the earlier writings and are not above correcting what they see as misinterpretations of the Buddha's original intention.

New ideas arose that were not found in the Pali scriptures. From the perspective of Zen, the most significant of these is the concept of an inherent Buddha-nature – a potential for self-realization – that exists in all sentient creatures. Another way of saying that self-realization is inherent in all of Being is to say that Buddha-nature manifests itself in all phenomenon. That is essentially the recognition that the universe is made up not only of matter, energy, and time but of Mind as well.[34]

This inherent potential for self-realization is not a "thing" – in the sense that it has no substance – and so it is termed *sunyata*, meaning void or empty.

---

33. There was a similar development in the Christian Middle Ages, which produced popular cults focused on the Saints as well as the obscurities of Scholastic philosophy.

34. Cf. Carl Sagan's famous assertion: "We are a way for the Cosmos to know itself."

The concept of Emptiness had been present in Theravada Buddhism, but it acquires a new emphasis and importance in the Mahayana. It is, however, a difficult concept to grasp because it's less a theoretical idea to be understood than it is an intuitive insight to be attained. As a consequence, attempts to explain sunyata are inevitably vague and even misleading.

In Theravada teaching, the focus had been on the Five Skandhas that are empty of a stable or permanent Self (Anatman). The Mahayana, while agreeing that there is no permanent Self, could be critical of the way in which the original teaching had been expressed. *The Lankavatara Sutra*, for example, dismisses the traditional enumeration of five skandhas as redundant:

> These five grasping aggregates are: form, sensation, perception, discrimination, consciousness. Of these, form belongs to what is made of the so-called primary elements, whatever they may be. The four remaining aggregates are without form and ought not to be reckoned as four, because they merge imperceptibly into one another.[35]

Emptiness in Mahayana writing can be understood on multiple levels. At the simplest level it is the recognition that all things – physical objects, events, thoughts – are, like the sense of Self, impermanent and interdependent. Consider, for example, where the experience we call "sound" resides. The act of striking a bell creates a wave or vibration that, if it travels through an appropriate medium such as the atmosphere, can set off sympathetic vibrations in the ear that are then interpreted by the brain as "sound." Sound does not exist in itself but is dependent upon an initiating cause, a series of intermediate linkages, and ultimately a receptor.

Further the very concept of "sound" is meaningless without the concept of silence, since the two can only exist in relationship to one another. If sound were to be constant and without modulation it would no longer be what we call "sound," just as if there were only "silence" it would cease to be identified as such. Oddly, it is because of its impermanence that one can distinguish sounds.

One impediment to understanding what is meant by sunyata is that words used to translate it have negative connotations. "Empty" and "void" both imply that something is lacking. The Buddhist concept is quite different. While having no substance of its own, it is from the void that all else proceeds. When the Buddhadharma arrived in China, it easily found a correspondence between the concept of sunyata and the Dao that is the

---

35. Dwight Goddard (ed.), *A Buddhist Bible* (Guildford, UK: Whitecrow Press, 2010), p. 65.

matrix – although empty in itself (like a hollow vessel) – from which all things come forth.

It remains, however, that the void is empty of all qualities and features and is beyond all dualism, including the fundamental dualism of is/is not. Therefore, it is beyond human imagination or thought, that is inevitably dualistic. But – since all things including one's self are a manifestation of this void – while it cannot be understood, it can be intuited. That intuitive realization, in the Mahayana perspective, is the enlightenment experience that Gautama achieved and by which he became the Buddha. From the Mahayana perspective, all Buddhist endeavor, all the Buddha taught, is intended to assist others in achieving that insight.

This does not change the fact that the goal of the Buddhadharma is to achieve release from the Wheel of Samsara. But that escape is now understood to be achieved through enlightenment because with self-realization one ceases to cling to a world that one recognizes is essentially illusory. Yasutani Hakuun Roshi,[36] who played a major role in establishing Zen in the West, put it this way (using the Japanese term "ku" for "sunyata"):

> Once you realize the world of ku you will readily comprehend the nature of the phenomenal world and cease clinging to it. What we see is it is illusory, without substance, like the antics of puppets in a film. Are you afraid to die? You need not be. For whether you are killed or die naturally, death has no more substantiality than the movements of these puppets.[37]

Emptiness is also perceived as a quality of Mind in a non-personal sense. Whereas the personal mind is cluttered with conditioned thoughts, habits, envy, ambitions, personal memories, and so forth, Mind in its pure state is empty. This is conveyed by the analogy of a mirror. It is precisely the emptiness of the mirror that allows it to reflect what is before it. The *Surangama Sutra* speaks of a Mind-Essence that is essentially the same thing as Buddha-nature. It is not personal and is, in fact, clouded by the personal mind. It abides eternally

> – as Suchness bright, illumining, all-pervading, and immovable. In this Essence of eternal truth there is indeed neither going nor coming, neither becoming confused nor being enlightened, neither dying nor being born; it is absolutely unattainable and un-

---

36. The title "roshi" in Japanese means "venerable old one;" it is essentially a title of respect. In North American Zen, roshi has come to mean someone who has full authorization to teach Zen independently.
37. Philip Kapleau (et al., eds), *The Three Pillars of Zen* (New York: Anchor, 1989), p.75.

explainable by the intellect, for it lies beyond all the categories of thought.[38]

The "Suchness" referred to here is "Tathata" – reality unfiltered by the mechanisms of human thought. From the perspective of the Mind-Essence all things, including one's individual existence are "as so many particles of dust, floating, rising, and disappearing like foam, in the vast emptiness of space that the one illuminative Mind-essence eternally pervades."[39]

The Trikaya

Mahayana thought developed a complex and baroque metaphysics in order to reconcile the concepts of a universal Buddha-nature, the historical Buddha Shakyamuni, and the plethora of Buddhas and Bodhisattvas posited as existing in the past and perduring into the endless future. This is explained by the doctrine of the *Trikaya* or Three Bodies.

Buddhas and Bodhisattvas are theorized to have three forms of being. The first form is the *Dharmakaya* – or Body of the Law. This is the Buddha-nature that pervades all existence, an undifferentiated universal principle that is manifested in the elements of creation. To borrow a term from the Christian theologian, Paul Tillich, the Dharmakaya can be considered "the ground of being."

The second form is the *Sambhogakaya* – or Body of Bliss. This is the existence of the Buddha or Bodhisattva in a supra-human realm, residing in one of various Heavens or paradises. These are essentially devotional figures – like Avalokitesvara and Amitabha – who are believed to have earned a superabundance of merit during their physical lifetimes that they can "transfer" for the benefit of others. This was the form the Buddha Shakyamuni was in while residing in the Heaven of Delight before taking upon himself his final birth.

The third form, then, is the *Nirmanakaya* – Body of Transformation. These are the historical Buddhas (whether Gautama or another) who, driven by compassion, accept rebirth (incarnation) and in their activity devise appropriate means (*upaya*) to suit the needs of particular populations. The teachings of incarnated Buddhas were addressed to audiences of a specific time and place but, in the case of Shakyamuni Buddha, also came to be recorded in written form for the benefit of future generations. Some of the teachings in these written documents had to wait for the sangha to mature sufficiently before they could be promulgated which is why – it is purported – they are not found in the earlier Pali scriptures.

---

38. D.T. Suzuki's summary of the *Surangama Sutra* in *Manual of Zen Buddhism*, p. 40.
39. Ibid.

Three Mahayana Sutras

While Zen describes itself as a "special transmission outside of the scriptures," there is a group of Mahayana documents – the Prajna Paramita Sutras[40] – which are commonly referenced in Zen discourse and with which the early Chan teachers in China were familiar. They share in common an emphasis on the issue of Emptiness, asserting that the reason humankind suffers (First Noble Truth) is because they believe themselves to be trapped on the Wheel of Samsara, whereas in fact there is neither such a wheel (which is merely a human concept) nor an actual Self to be trapped.

The Lankavatara Sutra

Like many of the Mahayana Sutras, the *Lankavatara* is characterized by the elaborate and fanciful style common to Indian and Himalayan religious writing. The sutra claims, for example, that one who attains Self-Realization

> – will find himself seated upon a lotus-like throne in a splendid jewel-adorned palace and surrounded by Bodhisattvas of equal rank. Buddhas from all Buddha-lands will gather about him and with their pure and fragrant hands resting on his forehead will give him ordination and recognition as one of themselves. Then they will assign him a Buddha-land that he may possess and perfect as his own.[41]

Sutra chanting was one of the upayas Mahayana Buddhists practiced in order to gain merit even when they took it for granted that they would probably not grasp the intent of the doctrines presented in the texts they recited. For some, the descriptions of lotus-thrones and other marvels were accepted as trustingly as Christian fundamentalists accept the various improbable elements of their faith, while more sophisticated individuals – both Buddhist and Christian – consider these elements to be figurative rather than literal.

The exalted nature of the teaching is emphasized by fact that the gathering at which it is delivered is outside the human realm. At the palace of the demon king Ravana – who had become a disciple of the Buddha – a miraculous assembly of Bodhisattvas and Mahasattvas[42] convenes.

---

40. "Perfect Wisdom" or "Perfection of Wisdom."

41. Passages quoted from the *Lankavatara Sutra* come from Dwight Goddard and D.T. Suzuki's abridged translation in *A Buddhist Bible* (Guildford, UK: Whitecrow Press, 2010).

42. Mahasattvas are essentially highly advanced Bodhisattvas.

Although all those present are mature spiritual practitioners, the Buddha senses that many of them still have "mental agitations" that – "moved by compassion" – he seeks to dispel. The sutra then goes on for an almost inordinate length – the "abridged" version I consulted was 38 pages long – to make the point, essentially, that words are unable to convey reality.

The visible world, the Buddha tells the gathering, is an illusion. People fail to understand this because they are deceived by language. Words and letters are "only sweet sounds that are arbitrarily chosen to represent things…[but they] are not the things themselves, that in turn are only manifestations of mind." For most people, words and letters become more real than that which they indicate. Because words are static – whereas reality is in a constant state of change – language becomes a distorting lens through which the real is viewed. It is for this reason that the Buddhas of the past and present "do not teach a Dharma that is dependent upon letters. Anyone who teaches a doctrine that is dependent upon letters and words is a mere prattler, because Truth is beyond letters and words and books."

Therefore, the Buddha warns, misunderstanding can't be dispelled by sutra study because the sutras themselves are unable to convey the truth. They are

> – only a finger pointing towards Noble Wisdom. They are like a mirage with its springs of water which the deer take to be real and chase after. So with the teachings in all the sutras: They are intended for the consideration and guidance of the discriminating minds of all people, but they are not the Truth itself, which can only be self-realized within one's deepest consciousness…(A)ll the Bodhisattvas must seek for this inner self-realization of Noble Wisdom, and not be captivated by word-teachings.

So it is that the Buddha can make the astonishing claim that "from the night of Enlightenment to the night of the Parinirvana, the Tathagata has uttered no word nor ever will utter a word." Noble Wisdom is the intuitive – rather than theoretical – understanding that all things are Empty. To even use the world "empty," however, is "false-imagination," but "because of one's attachment to false-imagination we are obliged to talk of emptiness, no-birth, and no self-nature."

The nature of reality, the sutra emphasizes, is beyond duality. It can only be apprehended by transcending such distinctions "as being and non-being, oneness and otherness, bothness and not-bothness, existence and non-existence, eternity and non-eternity." These concepts have no reality in themselves but are simply manifestations of the mechanics of the mind. This is not something so much to be understood intellectually as to be experienced directly in Self-Realization, that can only occur when the usual discriminating mind ceases to be entranced with name and form (nama-rupa). In order for that to happen, there must be

> – a "turning-about" in the deepest seat of consciousness. The mental habit of looking outward by the discriminating-mind upon an external objective world must be given up, and a new habit of realizing Truth within the intuitive-mind by becoming one with the Truth itself must be established.

The route to achieving this "turnabout" – and the reason the sutra became important to the Zen tradition – is through meditative concentration. Instructions on how to meditate are given, as well as a warning that the goal of such meditation is not to escape into a nirvana separate from the world of birth-and-death.

> [There are those] who, afraid of the suffering incident to the discriminations of life and death, unwisely seek Nirvana. They have come to see that all things subject to discrimination have no reality and so imagine that Nirvana must consist in the annihilation of the senses and their fields of sensation; they do not appreciate that birth-and-death and Nirvana are not separate one from the other.

The understanding of nirvana given in the *Lankavatara* is very different from the way it is understood in the Theravada tradition.

> Some philosophers conceive Nirvana to be found where the mind-system no more operates owing to the cessation of the elements that make up personality and its world; or is found where there is utter indifference to the objective world and its impermanency. Some conceive Nirvana to be a state where there is no recollection of the past or present, just as when a lamp is extinguished, or when a seed is burnt, or when a fire goes out; because then there is the cessation of all the substrata, which is explained by the philosophers as the non-rising of discrimination. But this is not Nirvana, because Nirvana does not consist in simple annihilation and vacuity.
>
> Again, some philosophers explain deliverance as though it was the mere stopping of discrimination, as when the wind stops blowing, or as when one by self-effort gets rid of the dualistic view of knower and known, or gets rid of the notions of permanency and impermanency; or gets rid of the notions of good and evil; or overcomes passion by means of knowledge...

All of these understandings of nirvana are inadequate because they conceive of it in dualistic terms. True nirvana comes about when "the mortal-mind ceases" to make dualistic discriminations, and, as a result,

> – there is no more thirst for life, no more sex-lust, no more thirst for learning, no more thirst for eternal life; with the disappearance of these fourfold thirsts, there is no more accumulation of habit-energy; with no more accumulation of habit-energy the defilements on the face of the Universal Mind clear away, and the Bodhisattva attains self-realization of Noble Wisdom that is the heart's assurance of Nirvana.

Further, the Buddha emphasizes, to seek nirvana as a form of deliverance for oneself is to fall short of the nirvana of the bodhisattvas. The Dharma turns the disciple's thoughts away "from themselves and…[encourages] them to a deeper compassion and more earnest zeal for others."

> Nirvana is where…compassion for others transcends all thoughts of self…
>
> Nirvana is…where the manifestation of Noble Wisdom that is Buddhahood expresses itself in Perfect Love for all; it is where the manifestation of Perfect Love that is Tathagata-hood expresses itself in Noble Wisdom for the enlightenment of all – there, indeed, is Nirvana!
>
> The true bodhisattva, thus, is one who does not seek to attain nirvana until all beings are saved.
>
> But no beings are left outside by the will of the Tathagatas; someday each and every one will be influenced by the wisdom and love of the Tathagatas of Transformation to lay up stock of merit and ascend the stages. But, if they only realized it, they are already in the Tathagata's Nirvana for, in Noble Wisdom, all things are in Nirvana from the beginning.

Diamond Sutra

The oldest extant printed book is a woodblock copy of the *Diamond Sutra* released in 868, nearly six hundred years before Gutenberg's Bible. One of the most revered of all Mahayana texts, it is replete with praise for itself:

> – wherever this sutra or even four lines of it are preached, this place will be respected by all beings including Devas, Asuras, etc., as if it were the Buddha's own shrine or chaitya; how much more a person who can hold and recite this sutra!…(S)uch a person achieves the highest, foremost, and most wonderful deed.

> Wherever this sutra is kept, the place is to be regarded as if the Buddha or a venerable disciple of his were present.[43]

The sutra begins with a homely description of the Buddha returning from his daily begging round, eating his single meal of the day, washing his feet, and then taking his seat before the assembled disciples. A monk named Subhuti – speaking on behalf of the 1250 monks gathered there – then asks the Buddha to describe how "good men and good women" should proceed who seek to "keep their thoughts under control" and so attain Supreme Enlightenment. The Buddha praises Subhuti for his question and explains:

> All the Bodhisattva-Mahasattvas should thus keep their thoughts under control. All kinds of beings such as the egg-born, the womb-born, the moisture-born, the miraculously-born, those with form, those without form, those with consciousness, those without consciousness, those with no-consciousness, and those without no-consciousness – they are all led by me to enter Nirvana that leaves nothing behind and to attain final emancipation. Though thus beings immeasurable, innumerable, and unlimited are emancipated, there are in reality no beings that are ever emancipated. Why, Subhuti? If a Bodhisattva retains the thought of an ego, a person, a being, or a soul, he is no more a Bodhisattva.

Throughout the sutra the formula "X is not X, that is why it is called X" is repeated several times: "– according to the teaching of the Buddha, Prajna Paramita is not Prajna Paramita and therefore it is called Prajna Paramita;" "– what is known as a true idea is no idea, and for this reason it is called a true idea." The point is essentially the same as that made in the *Lankavatara* that words fail to convey the reality of things. In this instance, however, the Buddha's statement is broader. All beings of whatever nature are already emancipated, even though there are no beings to be emancipated, because the only reason these beings have not achieved Supreme Enlightenment is that they fail to recognize they are already awakened.

Both sutras are unremittingly non-dual. Language, on the other hand, is dualistic by its nature and creates a false sense of the stability and independence of things that are in fact characterized by fluidity (impermanence) and dependency.

The Buddha quizzes Subhuti about whether the Buddha can be recognized by his bodily form, and Subhuti responds

---

43. Passages quoted from the *Diamond Sutra* come from D.T. Suzuki, *Manual of Zen Buddhism* (New York: Grove Press, 1960). "Devas" and "Asuras" are supernatural beings. "Chaitya" is another word for a shrine.

"No, World-honored One, he is not to be recognized after a body-form. Why? According to the Tathagata, a body-form is not a body-form."

The Buddha said to Subhuti, "All that has a form is an illusive existence. When it is perceived that all form is no-form, the Tathagata is recognized."

The Buddha then asks if it could be said that he had attained Supreme Enlightenment and has something about which to preach, and once again Subhuti demurs:

- as I understand the teaching of the Buddha, there is no fixed doctrine about which the Tathagata would preach. Why? Because the doctrine he preaches is not to be adhered to, nor is it to be preached about; it is neither a dharma nor a no-dharma.

The Buddha has no teaching in the sense that the path he demonstrates is founded on letting go of all teaching, concept, and theory. Therefore, Bodhisattvas should

- rouse a pure thought. They should not cherish any thought dwelling on form; they should not cherish any thought dwelling on sound, odor, taste, touch, and quality; they should cherish thoughts dwelling on nothing whatever.

In other words, the Bodhisattva - as it is expressed in other translations - should arouse his or her mind without resting it on anything. The normal mode of thought is through the discursive mind that is incapable of grasping reality or truth because it formulates reality into concepts. To "rouse the mind without resting it on anything" is to make use of the unconditioned mind, the mind not yet colored by cultural conditioning or language. This is the intuitive mind. The route to Perfect Wisdom – Prajna Paramita – is not through study of the sutras or any other system of thought but through personal insight. Therefore, even the Dharma itself should only be viewed as a raft that – once it has brought the disciple to "the other side" – will need to be abandoned as well.

The sutra considers human behavior in a similar manner. The Buddha instructs Subhuti that when, for example, a Bodhisattva practices charity

- he should not be cherishing any idea, that is to say, he is not to cherish the idea of a form when practicing charity, nor is he to cherish the idea of a sound, an odor, a touch, or a quality. Subhuti, a Bodhisattva should thus practice charity without cherishing any idea of form. Why? When a Bodhisattva practices charity without cherishing any idea of form, his merit will be beyond conception.

Likewise, one who enters the order or advances within it should do so without any sense of accomplishment. A distinction is implied here between action that is calculated, and action undertaken without self-interest. Non-dualistic action is spontaneous. One responds to a situation or the need of another without thought of oneself or other. Such people

> – are free from the idea of an ego, a person, a being, or a soul; they are free from the idea of a dharma as well as from that of a no-dharma. Why? Because if they cherish in their minds the idea of a form, they are attached to an ego, a person, a being, or a soul. If they cherish the idea of a dharma, they are attached to an ego, a person, a being, or a soul. Why? If they cherish the idea of a no-dharma, they are attached to an ego, a person, a being, or a soul. Therefore, do not cherish the idea of a dharma, nor that of a no-dharma.

The Heart Sutra

The most succinct summary of Mahayana teaching is found in the *Prajna Paramita Hridaya* or the *Heart of Perfect Wisdom Sutra*, that is regularly chanted – in a staccato tempo accompanied by the beat of a drum – in temples, monasteries, and practice centers throughout the Mahayana world.

As a document, it is incomprehensible. It cannot be read as a discourse providing information nor as a narrative. And yet when chanted, it has the capacity to reveal itself as something similar to poetry or even music, where meaning is revealed through intuition rather than through intellection.

> The Bodhisattva of Compassion,[44] from the depths of Prajna Wisdom,
> saw the emptiness of all five skandhas
> and sundered the bonds of suffering.
> Know then: form here is only emptiness, emptiness only form.
> Form is no other than emptiness.
> Emptiness no other than form.
> Feeling, thought and choice, consciousness itself are the same as this.
> Dharmas here are empty, all are the primal void.
> None are born or die,
> Nor are they stained or pure, nor do they wax or wane.

---

44. Avalokitesvara.

So in emptiness no form, no feeling, thought or choice,
nor is there consciousness.
No eye, ear, nose, tongue, body, mind;
no color, sound, smell, taste, touch, or what the mind takes hold of,
nor even act of sensing.
No ignorance or end of it, nor all that comes from ignorance:
no withering, no death, no end of them.
Nor is there pain, or cause of pain, or cease in pain,
or noble path to lead from pain.
Not even wisdom to attain; attainment too is emptiness.
So, know that the Bodhisattva holding to nothing whatever,
but dwelling in prajna wisdom, is freed of delusive hindrance,
rid of the fear bred by it, and reaches clearest nirvana.
All Buddhas of past and present, Buddhas of future time,
through faith in prajna wisdom come to full enlightenment.
Know then the great dharani, the radiant peerless mantra,
the supreme, unfailing mantra, the Prajna Paramita,
whose words allay all pain.
This is highest wisdom, true beyond all doubt,
know and proclaim its truth:

Gate, gate, paragate, parasamgate, bodhi, sva-ha![45]

The sutra appears to baldly refute the Four Noble Truths, the doctrine of the Skandhas, and the law of causality. All theory is negated. Only Prajna – Wisdom – has any reality, and that is not something that can be discovered through reason but, rather, must be directly encountered. If to understand something means to be able to make sense of it intellectually, the Prajna Paramita teachings of the Mahayana are truly incomprehensible. Which, of course, is why they are called…

---

45. Rochester Zen Center, *Chants and Recitations* (Rochester: Rochester Zen Center, 2005). A "dharani" is a chanted phrase, fundamentally the same thing as a mantra. The dharani at the end can be translated: "Gone, gone, gone beyond, gone altogether beyond, awakening, hurrah!"

When the highest type of men hear the Dao,
   they try hard to live in accordance with it.
When the mediocre type hear the Dao,
   they seem to be aware and yet unaware of it.
When the lowest type hear the Dao,
   They break into loud laughter –
If it were not laughed at, it would not be Dao.

Dao De Jing, poem 41
Lin Yutang's rendering (emended)

Daoism

THE CHINESE HISTORIAN, Sima Qian – writing five hundred years after the event – records that in 516 BCE two of Gautama Buddha's contemporaries met in the Royal Archives in Loyang, then the capital city of the Dong Zhou Dynasty. The younger of these, Kongzi – better known in the west as Confucius – was 35 years old, and he was seeking to define a philosophy based on traditional values that would bring humankind back into harmony with the universal order. To that end, he had traveled to Loyang in order to speak with the respected keeper of the Archives, Li Erh, now known by the honorific title Laozi,[46] or "Old Master," who was more than half a century his senior.

Confucius asked Laozi about teachers of former times and the ritual ceremonies they practiced. Laozi responded that "Those ancients you admire so much have been dead a long while now, and their bones have turned into dust. Only their words remain. The wisest rose to positions of leadership when times were good but slipped quietly away when times were bad. In the same way that it is said that a successful merchant will conceal his wealth and behave as if he has little, so the great man, while rich in talent and ability, maintains simple manners and an ordinary appearance, feigning ignorance in order to avoid attracting attention. My advice to you is to rid yourself of pride and affectation and your many extravagant ambitions."

Later, one of his disciples asked Confucius how the meeting with Laozi had gone. Confucius told him, "I know about great animals like elephants and how they walk, and I know about the giant beasts hidden in the ocean and how they swim. I even know of great birds that fly for thousands of miles. But this man is like none of these. He is a dragon, and no one knows how he proceeds nor how he lives. He is like an abyss."

Shortly after this visit, according to Sima Qian, Laozi became weary of the ineptitude of the political leaders of the time and the suffering resulting from their policies, so he left the capital to seek a place of retirement

---

46. In the older Wade-Giles form, Lao Tzu. See p. 15 above.

and solitude. When he came to the Hangyu Pass, the warden recognized him and asked if he would write a summary of his thoughts before he left the realm. On the spot, Laozi is said to have composed a book of 81 verses in two sections, after which he proceeded on his way and – following the example of the wise men of old about whom he spoken with Confucius – was never seen again. The slim volume he gave to the warden, only 5000 characters long, was the *Dao De Jing*,[47] and it became the central document of the tradition known as Daoism – the way of the Dao (Tao) – and for centuries stood as the most respected challenge to the Confucian perspective in Chinese thought.

The Three Sovereigns and Five Emperors

The American mythologist, Joseph Campbell, has pointed out that when Buddhism and Daoism are contrasted with the theocentric religious traditions of the West they are "clearly of a kind…[however] compared with each other in their own terms, they show a diametric contrast…"[48] Chan[49] Buddhism is the product of the encounter between these two traditions. And while the offspring was given its father's name (as is the custom), in many ways it has more in common with its maternal heritage.

Although popular folklore in China supposed that there had been a "Lord of Creation," Shangdi,[50] he was not a significant focus of worship or veneration. In that sense, ancient Chinese lore begins not with a creation story but rather with accounts of a series of mythic rulers beginning with the Three Sovereigns. The first of these, Suiren, taught humans the use of fire; he was followed by Fuxi, who taught them to domesticate animals. These two were succeeded by Shennong who introduced agriculture and thus provided the basis for a settled society and the building of cities.[51] Once these conditions were established, the people were governed by Five Emperors, beginning with the Yellow Emperor, Huangdi, who is venerated as the father of Chinese civilization. Huangdi's successors rose to the throne not only by inheritance but by merit. In addition to being political leaders, the five are referred to as sages whose wisdom and harmony with the natural order of things benefited all of their subjects. Human life became progressively better under their enlightened leadership culminating in the reigns of the Emperors Yao and Shun, when a Golden Age was

---

47. Still better known by the Wade-Giles rendering, *Tao Te Ching*.
48. Joseph Campbell, *Masks of God: Oriental Mythology* (New York: Viking Press, 1962), p. 29.
49. Which will be pronounced "Zen" by the Japanese.
50. Or simply Di (Wade-Giles: Shang Ti).
51. There are variations in this list. These are the three identified in the *Zhuangzi*.

achieved during which perfect accord was established between the human, celestial, and natural realms. Unfortunately, later emperors lacked the virtues of their predecessors and as a consequence conditions began to deteriorate.[52]

There were, of course, local gods and supernatural powers that the working classes appealed to for aid. There was also a general acceptance of the existence of ghosts, ancestral spirits, and gods who required placation and could impact human lives for good or ill. For the better educated classes, however, what we view as the traditional religious systems and scriptures of China do not focus so much on the relationship between humankind and the supernatural but rather define the qualities that the sage-emperor requires in order to restore the glory days of Yao and Shun. On one level, the *Dao De Jing* is such a text, as is *The Analects of Confucius*.

Dao

The word "dao" means "way" both in the sense of a "path" and "the way in which things work." In the latter sense, it is similar to the pre-Buddhist concept of Dharma, the way things are, the inherent natural order of the universe. The concept predates both Confucius and Laozi.

Fundamental to the metaphysics of Daoism is the concept represented in the Taijitu figure:

The symbol may have originally represented the phases of the moon and refers to the interplay of two alternate forces – yin and yang – that is the essential generative mechanism of nature. The glyphs for yin and yang denote the shady (yin) and sunny (yang) sides of a hill. Yang is masculine, light, dry, warm, active, and is represented in art as a dragon; yin is feminine, dark, moist, cool, passive, and is represented in art as a phoenix. Yang is also considered positive and yin negative, although these are neutral terms in Daoist thought – as they are when applied to electrical current. The essential quality of yin and yang is that they arise simultaneously and interdependently. As Laozi put it:

---

52. In an interesting contrast, older cultures tended to see the world in a state of general decline from a previous Golden Age, whereas contemporary culture – with its faith in technology – tends to view conditions in the world to be steadily improving.

> When the people of the Earth all know beauty as beauty,
>> There arises (the recognition of) ugliness.
> When the people of the Earth all know the good as good,
>> There arises (the recognition of) evil.
> Therefore:
>> Being and non-being interdepend in growth;
>> Difficult and easy interdepend in completion;
>> Long and short interdepend in contrast;
>> High and low interdepend in position;
>> Tones and voice interdepend in harmony;
>> Front and behind interdepend in company.[53]

As the Zen popularizer, Alan Watts – who was more a Daoist than a Buddhist – put it: "The yin-yang principle are not…what we would ordinarily call a dualism, but rather an explicit duality expressing an implicit unity."[54] Yin and yang can be thought of as separate (dual), but they form a unity insofar as one only exists in contrast to the other.

Human concepts of "good" and "bad" don't apply to the Dao, which is not – Laozi warns – "human-hearted." Nor is it in any sense personal; no one would pray to Dao or seek to petition it to intercede on one's behalf. The fundamental choice humans have in regard to the Dao is either to seek to live in harmony with it – live in harmony with the way things are – or not. One who does so, naturally finds satisfaction; those who do not are inevitably frustrated and unhappy.

In the Taijitu figure, there is a drop of the opposite color in each of the two halves, emphasizing that nothing is either wholly yang or yin. All things are a mixture of the two. In males, the yang is dominant but not exclusive; in females, the yin is dominant but not exclusive. On a cosmic level, the interplay between the two generates all that is.

The Dao itself is empty and consists of nothing, but this emptiness is the fruitful womb from which the "10,000 things" emerge in a natural process not dependent upon or responsible to any Supreme Being. In fact, Laozi asserts that the Dao existed before Shangdi[55] and even before Heaven and Earth came into being.

> Before the Heaven and Earth existed
> There was something nebulous:
>> Silent, isolated,

---

53. Lin Yutang (tr. ed.), *The Wisdom of Laotse* (New York: The Modern Library, 1948), poem 2.
54. Alan Watts, *Tao: The Watercourse Way* (New York: Pantheon, 1975), p. 26.
55. Cf. poem 4.

> Standing alone, changing not,
> Eternally revolving, without fail,
> Worthy to be the Mother of All Things.
> I do not know its name
> And address it as [Dao].[56]

There is a superficial similarity between the multiplicity of things arising from Dao and the Indian story of the original being that split itself into two and then generated all living creatures; however, the Dao is not self-aware nor are its actions in any sense willed. And while in both India and China meditation techniques were devised by which devotees were capable of turning inward and discovering their true nature (be it atman or Dao), in the "diametric contrast" Campbell mentioned there is a significant difference between the goals of these practices. In India, and particularly in early Buddhism, the practitioner seeks a means of escaping from the world and its concomitant suffering, first through meditative absorption and later through the ultimate extinction of nirvana. In China, on the other hand, the goal is to learn to accommodate oneself to the rhythm of the yin and yang as a means of entering more fully into a life that is in harmony with the Dao.

Harmony is sought with the Dao on both the macroscopic and microscopic levels. Individuals can seek to align their lives with the Dao, but it is particularly important that national leaders do so in order that their actions – like those of Yao and Shun – benefit all their subjects. The way in which this is to be accomplished is the focus of both Confucian and Daoist thought, although their approaches differ, and Daoism, to an extent, is a reaction to the more broadly accepted Confucian perspective.

Confucianism

While it is now generally accepted that Laozi was not an actual person, there is more evidence for the historicity of Confucius than there is for Siddhartha Gautama. The stories told of him in the classic histories of China, however, are largely popular legends elaborated over generations.

According to these, he came from humble origins but, through personal merit, was appointed to the court in the state of Lu, where he rose to a position equivalent to that of Prime Minister. The Duke, however, was a frivolous man who neglected matters of state, and eventually Confucius – accompanied by a small band of disciples – left Lu and traveled from one ducal court to another seeking a patron who would accept his advice and

---

56. Lin Yutang, op. cit., p. 145.

so restore the land to the glories of the past. He was unable to find such a ruler and died believing he had failed in his life's ambition.

As with the Buddha, no documents from Confucius's lifetime remain. The book ascribed to him – *The Analects* – is a collection of notes kept by his disciples and probably didn't acquire its current form until generations after his death.

Confucius was a social conservative who, in response to what he saw as the degeneracy of contemporary society, advocated a return to traditional values that would harmonize the rule of men with the celestial order of the universe. Just as there is an evident hierarchy of spheres in the Heavens that maintains a stable and predictable order, order should be established in human affairs by defining and entrenching the relationships between persons. Confucius compares the ideal ruler to the North Star that remains static while the rest of the Heavens revolve about it.

For Confucius, Dao is the natural order of society as well as of Heaven and Earth; it is the way human relations would be if individuals understood their proper place in the social order and behaved accordingly. When everyone is conscious of and performs the responsibilities and obligations attendant upon their social position, society is able to make optimal use of individual talents for the benefit of all persons. The "Superior Man" in Confucian terms, then, is one who brings himself into harmony with the social and political orders, with his family responsibilities, and with the celestial realm.

The system is grounded in what Confucians call the "rectification of names." This defines one's role or position within the five fundamental relationships, which are that between a prince and his ministers, that between father and son, that between spouses, that between elder and younger brothers, and that between friends. Benevolence, or *Ren*,[57] is the respectful relationship between individuals grounded in "human-heartedness" or empathy. Once one has defined their precise position, they can understand – or can be taught – their responsibilities within those five relationships and the proper etiquette to be maintained between persons of differing ranks. As in India, one's social position (caste) is part of the natural order; unlike India, however, the position is not a matter of birth alone but also of proven merit.

Confucianism also insisted on correct veneration and participation in the rites that maintain the social order. These rituals were associated with astronomical observations and so were believed to bring human conduct into line with the fundamental pattern of nature or Heaven.

Because one's position is part of the natural order, Confucius maintained that one can only find genuine satisfaction by fulfilling the obligations attendant upon one's station in life with "sincerity" or *zhi*.

---

57. "Jen" in Wade-Giles Romanization.

> The superior man does what is proper to the station in which he is; he does not desire to go beyond this. In a position of wealth and honor, he does what is proper to a position of wealth and honor. In a poor and low position, he does what is proper in a poor and low position. Situated among barbarous tribes, he does what is proper to a situation among barbarous tribes. In a position of sorrow and difficulty, he does what is proper to a position of sorrow and difficulty. The superior man can find himself in no situation in which he is not himself.[58]

Zhi is the wisdom that arises when virtue is fully integrated into one's life and one acts from internal rather than external compulsion. Genuine sincerity, in this sense, requires discipline and commitment in order to achieve, and Confucius admits he did not attain it himself until he was 70.

Whereas in India and elsewhere, it is religious ritual and doctrine that maintains the social order, Confucian China was unique in maintaining it through cultural institutions and the arts. "It is by poetry that the mind is aroused. It is by the rules of propriety (rituals, ceremonies, rules of proper conduct) that the character is established. It is from music that the finish is received."[59]

In many ways, Confucianism was a humane system, but, as it became institutionalized, it sought to define with greater precision the specifics not only governing human relationships – the rules of protocol and proper decorum – but also the rules governing all aspects of human activity that maintained the cultural integrity of the state, including the arts, medicine, and ritual observances. Confucians sought to impose order on the world by defining its elements and organizing them; thus they maintained the traditional Chinese mode of categorizing things in groups of five (the number of fingers on a hand), even though it is clear – as Daoists pointed out – that such attempts inevitably distort reality. So it was that in the same way that there had been five Emperors in the past, there are five fundamental human relationships, five fundamental colors,[60] flavors,[61] tones,[62] even five principle internal organs,[63] and five elements.[64]

---

58. Quotation from the *Chung Yung*, or *Doctrine of the Mean*, attributed to Confucius's grandson, Tzu Ssu. It is one of what are called the *Four Books of Confucianism*. Quotation from Campbell, op. cit., pp. 417-18. James Legge translation.

59. Ibid., p. 418.

60. Green, red, white, black, and yellow.

61. Salty, sour, bitter, pungent, and sweet.

62. The notes of the pentatonic scale.

63. Heart, spleen, gall bladder, and the two kidneys.

64. Water, fire, wood, metal, and earth.

It is easy to recognize that traditional social structures such as dividing categories into sets of five are wholly artificial. Daoists went further in their criticism of Confucianism, maintaining that the basic tenets on which it is based are equally artificial, and that, when they are mandated by the state, what had been a teaching grounded in benevolence becomes something harsh and rigid. It is also the case that such systems are inevitably promulgated by an elite who benefit from a stable social order built upon the labors of lower classes who have neither the time nor the education to benefit from poetry, music, or philosophy. The Daoist critic and humorist, Zhuangzi, has a simple farmer mock a passing Confucian scholar, accusing him of being "one of those people who read a lot of books to imitate the sages, who stretch and strive to benefit others and then play the string instrument alone and sing a sad song to sell their reputation to the world."[65]

Laozi and Zhuangzi

As in India, there were those in China who felt that the path to discovering the significance of life was to be found not in religious or philosophical texts or established systems of belief and behavior but by withdrawal from society into the forests and mountains, where – by a system of internal reflection – they could bring themselves into harmony with the natural flow (Dao) of being. Critics viewed this as a socially irresponsible form of quietism, but its advocates argued that it was precisely because the Emperors Yao and Shan had realized Dao and harmonized themselves with it – rather than relying on artificial rules of deportment and ritual activity – that they had been able to bring about the Golden Age for which they are held up as models of perfected human behavior.

The poems attributed to Laozi were collected from unknown Daoists who, following the advice given in the *Dao De Jing*, drew no attention to themselves. "Laozi" is not actually a name but a title meaning "Old Master." So, when later writers referred to the verses in the *Dao De Jing*, they were not necessarily attributing them to a particular individual but rather to an "old master" who was otherwise nameless. The book itself can be, and has been, read as a spiritual document, a document prescribing a way of political governance,[66] and a treatise on personal health. As Daoist master Li Xizhai wrote in the twelfth century: "Lao Tzu's 5000-word text clarifies what is mysterious as well as what is obvious. It can be used to attain the [Dao], to order a country, or to cultivate the body."[67]

---

65. Lin Yutang, op. cit., p. 268.
66. The founder of the Ming Dynasty – Ming Taizu – called the *Dao De Jing* the perfect book for guiding kings.
67. Red Pine (tr.), *Lao Tzu's Teaching* (Port Townsend, WA: Copper Canyon Press, 2009), p. 5.

The other great text of Daoism is known by the name of its putative author, Zhuangzi, believed to have lived from 369 to 286 BCE. It has been questioned whether he, too, was an actual person, and there is even more doubt that the book bearing his name was the work of a single author. Regardless of whether they were historical figures or not, Laozi and Zhuangzi have become personifications of a point of view that stands in contrast to Confucianism.

Like Buddhism, Daoism deals with human unhappiness and discontent; however, its analysis of the cause of that discontent and how best to respond to it is very different. Both the *Dao De Jing* and the *Zhuangzi* assume the social conditions of their time to be inferior to those of the past. In the days of the Three Sovereigns and Five Emperors, rulers governed so subtly and efficiently that – as Laozi puts it – the populace was unaware of them and believed the conditions in which they lived were simply the way things were. In those ancient times, the people and their rulers[68] were instinctively in harmony with the Dao and lived at ease, not seeking to promote themselves. They were happy, content, healthy, and unconsciously moral in their relationships with one another. As time passed, however, conditions deteriorated because of the artificial nature of civilized society and governance by law. Human behavior lost its spontaneity and freedom. When rewards and punishments were instituted, the inherent morality of people declined, and both rulers and their subjects were estranged from the Dao. People became dissatisfied and strove with one another for recognition. Zhuangzi summed it up this way:

> The ancient men lived in a world of primitive simplicity and the world was simple with them. That was the time when the yin and the yang worked harmoniously, and the spirits of men and beasts did not interfere with the life of the people, when the four seasons were in order and all creation was unharmed, and the people did not die young. Although men had knowledge, they did know what to do with it. This was the time of complete unity, when nobody interfered and lived according to their nature. Then man's character began to decline. Then [Suiren] and [Fuxi]…came to rule the world, and the world still lived in accord with nature but had lost its unity. Man's character declined again. When the Emperors [Shennong] and [Huangdi]…came to rule the world, the world was still at peace, but was already departing from nature.

---

68. The glyph Laozi uses for the term "ruler" is three horizontal lines representing the Heavens, humankind, and the Earth, united by a single vertical line: 王. The ruler is precisely the one who brings humankind into harmony with Heaven and Earth. "If princes and dukes can keep the [Dao], / The world will of its own accord be reformed." Poem 37, Lin Yutang, op. cit., p. 194.

Man's character declined again. Then Emperors Yao and Shun came to the world and began the spread of culture. Then falseness arose and the original simplicity of man was lost. Man departed from [Dao] in order to do good and performed commendable acts to win praise. Man abandoned nature and attended to the development of his mind. Mind rubbed against mind and produced knowledge, but as knowledge was not adequate to bring peace to the world, they resorted to cultural refinement and learning and scholarship. Cultural refinement destroyed the inner character of man and scholarship and learning submerged man's mind. From that time on, the people were perplexed and confused and lost the way whereby they could recover their original nature and return to the original state.[69]

The route to contentment, therefore, is to return to a more natural lifestyle grounded in the Dao. The Confucian effort to bring about social change through an enlightened system of governance is precisely the wrong way to go because of the artificial manner in which it seeks to arrange matters. Zhuangzi compares this to carpenters who seek to impose regularity on nature:

Those who rely upon the arc, the line, compasses, and the square to make correct forms injure the natural constitution of things. Those who use cords to bind and glue to piece together interfere with the natural character of things. Those who seek to satisfy the mind of man by hampering it with ceremonies and music and affecting humanity and justice have lost the original nature of man. There is an original nature in things. Things in their original nature are curved without the help of arcs, straight without lines, round without compasses, and rectangular without squares; they are joined together without glue and hold together without cords. In this manner, all things grow with abundant life, without knowing how they do so. They all have a place in the scheme of things without knowing how they come to have their proper place. From time immemorial this has been so, and it may not be tampered with. Why then should the doctrines of humanity and justice continue to remain like so much glue or cords, in the domain of [Dao] and character, to give rise to confusion and doubt among mankind?[70]

---

69. Lin Yutang, op. cit., pp. 116-17, emended. For Zhuangzi, the deterioration of the human condition begins long before the Emperors who followed Yan and Shun.

70. Ibid, p. 58, emended.

Basic Daoist Concepts
Dao

The concept of Dao (道) that predates both Laozi and Confucius is that of a natural order in things which it's futile to try to resist. The opening poem of the *Dao De Jing* asserts that it existed before Shangdi, the Lord of Creation, and is the "the origin of Heaven and Earth."[71] It is not, however, a willed process. The Dao acts with spontaneity but without volition. In this sense, it can be considered equivalent to *ziran* (自然), nature, or that which is spontaneously so of itself.

The sage is one who accommodates himself to this order; fools may try resist it, but to do so is futile because, as Alan Watts put it, there is no way to deviate from Dao:

> You may imagine that you are outside, or separate from the [Dao] and thus able to follow it or not follow; but this very imagination is itself within the stream, for there is no way other than the Way. Willy-nilly, we are it and go with it. From a strictly logical point of view, this means nothing and gives us no information. [Dao] is just a name for whatever happens.[72]

Other than to recognize that it is, Laozi and Zhuangzi insist there is nothing more one can posit about the Dao; therefore, one cannot discuss its characteristics. The Dao that can be spoken of is not the true Dao. The opening lines of the *Dao De Jing* make this point explicitly:

> The [Dao] that can be told of
>   Is not the Absolute [Dao];
> The Names that can be given
>   Are not Absolute Names.[73]

Likewise, in the *Zhuangzi*: "Dao cannot be heard…that which is heard is not Dao. Dao cannot be seen; that which is seen is not Dao. Dao cannot be told; that which can be told is not Dao."

---

71. Ibid, p. 41. Early Zen enthusiasts in North America had access to several translations of the – as it was then known – *Tao Teh Ching*. The three most popular were by James Legge (1891), Arthur Waley (1934), and Lin Yutang (1948). My decision to quote the Lin Yutang versions is a matter of personal preference. I also consulted the contemporary rendition of "Red Pine" (2012).
72. Watts, op. cit., p. 38, emended.
73. Lin Yutang, op. cit., p. 41, emended.

Sages cannot reveal the Dao to others not because of willful secrecy but simply because there is nothing that can be said about it. Dao is not a concept that can be intellectually understood; however, because human life is one element in the larger ecological whole that is the Dao, it can – like the Buddhist concept of the Void and for similar reasons – be intuited. Therefore, the intent of Daoist literature is not to explain or define the Dao but to lead people to a direct awareness of it. This intuition can be cultivated through meditative practice, the outline of which is suggested in the 10th poem of the *Dao De Jing*, where the breath is controlled to the point that it becomes as soft as that of a baby, and the mind, like a mirror, is wiped clean of dust. "When the eye is cleared of obstacles," Zhuangzi explains:

> – it sees sharply. When the ear is cleared of obstacles it hears well. When the nose is not blocked up, it smells well. When the mouth is cleared, it tastes well. When the mind is clear, it thinks well. When knowledge is cleared of obstacles, one attains the character of the [Dao].[74]
>
> ...
>
> When water is at repose, it is so clear that it can reflect a man's beard; it maintains absolute level and is used by the carpenter for establishing the level. If water is clear when it is at rest, how much more so is the human spirit? When the mind of the sage is calm, it becomes the mirror of the universe, reflecting all within it.[75]

The Uncarved Block

Things in their natural state, as they come forth from the Dao, are whole and complete just as they are and have an inherent power or force. The image Daoists use to convey this is "the uncarved block of wood" that represents the state of nature before being conditioned by human effort. Psychologically it is the state of mind before enculturation, artificial education, conditioning, and habit. It is a consciousness by which one can perceive clearly – without prejudice or evaluation – what is. The Tang Dynasty scholar, Su Che, wrote in his commentary on the *Dao De Jing* that "Uncarved wood reminds us to put an end to human fabrication and return to our original nature."[76] A thousand years later, the Seventh Patriarch of the Dragon Gate sect of the Golden Lotus lineage, Song Changxing, warned, "Before a block of wood is split, it can take any shape. But once split, it cannot be round if it is square or straight if it is curved. [Laozi] tells us to avoid being split. Once we are split, we can never return

---

74. Ibid., p. 87, emended.
75. Ibid., p. 195.
76. Red Pine, op. cit., p. 30.

to our original state."[77]

Allowed to remain in their natural state, things thrive. Difficulties arise when that natural state is interfered with. Zhuangzi used the example of a horse-trainer to make this point:

> Horses have hoofs to carry them over frost and snow, and hair to protect them from wind and cold. They feed on grass and drink water, and fling up their tails and gallop. Such is the real nature of horses. They have no use for ceremonial halls and big dwellings.
>
> One day Polo (famous horse-trainer) appeared, saying, "I am good at managing horses." So he burned their hair and clipped them, and pared their hoofs and branded them. He put halters around their necks and shackles around their legs and numbered them according to their stables. The result was that two or three in every ten died. Then he kept them hungry and thirsty, trotting them and galloping them, and taught them to run in formation, with the misery of the tasseled bridle in front and the fear of the knotted whip behind, until more than half of them died.[78]

Inutility

Related to this is the value of uselessness. As the 16th century commentator Jiao Hong noted: "Those who pursue the Way are natural. Natural means free from success and hence free from failure. Such people don't succeed and don't fail but simply go along with the successes and failures of the age. Or if they do succeed or fail, their minds are not affected."[79]

Rather than seeking advancement, the Daoist prefers obscurity and inutility. Zhuangzi makes the argument in one of his most memorable parables:

> A certain carpenter Shih was travelling to the Ch'i State. On reaching Shady Circle he saw a sacred li tree in the temple to the God of Earth. It was so large that its shade could cover a herd of several thousand cattle. It was a hundred spans in girth, towering up eighty feet over the hilltop, before it branched out. A dozen boats could be cut out of it. Crowds stood gazing at it, but the carpenter took no notice, and went on his way without even casting a look behind. His apprentice, however, took a good look at it, and when he caught up with his master, said, "Ever since I have handled an adze in your service, I have never seen such a splendid

---

77. Red Pine, op. cit., location 1394.
78. Lin Yutang, op. cit., 161-62.
79. Red Pine, op. cit., p. 47.

piece of timber. How was it that you, Master, did not care to stop and look at it?"

"Forget about it. It's not worth talking about," replied his master. "It's good for nothing. Made into a boat, it would sink; into a coffin, it would rot; into furniture, it would break easily; into a door, it would sweat; into a pillar, it would be worm-eaten. It is wood of no quality, and of no use. That is why it has attained its present age."

When the carpenter reached home, he dreamt that the spirit of the tree appeared to him in his sleep and spoke to him as follows: "What is it you intend to compare me with? Is it with fine-grained wood? Look at the cherry, apple, the pear, the orange, the pumelo, and other fruit-bearers. As soon as their fruit ripens, they are stripped and treated with indignity. The great boughs are snapped off, the small ones scattered abroad. Thus do these trees by their own value injure their own lives. They cannot fulfill their allotted span of years, but perish prematurely because they destroy themselves for the (admiration of) the world. Thus, it is with all things. Moreover, I tried for a long period to be useless. Many times I was in danger of being cut down, but at length I have succeeded, and so have been exceedingly useful to myself. Had I indeed been of use, I should not be able to grow to this height. Moreover, you and I are both created things. Have done then with this criticism of each other. Is a good-for-nothing fellow in imminent danger of death a fit person to talk of a good-for-nothing tree?"

When the carpenter Shih awaked and told his dream, his apprentice said, "If the tree aimed at uselessness, how was it that it became a sacred tree?"

"Hush!" replied his master. "Keep quiet. It merely took refuge in the temple to escape from the abuse of those who do not appreciate it. Had it not become sacred, how many would have wanted to cut it down! Moreover, the means it adopts for safety is different from that of others, and to criticize it by ordinary standards would be far wide of the mark."[80]

Laozi puts it more poetically and ironically:

The people of the world have enough and to spare,
But I am like one left out,
My heart must be that of a fool,
Being muddled, nebulous!
The vulgar are knowing, luminous:

---

80. Lin Yutang, op. cit., 137-38.

I alone am dull, confused.
The vulgar are clever, self-assured;
I alone, depressed.
Patient as the sea,
Adrift, seemingly aimless.

The people of the world all have a purpose;
I alone appear stubborn and uncouth.[81]

Li

Zhuangzi follows his description of the horse-trainer Polo with a discussion about craftsmen who use tools to impose order on natural materials.

> The potter says, "I am good at managing clay. If I want it round, I use compasses; if rectangular, a square." The carpenter says, "I am good at managing wood. If I want it curved, I use an arc; if straight, a line." But on what grounds can we think that the nature of clay and wood desires this application of compasses and square, and arc and line?[82]

Straight lines seldom occur in nature, save in the mineral realm. Rather, there is a spontaneous, irregular patterning that naturally arises, seen in the grain of wood, in the ripples left by waves on a beach, or in the branches of a tree. The Chinese term for this type of pattern is *li*, a word that originally referred to the markings in jade. It became a significant aesthetic as well as philosophical concept both in Daoism and Confucianism, although once again they interpreted the idea differently. For the Confucian, li referred to the ordering principle in nature that could be duplicated in human affairs. For Daoists, li is specifically the constantly new, non-repetitive, and creative patterns that arise naturally before carpenters, potters, and Confucians seek to regularize them. There is order in the formation of clouds, the striations in stone, the patterns of frost on a window, but it is not the type that can be predicted or defined. The path of a stream, for example, is not happenstance; water naturally flows around obstacles and finds a course appropriate to the conditions it encounters. In that way, the river fits naturally within the environment. Li, then, is the way the flow of the Dao naturally manifests itself in the physical world.

The li principle is apparent when contrasting Chinese visual arts with Western representational painting. Chinese paintings of a natural

---

81. Ibid., 128-29.
82. Ibid., 162.

scene – what are called *shan shui* paintings – are notable for their lack of symmetry,[83] whereas the Western painting may well have a very clear and geometrical sense of order adhering to the rules of perspective. The one is spontaneous, the other is calculated.

Wu wei

Instead of striving to become something, the Daoist practices *wu wei* (無爲), non-doing. Wei refers to a deliberate action; wu is a negative prefix. The term can be translated "non-action" or "non-interference," but not in the sense of inaction or stillness; rather in the sense of an action that comes about without intent, without effort. It is like a boat flowing with the current rather than struggling against it. Where Confucians seek to promote order by defining roles and establishing protocols for proper behavior, Daoists reject the idea that there are specific roles, protocols, or proper responses and, instead, advocate non-interference and spontaneity. Wu wei, in this sense does not seek results, and yet (as Laozi puts it) nothing is left undone.[84] When situations arise, one will respond not with self-conscious deliberation but naturally and appropriately, the way one bats an insect away from one's eye without thinking about it or planning to do so. In a similar manner, the wise ruler is one who does nothing "and the people are reformed of themselves."[85]

For Zhuangzi, wu wei is action carried out in such harmony with Dao that it appears as if nothing is happening.

> There is great beauty in the silent universe. There are manifest laws governing the four seasons without words. There is an intrinsic principle in the created things which is not expressed. The Sage looks back to the beauty of the universe and penetrates into the intrinsic principle of created things. Therefore, the perfect man does nothing, the great Sage takes no action. In doing this, he follows the pattern of the universe.[86]

The significant difference between the "pattern of the universe" and the created world of potters and carpenters is that one "grows" while the other is "constructed." The carpenter's work is an act of volition. There is no

---

83. Cf. the illustrations in my *Zen Masters of China* (Tuttle, 2012), especially *Lofty Hermitage in Cloudy Mountains* by Liang Kai (p. 68) and *Walking on a Path in Spring* by Ma Yuan (p. 124).

84. Poem 37: "The [Dao] never does, / Yet through it everything is done." Lin Yutang, op. cit., p. 194.

85. Poem 57, Lin Yutang, op. cit., p. 265.

86. Ibid., p. 68

volition in the growth of a tree, or the evolution of life, the solar system, and planets; these come about spontaneously.

Emptiness

An emphasis on "emptiness" was found in Daoist thought long before its contact with Mahayana Buddhism.

> The knowledge of the men of old reached the ultimate height. What was the ultimate height of knowledge? They recognized that nothing but nothing existed. That indeed was the limit further than which one could not go. Then there were those who believed that matter existed, but only matter unconditioned (undefined). Next came those who believe in conditioned (defined) matter, but did not recognize the distinctions of true and false. When the distinctions of true and false appeared, then [Dao] lost its wholeness. And when [Dao] lost it wholeness, individual bias began.[87]

The Dao is described as being empty like a valley, a vessel, or – as in the fifth poem of the *Dao De Jing* – a bellows.

> How the universe is like a bellows!
>   Empty, yet it gives a supply that never fails;
>   The more it is worked, the more it brings forth.[88]

De

The collection of poems attributed to Laozi takes its name from the ideograms beginning each of the two sections into which the book is traditionally divided – Dao and De – combined with the term jing meaning "ancient text." Literally *Dao De Jing* means "The Ancient Book of the Dao and De."

De has been variously translated as "virtue" or "power," in the sense of an innate quality such as the healing quality of a particular plant, an analogy used by Alan Watts:

> [De] is the realization or expression of the [Dao] in actual living, but this is not virtue in the sense of moral rectitude. It is rather as when we speak of the healing virtue of a plant...In theistic terms, [de] is what happens 'by the grace of God' as distinct from human nature, though without the implication of any supernatural intervention in the course of nature...[De] is also the unusual and

---

87. Ibid., pp. 43-44.
88. Ibid., p. 63.

thus remarkable naturalness of the sage – his unself-conscious and uncontrived skill in handling social and political affairs…[89]

The poet/translator Bill Porter (Red Pine) points out that De can "mean 'virtue,' in the sense of 'moral character' as well as 'power to act.'"[90] In Confucian thought, it refers to virtuous behavior, whereas in Daoist texts it more often refers to an ability or power that is the manifestation of an inherent personal accord with the Dao. In that understanding it can be thought of as an inherent quality which manifests in capacity, one's individual strengths and abilities. Dao itself is, as it were, the essence of being and as such is unknowable unless embodied in something specific. As Zhuangzi puts it, de is the specific – therefore knowable – qualities a thing or individual receives from Dao; water its fluidity, rock its obduracy, one person the quality of leadership, another the capacity to be nurturing. Therefore, he notes, what "is unified in [Dao] becomes differentiated in [De]."[91]

The 38th poem in the *Dao De Jing* – that begins what is traditionally considered the second part of the work – focuses on De. Red Pine translates it as "virtue," Lin Yutang as "character," and Arthur Waley as "power"; therefore, they each render the opening lines differently.

> Higher Virtue isn't virtuous
> thus it possesses virtue
> Lower Virtue isn't without virtue
> thus it possesses no virtue
> Higher Virtue involves no effort
> or the thought of effort[92]

> The man of superior character is not (conscious of his) character,
>   Hence he has character.
> The man of inferior character (is intent on) not losing character,
>   Hence he is devoid of character.
> The man of superior character never acts,
>   Nor ever (does so) with an ulterior motive.
> The man of inferior character acts,
>   And (does so) with an ulterior motive.[93]

---

89. Watts, op. cit., p. 107, emended.
90. Red Pine, op. cit., location 137.
91. Lin Yutang, op. cit., p. 173, emended.
92. Red Pine, op. cit., p. 76.
93. Lin Yutang, op. cit., p. 198.

> The man of highest "power" does not reveal himself as a possessor of "power";
> Therefore he keeps his "power".
> The man of inferior "power" cannot rid it of the appearance of "power";
> Therefore he is in truth without "power".
> The man of highest "power" neither acts nor is there any who so regards him;
> The man of inferior "power" both acts and is so regarded.[94]

Zhuangzi, as always, is eloquent on the issue. Following the passages quoted above regarding the horse-trainer who claimed to be good at managing horses and the potter who claimed to be good at managing clay, he presents this – albeit romanticized – vision of what the world was like when all things adhered to their true natures, or De:

> I think one who knows how to govern the empire should not do so. For the people have certain natural instincts – to weave and clothe themselves, to till the fields and feed themselves. This is their common character [De], in which all share. Such instincts may be called "Heaven-born." So in the days of perfect nature, men were quiet in their movements and serene in their looks. At that time, there were no paths over mountains, no boats or bridges over waters. All things were produced, each in its natural district. Birds and beasts multiplied; trees and shrubs thrived. Thus it was that birds and beasts could be led by the hand, and one could climb up and peep into a magpie's nest. For in the days of perfect nature, man lived together with birds and beasts, and there was no distinction of kind. Who could know of the distinctions between gentlemen and common people? Being all equally without knowledge, their character could not go astray. Being all equally without desires, they were in a state of natural integrity. In this state of natural integrity, the people did not lose their (original) nature.
>
> And then when Sages [such as Confucius] appeared, straining for humanity and limping with justice, doubt and confusion entered men's minds. They said they must make merry by means of music and enforce distinctions by means of ceremony, and the empire became divided against itself. Were the uncarved wood

---

94. https://terebess.hu/english/tao/waley.html#Kap38.

not cut up, who would make sacrificial vessels? Were [Dao] and character [De] not destroyed, what use would there be for humanity and justice? Were man's natural instincts not lost, what need would there be for music and ceremonies? Were the five notes not confused, who would adopt the six pitch-pipes? Destruction of the natural integrity of things for the production of articles of various kinds – this is the fault of the artisan. Destruction of the [Dao] and character in order to strive for humanity and justice – this is the error of the Sages.[95]

The Primacy of Yin

In his summary of the teachings of Laozi, Zhuangzi quotes the opening lines of the 28th poem in the *Dao De Jing*. The poem in its entirety touches on several significant Daoist concepts:

He who is aware of the Male
But keeps to the Female
  Becomes the ravine of the world.
Being the ravine of the world,
  He has the original character [De] which is not cut up.
  And returns again to the (innocence of the) babe.
He who is conscious of the white (bright)
But keeps to the black (dark)
  Becomes the model for the world.
Being the model for the world,
  He has the eternal power which never errs,
  And returns again to the Primordial Nothingness.
He who is familiar with honor and glory
But keeps to obscurity
  Becomes the valley of the world.
Being the valley of the world,
  He has an eternal power which always suffices,
  And returns again to the natural integrity of uncarved wood.
Break up this uncarved wood
  And it is shaped into vessels
In the hands of the Sage
  They become the officials and magistrates.
  Therefore the great ruler does not cut up.

Perhaps in response to the societal inclination to give primacy to the masculine/yang qualities, Laozi espouses the yin, noting that "Gentleness

---

95. Lin Yutang, op. cit., pp. 162-63.

overcomes strength."⁹⁶ The 16th century Daoist, Wang Dao, developed the point in his commentary on the poem:

> Sages recognize "that" but hold to "this." "Male" and "female" mean hard and soft. "Pure" and "base" mean noble and humble. "White" and "black" mean light and dark. Although hard, noble, and light certainly have their uses, hard does not come from hard but from soft, noble does not come from noble but from humble, light does not come from light but from dark. Hard, noble, and light are the secondary forms and farther away from the Way. Soft, humble, and dark are the primary forms and closer to the Way. Hence sages return to the original: a block of wood. A block of wood can be made into tools, but tools cannot be made into a block of wood. Sages are like blocks of wood, not tools.⁹⁷

The penultimate poem in the *Dao De Jing* presents Laozi's vision of a perfect society in which the more aggressive and assertive yang characteristics – that drive social and economic progress – are forsaken for the more passive yin.

> (Let there be) a small country with a small population,
> Where the supply of goods are tenfold or hundredfold, more than
>   they can use.
> Let the people value their lives and not migrate far.
>   Though there be boats and carriages,
>   None be there to ride them.
>   Though there be armor and weapons,
>   No occasion to display them.
> Let the people again tie ropes for reckoning,
>   Let them enjoy their food,
>   Beautify their clothing,
>   Be satisfied with their homes,
>   Delight in their customs.
> The neighboring settlements overlook one another
>   So that they can hear the barking of dogs and crowing of cocks
>   of their neighbors,
> And the people till the end of their days shall never have been
>   outside their country.⁹⁸

---

96. Ibid., poem 36. p. 191.
97. Red Pine, op. cit., location 1386.
98. Lin Yutang, op. cit., poem 8, p. 310.

Later Daoism

A third classic of Daoism is a book attributed to Liezi who is described by Zhuangzi as being able to fly (ride the winds). Although it was purported to have been written about the same time as the *Dao De Jing* (5th century BCE), scholars have determined that it was actually compiled some 900 years later (4th century CE) by which time Daoism as an established cult had undergone numerous changes. Given its nature, it is ironic that Daoism – which rejected the institutionalism of the Confucianists – should itself become institutionalized. A formal Daoist church evolved under the leadership of a patriarch known as the Heavenly Teacher and was even, for a time, the officially recognized state religion.

The focus of Daoist activity continued to be the search for satisfaction in this current life, not in a world to come or in reincarnation – and certainly not in extinction – so it was that Daoist alchemists laid the basis of Chinese science in their efforts to develop an elixir of longevity. Early Daoists had held that by following the Dao one would live longer than if one resisted it. In the first century CE, the Patriarch of the Way of the Celestial Masters – Zhang Daoling – put it succinctly: "Who follows the Way lives long. Who loses the Way dies early. This is the unbiased law of Heaven. It doesn't depend on offerings or prayers."[99] Longevity, thus, is the natural consequence of being in accord with the Dao. Over time, however, longevity became an end in itself. The emphasis became less on the Way per se than on efforts to prolong life and on cult activity, including divination. By that time, however, the spirit of Laozi and Zhuangzi had been passed onto the followers of a new religious tradition that had found its way into China from India.

---

99. Red Pine, op. cit., p. 49.

Part Two

A monk asked the Sixth Patriarch, Huineng, "Who now has the secret teachings of the Fifth Patriarch?"
"Someone who understands Buddhism," Huineng said.
"Do you, then, have them, Sir?"
"I don't understand Buddhism," declared Huineng.

Chan[100]

Bodhidharma

THE OLD SILK ROAD that linked India with both Europe and East Asia was established as early as 3000 years ago.[101] Ideas as well as goods were carried along this system of trails, and, sometime during the Han Dynasty (206 BCE–220 CE), Mahayana Buddhism made its way into China. Daoist scholars were intrigued by the Buddhadharma although they never quite accepted the concept of dukkha. The Chinese mentality was too optimistic to wholly subscribe to the tenet that "life is suffering." Happiness was to be found, they felt, not by turning away from life but by harmonizing one's life with the natural order – Dao – and in the cultivation of a calm mind.

The gradual process by which Daoism and Mahayana Buddhism eventually merged to form Chan took place over a period of some 500 to 600 years, coming to flower in the Tang Dynasty and to full fruit in the Song, by which time Chan had become the principal form of monastic Buddhism in China. The faux histories of the Song period – like the largely fictional *Transmission of the Lamp*[102] – simplified the complexities of cultural assimilation and posited that Chan had been brought directly to China during the reign of Emperor Wu Liang (464-549) by an Indian missionary named Bodhidharma.

The story asserts that in addition to the teachings found in the sutras, there had always been a special non-verbal teaching passed first from the Buddha to Mahakasyapa, who in turn, passed it onto Ananda, and so on for 27 generations until it came to Bodhidharma, the 28th Patriarch of the Dhyana – or meditation – School of Buddhism. A Song Dynasty poem

---

100. A fuller treatment of the material in this chapter can be found in my previous book, *Zen Masters of China* (Tuttle, 2012).

101. Fragments of Chinese silk have been found in Egyptian caches dated to 1000 BCE.

102. *Jingde Chuandenglu*.

attributed to Bodhidharma sums up the teaching in four lines:

> A special transmission outside the scriptures;
> Not dependent on words or letters;
> By direct pointing to the mind of man,
> Seeing into one's true nature and attaining Buddhahood.

The poem emphasizes a fundamental change of emphasis. The focus in earlier forms of Buddhism had been the relief of suffering. Chan is about attaining insight, "seeing into one's true nature." True, suffering may draw individuals to practice, and "seeing into one's true nature" may relieve suffering, but the change of emphasis remains significant and results in the development of a type of Buddhism very different than those that preceded it.

Buddhism was 1000 years old by Bodhidharma's time, and in India it had become more speculative and abstract with the passing of the centuries. Not unlike in Christian seminaries, the primary activity of monks was gaining an understanding of the teachings through the study of scripture – the sutras – personal discipline, and ritual activity. Mindfulness and meditation, as prescribed in the Noble Eightfold Path, were still taught, but the faith gradually had become more theoretical and orthodox with the passage of time.

Distressed by what he considered the degraded condition of the Buddhadharma in the land of its birth, Bodhidharma's predecessor – the 27th Patriarch, Prajnatara – advised his[103] disciple to go to China to determine if that land were a suitable environment in which to revitalize the meditative tradition of Buddhism.

Conditions turned out not to be so different in China. The Buddhism Bodhidharma found there was also largely academic. Scholars translated Indian sutras and composed elaborate commentaries on them. A variety of competing schools had evolved that based their teachings on one or the other of these scriptures. Devotional Buddhism was popular with the masses, in which the Buddha and various Bodhisattvas were treated as deities whose aid could be invoked through petition or ritual activity. There were meditation teachers as well, although none of them claimed to belong to the line of transmission descended from Mahakasyapa.

The Emperor was an adherent of Buddhism, and, when he learned that a monk from the land of the Buddha's birth had come to China, he invited Bodhidharma to his court. The monk was probably not what the emperor expected. Chinese portraits of Bodhidharma exaggerate his

---

103. Or possibly "her." A Tara is a female Bodhisattva, so the name means "Wisdom Tara," leading some to conjecture that Prajnatara may have been a woman.

foreign features. He is portrayed bearded, with shaggy eyebrows, large round eyes, and a stern expression. He was most likely shabbily dressed, poorly groomed, and smelling much the way one might expect someone undertaking a three-year journey under difficult circumstances to smell.

The emperor believed in karma and was concerned about the misdeeds of his youth – some of which had been responsible for bringing him to the throne – and in later life he had tried to compensate for them through a variety of pious acts such as sponsoring the translation of Buddhist texts, supporting large numbers of monks and nuns, and assuming the cost of building temples. Eager to be assured that his religious activities balanced his previous behavior, he described all he had done to promote Buddhism in his country then asked Bodhidharma, "What is your opinion? What merit have I accumulated as a result of these deeds?"

Bodhidharma responded bluntly: "No merit whatsoever."

"Why no merit?" the Emperor asked.

"Motives for such actions are impure," Bodhidharma told him, "undertaken for the purposes of attaining auspicious birth in the future. They are like shadows cast by bodies, following those bodies but having no reality of their own."

"Then what is true merit?" the Emperor asked.

"It is clear seeing, pure knowing, beyond the discriminating intelligence. Its essence is emptiness. Such merit cannot be gained by worldly means."

This was unlike any exposition of Dharma the Emperor had yet encountered, and he asked, "According to your understanding, then, what is the first principle of Buddhism?"

"Vast emptiness and not a thing that can be called holy," Bodhidharma replied at once.

Wu spluttered: "What does that mean? And who are you who now stands before me?"

To which Bodhidharma is said to have replied: "I don't know."[104]

Then he left the court and proceeded to the Shaolin Monastery on Mount Songshan, where he practiced silent meditation facing a cave wall for nine years and – at least according to some traditions – introduced the monks living there to kung fu, as well as miraculously creating the first tea plants, which sprouted from the eyelids he cut off to prevent himself from falling asleep during meditation.

When word of Bodhidharma's disrespectful behavior spread throughout the kingdom, most members of the Buddhist community avoided him. There was a scholar, however – Dazu Huike – who had been searching for

---

104. This story is presented as the first gongan (koan) in the *Biyan Lu*, or *Blue Cliff Record*.

a teacher to help him achieve peace of mind, and, in desperation, he went to see the barbarian monk from the land of the Buddha. When Huike presented himself at Bodhidharma's door, the old Indian suspected him to be another looking for an intellectual explanation of the Dharma, so for a long while he ignored Huike. The scholar, however, remained patiently outside Bodhidharma's cave for days, waiting to be acknowledged. One night, it snowed so heavily that by morning the drifts were up to Huike's knees. Seeing this, Bodhidharma finally asked, "What is it you seek?"

"Your teaching," Huike told him.

"The teaching of the Buddha is subtle and difficult. Understanding can only be acquired through strenuous effort, doing what is hard to do and enduring what is hard to endure, continuing the practice for even countless eons of time. How can a man of scant virtue and great vanity, such as yourself, achieve it? Your puny efforts will only end in failure."

Huike drew his sword and cut off his left arm which he presented to Bodhidharma as evidence of the sincerity of his intention. "My mind isn't at peace," he lamented. "Please, master, pacify it."

"Very well," Bodhidharma relented. "Bring your mind here, and I'll pacify it."

"I've sought it for these many years but still am not able to get hold of it."

"There! Now it's pacified!"

And at these words – as when Mahakasyapa saw the Buddha twirling the flower between his fingers – Huike came to awakening. In the terms of the tradition that would arise from this encounter, he moved beyond an intellectual grasp of the Dharma to attain the same experiential insight that the Buddha himself, Mahakasyapa, and the Indian patriarchs before Bodhidharma had achieved – that his basic nature, his "Buddha-nature," was no different from that of all existence.

What is not explained in either the story about Mahakasyapa or Huike is the mechanics of how this insight came about. It can be inferred that both of them had dwelled on issues such as the nature of mind, the significance of the Buddha's teaching, and the purpose of human life for a long while, but in the Chinese story it is emphasized that it was the awakened teacher, Bodhidharma, and not the questioning student, who was practicing meditation. Insight was transmitted, but the how had not yet been defined.

The Chinese Patriarchs

Huike is recognized as the Second Patriarch of the Chan tradition, followed by a leper, Jianzhi Sengcan. Sengcan came to Huike seeking freedom from the sins he believed must have been the cause of his condition.

Echoing his own teacher, Huike said, "Bring your sins here, and I'll rid you of them."

"When I reflect on my sins," Sengcan admitted, "I'm not sure what they are."

"Then you're cleansed," Huike told him. Once again, the challenge to identify the true nature of the source of one's concern – Huike's search for mind, Sengcan's attempt to define sin – is enough to bring about intuitive insight, and, although it can be inferred that the individual who achieved that insight had dwelled on the issue for a long while, it is not explicitly stated that he had been engaged in any sort of formal meditation practice.

After Huike's death, Sengcan became the Third Patriarch during a period when institutionalized Daoism was in ascendance and Buddhism was subject to persecution as a foreign – barbarian – teaching. Sengcan, therefore, retired to the mountains, away from the attention of authorities. There he was tracked down by another driven inquirer, Dayi Daoxin, who begged to be shown the way to achieve liberation. Yet again, the transmission of insight is brought about by challenging the questioner to consider his request.

"Who is it that holds you in bondage?" Sengcan asked.

"Well, no one," Daoxin admitted.

"Then why are you seeking liberation?"

But by this time, the idea of a defined spiritual practice is made explicit. One of Sengcan's legacies is a poem entitled the *Xinxin Ming*, that promotes the "serene" stilling of the mind in "the oneness of things." It also demonstrates the way in which Buddhist and Daoist concepts had begun to mingle.

> The Perfect Way [Dao] knows no difficulties
> Except that it refuses to make preference:
> Only when freed from hate and love,
> It reveals itself fully and without disguise.
>
> A tenth of an inch's difference,
> And heaven and earth are set apart;
> If you want to see it manifest,
> Take no thought either for or against it.
>
> To set up what you like against what you dislike –
> This is the disease of the mind:
> When the deep meaning of [Dao] is not understood
> Peace of mind is disturbed and nothing is gained.
>
> The [Dao] is perfect like unto vast space,
> With nothing wanting, nothing superfluous:

> It is indeed due to making choice
> That suchness is lost sight of.
>
> Pursue not the outer entanglements,
> Dwell not in the inner void;
> When the mind rests serene in the oneness of things,
> The dualism vanishes by itself.
> ...
> When we return to the root, we gain the meaning...
> ...
> Try not to seek after the true,
> Only cease to cherish opinions.[105]

By the time Daoxin followed Sengcan as fourth patriarch, the suppression of Buddhism had abated, monasteries were again open, and a formal tradition of meditative training started to evolve. Daoxin instructed his disciples to be earnest in their practice of *zuo chan* (*zazen* in Japanese) or seated meditation. "Zuo chan is basic to all else," he told them. "Don't bother reading the sutras; don't become involved in discussions. If you can refrain from doing so and concentrate instead on zuo chan, for as much as thirty-five years or more, you will benefit. Just as a monkey will eat a nut still in its shell although it's only satisfied when it has patiently extracted the nut from that shell, so there are only a few who bring their zuo chan to fulfillment." This is a significant departure from the usual practice not only elsewhere in China but throughout the Buddhist world. The emphasis of the emerging Chan tradition is not on study or ritual activity – although these are not entirely dispensed with – but on meditative practice, as a result of which it comes to be known as the "single practice" form of Buddhism. Taken at face value, the implication is that one does not need to know anything about the teachings of the Buddha as long as one commits oneself to zuo chan. Later Chan texts – including the *Platform Sutra of the Sixth Patriarch* discussed below – don't reject the importance of Mahayana teachings but suggest that without first achieving the intuitive insight that comes from meditation one would not be capable of understanding them.

Huineng

According to most contemporary accounts, Daoxin's heir, Daman Hongren, was succeeded by a monk named Shenxiu, whose official

---

105. D.T. Suzuki, *Essays in Zen Buddhism: First Series* (New York: Grove Press, 1994), pp. 196-201, emended.

epitaph identifies him as the Sixth Chan Patriarch. Within a short time, however, this was forgotten, and the title was bestowed instead on another of Hongren's disciples, a monk who had been relatively unknown until after both he and Shenxiu were dead.

At an assembly of Dharma teachers held in 734, one of the attendees, Heze Shenhui, challenged Shenxiu's right to be recognized as Hongren's successor. Heze Shenhui claimed Shenxiu had appropriated a title that rightly belonged to his own Dharma master, Dajian Huineng. Shenxiu's school, he argued, was actually a heterodox sect; the true line of transmitted descent went through Huineng and by inference to Heze Shenhui himself. As evidence of his claim, he recounted a story that related how Hongren had secretly given the robe and bowl of Bodhidharma to Huineng. Shenxiu's disciples at the assembly had not expected to have the authority of their teacher challenged and were unprepared to counter Heze Shenhui's assertions. And so the legend of the Sixth Patriarch – Huineng – came into being.

Ironically, although all existing Zen schools today trace their lineages back to Huineng, none of those lineages pass through Heze Shenhui.

The biography of Dajian Huineng promoted by Heze Shenhui is recorded in a document entitled *The Platform Sutra of the Sixth Patriarch*, a pious fiction composed to establish Huineng's credentials as Hongren's official heir and to support the claim of the Southern School – associated with him – to be the teaching coming from the Buddha through Mahakasyapa and Bodhidharma in an unbroken line to the present. To stress that the core of this teaching is "not dependent on words or letters," the story insists that Huineng was illiterate.

As a young man of 24, the tale goes, he chanced to hear a man chanting the *Diamond Sutra*. Although he was unfamiliar with the sutra, when Huineng heard the phrase "rouse the mind without resting it on anything" he came to a deep spontaneous awakening of the type Mahakasyapa and Huike had attained. Huineng asked the man about the sutra and was told that, if he wanted to learn about it, he should go to Hongren's East Mountain Monastery.

When Huineng presented himself to Hongren, the abbot asked where he came from. Huineng explained that he was from Guangdong in the South and that he had come to the East Mountain in order to attain Buddhahood.

"How is it possible for someone like you to attain Buddhahood?" Hongren asked. "Southerners are barbarians and don't have Buddha-nature."

Undeterred, Huineng responded: "There may be Southerners and there may be Northerners, but what has that to do with Buddha-nature?"

It was an astute answer, and Hongren recognized that the young man's insight was more profound than that of any of the ordained monks under his charge. "If they heard that a layman, an illiterate lad at that, had achieved awakening," Hongren told him, "they wouldn't believe it, and they might do you harm. Or they might come to lose respect for the teachings of Buddhism altogether. So for a while you and I will keep this secret."

Huineng agreed to do as the Master instructed. He kept away from the monks' quarters and the meditation hall and worked, instead, in the granary hulling rice and splitting firewood. Not long after this meeting, Hongren announced that he was retiring and needed to identify a successor. He challenged his monks to submit their understanding of the Dharma in a short poem, or gatha. The one whose poem demonstrated the deepest insight would receive the bowl and robe that Bodhidharma had passed onto Huike and that had eventually come to Hongren.

The monks were certain that the head monk, Shenxiu, would succeed their master and therefore none of them offered a poem for consideration. Shenxiu, however, was not confident of the depth of his understanding so decided to submit his poem anonymously. Without signing it, he inscribed it on a patch of bare wall:

> The body is like the Buddha-tree,
> the mind a stand with a mirror bright.
> Take care to wipe it clean,
> and don't let dust or dirt alight!

When Hongren found the verse the next morning, he had incense lit in front of it and said, "All those who practice as it describes will undoubtedly acquire great merit." Then he spoke to Shenxiu privately, telling him that it only expressed a theoretical understanding of the Dharma. "You have merely arrived at the gate, but you have not yet been able to enter it."

Huineng happened to hear a monk reciting Shenxiu's poem, and, because he could neither read nor write, he asked the assistance of a visitor to the monastery in replying to it. The visitor wrote Huineng's gatha beside Shenxiu's:

> The body is not a tree,
> nor the mind a mirror bright.
> Since from the beginning not a thing exists,
> where can dust and dirt alight?

The point Huineng's gatha makes is subtle. Instead of attempting to "clean the mirror," Huineng challenges the Chan student to see into the nature of mind itself, which is never dull nor in need of polishing but always remains clear. It can be compared with the sun that remains pure and bright regardless of the clouds or mist that may obscure it.

Hongren realized who the author of the second poem must be and secretly passed the robe and bowl onto Huineng. Then Hongren told Huineng to go into hiding because there would inevitably be those who objected to his selection as Sixth Patriarch.

A few days later, the story continues, a rumor went through the monastery that an illiterate layman had stolen the sacred relics of the First Patriarch and fled with them. Outraged at this sacrilege, a group of monks pursued the thief. They were led by a monk named Ming who, before entering the sangha, had been a general in the army. For two months the group followed Huineng, but, as the chase went on, the pursuers gave up one after another until only Ming remained.

Eventually Ming caught up with Huineng. When the new Patriarch saw the former soldier approaching, he placed the robe and bowl on the ground and said, "If you've come for these, they are merely symbols of our tradition and have no other value. If you want them, take them."

When Ming tried to pick the items up, however, he was unable to lift them. Shaken by this inability, he paused a moment, then said: "If that's so, I have no use for them. What I've come for is the Dharma. So if you are indeed the successor of Hongren, please dispel my ignorance."

"If you've come for the Dharma, then, without thinking about good or bad, show me your face before your parents were born."

As soon as he heard these words, Ming also attained awakening. He bowed before the younger man and asked to become his disciple. Huineng demurred, however, suggesting rather that they both consider themselves the disciples of Hongren.

Tradition maintains that Huineng remained in hiding until he was 39 years old, then established himself at the Baolin monastery in the South, where – at least according to the story promulgated by Heze Shenhui – thousands came to become his disciples. Shenxiu, however, was recognized as Hongren's successor by the monks of the East Mountain Monastery, and the teaching that descended from him became known as the Northern School to distinguish it from Huineng's Southern School.

It is likely that during their lifetimes, Shenxiu and Huineng considered each other colleagues rather than rivals, and there is evidence that for a long while Shenxiu's school had been the more prestigious. Eventually, however, the Southern School gained dominance and the Northern faded away.

Both history and legend are recorded by those who survive, so regardless of what Shenxiu actually taught, the version of his teachings we now have is as they were interpreted by Huineng's followers. The two schools were in the Bodhidharma tradition in that their focus was on meditation rather than sutra study or ritual activity. The controversy between them was whether the attainment of Buddhahood (awakening) came little by little or suddenly. In the gatha attributed to Shenxiu, awakening is presented as something acquired gradually, comparable to the process of burnishing a metal surface so that it slowly reflects a clearer and sharper image. Huineng's school, on the other hand, insisted that true awakening necessarily occurred instantly. Although there may be activity leading up to that experience, the experience itself comes all at once. The Southern School compared the process to chipping away at a stone barrier. While it could take a long while to pierce the barrier, once one does, the view on the other side become visible immediately.

The Platform Sutra

Some time around the year 780, nearly 70 years after Huineng's death, a document was composed purporting to be a transcription of several of his Dharma talks. The work underwent a number of revisions between the 8th and 13th centuries, and the earliest extant copies date to somewhere between 830 and 860. Its long title was: *The Southern School's Sudden Doctrine, the Prajna Paramita: The Platform Sutra Delivered by the Sixth Patriarch Huineng at Dafan in the Shao Prefecture*. Its importance to the Chan School is emphasized by the fact that it is accorded the status of a sutra, a term otherwise generally used to refer to the teachings of the Buddha.

While it is unlikely to be an actual transcription of Huineng's sermons, the material included in it provides useful information about the nature of the practice promoted by Huineng's successors. With its extended discourse and inflated style, it is more Indian in form than Chinese, and certainly the high degree of literacy and the academic tone evidenced in it is in stark contrast with the tradition that Huineng could neither read nor write.

Prajna Paramita means "perfection of wisdom." In Mahayana Buddhism, this referred to the advanced teachings suitable only for those on the Bodhisattva path, in contrast to more general teachings – such as the Noble Truths and the Twelvefold Chain of Dependent Co-Arising – available to both "stream-enterers" and lay people. The term was also applied to the collection of sutras that included the *Lankavatara*, the *Diamond*, and *Heart Sutras*. For Huineng, Prajna Paramita is the intuitive, non-conceptual insight that comes from meditation and that is essential for genuine understanding of the Dharma. As he states in the *Platform Sutra*, "If you do not know the original mind, studying the Dharma is to no avail."[106] What Huineng teaches is not a theory, not something "that can be discussed," but a practice, something the disciple himself must undertake.

In Huineng's analysis, Maha Prajna Paramita (Great Perfection of Wisdom) practice is based on the premise that all persons have innate intuitive wisdom (prajna/bodhi) but are unaware of it because of delusion and so require the assistance of a teacher who can "show them how to see into their own natures" and realize their Buddha-nature. He states that his

> – teaching of the Dharma takes meditation (ting) and wisdom (hui) as its basis. Never under any circumstances say mistakenly that meditation and wisdom are different; they are a unity, not two things. Meditation itself is the substance of wisdom; wisdom itself is the function of meditation. At the very moment when there is wisdom, then meditation exists in wisdom; at the very moment when there is meditation, then wisdom exists in meditation. Good friends, this means that meditation and wisdom are alike. Students, be careful not to say that meditation gives rise to wisdom, or that wisdom gives rise to meditation, or that meditation and wisdom are different from each other. To hold this view implies that things have duality…The practice of self-awakening does not lie in verbal arguments. If you argue which comes first, meditation or wisdom, you are deluded people…

Meditation and wisdom "are a unity, not two things" in the way a lamp and the light it casts are not separate.

> If there is a lamp there is light; if there is no lamp there is no light. The lamp is the substance of light; the light is the function of the lamp. Thus, although they have two names, in substance they are not two. Meditation and wisdom are also like this.

Wisdom is not knowledge of the Dharma as doctrine but rather the insight that derives from practice of meditation that he calls – borrowing a term from the *Xinxin Ming* – "straightforward mind." Nor is this meditation a matter of seeking to achieve a blank mind as it is commonly mistaken to be. Rather, it is clear awareness of the flow of sense of impressions, including thoughts, without being caught up in them or deceived by them. The point is similar to that made in the *Lankavatara Sutra*: Because of conditioning, the discriminating intellect fails to see reality clearly; through clear awareness, the conditioned perspective is overcome, and one attains

---

106. Quotations from Philip Yampolsky (trans.), *The Platform Sutra of the Sixth Patriarch* (New York: Columbia University Press, 1967).

direct experiential understanding of the interdependence of all of being and the essential emptiness of individual entities (in the sense that they have no abiding independent reality or self). As such, "straightforward mind" is not limited to periods of seated meditation – as important as that is – but should be maintained "at all times, walking, staying, sitting, and lying."

The *Platform Sutra* does not deny the value of traditional activities such ritual or sutra study. Although, in themselves, they will not bring about awakening, they do help maintain an atmosphere conducive to attaining "straightforward mind" and direct perception of one's True Nature – the unconditioned Mind unobscured by the clouds of discursive thought. The problem is that because "all sentient beings have of themselves deluded minds, they seek the Buddha by external" practices such as these, failing to recognize that awakening can only be attained – as the Bodhidharma poem emphasizes – by turning inward under proper guidance.

Transmission

The artificiality of the concept of a single line of descent from the time of the Buddha to the Sixth Patriarch is evident in the fact that Huineng had not one but several heirs[107] none of whom received the robe and bowl of Bodhidharma. Those items, it was claimed, were buried with their teacher. One of these heirs, Nanyang Huizhong, later came to be known as the "National Teacher" (Guoshi) because he served in the court of the Emperor.

The concept of transmission may originally have been a legal one. By the time of Hongren, both Daoist and Buddhist monasteries were complex operations in which the members formed a "tonsured family." Entry into the community could only be acquired by sponsorship. Novices had to be sponsored by a senior monastic, after which they became part of the "tonsure family associated with the monastery in which the sponsor resided and would enter into a complex and lifelong web of rights and obligations with the other members of the tonsure family."[108] Further, under normal circumstances monastic offices – including the abbacy – were passed down through the tonsure family. In this sense, the term "transmission" referred to the right transmitted through the community to hold office.

---

107. Ten are identified in the *Platform Sutra*.

108. Morten Schlütter, *How Zen Became Zen* (Honolulu: University of Hawai'i Press, 2008), p. 36. These monasteries are termed "hereditary" because their abbots come from within the "tonsure family." In the Song era, "public" monasteries arose where abbots could be appointed from appropriate candidates from other communities, although these appointments often needed to be approved by the state. In the Song Dynasty, Chan monasteries tended to be public in this manner.

In Chan parlance, however, transmission refers to the process of passing on (transmitting) direct awareness of one's inherent Buddha-nature. Thus, there is an elitist quality in the Chan traditions. While there are tens of thousands of monasteries and teachers throughout China, only a very narrow line of descent is credited as passing on the genuine awakening experience.

The mechanics of how this is accomplished is not clearly defined because it is less an actual passing on than it is an acknowledgement of attainment. It is not that the teacher gives anything to the student; rather he recognizes the student's achievement. The teacher's responsibility is to maintain an environment in which this achievement can occur and guide the student towards it.

Although the term "Chan" refers to meditation,[109] the stories of awakening seldom mention the practice and almost never is the awakening experience described as occurring during meditation, although, without a doubt, monastics spent considerable time in the practice, cultivating clear attention. The salient point is that awakening is experiential, not theoretical, not something to be attained through study and reflection. One of the most famous awakening stories is that of Xiangyan Zhixian, who, a century after the death of the National Teacher, Nanyang Huizhong, became the caretaker of his grave site.

Xiangyan had been a student of Baizhang Huaihai, a third generation Dharma descendent of Huineng, and had devoted himself to the study of Buddhist scriptures. After Baizhang died, Xiangyan presented himself to the master's successor, Guishan Lingyou, and asked to be accepted as a disciple. Guishan was reluctant to grant the request because he suspected Xiangyan's understanding was largely theoretical. To test him, he asked the question that Huineng had put to General Ming: "What is your true self, your self before your mother gave birth to you, before you came to know east from west?"

Xiangyan attempted several responses to the question, each of which Guishan dismissed. Finally, he said, "Please, then, teach me. Show me this original self."

"I've nothing to give you," Guishan told him. "Even if I tried to instruct you, that would only provide you an opportunity to ridicule me later on. After all, whatever I have is my own and can never be yours. How can that be of any help to you?"

Xiangyan searched through the books and notes he had collected over the years but found nothing to help him understand what Guishan was asking for. So, he gathered all of his papers together and set fire to them, declaring, "What's the use of studying the Buddhadharma, so difficult to comprehend and too subtle to receive instruction from another?

---

109. "Channa" is the Chinese pronunciation of the Sanskrit term "dhyana."

I'll become a simple monk, abiding by the precepts, with no desire to try to master things too deep for thought."

He left Baizhang's temple and traveled for many weeks, eventually coming to Mount Baiya in Nanyang, where the remains of Huizhong were buried. The tomb was in a state of deterioration, so Xiangyan built a grass hut nearby and took upon himself the responsibilities of caretaker. Adhering to the directives of the Noble Eightfold Path, he carried out his tasks as mindfully as he could. One day, as he was sweeping the grounds with a broom, a stone he cleared away struck a bamboo stalk. The sound, sharp and hollow, was clear in his attention, and the moment he heard it he came to a deep awakening. He was speechless for a moment, then broke out laughing. He went into the ruined temple, lit incense in gratitude, and bowed in the direction of Guishan's temple. Then he traveled to see the man who had refused to teach him. "Your kindness to me was greater than even that of my parents," Xiangyan told Guishan. "Had you tried to explain this truth to me in words, I would never be where I am now."

In this manner, Guishan is said to have "transmitted" the awakening experience to Xiangyan.

Multiple Lines of Descent

Although a teacher might have numerous students who had enlightenment experiences such as Xiangyan's, only those who went on to become teachers themselves were identified as "Dharma heirs" and had their names included in the written documents recording "transmission lines." In this sense, both insight and authority are "transmitted." The heir not only had attained, or surpassed, the degree of insight of the teacher, they also made a commitment to passing that insight on. Theoretically, therefore, a teacher could have a student whose level of insight was superior to that of his brothers but because he did not become a teacher – specifically the abbot of a monastery – he is not listed among that teacher's descendants. An heir needed not only insight (prajna) but also the administrative and organizational skills necessary to serve as the abbot of a monastery.

The first time the line of teaching derived from Bodhidharma is identified as "Chan Buddhism" occurs in the records of Mazu Daoyi, the only Dharma heir of Nanyue Huairang, one of Huineng's successors. Mazu would have 139 heirs. By the 9th century, there were many lines of descent, with the inevitable attendant rivalries. Most of these were short-lived. Later records will identify five primary lines – the so-called Five Houses of Chan – three of which also fell into abeyance by the year 1000. The two that remained – the Linji [J: Rinzai] and the Caodong [J: Soto] – would spread throughout Japan, Korea, Vietnam, and eventually to North America and Europe.

The Linji Line

Mazu Daoyi

Mazu Daoyi began his training under a teacher who seems to have been more in sympathy with the Northern than the Southern School. That instructor taught him to strive to keep an empty mind during meditation. When Mazu came to Nanyue Huairang's monastery, he continued to practice as he had been shown. Nanyue happened to notice the young man's dedicated sitting and asked him what he hoped to accomplish by it.

Probably surprised by the question, Mazu replied, "I want to attain Buddhahood."

Without a word, Nanyue picked up a piece of broken tile and began to rub it vigorously. He kept this up until Mazu asked what he was doing.

"I'm polishing this tile to make it into a mirror."

"But no amount of polishing will turn a tile into a mirror!"

"Neither will any amount of meditation, as you practice it, make you into a Buddha."

"What should I do then?" Mazu asked.

"If you were driving a cart and it stopped, would you strike the cart or the ox?"

Mazu did not know how to reply.

"Consider your intention," Nanyue continued. "Is it to become a master of sitting Chan? Or is it to attain Buddhahood. If what you wish is to study Chan, then know that Chan isn't a matter of sitting or lying down or any other position. If you wish to become a Buddha, then know that the Buddha is formless. Buddha has no particular posture, such as sitting in the cross-legged position. Trying to become a Buddha by sitting cross-legged kills the Buddha. Cling to this practice and you'll never attain the truth."

It is said that upon hearing these words, Mazu felt refreshed, as if he had had a cool drink on a warm day.

While the dialogue appears to question the value of sitting meditation, what is actually being challenged is the style of meditation being practiced. It is not by "wiping the mirror of the mind clear" and sitting passively that one comes to awakening but rather through seeing into the nature of Mind, which is identical with one's Buddha-nature (the Indian term) or the Dao (the traditional Chinese term). And, as the *Platform Sutra* emphasized, the action of Mind is not limited to a specific posture, such as sitting.

Once Nanyue confirmed Mazu's enlightenment, the latter sought to live a quiet and solitary life, but, wherever he went, people committed to achieving awakening found him. His manner of teaching was later described as "strange words and extraordinary actions." He did not comment on the sutras or engage in religious rites but rather took advantage of situations that arose during ordinary daily activities using whatever "skillful means" (upaya) were appropriate to the circumstances.

A monk, for example, was engaged in trimming a wisteria vine with him one day. The monk took the opportunity to pose the question, "Why did the First Patriarch come from the west?" This was a formula question meaning, "What was the significance or content of Bodhidharma's teaching?" He probably expected a verbal answer, but Mazu responded by motioning to him and whispering: "Come a little nearer, and I'll tell you."

When the monk went over to Mazu, the master kicked him so hard that he fell over. As he hit the ground, the monk came to awakening, and he sat up laughing heartily.

"What is the meaning of this laughter?" Mazu asked.

"How strange! How odd! The teachings of the Buddha are so vast they can't be numbered. And yet I now see them all revealed on the tip of a single hair."

The concept of *upaya* broadens in the Chan tradition. In this instance the skillful means is a kick that would have been both ineffective and cruel if the student had not attained a certain level of readiness through meditation and other traditional practices.

A scholar once visited Mazu, telling him: "I'm fairly-well acquainted with the literature of Buddhism, but I still don't understand why the Chan school claims that mind is Buddha."

"The very mind that doesn't understand is Buddha; there isn't any other," Mazu told him.

Still not grasping what Mazu was saying, the scholar persisted: "It's said that your First Patriarch brought a secret teaching from India, from where all the scriptures originate. Will Your Reverence please reveal that secret to me?"

"Well, I'm very busy just now. Perhaps you could come again at a later time."

Disappointed, the scholar bowed and turned to leave. Before he reached the door, however, Mazu called out: "Monk!"

The scholar turned back to him.

"What is it?" Mazu demanded sharply.

At that, the scholar came to awakening and understood the secret teaching of Bodhidharma. Full of gratitude, he bowed to Mazu.

"Don't be foolish," Mazu said. "What use is there in bowing?"

When another monk came to Mazu saying that he sought awakening, Mazu asked, "Why have you come to me? You have your own treasure house. Look there for what you seek."

"Where is this treasure house of mine?" the monk inquired.

"What you're asking is your treasure house."

Mazu's remarks in each case were appropriate to the supplicant's condition. Outside the specific context of the situation in which teacher and student were at the time, the answers make little sense. Stories such as these were referred to as *wenda*[110] or "encounter dialogues" and were routinely recorded in books called *Yulu* or "Records" kept by itinerant monks as they travelled between monasteries. These tales became the basis of a new canon of Buddhist writing. Individual incidents became the subjects of lectures given in the Dharma Halls, not unlike Christian sermons taking a verse from the Bible as their basis. Eventually they came to be used as subjects assigned to students for meditation and thus formed the basis of the *gongan* (*koan* in Japanese) system.

These stories are unlike anything found in the Buddhist literature of India. Instead of being lengthy abstract arguments, they are brief, anecdotal presentations of the Dharma, closer in style to Daoist tales than to the voluble presentations found in the *Platform Sutra* and its Indian models. Instead of putting forth an argument to be followed, they present a manifestation of the Dharma in action or dialogue to which one responds more as one does to poetry than to exposition. They are not about conveying information but are about encouraging a different way of seeing things.

Baizhang Huaihai

Mazu's most important heir was Baizhang Huaihai, a reformer whose restructuring of Chan monasteries helped the tradition survive the persecution that occurred just thirty years after his death. There were several reasons why members of the ruling classes continued to find fault with Buddhism. It was viewed by native Confucians as a foreign religion whose egalitarian sentiments were a threat to the existing social order. They objected to the fact that some of the monasteries had amassed great wealth and believed they were refuges for individuals seeking to avoid military service or payment of taxes. The monasteries depended upon the donations of the Buddhist faithful for their maintenance, and in many cases the monks supported by those donations had become drones who neither promoted the Dharma nor contributed to the society as a whole.

---

110. *Mondo* in Japanese.

Since the time of Sengcan, Chan centers tended to be located in remote regions and so did not draw the same attention the monasteries of other Buddhist sects had; however, Baizhang understood that they were not immune to the abuses found elsewhere. He determined that Chan monks should be self-sufficient and insisted that they produce their own food rather than depend upon the donations or labors of others. Since some Buddhist sects forbade their monks to engage in any activity, including farming, that might take the life of even the smallest creature, these reforms were controversial.

Baizhang formalized what had previously been traditional guidelines into a prescribed rule. The structure of his monasteries included both physical labor and meditation. Both were part of the practice and one was not to be considered superior to the other. On one occasion, when his disciples asked him to speak to them about the Dharma, he told them: "First prepare the fields for planting. After that I'll talk to you about the great principle of Chan." Once the monks completed their work, they presented themselves in the Dharma Hall. Baizhang took his place before them and extended his arms wordlessly.

In his own activity, he provided an example of the life he expected his disciples to lead. Well into his eighties, he continued to work in the fields every day. As he became frailer with age, however, some of his disciples decided he should refrain from such exertions, and they hid his gardening implements. When Baizhang could not find his tools, he went back to his room and remained there at meal time. He did not eat that day or the next. The disciples discussed this and wondered if he were angered by the missing tools, so they put them back in their usual place. Baizhang returned to his work in the fields and resumed his meals as well. He told his disciples, "A day of no work is a day of no food."

Huangbo Xiyun

A notable characteristic of wenda is that they seldom seem to focus on matters of Buddhist doctrine, and yet their proponents insist that they present the heart of the Dharma. For example, this story is told about Baizhang's illustrious disciple, Huangbo Xiyun – who is recorded to have been seven feet tall: He began his studies with another of Mazu's heirs, Nanquan Puyuan, who must have had a high regard for Xiyun because when the younger man departed to further his studies the master accompanied him to the monastery gate. There he held up Xiyun's hat and commented: "You're fairly large, but your hat isn't too big for you, is it?"

Xiyun accepted the hat saying, "That's so, but the entire universe is covered beneath it."

"And as for me?" Nanquan asked.

Xiyun put on his hat and departed.

When Baizhang acknowledged Xiyun as his Dharma heir, he declared, "If the disciple's insight is only equal to that of his teacher, the teacher's legacy is diminished. But when the disciple's insight surpasses that of his teacher, then, indeed, he's worthy of receiving transmission."

One of Xiyun's students, the governor of the local prefecture, was wealthy enough to finance a temple for his teacher. The mountain where the temple was built was named Mount Huangbo, and Xiyun came to be known as Huangbo Xiyun.

The central issue for Huangbo, as for most Chan teachers, was "mind" (xin). He pointed out that just as the eye cannot see the eye, so mind cannot be found by mind. All beings, he held, are the One Mind outside of which nothing exists. It was natural that the disciples who came to him often believed they were supposed to seek for their True Natures, but Huangbo insisted there was nothing to attain or to do because, like all other sentient beings, these disciples already were Buddha. "There's no distinction between Buddha and sentient beings," he taught. "Both are the One Mind. To awaken to the realization that your Mind, just as it is, is the Buddha, is to realize that there's nothing to be attained, nothing to be done. This is the Dao."

To seek what one already is or already has is to misunderstand the situation. Therefore, the act of seeking puts realization at a distance. The emphasis here is not on the Dharma as presented by Shakyamuni Buddha but on attaining one's own direct insight, realizing one's own Buddhahood. The goal is not to become a Buddhist but a Buddha.

Linji Yixuan

Linji Yixuan, like many of the Tang Dynasty Chan masters, began his studies in more traditional Buddhist schools that focused on the precepts and sutras. But he, too, found the intellectual study of the Buddhadharma unsatisfying and, while still in his twenties, sought a teacher who would be able to help him understand the teaching that was beyond words. So it was that he came to Huangbo's monastery. As a novice, Yixuan had almost no contact with the master. He was taught how to meditate and was given a work assignment, and in this way three years passed. The head monk of the monastery observed Yixuan's practice and recognized the sincerity of his effort. One day he asked the younger man if he had yet presented a question to the master. Yixuan admitted that he had not done so and was unsure what question to pose.

"Ask him what the basic teaching of the Buddhadharma is," the head monk suggested.

Following the advice of the head monk, Yixuan sought an audience with Huangbo, and, after making his formal bows, he asked, "Master, please, what is the basic teaching of the Buddhadharma?"

He had barely got the question out, when Huangbo leaned forward and slapped his face. Nonplussed, Yixuan bowed again and withdrew. The head monk asked how the interview had gone.

"I'd hardly put my question when the master struck me!" Yixuan complained.

"Very well. Ask him again."

So twice more, Yixuan asked Huangbo about the basic teaching of the Buddhadharma, and both times Huangbo replied with a slap.

Yixuan decided that he had either offended the master or had failed him in some manner, so he told the head monk, "I thank you for your efforts on my behalf, but whenever I speak to our master, his only response is to strike me. Apparently I have some karmic obstruction that prevents me from understanding the matter of Chan. So I've determined to leave the monastery."

"That's for you to decide," the head monk admitted. "But if you're leaving the monastery, it is customary for you to take formal leave of the master first."

Yixuan promised to do so.

Before Yixuan arranged for his final meeting with Huangbo, the head monk went to the master and told him, "The young monk who's been to see you three times is a sincere seeker of the truth. When he presents himself again, please treat him appropriately. Provided he receives proper training, he'll become a great teacher and become a large tree under which many will be able to take shelter."

When Yixuan came before Huangbo to announce his departure, the old master told him: "If you must leave, you should go from here to see Master Dayu. He alone can answer your questions."

Yixuan was still hopeful that if he found the appropriate teacher, he would be able to understand Chan, so he sought out Dayu's temple and presented himself to the master. Dayu asked him where he had come from.

"I've spent the last three years at the temple of Master Huangbo."

"And what is the teaching of Huangbo?" Dayu asked.

"I don't know," Yixuan admitted. "Three times I've asked him to explain the basic teaching of Buddhism, and each time he's struck me. I don't know what my fault was."

"Such ingratitude!" Dayu exclaimed. "Huangbo has exhausted himself with grandmotherly kindness on your behalf, and you wonder what your fault was!"

As soon as he heard these words, Yixuan came to enlightenment. "Aye! There's not so much to Huangbo's Buddhism after all!" he exclaimed spontaneously.

Yixuan traveled back to Huangbo's temple. The master, who was standing by the gate at the time, happened to see him approaching. "Here's that fellow again!" Huangbo called out. "Coming and going. Going and coming. When will it ever end?"

"It's the result of your grandmotherly kindness," Yixuan said.

"Who's gone and who's returned?" Huangbo asked.

"You were kind enough to send me to Dayu."

"And what did he have to say?"

Yixuan described his meeting with Dayu. After listening, Huangbo remarked, "That scoundrel! The next time I see him, I'll give him twenty blows."

"Why wait?" said Yixuan. "Have them now!" And with that he slapped Huangbo.

"What arrogance! What impudence!" Huangbo exclaimed.

Yixuan replied by shouting, "Ho!"

"Where's my attendant?" Huangbo called. "Take this madman away and house him in the monks' quarters!"

Although Huangbo appeared to be angry with Yixuan, he was, in fact, proud of the younger man's attainment. The give and take between master and student continued through the remainder of Yixuan's time with his teacher.

On one occasion, Huangbo was working in the fields with a hoe when Yixuan walked by.

"Why don't you have a hoe?" the teacher demanded.

"Someone's taken it," Yixuan shot back.

Huangbo raised his own hoe and said, "Only this, but the whole world is unable to hold it up."

Yixuan took the hoe away from Huangbo and asked, "So how is it that it's in my hands?"

"Here's a man doing a great work today!" Huangbo remarked.

After completing his studies with Huangbo and receiving transmission, Yixuan undertook the traditional pilgrimage to visit other Chan masters throughout China. Once he completed his pilgrimage, he settled in a small temple on the banks of the Hutuo River. The temple was known as Linjiyuan (J: Rinzai-in), the "Temple Overlooking the Ford." So Yixuan acquired the name Linji by which he and the school descending from him are best known. Although he received disciples at the temple, their numbers were never large. The tradition they established, however, proved to be enduring.

Linji had a reputation for the rough treatment he dealt out to his followers, but it was also recognized that his methods were effective. Two stories are told about the treatment meted out to a disciple named Dingzhou Shizang.

One day Linji told his disciples: "Over a mass of reddish flesh there sits a true man of no rank." In Chinese society, the idea of a man without rank was difficult to comprehend; each person was expected to know his place within the Confucian hierarchy of responsibilities and obligations. "This true man of no rank comes in and goes out of your face all of the time. If you haven't identified him yet, do so now. Look!"

Dingzhou stood and asked, "Who is this man of no rank?"

Linji, true to form, stood up, took hold of the monk's robes, and shook him. "Speak! Speak!" he demanded.

Dingzhou, not knowing how to reply, remained silent.

"What a piece of dried shit this true man of no rank is!" Linji said, releasing the monk.

On another occasion, Dingzhou asked, "What is the purpose of the Buddhadharma?"

This time, Linji slapped his face.

Dingzhou was as confused as Linji had been when he had first been struck by Huangbo. Not knowing what to do, he stood where he was. A fellow monk leaned towards him and whispered, "Why don't you bow?"

And just as Dingzhou started to bow, he came to awakening.

"Your body is composed of the four elements – earth, water, fire, and air," Linji told his disciples. "None of these can hear or understand my preaching. Your stomach, your liver, they can't understand this preaching. Nor can empty space understand it. So, who, then, is hearing? Who understands?"

He made a similar point when he demanded of his assembled monks, "Just at this moment, right before your eyes, who's the one listening to this lecture?"

When asked how one should go about seeking awakening, Linji said: "All one has to do is to attend to the circumstances of his life. Rise in the morning and put on your clothes, then go to work. When hungry, eat; when tired, rest. Don't have a desire to attain Buddhahood. Don't have even the least thought of it. A wise man of old warned, if you strive for Buddhahood by any conscious deed, this will only lead to constant rebirth."

Linji Yixuan was one of the great personalities of Tang Dynasty Chan. His descendants over the next several generations, however, were not as well known, in part because, rather than developing their own styles, they dedicated themselves to carrying on the traditions associated with their teacher. The distinctive characteristics of the school – including the liberal use of the stick and shouting "Ho!" – were techniques copied from Linji. The most important line descending from Linji was that of Xinghua Cunjiang, who warned his followers of the danger of merely aping the mannerisms of his late master. "All day long I hear monks shouting 'Ho!' in the corridors and in the halls. But you must beware of shouting for its own sake. Even if you were to shout so loudly that it took my breath away, when my breath returned, I'd tell you, 'Still not it!' I haven't been passing out gift-wrapped gems to you. What's all this shouting about?"

The Caodong Line

Shitou Xiqian

Mazu's great contemporary was Shitou Xiqian, whose name meant "Stone Head" or, more literally, "The Monk Who Lives on Top of the Stone." His fame rivaled that of Mazu during their lifetimes. Both gathered disciples in rural rather than urban settings, Mazu "west of the river" and Shitou in Hunan "south of the lake."

At the age of thirteen, Shitou sought admission to Huineng's community. The patriarch died within a year, and Shitou continued his study with Huineng's heir, Qingyuan Xingshi. His awakening experience came about as a result of a passage he read in a sutra commentary that declared: "Only those can be called holy who view the world in such a way that they see themselves in all things." Shitou realized that this statement did not go far enough. He slammed his fist on the table, exclaiming: "Only those are holy who have no selves, for everything is their self. Who, then, can speak of you and me, of one's self and another's self?"

After Qingyuan recognized Shitou as a successor, the younger man retired to the temple on Mount Heng where he built a hut on the large flat rock from which he derived his name. Here he attracted his own disciples and taught for twenty-three years. His style of teaching lacked the dramatic elements – the "strange words and extraordinary actions" employed by Mazu and Linji – and he was more open to the value of traditional devotional practices. In an often-quoted sermon, he states:

"I received my dharma, my teaching, from a preceding Buddha [Qingyuan]. It doesn't matter what method one uses – sitting meditation or chanting sutras or other means of devotion. All that matters is attaining Buddha-wisdom. This very mind – this is Buddha. Mind, Buddha, sentient beings, pure wisdom, even defiling passions, these are all different names for one reality; they're all names for one and the same substance.

"What you must discover is your own Mind-essence. Realize that it's separate from creation and destruction, from permanence and extinction.

Its nature is neither stained nor pure. It's absolutely still and completely whole. It makes no distinction between sacred or profane. It has countless ways of responding to circumstances. And although I call it Mind, it's distinct from both mind and consciousness. The various modes of being and the different manners of birth are all only appearances that have been produced by Mind, like the reflection of the moon in water or of images in a mirror. How can Mind be subject to birth and death? If you understand this, you won't lack anything."

Dongshan Liangjie

About twenty-five years after Shitou Xiqian's death, a child named Liangjie was sent to a local Buddhist temple to begin his education. His teacher was a modest local priest without pretensions about his own attainments. He recited the sutras, carried out the various devotional duties the community expected of him, and shared what he knew with Liangjie.

One day, as he had been instructed, the boy was reciting the *Heart Sutra*. When he came to the line which asserts that there is "No eye, ear, nose, tongue, body, mind," Liangjie paused. It seemed the most common-sense thing in the world that he did, in fact, have eyes, ears, a nose, and so on; that there were colors, sounds, smells, and taste. Confused by this, he asked his teacher why the sutra would declare something so obviously false. The priest admitted he didn't know and suggested the boy continue his studies with one of the growing number of Chan teachers living in the mountains.

Liangjie left the temple and pursued his formation under the guidance of several Chan masters before working with Yunyan Tansheng, a second-generation Dharma heir of Shitou. When they first met, the young man asked the master about a remark attributed to the National Teacher, Nanyang Huizhong, who was supposed to have said, "Inanimate objects such as walls, tiles, and stones are continuously preaching the Dharma. Who can hear such teaching?"

"The inanimate hear them," Yunyan told him.

"Do you hear them?" Liangjie asked.

"If I heard them, you wouldn't be able to hear me."

"Why can't I hear them?" Liangjie persisted.

Yunyan raised his staff. "Do you hear it?" he asked.

"No."

"When you can't hear my preaching, how can you hope to hear the preaching of the inanimate?" Then Yunyan asked: "Do you know the *Sutra of the Amituo Buddha*?[111] It tells us: 'Streams, birds, trees and forests,

---

111. J: Amida Buddha; the Buddha whose name is chanted by practitioners of the Pure Land sect.

all chant the name of Buddha.'"

Hearing this, Liangjie achieved his first awakening. Although he realized it was fairly shallow, he wrote a poem to commemorate the event:

> How wonderful, how very wonderful!
> The preaching of the sentientless is inconceivable!
> Listening with the ear, it is difficult to understand,
> Hearing with the eye, then you know it.[112]

After remaining with Yunyan for a while, Liangjie set out on a pilgrimage to meet other Chan teachers in order to deepen his understanding. Prior to his departure, Liangjie asked, "If, in some future time, someone were to ask me to describe your teaching, what should I say?"

"Say only this: 'Just this is it.'"

Liangjie was confused by the statement, and his expression showed it.

"In undertaking this matter you must investigate it minutely," Yunyan counseled him.

Liangjie's great awakening finally occurred as he was crossing a stream. The man whose quest had begun by wondering about the assertions of the *Heart Sutra* happened to see his own reflection on the water and that was the cue he needed to understand Yunyan's parting instructions. He commemorated the event with a poem:

> Long seeking it through others,
> I was far from reaching it.
> Now I go by myself;
> I meet it everywhere.
> It is just I myself,
> And I am not itself.
> Understanding this way,
> I can be as I am.[113]

He eventually settled on Mount Dong (Dongshan), thus acquiring the name he came to be known by. Here he built a hermitage and dedicated himself to practice. Mindfulness in daily activity became a hallmark of Dongshan's Chan. Slowly, he began to gather his own disciples and guided them in the spirit of the *Xinxin Ming*, bringing them into the present moment, experiencing events without judgment as they arose.

---

112. Isshu Miuru and Ruth Fuller Sasaki, *Zen Dust* (New York: Harcourt, Brace & World, 1966), p. 297.

113. Katsuki Sekida, *Two Zen Classics* (Boston: Shambhala, 2005) p. 267.

The teachings of Dongshan as promulgated by his heir, Caoshan Benji, became the basis of the largest of all the Chan schools, the Caodong, which derives its name from the initial syllables of the mountain names of these two masters. In Japanese, where their names are Sozan Honjaku and Tozan Ryokai, the school is known as Soto.

The Song Dynasty

The majority of the Chan tales that form the basis of the gongan – koan – system come from the Tang Dynasty. After the collapse of the Tang, China was subjected to the cultural chaos of five dynasties succeeding one another in the fifty-three-year period between 907 and 960. Conditions stabilized again with the establishment of what is known as the Northern Song. Later, in 1127, when the Northern provinces broke away from the South, the Song leadership simply moved their capital south and continued to govern a smaller but more stable country during the period known as the Southern Song which lasted until Kublai Khan established the Yuan Dynasty in 1279.

Following the collapse of the Tang Dynasty, two of the Five Houses of Chan faded away, and the Caodong seemed on the verge of disappearing as well. The two dominant houses of what was known as "single practice" Buddhism at the beginning of the Song era were the Linji and Yunmen lineages. Their monasteries spread throughout the land, attracting numerous adherents. As the number of monks increased, the monasteries needed to find ways of accommodating and dealing with larger numbers and with persons of varying aptitude. Consequently, while, the monasteries thrived, they also became more formalized. The innovative techniques of the teachers of the Tang Dynasty, who often worked with only a few close disciples, needed to be replaced by disciplines designed for larger communities.

Because the story of Chan stresses that it is a continuous transmission from the Buddha down to the present time, the authority of Chan masters depended as much on their ability to trace their lineage back to Huineng and Bodhidharma as it did on their personal insight and skills, so at times lineage documents were fudged to provide this proof. For example, the Caodong master, Touzi Yiqing, is said to have been the Dharma heir of Dayang Jingxuan, even though the two never met. This is explained in the records by the assertion that Yiqing received the transmission from another teacher who "held it in trust" for Jingxuan – which, even if true, demonstrates that "direct transmission" was not always the only way to be proclaimed an heir.

Furong Daokai

The reason the legitimacy of Yiqing's transmission is important for the Caodong School is that his heir, Furong Daokai, is credited with reviving the school when it was on the verge of extinction.

Daokai was an influential teacher much admired by government officials and the educated classes of the day, and several of his career appointments were brought about by imperial decree. The way in which he responded to these honors enhanced his reputation. The emperor of the day, Huizong, considered himself a patron of Buddhism but also assumed he had the right to place talented people in positions he thought appropriate for them. In 1104, he assigned Daokai to a temple in the capital city, Kaifeng. Three years later, the emperor bestowed a purple robe – a notable honor – on Daokai, as well as the title Dingzhao, and ordered him to take up a new position at the Chongning Temple which had been specifically established so that the monks could pray to the Celestials for the long life of the Emperor. Daokai expressed his gratitude for these honors but insisted he could not accept them; it was, he argued, inappropriate for a monk to seek profit or fame. The emperor, who was used to monks routinely accepting imperial gifts, was surprised by this scrupulousness and sent a high court official to urge Daokai to change his mind. When Daokai refused to do so, the emperor, in a fit of pique, stripped him of his monastic robes and exiled him to his home province.

Although he no longer had official standing within the Buddhist community, Daokai's integrity attracted followers who sought him out during his period of exile. Probably responding to popular pressure, the emperor rescinded the exile a year later. Daokai was reinstated in the clergy and established a new monastery near Lake Furong, from which he took his name.

Caodong Meditation Practice

Early Chan literature includes little description of meditation techniques because it was almost exclusively a practice for those living in monastic communities where instruction was given face to face. It is not until the Southern Song period that lay members of the educated classes began to practice meditation as well and written instructions needed to be provided. One of these, the *Manual for Sitting Meditation*,[114] describes the practice that, in all likelihood, had been common since the time of the Fifth Patriarch. The instructions begin with detailed descriptions about the proper way to sit, how the body should be aligned, the legs folded, and the hands placed. Eyes are lowered but not closed, and the breath is relaxed and regular. In the Caodong tradition, meditators sit facing a wall in emulation of Bodhidharma. The work then states:

---

114. *Zuo Chan Yi*.

Do not think of any good or evil whatsoever. Whenever a thought occurs, be aware of it; as soon as you are aware of it, it will vanish. If you remain for a long period forgetful of external conditions [*wangyuan*], you will naturally become unified. This is the essential art of seated meditation.[115]

This form of meditation was known as "silent illumination" until that term was appropriated by critics of Daokai and his descendants and used as an expression of derision. It is the basis of what, in the Japanese Soto School, came to be called *shikan taza* – "just sitting so." An essential element of the practice is not to seek to attain anything from it. This is grounded in the basic premise of Mahayana belief that all beings have inherent Buddha-nature that, therefore, is not something to be acquired but rather to be realized. In the story of the Buddha's awakening as passed down through the Chan and Zen lines, he is said to have proclaimed at the moment of his enlightenment, "Wonder of wonders, all things, just as they are, are whole and complete. All beings are endowed with Buddha-nature." In a similar fashion, from the Daoist perspective, one does not seek to align oneself with the Dao because one cannot separate oneself from it. It is only delusion that prevents one from realizing this. The Caodong – and later Soto – teachers thus maintained that sitting in meditation is itself the same as attainment. They encouraged students to become still, like an old incense burner in a temple or a dry log or even a corpse with white mold forming at the sides of the mouth.[116] It is the cultivation of that state of mind that the Daoist Zhuang Zhou had compared to still water: "If water is clear when it is at rest, how much more so is the human spirit? When the mind of the sage is calm, it becomes the mirror of the universe, reflecting all within it."[117]

Critics of this approach claimed it amounted to sitting in a dark cave accomplishing nothing; supporters viewed this form of meditation as essentially an exercise in stilling the mind. Once the mind was still, any activity could trigger awakening – the appearance of the morning star on the horizon or even the sound of a stone striking bamboo. The only difference between the teachings of Daokai and his descendants from earlier generations of Chan teachers appears to be a greater emphasis on sustained periods of sitting without deliberately seeking anything from the practice.

---

115. Quoted in Morten Schlütter, *How Zen Became Zen* (Honolulu: University of Hawai'i Press, 2008), p. 170.

116. Cf. Zhuang Zhou who wrote of one's body becoming like dead wood and one's mind like cold ashes.

117. Lin Yutang, op. cit., p. 195.

The most vociferous critic of the Caodong approach to meditation was Dahui Zonggao, a master in the Linji lineage of Wuzu Fayan.

Wuzu Fayan and Gongan Practice

Wuzu Fayan was born in 1024, sixty-four years after the establishment of the Song Dynasty. He began his studies in the Yogacara tradition, a speculative school based on the study of original Indian texts. One day he was reading an argument between adherents of the Yogacara tradition and their opponents on the nature of "knowing." He could not tell from their reasoning which side was correct. Then he came upon a commentary on the argument by the Chinese translator, Hsuan Zhuang, who wrote: "It is like drinking water. One knows for oneself whether it is cool or warm." This passage made Fayan realize that what he hungered for was an actual, rather than intellectual, understanding of the Buddhadharma.

Coming to believe that he would not be able satisfy this desire in the Yogacara community, he sought a teacher who might be able to help him. The first Chan teacher he met was Yuanjien Fayuan who enigmatically told him, "Shakyamuni Buddha had a secret word which he passed onto Mahakasyapa, but Kasyapa couldn't keep it hidden."

Fayan meditated on this statement for a year. Then Yuanjien, who was elderly at the time, told him he needed to work with a younger teacher who would be able to dedicate more attention to him. Yuanjien suggested that Fayan go to Boyun Shoutuan.

Boyun presented Fayan with Zhaozhou Congshen's *Wu* as a gongan. The word gongan refers to "a public record," in the sense of records kept by law courts to establish precedent in jurisprudence. They derived from the "encounter dialogues" commonly used in lectures and as testing questions to determine the depth of a student's understanding. When later teachers added commentaries to these stories, they acquired the status of precedents and were then termed "gongan." They appear to have first been used as teaching techniques in the early Song period. In the later Song they were gathered into collections, like the *Biyan Lu*,[118] or *Blue Cliff Record*, that was expanded and annotated from an earlier source by Wuzu's heir Yuanwu Keqin.

---

118. In Japanese, *Hekiganroku*. "The volume of literature produced by the Chan school far outweighs anything produced by any other groups of Buddhism in the Song. The irony of the Song Chan school's claim to embody 'a separate transmission outside the teachings, not setting up words' was not lost on contemporaries, including the bibliophile Chen Zhensun (ca. 1190–after 1249), who pointed out that four of the Chan transmission histories together consisted of 120 fascicles comprising several tens of millions of characters, and who mockingly twisted the Chan school's self-description as 'not relying on words' (bu li wenzi) to read as its homophonic 'never separated from words.'" Schlütter, op. cit., p. 8.

Gongans are usually posed as questions that cannot be answered rationally but can be resolved intuitively. The goal is not for a student to learn a particular doctrine as an article of faith but to experience for themselves the significance of the doctrine. The focus is on realization, rather than study, and it was realization that Wuzu sought.

The *Wu*[119] gongan is very short. A monk asks the Tang Dynasty Chan Master, Zhaozhou Congshen, whether or not a dog has Buddha-nature. Zhaozhou replies with a single syllable, "Wu!" which means "No!" or "Nothing!"

As I have written elsewhere, the story is more complex than it may appear. The monk who put the question would have known that Buddhist teaching affirms that all creatures have Buddha-nature, not only dogs but even mosquitoes and worms. What the monk was looking for was reassurance. Although he knew in theory that he had Buddha-nature, he still had not realized it. He may have begun to wonder whether Buddha-nature was innate or if it were something to be acquired through technique. His question, therefore, was sly. Instead of asking about his own condition, he asked whether even a dog – a despised animal in Chinese culture – had Buddha-nature. Zhaozhou's reply was not a literal negative. In fact, on another occasion, when posed the same question, he said, "Yes!"

It was while working with Wu that Fayan eventually came to awakening, and consequently he became an enthusiastic advocate of the use of gongan.

After receiving transmission from Boyun, Fayan took up residence on Mount Dong, which was popularly known as the Fifth Patriarch's Mountain (Wuzu-shan), and it was from this that he derived his teaching name.

Wuzu had a gentle, humorous, and self-effacing manner. He referred to himself as "that fellow who lives somewhere-or-other at the foot of the East Mountain." D.T. Suzuki, in his first volume of *Zen Essays*, provides this example of Wuzu's dharma talks:

> "Yesterday I came across one topic which I thought I might communicate to you, my pupils, today. But an old man such as I am is apt to forget, and the topic has gone off altogether from my mind. I cannot just recall it." So saying, [Wuzu] remained quiet for some little time, but at last he exclaimed, "I forget, I forget, I cannot remember!" He resumed, however: "I know there is a mantra in one of the Sutras known as The King of Good Memory. Those who are forgetful may recite it, and the thing forgotten will

---

119. In Japanese, *Mu*.

come again. Well, I must try." He then recited the mantra, "Om o-lo-lok-kei svaha!" Clapping his hands and laughing heartily, he said: "I remember, I remember; this it was: When you seek the Buddha, you cannot see him: when you look for the patriarch, you cannot see him. The muskmelon is sweet even to the stems, the bitter gourd is bitter even to the roots."[120]

He then came down from the pulpit without further remark.

Dahui Zonggao

Wuzu's principle heir was Yuanwu Keqin who, in turn, was the teacher of Dahui Zonggao.

Before becoming Yuanwu's disciple, Dahui Zonggao had studied with several other masters and had a number of what he called "fragmentary experiences of awakening." He was not, however, satisfied with the depth of his insight. During a chance visit to Yuanwu's monastery, he heard the master giving a Dharma talk about the Tang dynasty teacher, Yunmen Wenyan:

"A monk," Yuanwu told the assembled monks, "once asked Master Yunmen, 'Where do all the Buddhas come from?'" "And Yunmen told him, 'The Eastern Mountain walks on water.' But that's not what I say. When I'm asked, 'Where do all the Buddhas come from,' I say, 'A fragrant breeze blows from the south and cools the Dharma hall.'"

Hearing these words, Dahui later reported, "I felt as if I were cut free from space and time. It was as if a sharp knife had cut the tangled knot of a cord. I was dripping sweat from every pore of my body."

He sought a private audience with Yuanwu and reported his experience. Yuanwu tested him, then acknowledged that he had had a genuine awakening; however, he added: "While it's difficult for people to achieve the level of insight you've attained, you still haven't understood everything yet, as you probably realize. You've died, but now you have to come back to life."

Yuanwu then presented Dahui with this gongan: "Being (u) and not-being (wu) are like a wisteria vine wound about a tree."

For six months, Dahui meditated on the gongan, but every time he tried to offer Yuanwu an explanation of his understanding, the master stopped him, saying, "No! It's not like that!"

Slowly the gongan came to occupy all of Dahui's attention, and one day, while he was eating, he was so absorbed in the gongan that he forgot how to use his chopsticks and let them fall to the floor.

---

120. Suzuki, op. cit., p. 286.

"That's the Chan of the boxwood tree," Yuanwu remarked, referring to the tree from which chopstick wood was harvested.

"I'm like a dog beside a pot of boiling fat," Dahui complained. "It can smell the fat but can't get at it no matter how much it tries. But it can't leave it either."

"You've fallen into a deep pit," Yuanwu admitted. "You might need to stay there for a while."

Some time later, Dahui asked Yuanwu, "I heard that when you were a student in the assembly of Wuzu Fayen, you asked him to resolve this matter of u and wu. Is that true?"

"I asked my master the meaning of the statement, 'It's said that being (u) and not being (wu) are like a wisteria vine wound about a tree.' And he told me, 'You can't picture it however hard you try.' Then I asked, 'And what if the tree is blown over and the vine dies?' My master told me, 'You're still caught up in words.'"

There was a moment's pause, then Dahui laughed aloud. "I understand!" he exclaimed.

"Today you now know that I haven't deceived you," Yuanwu told his pupil.

As a result of his own experience, Dahui also became an advocate of the gongan system, which he used as a "skillful means" to help students first to achieve awakening and then to deepen their original insight. He viewed awakening not as a single event but an on-going process. He told his students that he had had eighteen major awakenings and countless smaller experiences.

"There aren't any words in Chan," he told them. "It's all awakening. When you have awakening, you've got it all."

The gongan he most frequently assigned to those who came to him for instruction was Zhaozhou's "Wu." His approach to the gongan, however, was not the same as Boyun Shoutuan's when he'd presented it to Wuzu Fayan. Dahui instructed his students to focus not on the story but solely on the one word "Wu!" This type of focused concentration on a key phrase, or "head word" – *huatou* – from a gongan came to be known as Kan Hua Chan or the Chan of the Head Word and would come to be the preferred meditation technique used in the Linji tradition.

Dahui instructed his students to focus attention on the syllable Wu – without thinking what it meant – not only during formal meditation but while engaged in other activities as well.

> Whether you are walking or standing, sitting or lying down, you must not for a moment cease [to hold this 'no' (wu) in your mind].

> When deluded thoughts arise, you must also not suppress them with your mind. Only just hold up this huatou ['no' (wu)]. When you want to meditate and you feel dull and muddled, you must muster all your energies and hold up this word. Then suddenly you will be like the old blind woman who blows [so diligently] at the fire that her eyebrows and lashes are burned right off.[121]

Dahui expected his students to achieve intense awakening experiences, and he believed that the usual meditative practices, as continued in the Caodong tradition, did not elicit these but kept students in a dull or torpid state. Because "silent illumination" was undertaken without expecting anything from it, it could not be a means to attain that awakening experience that was fundamental to Dahui's understanding of Chan. The Caodong School, for its part, argued that Dahui's approach was heretical in that it sought to attain something – awakening – that Mahayana teachings asserted did not need to be attained but rather only realized.

At the beginning of the Song Period, there had been minor disagreements between the various Chan sects and their lineages, but largely their relations were amicable, and students routinely worked with teachers from various schools without distinction. By the end of the Song Period, as the methodologies of the Caodong and Linji lineages hardened, two distinct "single practice" traditions with very different perspectives – both tracing their heritage back to Bodhidharma through Huineng – emerged. Students might still work with teachers in both lines but were usually discouraged to do so. By the time the first Japanese inquirers came to the Chinese mainland seeking the Dharma, the lineages were well established rivals.

Chinese Buddhism was not monolithic. There were multiple presentations of the Dharma available, the most popular being devotional practices that the general population found accessible and comforting. And while Chan monasteries weathered occasional anti-Buddhist suppressions, they did so because they tended to be small and were located in isolated mountain settings distant from cities. Chan flourished in the Tang and Song dynasties but flourished in relative terms. It remained a monastic teaching and practice, and, of course, only a minority of the population were drawn to monastic life. Chan was not a dominant cultural influence in China the way that Daoism and revised Confucianism (Neo-Confucianism) remained.

Chan was very much a product of Chinese culture. The form of the Dharma that came about as a result of the encounter between Buddhism

---

121. Quoted in Schlütter, op. cit., pp. 107–08.

and Daoism in China was strikingly different from the teachings that had first evolved in the foothills of the Himalayas. Chan would, however, achieve its full potential not in the land of its birth but on the islands to the east, and the form it was to take there would be even more different still.

When the monk Kakua returned to Japan from China, the Emperor ordered him to come to the capital to explain what wisdom he had acquired from the study of Chan. Standing before the emperor and his retinue, Kakua brought out a flute from the sleeve of his robe, blew a single note on it, then bowed and left the court.

Zen[122]

The Buddhadharma Arrives in Japan

In 552, a diplomatic delegation from Korea arrived at the court of the Japanese Emperor. Compared with conditions in Korea and China, those in Japan at the time were relatively primitive, and the court may well have seemed a shabby affair to the visitors. Isolated from the mainland of Asia, Japan had been protected from invasion and conquest, but for a long while it had also been cut off from contact with the technological and social advances occurring elsewhere. The Japanese had, as yet, no written language. The first steps were just being taken to establish a central government capable of controlling the clans that, lacking other enemies, warred with one another.

There was no organized religion on the islands. There was a folk tradition that honored the spirits (kami) associated with certain sacred places and times of year, and there was a tradition of venerating ancestors. But there was no official priesthood; it was the responsibility of individuals or families to conduct appropriate rituals. Householders maintained a family shrine, the clan or tribe a collective shrine, and there was a national shrine in honor of the imperial household. There was no organized philosophical or moral code associated with these traditions, and it was not until they were challenged by the arrival of foreign traditions such as Buddhism that this collection of practices evolved into *Kannaga-no-michi*, or Shinto, "The Way of the Gods."

Shinto did not bother to develop a theology or a philosophy. It sought not to compel faith but to evoke a sense of that awe "which is," as Joseph Campbell notes, "a sentiment which may or may not produce words, but in either case goes beyond them."

---

122. A fuller treatment of the material in this chapter can be found in my previous book, *Zen Masters of Japan* (Tuttle, 2014).

> A Shinto rite...can be defined as an occasion for the recognition and evocation of an awe that inspires gratitude to the source and nature of being. And as such, it is addressed as art (music, gardening, architecture, dance, etc.) to the sensibilities – not to faculties of definition. So that living Shinto is not the following of some set-down moral code, but a living in gratitude and awe amid the mystery of things...The basic moral idea is that the processes of nature cannot be evil. And to this there is the corollary that the pure heart follows the processes of nature.[123]

This is a sensibility that would characterize the form Chan Buddhism would come to take in Japan.

The Korean delegation of 552 brought a number of gifts including a statue of the Buddha and copies of several sutras. This is the first known introduction of the Buddhadharma to Japan. Certain factions – led by the Soga clan – were impressed by the sophistication of the Korean visitors and believed it was important for the Japanese to cultivate relationships with other nations; the Mononobe and Nakatomi clans, on the other hand, sought to preserve national purity and unity through isolationism. This rivalry was put to rest when, in 587, Soga no Umako destroyed the Mononobe clan, assassinated the reigning emperor, and installed his niece – Suiko, the widow of a prior emperor – on the throne, after which he then appointed her husband's younger brother, Prince Shotoku, to be her regent. Having transferred power in the land to his own clan, Soga was content to remain in the background while Shotoku ruled so ably that he is still honored as one of the most significant figures in the development of Japanese culture. Until 1986, his image had variously been printed on the ¥100, ¥1000, ¥5000, and ¥10,000 notes.

Prince Shotoku was an admirer of Tang culture and arranged for a number of expeditions to China from which courtiers, scholars, craftsmen, and monks brought back concepts that the Japanese assimilated and modified in their unique fashion. Using Chinese models, Shotoku reformed Japanese institutions, governance, the legal system, the calendar, and other branches of learning. The Chinese mode of writing was adopted, with the result that while a particular character would have the same meaning in both languages, the sound used to express it was different, so the glyph for Chan was pronounced Zen in Japanese. Shotoku established a bureaucracy based on that of the Chinese and promoted a central government in which local barons owed allegiance to the divinely descended emperor.

Shotoku is also recognized as the "father of Japanese Buddhism," and the expeditions to China he sponsored brought back Buddhist texts, ritual

---

123. Campbell, op. cit., pp. 476-77.

items, and missionaries. The forms of the Buddhadharma early Japanese visitors encountered were those popular in the port cities of the Chinese coast; there was no contact at this point with the remote Chan communities still hidden in the mountains. By the beginning of the Kamakura Era (1185-1333) three schools of Chinese Buddhism flourished in Japan – Tendai, Shingon, and Pure Land.

The Tendai School was the first wholly Chinese School of Buddhism. For years before Bodhidharma's supposed voyage from the west, Chinese travelers had brought back Buddhist documents from India. Often these were stored for years before scholars were able to translate them and discovered that they reflected a wide range of perspectives within the long history of Indian Buddhism. The teachings proclaimed in one document could be difficult to reconcile with those in others although they all purported to reflect the instructions of the Buddha. The founders of the Tendai School based their exposition of Buddhist doctrine on the *Lotus Sutra*, that they believed to be the least corrupt of the documents available.

Whereas the focus of the Tendai School was on scripture, the focus of the Shingon School was on ritual. When Emperor Junna [786-840] decreed that official rites for the state should be carried out in the Shingon Temple in Kyoto, many influential families professed allegiance to the sect hoping that doing so would benefit them in their quest for political prominence.

The Pure Land Sect became popular among the general populace that by and large lacked the education to read or understand the bewildering Mahayana documents but who found comfort in the Buddhist doctrine of reincarnation and the possibility of a better life to come. Pure Land Buddhism taught that the repetition of a mantra called the *nembutsu* – "*Namu amida butsu*"[124] – was adequate to ensure the devotee rebirth in the Pure Land or Western Paradise. Nothing more was required.

Although later Zen teachers would occasionally advocate the practice of *nembutsu* for the laity, the two traditions represent opposite approaches. Pure Land Buddhism is founded on the concept of *tariki* – "other power" – by which the devotee turns to a power outside of him or herself for assistance. Nor does Pure Land seek absolute release but, instead, rebirth in the Pure Land that is temporary and where the process of working towards eventual awakening or Buddhahood continues. In contrast, Zen advocates *joriki* – "one's own power" – in which the practitioner relies on his own resources for deliverance and the attainment of awakening in this lifetime. The simplicity of the Pure Land teaching had great appeal, however, and it remains the most popular form of the Buddhadharma in Japan.

---

124. "I take refuge in Amida Buddha."

The first recorded Japanese student of Zen was a monk named Dosho. Dosho took part in one of Shotoku's expeditions to China where he spent time with several meditation teachers including the Fourth Patriarch, Dayi Daoxin.[125] Over the following six centuries, other Japanese monks made their way to China to seek Chan training, but they were few in number, and it wasn't until the 12th century that Chinese Chan began to evolve into Japanese Zen. Several schools of Zen practice arose, but the two most enduring were the Rinzai (Linji) and Soto (Caodong). Two towering Japanese personalities adapted these traditions to Japanese conditions so effectively that they flourished in their new home with even greater vigor than they had had in the land of their births. The Soto priest, Dogen Kigen, established Zen practice in Japan in the 13th century, and, four hundred years later, Hakuin Ekaku reformed the, by then corrupt, Rinzai school.

Dogen Kigen

Dogen Kigen's mother was a concubine of a lord in the imperial household, and their son spent his earliest years in the rarefied atmosphere of the court. His father died while Dogen was still a child, and his mother a few years later. She was a devout woman, who, during her final illness, encouraged her son to become a monk and seek a way to relieve the sufferings of humankind. Dogen was eight years old when she died. As he sat beside her corpse during the official mourning period, he watched the smoke from a burning stick of incense rise into the air and dissipate. Observing it, he thought about his mother's words and was struck by the impermanence of all things.

An uncle adopted Dogen and took charge of his education with the intention that the boy eventually serve in the imperial court. But at the age of thirteen, Dogen left secular life to become a novice at Enryakuji,[126] the Tendai Monastery on Mount Hiei in Kyoto. It was during his ordination ceremony that he was given the Buddhist name Dogen, which means "Foundation of the Way."

Novice training focused on sutra study. Dogen was well versed in the Chinese language and took to it easily, but, while he found wisdom in the scriptures, he felt they were abstract and far removed from the actual world in which people were born, lived, suffered, and died. The sutras, for example, asserted that all sentient beings had Buddha-nature, but this was accepted as a tenet of faith and was not understood as something

---

125. "Doshin" in Japanese.

126. The suffix "ji" in Japanese denotes a temple, so the literal translation would be Enryaku Temple.

one should aspire to realize for oneself. For Dogen, this teaching posed a problem. If all beings had Buddha-nature and thus – as the Buddha himself had declared – all beings were inherently perfect, then why had it been necessary for the Buddha to strive to attain awakening, and why had Bodhidharma spent nine years gazing at a wall in China? If one were already a Buddha, why did the masters of old have to make such efforts to become aware of their Buddha-nature?

He presented his concern to another monk who advised Dogen to seek the counsel of Myoan Eisai who had recently returned from China. Although Eisai remained a Tendai monk throughout his life, he had also trained in the Linji School of Chan, and, in 1191, he received "transmission," official acknowledgement that he had seen into his own Buddha-nature and was authorized to teach others. In his case, he was specifically approved to promote the Chan tradition in Japan.

Dogen travelled to Eisai's temple, Kenninji, and posed his question to the master, "If, as the scriptures assert, all of us already have Buddha-nature, why is it that the masters of old had to struggle to attain awareness of it?"

Eisai told him, "No Buddha is conscious of having Buddha-nature, only the shallow are aware of it."

Dogen sensed something profound in that answer and became Eisai's student. Within a year, Eisai died, and Dogen continued his studies under his successor, Ryonen Myozen. When Myozen, following the example of Eisai, traveled to China to study Chan there, Dogen accompanied him.

They left for the Asian mainland in 1223; however, when they landed at the port of Mingzhou, only Myozen was allowed to proceed. Dogen was confined to the ship and dock for three months, perhaps in medical quarantine. Although he was unable to venture outside the restricted zone, there was enough traffic at the docks that he was able to learn a great deal about what was happening in the city and country. He was disappointed by what he discovered about the apparent state of Buddhism in China. If Japanese Buddhism was still immature and caught up in ritualism and magical rites, Chinese Buddhism had grown stale and decrepit.

Then a cook from one of the Chan monasteries came to purchase dried mushrooms from the ship's galley. Dogen was struck by the monk's deportment and wanted to quiz him about Chan practice. He invited him to remain on board the ship that night as his guest. The visitor declined, explaining that he was the head cook of his monastery and had to return to his duties. Dogen asked if spending his days in meditation wouldn't be more profitable than cooking. The cook gently suggested that the young Japanese visitor didn't know very much about Chan and took his leave.

Once allowed to leave the docks, Dogen followed Myozen to the monastery at Tientong. There he was received by Master Wuji Liaopai[127] of the Soto School, who introduced him to the "silent illumination" practice that would later be called shikan taza in Japanese.

After Myozen died in 1225, Dogen chose to remain at Tientong. He admired the strict discipline the monks adhered to, but he was angered that according to their regulations he – as a foreigner – was considered subordinate to native born novices younger than he. He protested that Myozen had named him an heir and that his rank should not be dependent upon his nationality. His protests weren't well received and may have made his position at the monastery more difficult than it needed to have been.

When his situation failed to improve, Dogen left Tientong and embarked on a tour of other monasteries, still seeking the enlightenment experience that, as yet, he knew of only from his reading. He also familiarized himself with the lineage charts of the various monasteries he visited and became well versed in the historical records of Chinese Chan. He would bring this respect for accurate records of transmission and succession back to Japan.

In the course of his travels, he had a second encounter with a cook whom he found working hatless in the heat of the day preparing food. Dogen asked the man how old he was, and the monk replied that he was approaching his seventieth year.

"Are there no younger monks who could assist you?" Dogen asked.

"Others are not me," the cook said. "These are my duties, how can someone else fulfill them?"

"But surely there's no need to carry them out during the hottest period of the day," Dogen persisted.

"If not now, when?" the monk asked.

"I can see that you are a man of the way (Dao)," Dogen said. "Please tell me, what is the true Way?"

"The universe has never concealed it," the cook said and turned back to his work.

The conversation struck Dogen profoundly, and the memory of it would stay with him long after he returned to Japan.

Dogen came back to Tientong despite his displeasure over his status at the monastery. A new abbot had been installed, Tientong Rujing,[128] with whom Dogen was greatly impressed. Here, he felt, was the "authentic" teacher for whom he'd been searching. In later years, he would refer to

---

127. J: Musai Ryoha.

128. J: Tendo Nyojo.

Rujing as the "Old Buddha." Rujing was a voluble critic of the koan study current in the Chinese Linji School that had replaced other forms of meditation and practice, and Dogen would come to share this point of view. Rujing stressed that seated meditation was the preeminent Buddhist activity. For three years, Dogen stayed with him, dedicating himself to the practice.

Rujing's sitting schedule was strenuous. Monks sat from early in the morning until late at night, and during the retreat periods, known in Japanese as sesshin, the sitting schedule was even more onerous. At one such retreat, the participants were sitting late into the night when Rujing noticed a monk had fallen asleep. He roused the group, shouting, "You must practice with all of your energy, even at the risk of your own lives. You must discard both body and mind!"

These words finally brought Dogen to a deep awakening. When it was time for the monks to present themselves for individual meetings[129] with the teacher, Dogen strode into the room confidently and lit a stick of incense, an act reserved for rituals or significant celebrations.

"What is the point of this incense?" Rujing demanded.

"I have discarded body and mind," Dogen said.

"You have discarded body and mind. Body and mind have indeed been discarded."

Rujing was so impressed with the depth of Dogen's awakening that he acknowledged the younger man as a Dharma Heir. In 1227, Dogen returned to Japan with – as he put it – "empty hands." Whereas previous visitors had returned from China with Buddhist sutras and artifacts, he brought back only a portrait of Rujing, his documents of succession, and the ashes of Ryonen Myozen. When asked what he had learned during his time in China, his self-deprecating reply was

> – that the eyes are horizontal, and the nose is vertical; thus I am unable to be deceived by others. There is not even a hair of Buddhism in me. Now I pass the time naturally. The sun rises in the east every morning, and every night the moon sets in the west. When the clouds clear, the outline of the mountains appears, and as the rain passes away, the surrounding mountains bend down. What is it after all?[130]

The Fukanzazengi and The Shobogenzo

Back at Kenninji, Dogen found a few students with whom he was able to share what he had learned in China. He also composed a summary

---

129. Called *dokusan* in the Japanese Soto tradition and *sanzen* in the Rinzai.
130. Quoted in Peter Matthiessen, *Nine-Headed Dragon River* (Boston: Shambala, 1998), p. 169.

of what he taught them in a short work called *Fukanzazengi* or *Universal Recommendations for the Practice of Zazen*. Because he felt that he was introducing Japanese students to true zazen practice for the first time, the instructions were very exact. One must, he wrote, follow the examples of the Buddha and Bodhidharma who both committed themselves to prolonged meditation practice. Echoing Chinese teachers like Nanyue, he wrote:

> – you must suspend your attempts to understand by means of scrutinizing words, reverse the activity of the mind that seeks externally, and illuminate your own true nature. Mind and body will fall off spontaneously, and your original face will be revealed…
>
> For zazen, you will need a quiet room. Eat and drink in moderation. Forget about the concerns of the day and leave such matters alone. Do not judge things as good or evil, and cease such distinctions as "is" and "is not." Halt the flow of the mind, and cease conceptualizing, thinking, and observing.[131]

As in the Chinese *Manual for Sitting Meditation*, he provides explicit directions on the physical aspects of zazen, explaining in detail how to place a cushion on a mat and sit upon it in either the traditional full lotus or half-lotus postures; he describes the proper alignment of the body, how to hold the hands in the lap with thumb tips touching, and stresses the importance of keeping the eyes open. Finally, one is to regulate the breath (taking long deep breaths, following a natural rhythm), and, sitting "firmly and resolutely," one thinks "about the unthinkable. How do you think about the unthinkable? Non-thinking. These are the essentials of zazen."[132]

As Dogen began to attract students, he also attracted the enmity of other schools of Buddhism, in particular the Tendai which sought to use its connection to the ruling powers to suppress their rivals. Dogen chose to avoid confrontation and left Kyoto, relocating to the Fukui Prefecture where he established Eiheiji. Although the original buildings have since been destroyed, Eiheiji remains, along with Sojiji, one of the two primary temples of the Soto Sect.

It was at Eiheiji that Dogen composed most of the essays brought together in his masterwork, the *Shobogenzo* or *"The True Eye of the Dharma"* – the "eye of the Dharma" that Gautama Buddha had passed onto Mahakasyapa. It is a collection of ninety-two essays on a wide variety

---

131. Francis Dojun Cook [trans.], *How to Raise an Ox* (Boston: Wisdom Publications, 2002), pp. 65-66.

132. Ibid., p. 66.

of topics written not in Chinese – the preferred ecclesiastical language of Buddhist writings in Japan – but in the vernacular. Throughout the collection, Dogen maintains that practice and enlightenment are one. The Buddha had taught that all beings, just as they are, are whole and perfect, that all beings had "Buddha-nature." Dogen asserts that while seated in meditation, enlightenment is present, even if the individual is unaware of it. All one needs to do is to forget the "self" (one's personality), and the larger Self (Buddha-nature) is present.

For Dogen, zazen was shikan taza, just sitting rather than reflecting on koans; however, while he remained critical of the Rinzai School and its use of koans, several of the essays in the Shobogenzo are based on koans. Dogen's criticism may have been based in part on his irritation over increased government support for the Rinzai School. More importantly, he felt that Rinzai students were, at times, more concerned about passing koans than they were in understanding the teachings of Buddhism. He had also discovered during his time in China that there were monks who had the developed the ability to answer koans without actually attaining insight, and he did not want this empty practice to emerge in Japan as well. On the other hand, he acknowledged his primary Dharma Heir, Koun Ejo, after he had resolved the koan "one thread [hair] passes through many holes."

Keizan Jokin

One of the recurring themes in the story of Zen is that often the immediate heirs of a charismatic teacher are unable to match his ability to teach, inspire loyalty, or provide leadership to the sangha. This was the case with Dogen. After his death, the community he had founded at Eiheiji split into rival factions which argued about doctrinal issues, the use of koans, the value of ritual activity, and whether zazen was necessarily the only appropriate form of practice. Then in 1297, the monastery complex was severely damaged by fire and the current abbot, Gian, didn't have the financial resources to rebuild it. Many monks left Eiheiji for other monasteries, and Gian himself retired to a hermitage. Within two generations of Dogen's death, both Eiheiji and the Japanese Soto School seemed in tatters.

That the school did not dissolve was largely due to the efforts of Keizan Jokin who is held in almost as much esteem by Soto Zen as Dogen himself, although the two men could not have been more different in character or approach.

Dogen was a forceful personality and, especially in his later years, could be inflexible and harsh. Keizan, on the other hand, was noted for his gentleness. The two men complemented one another. Dogen's strict formalism was needed to ground the Soto tradition in Japan; Keizan's warm and inviting personality helped to spread the tradition and make it attractive to laity and religious alike. While Dogen had few disciples, Keizan would have many. Dogen is honored as the First Patriarch of Soto Zen in Japan, but Keizan is often considered the Patriarch of Greater Importance.

Keizan became a novice at Eiheiji at the age of eight. The abbot at the time, Tettsu Gikai, was a second generation Dogen heir who employed koans in his teaching. Gikai assigned Keizan the koan from the *Mumonkan* in which Joshu asked his master, Nansen, "What is the way (Dao)?" To which Nansen replied, "Ordinary mind is the way." During one of their formal interviews, Keizan started to explain his understanding of the koan when Gikai stopped him by slapping his face. With that slap, Keizan came to awakening.

Gikai's chief rival – and successor – at Eiheiji, Gian, also recognized Keizan's enlightenment and officiated at the ceremony in which Keizan vowed to maintain the strict code of conduct that senior monks could choose to adopt. Keizan was, thus, acknowledged by both factions within the community.

His gentle and compassionate approach to promulgating the Dharma attracted both lay people and monks. He was appointed the abbot of Daijoji, formerly a Shingon temple that had become a Zen temple under Gikai's leadership. While there, he wrote the *Zazen Yojinki* that continues to be used in the Soto tradition as a basic introduction to meditation. In it, he wrote:

> *Zazen* clears the mind immediately and lets one dwell in one's true realm. This is called showing one's original face or revealing the light of one's original state. Body and mind are cast off, apart from whether one is sitting or lying down. Therefore, one thinks neither of good nor of evil – transcending both the sacred and the profane, rising above delusion and enlightenment – and leaves the realm of sentient beings and Buddhas.[133]

In a manner similar to the Chinese *Manual for Sitting Meditation* and Dogen's *Fukanzazengi*, the *Zazen Yojinki* provides detailed instructions on what is conducive to and what is harmful to zazen. Practitioners are advised to choose a place neither too hot nor too cold, neither too dark nor too bright. The most appropriate is a temple in a rural setting where the changes in the natural world provide a constant reminder of the law of impermanence.

He reviews the matters of proper posture and breathing, as had Dogen. But Keizan differed from Dogen in advocating the use of koans,

---

133. Heinrich Dumoulin, *Zen Buddhism: A History – Japan* (Bloomington: World Wisdom, 1990), p. 140.

such as Mu, when the student found it difficult to remain focused during shikan taza. He did, however, agree with Dogen that shikan taza was the purest form of zazen. The challenge of shikan taza is that there is no object, either the breath or a koan, for the practitioner to focus upon. One must sit alert and conscious, but, on the other hand, the goal is not to empty the mind entirely as other meditation techniques attempt to do. The movement of the mind is one of the things of which the meditator is aware, without allowing the flow of the mind to capture one's attention and carry it off into reflection or day-dreaming. It is a difficult balance, to be alert and yet not to fall into reverie. Although with practice the mind will gradually become quieter, it will never become entirely silent. In the same way that as long as the eye is open, there will be sight, so, as long as one is conscious, there will be thoughts. Keizan described this in a poem:

> Though you find clear waters ranging
> to the vast blue skies of autumn,
> how can that compare
> with the hazy moon on a spring night?
> Some people want it pure white,
> but sweep as you will,
> you cannot empty the mind.[134]

In 1311, Keizan turned Daijoji over to one of his Dharma successors and began a period of expansion, founding a number of monasteries. One of the most significant was the transformation of the Shingon Shogakuji on the Noto Peninsula into a Zen temple now known as Sojiji, which remains the primary Soto training temple in Japan to this day.

While remaining faithful to Dogen's focus on monastic meditation, Keizan also realized that if Soto Temples were to be supported by the people in the communities in which they were located, they would have to be responsive to the spiritual needs of those communities. His temples included both a meditation hall and a ceremonial hall in which ritual activities took place for the benefit of the laity. As well, monks supervised funerals, memorial services, and other rites for the benefit of their congregations.

As a result of Keizan's decisions, Soto Temples flourished throughout rural Japan. This would later, however, have an unintended consequence. As it became necessary to provide large numbers of priests to serve these temples, Soto training necessarily became less rigorous. It was not always possible to provide fully awakened teachers for each of these, often very

---

134. John Tarrant, *The Light Inside the Dark* (New York: Harper, 1998), p. 210.

small, temples. So while people still came to Soto monasteries seeking awakening, there were also many who simply wanted authorization to provide religious services for their communities. For those priests, meditation was performed as a devotional activity, but rarely did it result in the awakening experience called *kensho* in the Rinzai Tradition.

Rinzai Zen

Myoan Eisai – whom Dogen had sought out – founded the first Japanese Rinzai temple, Shofukuji, in 1195. Eisai himself was a synchronist who presented Zen as supplemental to the more ceremonial and ritualistic forms of Buddhism popular among the upper classes of Japanese society. It was left to later generations to begin the process of establishing Rinzai Zen as a separate and autonomous school.

Mugaku Sogen [Bukko Kokushi]

Many of the early Rinzai teachers in Japan were, like Mugaku Sogen, from China. Mugaku is better known by the posthumous name Bukko and the honorific title Kokushi, meaning "National Teacher." He was a Linji monk who gained fame when Mongol soldiers raided his temple intending to put all the monks there to death as they had elsewhere. Bukko remained calm in the face of the attack and asked the commander to allow him time to compose a poem to mark the occasion of his death. While the soldiers waited with drawn swords, Bukko took up his calligraphy brush and wrote:

> In all this world there is no place for me to lay down my staff
> Subject and object are totally empty! How delightful!
> The great sword of a famous warrior of the past –
> It is as if a spring breeze were split by a bolt of lightning.

Impressed by the equanimity with which the monk faced his impending death, the soldiers retreated without harming any of the members of the community.

The story of this encounter reached Hojo Tokimune in Japan. Tokimune was the *shikken*, or regent, to the Shogun, and in fact held the reins of power in the country. He was credited with repelling the Mongol attempt to invade Japan in 1274 but realized it had been good fortune that had prevented the invasion from succeeding.[135] He fully expected the Mongols to make a second attempt, and, to help him prepare for that, Tokimune invited Bukko to come to Japan in 1279 to serve as his advisor and teacher.

---

135. Kublai Khan had sent a fleet of 500 ships transporting 40,000 soldiers to invade the

Bukko asked Tokimune what he was seeking from the practice of Zen. Tokimune explained that he sought to conquer all fear. Bukko instructed him to search within himself for the source of fear; this became, in effect, a koan for Tokimune – "Where is my fear located?"

After the Mongol were once again defeated, Tokimune built Engaku Temple as a memorial for all those who had lost their lives defending Japan. Bukko was installed as its first head priest.

Seeing the esteem Tokimune had for Zen, samurai warriors were drawn to the practice as well, and – in an odd turn of fate – the teaching of the pacific Buddha came to be associated with the warrior class in Japan, although the samurai saw Zen not so much as a religion but as a practical discipline that helped them overcome fear and face death with equanimity.

Enni Ben'en [Shoichi Kokushi]

Although Zen teachers – immigrants as well as native born – could readily be found in Japan by the 13th century, some of the more serious students still felt it necessary to travel to China to deepen their training. One of these was Enni Ben'en, also known as Shoichi Kokushi – Shoichi, the National Teacher. The syncretic Zen of Myoan Eisai was short-lived. It would be the form of Rinzai brought back from China by Shoichi that would persevere in Japan.

When he returned from China, he was appointed abbot of Tofukuji in Kyoto. There he told his disciples that Zen was not a system of thought like other Buddhist traditions but was the vehicle by which one achieved the same state of mind as the Buddha himself. "When one practices Zen, one is Buddha! If one practices for a day, one is Buddha for a day. If one were to practice one's whole life, one would be Buddha one's whole life."

The form of Rinzai Enni promoted took an aggressive approach to zazen. Students were advised to put all their energy into their practice: "Imagine that you've fallen into a deep well. In such a situation, your only thought would be how to escape. All your attention, all your energy would be focused on that alone. Day and night, all you would dwell on was how to escape."

---

islands. The Japanese defense force consisted of less than 10,000 samurai, who fought valiantly in what seemed a hopeless cause. After the first day of battle, the samurai withdrew from the beachhead to rest, fully intending to resume the fight in the morning although it was almost certain they would be annihilated. During the night, the Mongol forces reboarded their ships and sailed out into the bay because the sailors were afraid that the high winds which had arisen might drive their ships onto shore and ground them. That decision was a grave error; the fleet sailed directly into the path of a typhoon which sank a third of the boats. The remaining vessels were heavily damaged and forced to retreat back to China. The Japanese believed that the storm – which they termed "*Kamikaze*" or "divine wind" – was evidence that the Shinto gods still protected the isles.

The use of koans gave an energy to meditation that was not always present in Soto practice. In a formula that became popular in Rinzai practice, three components were deemed necessary to achieve awakening: Great Faith, Great Perseverance, and Great Doubt. Great Doubt was the driving question that compelled one's practice – such as Tokimune's question about the location of his fear. Koans forced the practitioner to approach his or her meditation with an inquiring frame of mind, and that spirit of questioning proved to be an effective tool – upaya – for arousing the "Great Doubt" needed to bring aspirants to awakening.

In spite of the preferential status he gave Zen, Enni also honored the Shingon and Tendai teachings and so was eventually able to win respect for the Zen school, that was beginning to be seen less as a Chinese oddity and more a mainstream tradition in Japan. But Enni understood that Zen was still young in Japan and accommodations needed to be made. His Rinzai practice was not yet independent of Shingon and Tendai teachings, but it was on its way.

Emperor Hanazono and Shuho Myocho [Daito Kokushi]

The imperial household had little actual practical power during the Kamakura Shogunate. Emperors often came to the throne while still children and were pressured to retire in early youth in order to ensure that they didn't acquire genuine personal power, although the "retired" Emperor – who technically entered a monastery and became "cloistered" – was often able to exert influence over his younger successor. One such cloistered emperor who actually became a serious student of Buddhism was Hanazono who reigned from 1308-1318.

According to a story that is more likely legend than history, the retired Emperor heard a rumor that a Zen master of exceptional ability had come to Kyoto. Instead of establishing himself at one of the city's numerous temples, however, he chose to live among the derelicts and beggars residing under the Gojo Bridge. Intrigued, Hanazono asked his informant if there were any way to identify which of the beggars was the modest Zen Master. All the informant could report was a rumor that the master was particularly fond of honeydew melons.

Hanazono disguised himself as a fruit peddler and pushed a cart laden with melons to the region by the bridge. As the residents gathered around him, he held up a ripe melon and announced, "I will give this melon freely to anyone who can claim it without using his feet."

One of the beggars challenged him, "Then give it to me without using your hands."

It was as much the gleam in the eye of the beggar as his reply which told Hanazono that he had found the Zen teacher he was seeking. His name was Shuho Myocho and would later come to be known as Daito

[Great Light] Kokushi [National Teacher].

Shuho had studied with Zen Master Nampo Jomyo and had still been relatively young when recognized as an heir. Nampo advised him, however, to refrain from taking students of his own for another twenty years; instead, he should use the time to continue his meditation and deepen his understanding. When Nampo died, Shuho left the monastery and spent the next twenty years residing among the indigent and street people of Kyoto until – as the story goes – Hanazono found him under the Gojo Bridge.

Hanazono donated grounds for a new temple to be called Daitokuji, and Shuho was installed as its first abbot. Daitokuji would play a significant role, centuries later, in introducing Rinzai Zen to the west.

Muso Soseki

The most important proponent of Rinzai Zen in the 14th century was Muso Soseki. Orphaned at the age of four, he was placed in a Shingon monastery. He had an academic nature and enjoyed studying the doctrines and rituals of the Shingon and Tendai Schools. When Muso was eighteen, a teacher he was particularly fond of died in difficult and painful circumstances. Suddenly and directly confronted with the issue of the frailty of life, Muso found the issues he had been studying no longer abstract. He prepared a hermitage and determined to do a 100-day silent retreat in the hope that through meditation he might gain insight into these matters. Before he completed the 100 days, he had a dream in which two famous Tang Dynasty monks appeared to him – Sozan Konin and Sekito Kisen.[136] They presented him with a portrait of Bodhidharma and instructed him to safeguard it.

The dream left such a powerful impression upon him that he took the first characters of the names of these two masters ("So" and "Seki") and combined them to form the name "Soseki," by which he was known for the remainder of his life. This dream, he believed, was a call from his "true nature" to follow the path of Zen. He left his hermitage and sought out Issan Ichinei,[137] a Chinese Zen master who taught in Kamakura. Issan was concerned that his students be well grounded in Chinese Zen theory and much of his teaching was in the form of lectures. Muso himself would later want to make certain his own disciples had an understanding of the basic tenets of Buddhist doctrine, and he would assert that to preach about the sutras was to preach Zen. But as a young man, he found Issan's approach too academic. He lamented that with Issan he had traded the study of Buddhism for the study of Zen; the content was different, but these were still intellectual structures that only "darkened the mind."

---

136. Sushan Kuangren and Shitou Xiqian in Chinese.
137. Yishan Yining in Chinese.

Soseki chose to meditate on his own, without a teacher, demonstrating his life-long tendency towards solitude. In this way, he attained a number of insights into Buddhist doctrine but was astute enough to realize that those insights were not the same thing as awakening.

One spring evening, he was meditating under a tree outside of his hermitage. When it was night, he stood up to return to the hut. It was too dark for him to be able to see, and he reached out to where he thought the hermitage wall should be. There was nothing there, and he stumbled and fell. At that moment, it was as if he had fallen through a "wall of darkness" into light. The "unity of all things" was no longer a concept but rather an achieved experience.

He traveled to Kamakura and met with the Zen teacher, Koho Kennichi, who authenticated his awakening and presented him with a certificate - *inka shomei* - acknowledging that accomplishment.

All of his life, Soseki would be drawn to solitude, but he acquired such stature within the Zen community that time and again he was called upon to take on responsibilities at various temples. The Emperor Go-Daigo – who bestowed the title Kokushi on Soseki during his lifetime – appointed him the abbot of Nanzenji in Kyoto. Soseki tried to avoid the placement, as he had several earlier ones, but this time was unable to do so. Nanzenji was the most prominent Zen temple in the country, and, as its abbot, Soseki became a national figure.

This was a particularly unstable period in Japanese history. Emperor Go-Daigo with the assistance of a general, Ashikaga Takauji, wrestled power away from the Shogunate of the Hojo family ending the "Kamakura Period." Go-Daigo then sought to re-establish the political power of the Imperial Household, assigning positions of authority to various members of the nobility. Ashikaga Takauji felt that his contributions to the restoration of the Emperor were inadequately appreciated and was angered at being excluded from political power in the new government. Muso was astute enough to see that the Ashikaga were unlikely to accept the current situation, so he forged an alliance with the family and in particular with Takauji.

The samurai classes were restive under Go-Daigo, and when the emperor sought to impose a tax for the purposes of building a new palace, Takauji led a coup that ended the so-called "Kemmu Restoration," which had only lasted for three years. Takauji declared himself Shogun, initiating the Muromachi Period. Go-Daigo fled north from Kyoto and sought refuge in Yoshiro. Takauji raised the Crown Prince Komyo to the status of a rival emperor to Go-Daigo, and for the next 60 years (1331 to 1392) there would be two claimants to the Chrysanthemum Throne, one in the north and one in the south.

During the conflict between the Emperor and the Ashikaga family, Muso went into retirement and composed the *Rinsen Kakun*, a rule for the monastic life in which he emphasized the importance of zazen over ritual activity of the type increasingly being conducted in Soto temples.

As a practitioner within the Rinzai tradition, Muso made use of koans but recognized they were not necessarily suited to all monks. He pointed out that the koan tradition was relatively new in Buddhism; the earliest Buddhists had not made use of them. The practice arose in later generations as the zeal of monks for awakening had lessened and special incentives needed to be devised to spur them on. For him, as for the teachers of Enni Ben'en's day, the power of koan study was its ability to promote the necessary "Great Doubt" needed to bring the student to awakening.

In 1339, the year Emperor Go-Daigo died, Muso petitioned Ashikaga Takauji to convert one of the imperial palaces in Kyoto into a Zen temple dedicated to the memory of Go-Daigo. In this way the shogun could atone for any responsibility he had for dividing the country. The temple was called Tenryuji – Heavenly Dragon Temple. Muso – who was famed as much for his skill as a landscape artist as a Zen teacher – designed the temple grounds. His intention was to make gardens – which are artificial constructions – appear as natural as possible by incorporating not just plants but also stones and mosses. A significant part of his legacy is the association he established between Zen Temples and gardens.

The Cultural Impact of Zen

By the 14th century, Rinzai Zen had been adopted as the semi-official religion of the samurai class. The national leadership in Kamakura and later in Kyoto (after the Ashikaga returned the capital there) were patrons of the Rinzai tradition, and it became the form of Zen favored by the upper classes. By contrast, Soto Zen was more popular in rural areas and with the working classes.

Official support of the Rinzai tradition perhaps had as many negative consequences as positive ones. Rinzai temples were given responsibility for schooling the sons of the upper classes, and therefore the government had an interest in how they were organized. An administrative structure known as the *Gozan*, or Five Mountains, was established to govern both temples and their abbots. It was modeled after a system established in China where Chan Temples actually had been located in and named after mountains. The government assigned certain temples priority and designated them the "Gozan"; five were identified in Kamakura and another five in Kyoto; eventually the Kamakura Temples would become subservient to those in Kyoto. Beneath these chief temples there were ten mid-level establishments (called *jissetsu*) and then a national network of lesser, *shozan*, temples.

Once established, the system inevitably led to greater secular interference in the operation of those temples. The government approved abbots and controlled the curriculum. Gozan schools became training grounds for students entering the civil service and became a vehicle for promulgating government policies in remote districts. As centers of growing cultural importance, they lost something of their credibility as spiritual centers. Students without religious interest were sent to them in order to acquire basic literacy skills. Other students were drawn by a desire to become proficient in the various arts that had become associated with Zen.

Having acquired official status within the machinery of state, Gozan Temples performed a number of functions in addition to being training grounds for monks. While the sons of the nobility and the warrior classes attended the schools associated with the five major temples, feudal lords outside of Kyoto recruited Zen monks to establish schools at their courts, extending the influence of the system. Temples could be commercial establishments. Some acted as banks; others were publishing centers where school texts, along with both Buddhist and Confucian documents from China, were made available in woodcut prints. The temples also carried out ritual activities for the benefit of the national government. In many temples, religious teaching became slack. Documents attesting that a monk had attained "enlightenment" could be purchased by individuals unable to earn them. Very probably the majority of youth enrolled at Gozan temples had no more religious aspiration than students attending parochial schools in North America.

Regardless of the young person's religious interest, all students were introduced to the practice of zazen. Although it is a primarily a spiritual exercise, zazen does not work automatically. It isn't a technique for awakening so much as it is a means of putting oneself into a condition where one is susceptible to awakening. The practice, however, does help the individual develop other qualities that Gozan students discovered had practical applications outside monastic life. These skills included discipline, concentration, and the cultivation of *mushin* – or "no mind."

Mushin is the state Dogen described in an essay in which he wrote: "Studying the Buddha Way is studying oneself. Studying oneself is forgetting oneself. Forgetting oneself is being enlightened by all things."[138] Through zazen, one's personal ego – what one generally thinks of as one's "self" – is discovered to be an "illusion" in that it is the product of training, habit, and environment. It is the self that analyzes, plots, and plans; those are its strengths and why it is important. However, it is not usually particularly creative or spontaneous. The "emptiness" that is spoken of in the *Heart Sutra* is, at least in part, to be "empty of ego." It is a state familiar to

---

138. From the *Genjokoan*. Thomas Cleary (trans.), *Shobogenzo: Zen Essays by Dogen*

and valuable to artists and athletes. Once one has mastered the mechanics of one's craft or sport, inspiration is often liberated when the ego-self is abrogated; what one cannot do consciously, one may be able to accomplish instinctively. In sport, for example, there is no time for the athlete to think about his or her moves during competition. Likewise, the painter who seeks to achieve an effect through effort will almost inevitably produce a work inferior to one in which the hand moves, as it were, without intention; improvising musicians learn not to "think" when they play but, rather, allow the music to pour through them uninhibited.

Students who had no particular desire to achieve awakening discovered that their practice of zazen helped them in other ways. Kyoto temples had become repositories of Chinese artworks brought back to Japan by visiting monks and became models for Japanese artists. Chinese calligraphy was also much admired and imitated. Students in Gozan schools were introduced to a variety of arts, and, as these arts were further developed, a Zen style began to emerge. Far more so than in China, where there had been older and more powerful influences to compete with, this Zen style permeated Japanese arts and left a lasting impression on the national culture.

Zen masters themselves could be artists of rare merit, as was Muso Soseki in landscape design. Since the monasteries outside of Kyoto were often located in isolated rural settings, it was likely that the monks in residence would develop an appreciation of natural beauty. But even in the larger cities, the gardens attached to Zen monasteries were noted for their elegance. The designs ranged from reproductions of wild landscapes to the famous austere raked sand and boulders of *karesansui* gardens such as the often photographed one at Ryoanji.

Soseki and Dogen were both known for the quality of their calligraphy. Chinese characters, used in formal Japanese writing, are so expressive in themselves that they lend themselves to calligraphy in a way that the simpler Roman alphabet does not, and so it evolved into a serious art form in both China and Japan. Calligraphy is known as *shodo* in Japanese – the way (do) of writing. It is done with a brush, rather than a pen, and thick ink. The absorbency of the paper used does not allow for hesitation or correction. The artist's hand needs to move smoothly and with assurance. The writing has to be spontaneous and fluid. One cannot think about what one is doing. Mushin is the ideal state for the calligraphers who allow the work to flow through them rather than being consciously carried out.

The same fluidity of style characteristic of the best calligraphy is also required in brush painting. The materials used are the same, and – unlike the oils or acrylics of western artists – do not allow for changes to be

---

(Honolulu: University of Hawaii Press, 1986).

made after the ink is on the paper. Calligraphy and painting were often combined.

Painters who received their training in the Gozan Schools naturally chose Zen subjects, such as masters from the past and incidents of Zen history, but, like their Chinese predecessors, they also a demonstrated of love of landscape painting and the natural world.

The Way of Tea

The art in which Zen style is most fully evident is chanoyu – the tea ceremony. This evolved from the Chinese monastic practice, carried over to Japan, of serving tea to visitors. The lay ceremony in Japan is traced back to Murata Shuko who once declared that the taste of tea and the taste of Zen were the same. His Zen teacher, Ikkyu Sojun, had taught him that by paying appropriate attention to all the elements of the homely activity of steeping and serving tea he could bring the act to sacramental status. This awareness or mindfulness, however, cannot be forced; one can't be truly aware if one is making an effort to be aware. Therefore, to properly serve tea one needs to be in the same state of mushin as the calligrapher.

The ceremony Shuko developed was both formal and aesthetic. A special tea-house was designed and deliberately kept small. Indoor space was measured by the size of tatami mats, which were slightly less than 3' x 6'. A tea house was traditionally four and a half mats, or approximately 9 foot square. The doorway was low, so that all who entered had to bow in order to do so. The interior space was sparsely decorated, with perhaps a painting or an example of calligraphy on the wall, and a small alcove in which a simple floral arrangement – the predecessor of the art of *ikebana* – was displayed.

Shuko explained the atmosphere he sought to achieve by relating the story of a Chinese poet who had described the vivid contrast between blossoms on a plum tree in early spring against the woods still covered with snow. A friend of the poet suggested the poem would be more effective if only a single flower had bloomed against the white background. The starkness of that contrast is what Shuko achieved by placing just one flower in a vase within the austere tea shed.

The implements are chosen for their beauty as much as for their function. And in this highly stylized environment the tea master prepares and serves the beverage for a group of no more than four guests. Etiquette limits conversation to a discussion of the artistic merits of the wall hanging or the utensils. Affairs of state or other matters were proscribed. The tea house, thus, became a refuge from daily cares and concerns, and, as such, became popular with both military leaders and the nobility. Shuko, for example, was employed as tea-master to Yoshimasa, the eighth shogun of the Ashikaga Era.

The Way of the Sword

The qualities, grounded in Zen discipline, that contributed to making a master of calligraphy or a master tea-man were also applicable to the martial arts, and the Zen master who explored that relationship most thoroughly was Takuan Soho.

Although he left no lineage to succeed him, Takuan was exemplary of the wide scope of Zen influence at the beginning of the Edo period [1603 – 1868]. In addition to being a transmitted Zen teacher, he was also skilled in poetry, chanoyu, calligraphy, and painting. He is even credited with having invented the recipe for the popular pickled daikon radish which is called a "Takuan." He was also a respected scholar and a prolific author. His letter to the kendo[139] master at the Shogun's court, Yagyu Munenori, on Prajna Immoveable and its relation to swordsmanship is one of his best-known pieces and a seminal work on the application of Zen principles to other disciplines.

The letter begins by describing the tendency of the mind to "stop" or "abide" with things rather than flow naturally from one object to another. This is characteristic of *avidya*, or the ignorance that is the opposite of enlightenment. In kendo, if the swordsman's attention is stopped in this manner, he will be unable to respond to the moves of his opponent.

> No doubt you see the sword about to strike you, but do not let your mind "stop" there. Have no intention to counterattack him in response to his threatening move, cherish no calculating thoughts whatsoever. You simply perceive the opponent's move, you do not allow your mind to "stop" with it, you move on just as you are toward the opponent and make use of his attack by turning it on to himself. Then his sword meant to kill you will become your own and the weapon will fall on the opponent himself.[140]

This is the sword of "no-sword," in the sense that one is not consciously aware of self or sword but responds spontaneously and naturally to the situation in which one finds oneself. In this state of mind, Takuan writes, even if one were facing ten opponents at once, as long as one's mind does not "stop" with any one of them, one will emerge victorious.

In contrast to the "stopping" mind, or mind of delusion, is Prajna [Wisdom] Immoveable. The mind of delusion is the ego-consciousness; but behind it, underlying it, is the unmoved Prajna that is the source of one's ego-consciousness, the Self before thoughts arise. While this Prajna/

---

139. The way (do) of the sword.
140. Passages quoted from D.T. Suzuki, *Zen and Japanese Culture* (Princeton: Princeton University Press, 2010).

Wisdom is itself "unmoving" (because it does not "stop" with things), it is the source of spontaneous movement. Prajna Immoveable is the destroyer of illusion.

Takuan goes on to note how new kendo students, before they have received any training at all, are often more effective than students who have begun to learn proper technique. The untrained student responds to attacks spontaneously, instinctively moving to ward off blows. Once the student begins to train, he is taught how to stand, how to hold the sword, and is taught a variety of strikes. As the student acquires more and more knowledge, he inevitably starts to think about what the appropriate response to a situation should be. This thinking is an example of "stopping." But as the student continues to train, he eventually comes to a point where he has absorbed the training so thoroughly that he no longer needs to think about his actions. At this point, he approaches the state of mind he had had before beginning training, when he knew nothing. He has attained no-mind-ness, or mushin – "body and limbs perform by themselves what is assigned to them to do with no interference from the mind."[141]

The purpose of spiritual training, Takuan points out, is to overcome ignorance and attain no-mind-ness, and, as he demonstrates in his letter to Munenori, that training has as much practical application for swordsmanship as it has for the other Zen-inspired arts.

Hakuin Ekaku

Hakuin Ekaku was born in 1686. His importance to Japanese Zen is rivaled only by that of Dogen, who lived almost five centuries earlier. His influence was so pervasive that Rinzai Zen came to be known as Hakuin Zen, and virtually all current Rinzai teachers trace their transmissions back to him.

Hakuin's father was a samurai of limited means who had been adopted into his wife's family. His mother was a devout practitioner of Nichiren Buddhism, an offshoot of Tendai developed by the 14th century Japanese monk for whom the sect was named. Their youngest child was an intellectually gifted boy, but somewhat sickly and over sensitive.

When he was about eight years old, his mother took him to a public talk given by an itinerant Nichiren priest. In the sermon, the priest described the Eight Fiery Hells to which the wicked were condemned in order to expiate their sins before rebirth. His description included details of the torments to which the damned were subjected, such as being immersed in cauldrons of boiling water. Because of his sensitive and emotional temperament, Hakuin had an inflated sense of his personal failings.

---

141. Ibid., p. 100.

The sermon terrified him, and he came away certain he would be doomed to one of those hells when he died.

Not long afterwards, he was having a bath with his mother. When the water grew tepid, she asked the servant to add more wood to the fire heating it. As the water became warmer, her son burst into tears. When his mother asked why he was crying, he told her of his fear of being sent to one of the Eight Fiery Hells. "Even a little bit of hot water hurts!" he wailed. "How could I bear the torments of the Fiery Hells?"

She tried to console him by counseling him to think of the infinite mercies of the Bodhisattva Kannon. The boy took her words to heart and acquired a picture of the Bodhisattva which he enshrined in his sleeping quarters. Regardless, his anxiety remained unassuaged. He had a very literal and naïve faith. Once when he was reciting the *Lotus Sutra*, he was struck by a passage which promised that if one were to chant a particular mantra with sufficient zeal one would be exempt from harm by either fire or water. Hakuin chanted the mantra unremittingly for several days then tested its efficacy by taking up a heated poker from the hearth and touching it to his thigh. Either the mantra or his zeal failed.

Eventually he decided the only hope he had of avoiding condemnation after death would be to enter monastic life, which he did at the age of 15. His first community was the local Zen temple, Shoinji – which would later become his teaching center. Here he was given the Buddhist name "Ekaku." He adopted the name "Hakuin" later in life.

When he was 19, he came across the story of the death of the Chinese Zen Master, Ganto Zenkatsu.[142] The region where the master's temple had been located was overrun by bandits, and, in fear for their lives, all of the monks fled. Ganto alone remained in the temple. When the bandits arrived, they found him seated in zazen. They searched the temple for valuables and, frustrated not to find any, took out their anger by slaying Ganto. It was said that as their swords pierced him, he let out a scream so loud it could be heard for miles around. That scream distressed Hakuin, who wondered what use Ganto's Zen had been in the end. This story – on top of a general feeling of tedium and a sense of futility he'd felt since becoming a monk – drove him to return to lay life.

He had some talent as a poet and a painter and turned to these, but he came to find the artistic life no more satisfying than his time at the monastery had been.

One day, the abbot of the local temple brought the manuscripts and books of the temple library out into the courtyard and placed them in the sun to dry out any dampness they'd acquired. Young Hakuin took up a volume by chance that happened to be a collection of Chinese Zen tales.

---

142. Yantou Quanhuo in Chinese.

Allowing it to open at random, he came upon the story of Sekiso Soyen[143] who had been so committed to the quest for enlightenment that he did zazen day and night without interruption, stabbing himself in the thigh with an awl to stave off drowsiness.

The story made Hakuin ashamed of the puniness of his prior efforts. Shortly after this, he learned that his mother had died. His immediate thought was to travel home in order to pay his respects at her grave site, but, upon reflection, he decided a more appropriate way to honor her would be to rededicate himself to Zen practice.

He began a tour of temples, seeking instruction from various teachers, and he had an initial "tongue-tip" taste of awakening upon hearing the chirp of a cricket; it was a shallow experience but spurred him onto greater effort.

At the age of twenty-two, his travels brought him to Eiganji, where he attended a series of lectures given by the Rinzai teacher, Master Shotetsu. Between talks, Hakuin spent his time focused on Joshu's *Mu*.[144] He became so absorbed in the koan that he felt as if he were frozen in the midst of a glacier. Not a thought remained in his mind save for the repetition of Mu with each breath. This condition persisted for several days, and then he chanced to hear the toll of a temple bell. At that moment, it was if the ice had shattered or a jade tower had come crashing down. Not only was the question of Mu resolved, so too was the question of Ganto's death.

"*I* am Ganto!" he declared. "Wonder of wonders, there is no birth or death! There is no enlightenment to seek! The 1700 koans are of no value whatsoever!"

His pride, he later confessed, soared up "like a mountain," and he believed that no one for the last three hundred years could possibly have had as profound an awakening as he had experienced. So he was entirely unprepared when he went to Shotetsu to have his awakening acknowledged and Shotetsu refused to do so, expressing some doubt about Hakuin's attainment. Shotetsu, himself, did not take students, but he suggested that Hakuin needed to work with a teacher to clarify what he had accomplished.

Another monk, Doju Sokaku, had also been attending Shotetsu's lectures, and he advised Hakuin to meet his teacher, Dokyo Etan, also known as Shoju Rojin, or "The Old Man of Shoju Hermitage." So in 1708, the two set out for the master's temple. As they approached, they saw the old teacher chopping firewood. Shoju welcomed his disciple back and invited the two travelers into his hut. There Hakuin, following the customary practice, presented the master with a verse in which he summed up his

---

143. Shishuang Chuyuan in Chinese.

144. In Chinese, *Wu*.

understanding. Shoju looked at the poem briefly then tossed the paper aside, saying, "These are just words. Show me what you know."

Hakuin made a gagging sound and replied, "If I had anything to show you, I would vomit it up."

"Show me how you understand Mu," Shoju demanded.

"How can one touch it?" Hakuin said,

Shoju reached forward, grabbed Hakuin's nose, and gave it a sharp twist. "Here is how one can touch it!"

Hakuin was stunned and didn't know how to reply.

"You poor cave-dwelling demon," Shoju said dismissively. "Are you really so easily satisfied with this meager understanding?"

Hakuin's former pride in his attainment withered, and he asked: "What's missing?"

"When Nansen was dying, his disciples asked where he would be a hundred years to come…" Shoju began, relating the story of that Chinese master's last conversation with his disciples.[145] Before he could go any further, Hakuin put his hands over his ears and rushed from the room.

"You cave-dwelling demon!" Shoju called out after him.

Hakuin was sufficiently humbled by the experience to remain at the hermitage, meeting with Shoju regularly in the hope of having his awakening confirmed. But each time he presented himself to the old master, Shoju called him a "cave-dwelling demon" and sent him on his way.

One evening, Hakuin brought Shoju another verse. Shoju was seated on the veranda of his hermitage enjoying the warm sun after several days of rain. He looked at Hakuin's poem, then crumbled it up, saying, "Stuff and nonsense."

"Stuff and nonsense!" Hakuin shouted back at him.

Shoju gripped the lapels of Hakuin's robe in his left hand and beat him with his other fist. Then he threw the startled student off the porch into the mud. Hakuin lay there for a while, stunned, listening to Shoju laugh at him. After a while, Hakuin gathered himself together and rose to his feet. He made his formal bow to Shoju and returned to his quarters.

With renewed vigor, he threw himself into the koan about Nansen's death. One morning sometime later, he was engaged in *takahatsu*[146] and

---

145. The story is that when Nansen Fugan (Ch.: Nanquan Puyuan) was dying, his disciples crowded about his bed. The head monk asked, "Master, after your death, a hundred years from now, where will you be?"
 "I'll be a water buffalo," Nan-ch'uan told him.
 "And will I still be your disciple?" the head monk asked.
 "If you want to be my disciple, you'll need to chew grass."
146. The formal round of begging by which monks supported themselves, following the model provided by the Buddha and his disciples.

was so caught up in the koan that he stood in front of one house as if in a trance. The woman of house watched him with suspicion for a while then rushed out waving her broom at him.

"Go!" she screamed at him. "Go away! Go somewhere else! If you don't go away, I'll hit you!"

He was so absorbed that he ignored her. She hit him with the broom, knocking his hat off, and kept beating him until he fell to the ground unconscious. After the woman returned to her house, a passerby helped Hakuin sit up, patting his cheeks to revive him. When Hakuin came to, he realized he had resolved not only the koan about Nansen's death but several others as well which until that time had puzzled him.

He gathered himself together and rushed back to Shoju's hermitage. The master saw him coming and, when Hakuin was within speaking range, shouted at him: "I see something has happened to you. So, tell me about it."

Hakuin described all that had taken place.

"Now you have it!" Shoju told him and never again referred to Hakuin as a "cave-dwelling demon."

Following his awakening, Hakuin remained with Shoju for another eight months. Then Shoju told him it was time to begin gathering his own disciples. Underestimating the impact his student would have, he advised Hakuin to have modest expectations; it would be enough if Hakuin were able to find two or three disciples to continue the tradition.

Hakuin undertook a pilgrimage during which his understanding deepened. In 1716, he returned to Shoinji and found it in poor repair with neither roof nor floor boards. When it rained, Hakuin had to wear a rain hat and high *getas*[147] even indoors. The land and furnishings were mortgaged to local creditors. Undaunted, Hakuin set about rebuilding it, and, subsequently, his small rural temple became a center to which students from throughout Japan flocked for the next fifty years. Although Hakuin did not actively seek disciples, his character was such that genuine aspirants were drawn to him. Word spread throughout the land that a fully enlightened teacher lived in this small community. When Shoinji was no longer able to accommodate all those who sought to work with Hakuin, a number of additional buildings were constructed to house them. He would later have opportunities to become the abbot of larger temples in Edo and Kyoto but chose to remain at Shoinji.

Although the primary focus of his life's work was renewing the Rinzai School and training the monks under his direction, Hakuin also retained

---

147. Sandals with wooden slats on their soles.

a commitment to the working classes with whom he had great sympathy. He took lay disciples and was sensitive to the challenges they faced. While monastic life provided an opportunity for meditators to spend hours each day in formal zazen, lay people had myriad obligations and responsibilities to which they needed to attend. Hakuin taught them how they could transform their involvements in daily life into opportunities for practice. He wrote poems for the laity that were sung to popular folk melodies.

Hakuin returned to art around the age of sixty. He was an accomplished calligrapher and painter; his pieces displayed a sense of humor and proved to be effective tools in teaching the Dharma to people unable to read.

Hakuin took upon himself the responsibility of effecting a complete reform of the Rinzai School. Central to that reform was ensuring that only individuals who had legitimately received *inka*[148] be allowed to teach. It was essential that students work with genuinely awakened teachers.

Awakening was fundamental to Hakuin's Zen. One was not, in his opinion, a member of the Zen community until one had "seen into one's true nature." He believed that those – like some Soto teachers – who held that awakening was not important did so only because they hadn't achieved it themselves. He described them as being like one too weak to feed himself but claiming that the reason he wasn't eating was because the food had spoiled. While Hakuin was respected as a genial and kind man with great generosity of spirit and compassion, he could work himself into a furor about teachers he believed were compromising the Zen tradition.

Hakuin recognized that it was possible to achieve kensho through a number of practices. He often prescribed that lay people recite the nembutsu, but he maintained that the most effective route, and the only suitable route for monks, was koan study. He was dubious about the value of the Soto tradition of shikan taza and described the monks who engaged in it as being like incense burners in a mausoleum.

Awakening wasn't something that came about automatically from the practice of zazen or koan study. One's practice had to be entered vigorously, fueled by great faith, great determination, and great doubt. He advised both monks and lay people to ask, "Who sees? Who hears? When walking, when standing, when sitting, or lying down, in all circumstances, whether favorable or unfavorable, who is it that sees? – who is it that hears?"

After being taught to focus the attention through concentration on the breath,[149] students were given a first koan, which in the Rinzai tradition,

---

148. Or *inka shomei* – official documentation of attainment and authorization to teach.
149. Susokkan.

was usually Mu! With some Rinzai teachers since the establishment of the Gozan system, koan work had degenerated into an elite literary exercise in which students sought quotations from classic literature to demonstrate the spirit of the koans they were assigned. Hakuin dismissed this practice and insisted his students find a physical way to demonstrate the significance of the koan. Hakuin coined his own koan, which has become one of the best known: "You know the sound of two hands clapping. But, tell me, what is the sound of one hand?" The respondent was required to reply to the koan without using words.

After the initial breakthrough, practitioners were guided through a program of later koans each of which enhanced the student's original understanding and aided them in grasping experientially many of the teachings presented in the sutras. It was a process that could take many years. Hakuin knew from his own experience that the initial kensho could mislead one into believing one was fully awakened. He argued, instead, that after the first kensho one was like a new born child; one has all one's faculties, but those faculties still need to be cultivated.

Torei Enji

Torei Enji was one of the many students who attained awakening under Hakuin's guidance. Before he could begin his own teaching career, however, he contracted tuberculosis and feared that he wouldn't live long enough to repay Hakuin by passing on what he had learned. So he undertook to write a guide for new Zen practitioners entitled *A Discourse on the Inexhaustible Lamp of Zen*.[150] As it turned out, Torei recovered and, unsure what to do with the manuscript, showed it to Hakuin who approved it and advised him to complete it. The document remains the clearest exposition of the teachings of the early Hakuin School.

Torei begins by defining what distinguishes the Zen School from other forms of Buddhism. It isn't that these schools are in error but that they are inadequate. They are only able to discuss and theorize about awakening but are incapable of bringing people to awakening. They teach "the beginning and the end" of the path, whereas Zen points beyond the path to awakening itself. He compares the difference to that between a poor man and a rich man; the poor man can discuss the rich man's wealth, but he can't make use of it. "So then, of what use is it to him?" Torei asks.

One must undertake Zen practice with proper intent and motivation. The path is difficult and requires persistence, therefore one needs to be properly grounded before proceeding. For Torei, this requires making a

---

150. *Shumon Mujinto Ron*.

whole-hearted commitment to the Four Vows,[151] which, he stressed, are based on compassion. One must undertake Zen for the benefit of all beings; to do otherwise is to practice in vain. The way in which the Zen aspirant fulfills these vows is by committing him or herself to equal the attainments of the Buddhas and Patriarchs of the past and then to pass that attainment on to "one or two" others.

Nor can one undertake the way on one's own. It requires the guidance of a fully awakened teacher. Torei admits that it's difficult to find such a teacher in these "degenerate times," and he laments the number of unqualified teachers whose inadequate instruction only misleads their students. But without a qualified teacher, students are susceptible to shallow understanding and misleading visions. He compares proceeding without a teacher to setting out on a journey to a distant land without a knowledgeable guide; one has a particular destination in mind, but, because one lacks proper guidance, one may end up somewhere altogether different than where one had intended to be.

While the guide is necessary, one must also recognize that the path isn't an external one. What one is seeking can't be had from another but can only be found by turning inward. Buddha-nature is not found by learning a doctrine but by searching one's own mind. The basis of this practice is Right Mindfulness, that in turn is cultivated through Right Meditation (zazen). The various regulations associated with monastic life are solely intended to promote Right Mindfulness.

If one practices under appropriate guidance and with correct intention, one will develop a capacity for concentration so strong that conscious thought comes to an end. This is the Entrance to the Great Way and when attained, Torei warns, one must proceed with care, persisting without seeking anything in particular; because to do otherwise would be to seek only for something one has imagined. If one can let go of both body and mind, one will come to awakening, the understanding of one's True Nature and the nature of all Being.

Paraphrasing the instructions given by the Sixth Patriarch to General Ming, Torei challenges the student: "Without thinking 'yes' or 'no,' tell me: Who is it that sees? Who is it that hears? If one persists in this manner, the answer will arise of itself at the appropriate time without the need of discriminating dualistic thought."

Torei cautions the student not to suppose his or her efforts are complete with an initial kensho. From his own experience, as well as Hakuin's, he understands the importance of "Progressive Enlightenment," and he cites examples of masters from the past whose initial awakenings were deepened by continued practice after kensho.

---

151. Page 89 above.

The koan tradition that Hakuin and his heirs established evolved into what contemporary teacher, John Tarrant, describes as a "designed learning system."[152] The number of koans studied varies between lineages,[153] but the sequence is not arbitrary. The goal is to deepen the initial awakening insight, integrate it into the student's life in a holistic manner, and then understand the range of Buddhist teaching experientially. The approach is that expressed in the often-quoted remark of the Chinese master, Yantou Xuanjian, that helped his friend, Xuefeng Yicun, attain awakening: "Do you not know that what enters by the gate is not the family treasure? The Great Teaching must rise within your own breast and then cover heaven and earth."

In many obvious ways, the form of the Buddhadharma presented in Japanese Zen is very different from the practice of Gautama's original disciples, but the fundamental insights are the same. The complexities of Buddhist thought, the analysis of causality, the deep understanding of human psychology and the workings of the mind are part of the perspective shared by all Buddhist sects and provide the context of Zen practice. The manner in which they are conveyed through koan practice, however, has the unique characteristic that, with the guidance of a skillful teacher, students are able to realize the intention of these tenets not through abstract reflection but through direct personal intuition.

---

152. Richard Bryan McDaniel, *Cypress Trees in the Garden* (Richmond Hill, ON: Sumeru, 2015), p. 166.

153. Between 500 to 1700.

The Japanese doctrines teach absolutely nothing concerning the creation of the world, of the sun, the moon, the stars, the heavens, the earth, sea, and the rest, and do not believe that they have any origin but themselves. The people were greatly astonished on hearing it said that there is one sole Author and common Father of souls, by whom they were created. This astonishment was caused by the fact that in their religious traditions there is nowhere any mention of a Creator of the universe.

Francis Xavier

Encounter

"Oh, East is East, and West is West…"

MEDIEVAL CHRISTIANS attending mass on November 27th heard the story of Saints Barlaam and Josaphat, whose feast day it was. It was a familiar tale, included in popular collections of the lives of the saints, taking place in India, where it was believed the Apostle Thomas had gone after the Resurrection and Ascension of Jesus. Tradition held that Thomas had great success spreading the gospel in the East, and that a powerful Christian nation had been established on the Indian sub-continent which still existed under the rule of a mysterious king known as Prester John. According to the story, however, in the 4th century – shortly after Constantine signed the Edict of Milan ending the persecution of Christians in the Roman Empire – a man named Abenner assumed the Indian throne and sought to restore the old ways of worship by suppressing Christianity.

When Abenner's first child, a son named Josaphat, was born, the king – according to custom – called in astrologers to read the boy's destiny, and they predicted that the child would become a great Christian saint. Determined not to allow this to occur, Abenner kept his son confined in a luxurious palace where all his whims were catered to and where no mention of Christian doctrine was permitted. Eventually, however, Josaphat – while on a pleasure jaunt – met the holy hermit Barlaam who converted and baptized him. When Abenner realized that God had thwarted his efforts to shield his son from the gospel, he himself became a Christian and turned the throne over to Josaphat. Josaphat ruled wisely and justly for a period, then he too abdicated the throne, rejoined Barlaam, and spent the remainder of his life in prayer and worship. The story ends with accounts of the miracles that had since taken place at their combined grave site.

The origins of the story can be traced by the etymology of the name "Josaphat," which is the Latinized form of the Greek "Ioasaph." It, in turn, is derived from "Yudhasaf" which was probably originally "Budhasaf,"[154] the Arabic rendering of the Sanskrit word "Bodhisattva."

The simple reason no one in the Middle Ages recognized this as a retelling of the Buddha story was that not even educated Europeans knew anything about either the Buddha or his Dharma.

It hadn't always been the case. Trade with India and Ceylon had brought snippets of Buddhist thought and legends to the commercial centers of the Greek and Roman empires, and arguments have even been made that elements of the Buddha's biography were the basis of some of the traditional stories told about Jesus – his miraculous and virgin birth, holy men making prophecies about his destiny while he was still an infant, the period of temptation before taking up his public life, the traitor among his closest followers, and sending his disciples out to spread his teaching.

With the fall of the Roman Empire, the advent of the Dark Ages, and the disruptive impact of Islam, communication between East and West was obstructed. As Europe became Christian, Buddhism spread throughout India, Nepal, Tibet, Central Asia, China, Korea, and eventually Japan. But, as Stephen Batchelor notes:

> – the growth and consolidation of two of the world's major religions occurred in complete ignorance of each other. Absorption in their own doctrinal and institutional concerns combined with the rise of Islam from the 7th century onwards, closed the possibility of communication between them…[155]

When European merchants and missionaries came into contact with Buddhism in the 13th century, they weren't in a position to understand or appreciate it. They uniformly believed that the Christian faith alone expressed God's will; all other belief systems were not only in error; they were the work of the Devil who sought to bring about the damnation of humankind by seducing them to false doctrines. One of the earliest reported contacts with Buddhism is found in the travel memoirs of the Venetian, Marco Polo, who heard about the life of the Buddha while serving in the court of Kublai Khan. He laments that it was a shame Gautama had not been baptized. Had he been, he would very likely have been a very good Christian; as it was, Polo had no doubt that – like all other heathens – Gautama was damned to eternal perdition.

---

154. According to the Wikipedia entry on Barlaam and Josaphat, Yudhasaf was a variant which first showed up in Persian texts of the 6th or 7th century, possibly because the "Arabic initial 'b' changed to 'y' by duplication of a dot in handwriting)."

155. Stephen Batchelor, *The Awakening of the West* (Williamsville, VT: Echo Point Books, 2011), p. 32.

A fuller account of Buddhism was provided in a report prepared for Louis IX of France by the Franciscan, William of Rubeck. In 1253, William traveled to Asia hoping to bring solace to Christian slaves taken by Mongol invaders. When he arrived at the court of Kublai Khan's brother and predecessor, Mongke Khan, he was invited to participate in a debate between representatives of Christianity, Islam, and the Buddhadharma intended to determine which tradition Mongke would adopt for his realm. According to William's account, he bested his opponents easily, but the obdurate Khan remained unswayed and, in fact, ordered William to leave his territories.

William and later missionaries were hampered in their encounters with other faith traditions by their conviction that these were the works of Satan and so unworthy of serious study. With the rise of Scholasticism, the doctrines of Christianity were held to be self-evident to both reason and faith, and the study of other religious perspectives was permitted only in order to better refute them. The fact that so often the reasoned arguments of the Christian missionaries failed to convert their audiences was assumed to be due to willful ignorance on the part of the heathens. What the missionaries did not recognize – were almost incapable of recognizing – was that the basic premises upon which their arguments were based differed so much from those of the peoples of Asia that genuine discussion was virtually impossible.

The Evangelization of Japan

The first European to have any contact with Zen – the first European to enter the Japanese city of Kyoto – was St. Francis Xavier, one of the founding members of the Jesuit congregation in the 16th century. No order of missionaries was more committed to the belief that Christian doctrine was in accord with human reason and could be demonstrated through logical discourse. Xavier had conclusively demonstrated this to his own satisfaction by the success of his work in the Portuguese territories along the west coast of the Indian sub-continent. There he had converted tens of thousands of former Hindus to Catholicism and established some forty churches. The region still has a substantial Christian population, and Xavier's mummified corpse – minus an arm which is kept in Rome – remains on display at the Basilica in Goa. On special festivals, it's paraded through the streets. The arm has its own touring schedule.

While in Malacca, Xavier had made the acquaintance of a young exiled samurai named Anjiro. Anjiro is the first known Japanese convert to Christianity, and Francis was struck by the young man's cultural and intellectual sophistication, which he considered superior to anything he had previously encountered in Asia. He asked Anjiro if the people of his homeland were similar to him; would they, too, be receptive to Christianity. Anjiro replied that conversions might not be immediate; however, the people of Japan would inquire deeply into Christian teaching and observe the conduct of the Europeans. If they saw that the behavior of the missionaries was in accord with their teachings, then doubtless the leaders of the country would be drawn to the faith, and within no more than six months – by Anjiro's estimate – the majority of the population would follow, because Japan was a land "guided by reason."

Encouraged by Anjiro's optimistic assurances, Xavier sailed to Japan in 1549. What followed was a comedy of errors of Shakespearean proportions.

The Christians landed in Kagoshima, on the island of Kyushu. In his reports back to Goa, Xavier wrote that they had been welcomed with great enthusiasm by the local daimyo,[156] Shimazu Takahisa, who was particularly pleased with a portrait of the Virgin and Christ Child they had presented to him and to which he had spontaneously paid great reverence. Xavier observed that the daimyo's coat of arms consisted of a cross within a circle. In addition, he noted that the Buddhist clergy made use of bells and rosaries and "prayed" with folded hands. The respect they exhibited for bodhisattvas appeared similar to the veneration of the saints. Monks lived in communities that came together at regular intervals during the day to "pray." From these coincidences, Xavier wondered if at some time in the past Christianity had been brought to Japan, possibly by missionaries from the supposed Christian community founded in India by the apostle Thomas, and then had fallen into abeyance.

On his part, when Takahisa – whose family crest represented a horse's bit with a cross-like shape in the middle – learned that a group of foreign priests from the homeland of Shakyamuni Buddha had arrived in his fiefdom, he assumed that they were adherents of a new school of Buddhism, an assumption that was strengthened when they presented him with a lifelike portrait of the Bodhisattva Kannon holding a child.

> The foreign bonzes [priests/monks] from Tenjiku, the homeland of Shaka [Buddha], wore long black robes, had partly shaved heads, were said to have no intercourse with women, refrained from eating animal meat and kept speaking of the very things Buddhist priests were so fond of.[157]

---

156. Lord.

157. Urs App, "Saint Francis Xavier's Discovery of Japanese Buddhism," *The Eastern Buddhist* XXX: 1, 1997. pp. 53-76. http://universitymedia.org/downloads/app_francis_xavier_123.pdf.

Based on these misunderstandings, the Jesuits' relations with the Buddhist clergy were easy at first. Since Xavier thought Buddhism was probably a degraded form of Christianity, he felt that if he were able to win the support of the local clergy their congregations would follow. To that end, he made a point of meeting Buddhist leaders and entering into debate with them, expecting to have the same success in Japan as he'd had in India. He didn't.

Early on, Xavier met and formed a friendship with the abbot of Fukushoji, a Soto Zen monastery. The abbot's name is recorded as Ninshitsu, which Xavier reported meant "Heart of Truth." Xavier described Ninshitsu in fulsome terms, asserting that he was the equivalent of a bishop and "an amazingly good friend. Both the laity and the bonzes," Xavier wrote proudly, "are delighted with us, astonished that we have traveled from lands as far away as Portugal – more than 6000 leagues – for the sole purpose of speaking of the things of God."

He discussed the concept of an immortal soul with Ninshitsu but had to report that the Zen Master was "hesitant and unable to decide whether our soul is immortal or if it dies along with the body. At times, he has said that it is immortal, at others that it is not. I am afraid that it is the same with the other scholars." Ninshitsu and Xavier could not even agree upon what an individual's "self" consisted of. It never occurred to the Jesuits that anyone would consider the "self" to be anything other than the personal self, with its memories, habits, and individual quirks. For traditions that accepted the concept of reincarnation, however, one's self is not the present personality conditioned by a particular set of circumstances but that which – however understood – is incarnated in a number of successive personalities.

Nor could Xavier get Ninshitsu to acknowledge the necessary existence of a Supreme Being external to and responsible for Creation, something which the Jesuits assumed was as self-evident as the fact that the Sun circled the Earth. Although he hardly felt it was necessary to do so, St. Thomas Aquinas had famously posited five rational proofs for the existence of God. For example, he argued, it was obvious that nothing which is inanimate can move without an external cause for that motion. The sun and the moon are not animate objects, consequently there must be an external power – what Aquinas termed a Prime Mover – responsible for their movements. When the Jesuits put this argument to the Buddhists, they dismissed it out of hand. There was no reason, they maintained, why natural laws – the Dharma or the Dao – required an external force in order to function.

The more familiar the missionaries came to be with Buddhist teachings, the more bewildered they were by them. One of the Jesuits who accompanied Xavier to Japan, Cosme de Torres, expressed his frustration in an account to his superiors in which he described a conversation he had

had with a Buddhist abbot. The abbot asserted that the idea of a God such as de Torres described was foolish and, instead, outlined the concept of sunyata, the Void or Emptiness, which de Torres interpreted as a "great Nothingness." In his perplexed report, de Torres explained that after

> – the great Nothingness has entered existence; it can do nothing than to return to the same Nothingness…This is a principle from which all things proceed, whether human beings, animals, or plants. Every created thing contains this principle in itself, and when humans or animals die, the four elements revert into that which they had been at first, and this principle returns to that which it is…This principle is neither good nor evil. It possesses neither bliss nor pain. It neither dies nor lives, so that it is truly a Nothingness.[158]

Another Jesuit, Padre Luis Frois – who came to Japan after Xavier and de Torres – summed up his understanding of Zen this way: "The sect believes there is nothing more than birth and death, that there is no later life, nor a creator who governs the universe." It was difficult for Padre Frois to imagine how such an arid doctrine qualified as a religion.

It didn't take long for the Japanese to understood that what the Jesuits were presenting was not a new form of Buddhism but a rival faith which denied the validity of all other points of view. At that point the Japanese became less welcoming. There were, however, conversions. One of the appeals of the Christian doctrine is the possibility of salvation after death and a righting of wrongs in the world to come. To a populace weary of war, poverty, and turmoil, these were attractive concepts. So there were baptisms in Japan, although nothing like the number that Xavier had had in India.

The Chancellor of the Realm, Toyotomi Hideyoshi, viewed these conversions with suspicion. Hideyoshi was determined to unify the fractious Japanese people under a single authority, and he considered Christianity a potential political threat. So, in 1587, he issued an edict ordering the missionaries out of the country. The edict wasn't enforced and, indeed, a second missionary order – Franciscans from Spain – arrived to contest the hegemony of the Jesuits. When it became clear that in addition to sending missionaries, both Portugal and Spain had colonial aspirations in Japan, Hideyoshi responded by having six Franciscans, three Jesuit lay-brothers, and nineteen recent Catholic converts executed by crucifixion in 1597.

---

158. Quoted in Heinrich Dumoulin, *Zen Buddhism: A History – Japan* (Bloomington, IN: World Wisdom, 2005), p. 267.

Assuming he had made his point, Hideyoshi took no further action. He died the following year and was succeeded by Ieyasu Tokugawa, the first Shogun of the dynasty that would control Japan for the next two and a half centuries. Ieyasu established trading relationships with the Dutch – who supplied him with European weapons – and Holland reciprocated by sending Protestant missionaries who openly vied with the two Catholic orders for converts.

Ieyasu shared Hideyoshi's ambition to unify Japan politically and culturally, and he viewed Catholicism in particular as a subversive teaching that might draw the loyalty of the people from the Emperor to a foreign Pope. The population of Catholics in Japan at that time has been variously estimated to have grown to between 250,000 and 750,000 persons, a number too large for Ieyasu to ignore, so, in 1614, he ordered all foreigners expelled from the islands. An artificial island was built in Nagasaki harbor on which Dutch merchants were allowed to land; all other contact with Europe was severed by 1639. Japan isolated itself from the rest of the world for the next two hundred years, until, in 1853, the United States sent Commodore Matthew Perry and a flotilla of gunships into Tokyo harbor, compelling the Japanese to reopen their ports to Western shipping.

The West Turns East

As Japan withdrew from contact with the West, the West began to develop a fascination with the East. Jesuits – who had little tolerance for the obscurities of Buddhism – admired the writings of Master Kongzi so much that they graced him with the Latin name, Confucius, by which he is generally known outside of Asia. A full translation of the classic Confucian texts, including the *Analects*, was first published in Paris in 1687 by a Jesuit, Thierry Meynard, and was received with unexpected respect by Christian readers.

During the European Age of Enlightenment, in the mid-18th century, there was an upsurge in scientific and philosophical speculation that cast doubt on the supremacy of Christian doctrine. Rationalists like Voltaire and John Locke advanced the theory of Deism which – while it still took the existence of a Creator for granted – held that this Creator took no further role in governing after bringing creation into being. It was a perspective which they felt was similar to that espoused in Asian texts which were then becoming available. By the early 19th century, the Transcendentalists of New England – including Ralph Waldo Emerson and Henry David Thoreau – were studying Hinduism and Buddhism and publishing their findings.

Rationalism became even more broadly accepted after the publication of Charles Darwin's *Origin of Species*, which was released just six years after Commodore Perry's ships entered Tokyo harbor. Vilified by Protestants and Catholics alike, Darwin's work altered the relationship between science and religion for all time.

While many people began to have difficulty accepting the absolutes of the Christian creed, they frequently still wanted to believe that there was a spiritual dimension to human life. As a result, even the educated became susceptible to a bizarre range of new beliefs, such as in the existence of fairies (Arthur Conan Doyle was a true believer), spiritualism and communication with the dead, various forms of psychic phenomenon, even telepathic communications with mystic spiritual masters in the Himalayas.

In popular culture, these ideas were often associated with the Mysterious East – a region where it was imagined exotic powers were common and life was free of the more restrictive elements of Christian morality. Sir Richard Burton's translations of works like *The Arabian Nights*[159] and the *Kama Sutra* were popular not only for their fantasy elements but for their erotic content.

It was a period of serious academic research as well, and, by the end of the 19th Century, Asian studies had not only acquired a degree of respectability in western universities they also attracted a popular interest unimaginable a few decades earlier. Sir Edwin Arnold's verse biography of the Buddha – *The Light of Asia* – became a late Victorian best-seller. The same year Arnold's book came out, the Oxford scholar, Max Müller, released the first in what would be a fifty-volume series entitled *The Sacred Books of the East*, a collection of translations he and others had made of Hindu, Buddhist, Confucian, and Daoist texts, as well as works from the Muslim, Jain, and Zoroastrian traditions.

The form of Buddhism with which the West first became familiar was the austere doctrine of the Theravada School as found in Sri Lanka. There a British civil service officer, Thomas Rhys David, translated works which would be included in Müller's series. Rhys David would go on to found the Pali Text Society, committed to preserving the literary heritage – including the *Tripitaka* – of what was then known as Ceylon. As documents became more accessible in the West, some thinkers began to wonder if non-theistic Theravada Buddhism might not be a faith system better suited to bridge the growing rift between science and religion than Christianity.

Knowledge of Mahayana Buddhism came later, when missionaries and philologists began the process of translating Tibetan texts; however, the consensus of scholars like Rhys David was that the Mahayana – with its lurid artwork and suspiciously papist pantheon of Bodhisattvas – was a decadent corruption of the Buddha's original teachings. The

---

159. The actual title was *The Book of the Thousand Nights and a Night*.

post-Darwinian age may have been a time of rapid change and intellectual growth, but it remained staunchly Victorian.

Once Western commerce with Japan resumed, art enthusiasts like the Harvard graduate, Ernest Francisco Fenollosa, became entranced by the poetry, calligraphy, and scroll painting of that country. Fenollosa accepted a position at the Tokyo Imperial University in 1878 and was instrumental in establishing both the Imperial Museum and the Tokyo School of Fine Arts. The works in his personal collection became the basis of the Weld-Fenollosa collection of Japanese art currently housed in the Museum of Fine Arts in Boston. During his time in Japan, he became a serious student of Buddhism and formally took the precepts, the ceremony by which one declares his or her commitment to the Dharma.

Although only a handful of Westerners avowed Buddhism in the 19th century, Fenollosa was not alone. In fact he had been preceded in 1880 by two of the most unlikely figures in the history of the transition of Buddhism to the West.

Blavatsky and Olcott

The major role Theosophy played in the transference of Buddhism and Zen from Asia to the West can't be ignored, but neither can the fact that the woman who inspired the movement – Helena Petrovna Blavatsky – was, at the very least, a hoaxer and probably a conscious charlatan. Blavatsky was born in what is now the Ukraine to a family of German descent. Her father, Pyotr Alexeyevich von Hahn, was a nobleman in the royal horse artillery, and her mother, also named Helena, was a writer. Blavatsky later fictionalized much of her personal history, so a great deal of her biography is based on speculation, but it's probable that her first contact with Tibetan Buddhism occurred when her father's career took the family to Astrakhan. It wouldn't have been a very serious study, but apparently the young Helena was taken with the elements of Tibetan culture that had seemed exotic and magical to her. Eventually her parents decided a military environment was an inappropriate one in which to raise children, and Helena was sent to relatives in Europe, where she had access to a cosmopolitan education including an introduction to popular lore on the paranormal. While still a teenager, she claimed to have had visions of a "Mysterious Indian man" who guided her to out-of-body experiences through astral projection.

In 1849, at the age of 17, she married Nikifor Vladimirovich Blavatsky – a man more than twice her age – who intrigued her by his interest in the occult. The marriage lasted three months, after which she traveled throughout Europe, North America, the Middle East, and India. She later claimed that during this period she met the "Mysterious Indian Man" who now directed her to go to Tibet. There she was introduced to a group of spiritual adepts she referred to as the Masters of Ancient Wisdom under whose direction and guidance she developed psychic powers.

Around 1858, she returned to her family in Russia and demonstrated her advanced spiritual training with table rappings and the ability to move furniture without physically touching it. She also claimed to be in telepathic contact with two Kashmiri masters, Koot Hoomi and Morya, with whom she engaged in deep study from 1868 to 1870. This was accomplished by means of astral projection, so that, even though her body remained behind, her spirit was able to travel to the Himalayas to be with her tutors.

She moved to New York City in July of 1873 at the age of 41. At first, she needed to support herself as a seamstress, but when her father died, she inherited a modest fortune and was able to live more lavishly, all the while courting publicity with her supposed powers. She had psychic rivals, most of whom she boldly denounced as frauds, and it was while investigating two of these in Vermont – William and Horatio Eddy[160] – that she met Henry Steel Olcott, who was himself researching the brothers for a newspaper article.

The worst that can be said of Olcott is that he was naïve. He had served as an officer in the Union army during the American Civil War, rising to the rank of Colonel, and was involved in the investigation into the assassination of Abraham Lincoln. Although he was a lawyer specializing in financial fraud, he was oddly susceptible to the claims both of the Eddys, whose deceptions were later easily exposed by a vaudeville magician, and of Madame Blavatsky, as she was then known.

The two formed a close friendship. He became her student, and she introduced him to the Masters, who communicated with him through her. Slowly a group of like-minded people gathered around them who would become the nucleus of the Theosophical Movement. The term Theosophy was coined from the Greek words theos (god) and sophia (wisdom) and was intended to convey the idea of a "divine wisdom" universal to all world religions. Blavatsky outlined the fundamental concepts in a two-volume work, *Isis Unveiled*, the content of which she claimed was revealed to her by her psychic masters. The first printing, 1000 copies, sold out within ten days. It has remained in print ever since and is still available in e-editions.

The book posits that all religious and philosophic systems are derived from a single Ancient Wisdom tradition preserved more purely in the East – particularly in Buddhism – than in the West. Blavatsky had read extensively and may well have had an eidetic memory, and the book is

---

160. The Eddy brothers claimed to be able to summon ectoplasmic materializations of the dead.

so exhaustive in its reference to various systems of thought that people as savvy as Thomas Edison found it convincing.

The movement based on her teachings eventually had chapters in several countries. Many of the first westerners to show interest in Zen came to it from Theosophy. As it became more formally institutionalized, Theosophy eventually defined its aims as three: 1) To establish a universal brotherhood of all humankind without distinction of race, gender, or creed; 2) To promote the study of comparative religion, philosophy, and science; and 3) To investigate "unexplained laws of nature and the powers latent in" human beings.

It's impossible to distinguish between what Blavatsky actually believed and what she only feigned to believe. There is no doubt that she used pretty basic stage gimmicks to cause phenomena such as "astral bells" and the materialization of "letters" from the masters. However, at some point she seems to have come to believe that behind all the mummery there was something real. In 1880, she and Olcott left America and moved to India. Not long after, while visiting Ceylon, they became the first Westerners ever to officially convert to Buddhism.

Five years later, Blavatsky returned to Europe in poor health, but Olcott remained in Asia and became deeply engaged in the Buddhist-based nationalist movement in Ceylon as well as an effort to reclaim the site at Bodh Gaya in Northern India where it was believed the Buddha had attained enlightenment.

Although Buddhism was the dominant spiritual tradition in Ceylon, it had been essentially eradicated in the land of its birth as the result of Hindu revivals and Muslim invaders. When Olcott and Blavatsky came to India, they found the temple commemorating the spot where the Buddha attained enlightenment in ruins and the site itself the property of a private Hindu land-owner. Along with a young Ceylonese – Anagarika Dharmapala – Olcott sought to rescue the site and return it to Buddhist control.[161] It was a project he was confident that all Buddhists, wherever they resided, would support. The unexpected challenge he encountered was that practitioners in different parts of the world didn't necessarily have a sense of fellowship with those in other areas; often even differing sects in a single country had little communication with one another.

Asian practitioners had never had a sense of there being a single tradition that could be identified as "Buddhist." There was almost no means of communication between the adherents of the Buddhadharma in one nation and those in another and so no sense of solidarity. It was the

---

161. The effort was only partially successful. The site is now a UNESCO world heritage site maintained by a committee made up of both Hindus and Buddhists. By the terms of the Bodh Gaya Act of 1949, there are five Hindus and four Buddhists on the committee.

western need to classify and categorize that resulted in things as disparate as Japanese koan practice and Tibetan tantrism being identified as elements of a single system that the West defined as "Buddhism."

Olcott believed it was important to unite the various expressions of the Buddhadharma and sought ways to achieve that end. In 1890, he organized a conference of Buddhists from Ceylon, Japan, and Burma at which he presented a document identifying fourteen beliefs "upon which all Buddhist sects could agree if disposed to promote brotherly feeling and a mutual sympathy between themselves."[162] After the conference delegates agreed to the terms of the document, Olcott traveled to the three countries seeking ratification of the document from the Buddhist authorities in those communities. He had no difficulty in Sri Lanka and Burma, but the Japanese abbots with whom he met objected that the fourteen principles only represented the Theravada perspective and failed to take into consideration the broader understanding of Mahayana Buddhism. According to a story one hopes isn't apocryphal, Olcott is said to have asked them, "If I were to bring a basketful of soil from Mount Fuji, would it not be part of the sacred mountain? In the same way, even if this is only a small basket, is it not also a portion of the Buddhadharma?" The analogy, it is said, was enough to sway representatives from Nichiren, Pure Land, Tendai, and Zen schools to sign the document.

19th Century Japan

After controlling Japan for more than 250 years, the Tokugawa Shogunate came to an end twenty years before Olcott's arrival. It was followed by the Meiji Restoration, a period during which Japan made significant strides towards becoming a major global industrial and military power.

During the period of isolation from the west, the Tokugawa had effectively enforced a truce between the previously warring clans as a result of which local daimyo lost a great deal of their personal powers. The daimyo naturally resented this, but the political stability that had been imposed stimulated a vibrant cultural growth on the islands. An urban class developed with refined tastes, and Zen-inspired disciplines like the tea ceremony flourished, as well as the visual and literary arts.

But when the Tokugawa proved powerless to prevent US intervention in Japanese affairs, its hold on the nation was shaken. Young members of the military class, in particular, resented the humiliation of the national capitulation to foreign influences and in response formed a society called Ishin Shishi – the Men of High Moral Purpose – that advocated a return

---

162. Quoted in Rick Fields, *How the Swans Came to the Lake* (Boston: Shambhala, 1992), p. 114.

to imperial rule. Not only did they hold that political power should be restored to the divinely-born Emperor, but that Japan needed to be cleansed of foreign influences, including both Buddhism and neo-Confucianism which were considered imported traditions.

Although Shinto was declared the state religion during the Meiji Restoration, the population largely remained Buddhist. Nor did the authorities rescind a law – which had been enacted to prevent a resurgence of Christianity – that required families to be registered members of a Buddhist temple. The most popular form of Buddhism remained Pure Land, but the Soto and Rinzai schools also had significant followings.

Soto Zen was predominant in rural areas and, numerically, was the larger of the two. Temples, at times very small, had been established throughout the countryside, requiring large numbers of priests to service them. The major Soto training centers still taught a highly disciplined form of Buddhist practice focused on shikan taza meditation, but most of the students they trained would spend their careers tending to the needs of their parishioners instead of focusing on personal spiritual development.

Meiji authorities, in an attempt to diminish Buddhist influence, enacted laws that allowed and even encouraged Buddhist clergy to marry. An unintended consequence of this law was that responsibility for many Soto temples came to be passed down from father to son. Students who were training to take up the family business, as it were, often had a pragmatic attitude to their Zen studies and little interest in undertaking a lengthy and arduous quest for awakening.

Rinzai was the dominant form of Zen in urban centers and faced a different set of challenges. Rinzai temples no longer functioned as schools for the upper classes, as they had under the Gozan system, but they remained among the foremost cultural institutions in Japan. Consequently, abbots were expected to be men of refinement and sophistication. Not only did they need to demonstrate their spiritual credentials by passing as many as 1700 koans, they also needed to be proficient in Zen-inspired arts such as *ikebana* (flower arranging), the tea ceremony, and calligraphy, to be well-versed in classical Chinese poetry, and even to be above average players of the game of Go.

Both Rinzai and Soto monasteries continued to attract people who sought not to just understand Buddhist doctrine but to have experiential insight into it; however, they also drew individuals motivated by ambition or seeking to establish careers. And both sects suffered from the inevitable compromises and abuses that accompany institutionalization.

Ethnic Buddhism in America

Of course, even though the dominant culture in the United States had been unaware of it, Buddhism – and Mahayana Buddhism at that – had crept in the back door and established itself in America decades before Olcott and Blavatsky took their refuge vows. It came with the successive waves of Chinese migrants who made their way to California to work the gold fields and later on the transcontinental railroad. The first Buddhist temple in America was established in San Francisco in 1853; before the end of the century there would be more than 400 temples on the west coast stretching from California to British Colombia.

When Commodore Perry opened Japan to the West, he also opened the West to Japan, and, starting in 1868, Japanese laborers made their way to the Hawaiian Islands to work in the sugar cane fields. In 1889, the first Japanese temple outside of Japan was established on those islands for the benefit of these migrants.

The situation that Asian immigrants knowingly accepted when coming to America and Hawaii indicates just how difficult things must have been in their homeland. Working conditions in the west were deplorable. Migrants faced discrimination, violence, and even lynching. Laws were enacted to prevent them from attaining citizenship. They were subject to unequal taxation. In Hawaii – which at the time was still independent of the US – Japanese farmers were drawn by promises that were not kept:

> – workers were sent to outlying plantations where the work was long and hard…Men fell in debt to company stores, and gambling, drinking and prostitution spread through the camps.
>
> "Hawaii, Hawaii," went a song the Japanese made up as they worked in the hot sun, sweating under the heavy clothes they wore as protection against the thorny leaves of sugar cane.
>
> Like a dream so I came
> But my tears are flowing now
> In the canefields.[163]

The temples on both the islands and the mainland were more than places for devotional activity. They were cultural centers where the traditions of the homeland were treated with honor. The forms that first established themselves in the west were Pure Land in Hawaii and an eclectic mix of Daoism, Confucianism, and Buddhism in California.

Zen didn't make its way to the New World until 1893, and when it did it first appeared neither on the West Coast nor in Hawaii but in Chicago.

---

163. Fields, op. cit., p. 78.

Imakita Kosen and Soyen Shaku

Imakita Kosen was raised in an upper-class Confucian family at the end of the Tokugawa Era. He had been trained in both Neo-Confucianism and Daoism before beginning Zen studies at Sokokuji in Kyoto and later at Sogenji in Okayama. His study of Daoism led him to Zen, but his Neo-Confucian training also played a major role in his formation. His Zen would later be said to have the "savor of Confucianism," with its strict sense of social obligations.

While studying with Gisan Zenkai at Sogenji, Kosen had a powerful awakening experience:

> One night during *zazen* practice the boundary between before and after suddenly disappeared. I entered into the blessed realm of the totally wondrous. It was as if I had arrived at the ground of the Great Death, with no memory of the existence of anything, not even myself. All I remember is an energy in my body that spread out over ten times ten-thousand worlds and a light that radiated endlessly. At one point, as I took a breath, seeing and hearing, speaking and moving suddenly became different from what they had normally been. As I sought for the highest principle and the wondrous meaning of the universe, my own self became clear and all things appeared bright. In this abundance of delight, I forgot that my hands were moving in the air and my feet were dancing.[164]

In spite of Meiji opposition to Buddhism, Kosen was a staunch nationalist and supported the aims of the Restoration. During his tenure as abbot at Engakuji in Kamakura, he also served in the office of the national Superior Overseer of Religious Teaching in Tokyo. Kosen understood the reservations government officials had about Zen and recognized the need to transform some of its more archaic structures. To that end, he advocated promoting meditation training not only to monastics but to the lay population as well. At this point in the history of Zen, that was a revolutionary idea. Kosen created the *Ryomo Kyokai* – the Society for the Abandonment of Concepts – which introduced both university students and young Japanese professionals to Zen practice.

It was an ordained monk, however, who would become his heir – a young man whom Kosen would describe as a "born Bodhisattva." Soyen Shaku would also become the first Zen master to set foot in America.

---

164. Heinrich Dumoulin, *Zen Buddhism: A History – Japan* (Bloomington, IN: World Wisdom, 1990), p. 408.

He was born in 1859, just six years after the opening of Japan to the west, and as a child was enrolled in a temple school where – according to his own assessment – he learned to be filial to his parents, helpful to his siblings, loyal to his country, faithful to his compatriots, and respectful of the Three Treasures.[165] When he was 12, he became a monk, which wasn't an unusual age for that step.

After working with two prior teachers, Soyen eventually came to study with Imakita Kosen. He mastered the koan system quickly and easily and received inka from Kosen when he was only 25 years old. Normally after receiving transmission, a monk would undertake a pilgrimage to other Zen temples throughout the country to have his understanding tested and deepened, but Kosen encouraged Soyen, instead, to enroll in the newly established Keio University in Tokyo.

Soyen spent three years there during which he learned about other forms of Buddhism and developed a desire to deepen his understanding of the Buddhadharma by traveling to Ceylon in order to explore Theravada teachings. Before the restoration, travel restrictions had prevented Japanese from leaving the country and such a journey would have been impossible, but, now that these had been lifted, he was free to undertake the voyage.

It proved to be more challenging than he had anticipated. He admired the life-style of the Ceylonese monks and their commitment to the precepts; however, he was never able to communicate with them very well, and he realized that they would be bewildered if he attempted to explain Zen with its emphasis on personal enlightenment. An even greater frustration was the climate. Unused to the heat and humidity of the tropics, he didn't have the physical endurance to take part in the begging rounds – called takahatsu in Japanese – by which the monks traditionally supported themselves. In a letter he wrote to Kosen, he remarked that things in Ceylon were so different that only the barking of the dogs seemed familiar

Shortly after Soyen returned to Japan, Kosen died, and Soyen succeeded him as the abbot of Engakuji.

Like Kosen, Soyen was a political conservative and generally accepted the social and economic policies of the Meiji government. He was a product of his era and environment and, as such, took for granted the belief that the Japanese people were the unique descendants of a sacred royal household.

His education, which had trained him to be loyal to his nation and faithful to his compatriots, led him to support the country's military incursions into China and Russia, explaining in a letter to Leo Tolstoy – who had asked him to condemn the actions – that "sometimes killing and war are necessary to defend the values and harmony of an innocent country, race, or individual." During the Russo-Japanese War [1904-05], Soyen

---

165. Buddha, Dharma, and Sangha. Cf. pp. 40-41 above.

took leave from his duties at Engakuji to serve as a chaplain in the First Army Division and would later argue that Japanese victory was due, in part, to the strength the nation derived from Buddhist culture and specifically from Zen training which instilled a "Samurai spirit" in the population. It was a perspective that gradually came to be shared by government officials who'd previously been distrustful of Buddhism. By the end of the Russo-Japanese War, Zen practice was no longer considered suspect.

The World Parliament of Religions

The 1893 Chicago World's Fair – also known as the Columbian Exposition – was a celebration of the material progress humankind had made in the four hundred years since Columbus's arrival in the islands of the Caribbean. Twenty-seven million people attended the event that was unashamedly an expression of American Exceptionalism. No mention, naturally, was made of the negative impact of European arrival on indigenous populations or of other social, environmental, and human costs associated with the march of human progress, such as the still unknown number of Chinese laborers who died during construction of the trans-continental railroad.[166]

A group of Protestant clergymen saw the fair as an opportunity to hold a World Parliament of Religions in the city at the same time. The Parliament organizers intended to demonstrate that, rather than casting doubt on religion as the evolutionists appeared to have done, modern scholarship – which had now resulted in English translations of most of the world's scriptures – proved that humankind had been guided by "divine providence through all ages and all lands." In the same way that

---

166. "The Central Pacific did not keep records of the deaths of any workers on the railroad. Some historians estimate from engineering reports, newspaper articles and other sources that between 50 to 150 Chinese were killed as a result of snow slides, landslides, explosions, falls and other accidents. Chinese practice was to bury the deceased temporarily and at a later date collect the remains in a box in a ritual fashion. The bones would then be shipped back to China to be reburied in the worker's home village. One newspaper article entitled 'Bones in Transit' of June 30, 1870 in the Sacramento Reporter reported that 'about 20,000 pounds of bones' dug up from shallow graves were taken by train for return to China, calculating that this amounted to 1,200 Chinese. Another article published on the same day in the Sacramento Union stated that only the bones of about 50 Chinese were on the train. Others believe that some Chinese must have also died in a smallpox outbreak among railroad workers, although there are no records if any of the dead were Chinese. In addition, there were reports of Chinese workers being killed in Nevada as the result of Indian raids. Charles Crocker, testifying before Congress after the line was completed, acknowledged that a great many men were lost during construction – and most of those workers were Chinese." From the Stanford University "North America Project," http://web.stanford.edu/group/chineserailroad/cgi-bin/wordpress/faqs/.

the World Fair presented America as the pinnacle of material success, so would the Parliament demonstrate the superiority of Christianity over all other faith traditions. In the closing ceremonies, the Chairman of the Parliament, John Henry Barrows, confidently proclaimed that it had "shown that Christianity is still the great quickener of humanity…that there is no teacher to be compared with Christ, and no Saviour excepting Christ…I doubt if any Orientals who were present misinterpreted the courtesy with which they were received into a readiness on the part of the American people to accept Oriental faiths in place of their own."[167] One of those visiting Orientals to whom Barrows referred was Soyen Shaku.

Soyen had only been abbot of Engakuji for a year when he received the invitation to take part in the Parliament. Other, more experienced, abbots advised him to refuse it on the grounds that the barbarians of the United States couldn't possibly understand or appreciate the Buddhadharma. After careful consideration, however, Shaku decided to take part. He composed two papers to be presented at the Parliament but, because he had only a rudimentary knowledge of English, asked one of his students, Teitaro Suzuki, to translate them for him.

His principal paper dealt with Buddhist teachings on "cause and effect" and was read to the participants by Barrows. It was received politely but without the enthusiasm that the audience demonstrated for some of the more charismatic Asian presenters, such as Olcott's collaborator, Anagarika Dharmapala. One attendee who was impressed by Soyen's paper, however, was Paul Carus, a publisher and editor who was one of a growing number of people who wondered if Buddhism might not be better able to overcome the rift between the religion and science than Christianity could. Soyen's paper was in accord with his own thought, and Carus asked Soyen if he would consider remaining in the United States a while longer to participate in a project to prepare translations of Buddhist – in particular, Mahayana – texts for publication in English. Soyen demurred, stating that he was not qualified to do so and that his duties at Engakuji prevented him from taking on other responsibilities; he noted, however, that he had a student he thought was suitable for the task.

D.T. Suzuki

Teitaro Suzuki was born in 1870 to a samurai family, that – prior to the Meiji Era – would have been a privileged position in feudal Japan. After the Meiji reforms, however, those privileges were lost. His father died when Teitaro was only six years old, leaving the family in poverty. His mother – who suffered from failing eyesight – received a small widow's

---

167. Quoted in Fields, op. cit., p. 129.

pension that she supplemented by taking in boarders. A year after their father's death, Teitaro's older brother also passed away. So it was that while still very young, he came to wonder why he had had to face so many difficulties in life. He took his concerns to the priest at the Buddhist temple to which his family belonged and to the Christian missionaries proselytizing in his community, but neither could give him an answer.

His introduction to Zen came while he was attending Upper Middle School. One of the teachers was a lay disciple of Imakita Kosen and hosted a discussion group about Zen for students. This teacher gave Suzuki a copy a collection of letters written by Hakuin Ekaku. Although he found the book difficult to understand, it was enough to goad him to seek out an authorized Zen teacher.

The nearest Zen temple was at Kokutaiji in the adjacent prefecture of Etchu. It was there that the young Suzuki had the discouraging experience of being told to wait in a private room and meditate – with no further instruction – until the teacher returned to the monastery. When the teacher did finally see the boy, he dismissed his questions as being of no importance and ended the interview.

Suzuki was a good student and learned what passed for English in the Japanese school system of the day. While still engaged in his own studies, he found work teaching English at a primary school although, when he later attended Waseda University in Tokyo and encountered spoken English for the first time, he discovered that what he had been teaching bore little resemblance to the actual language.

His childhood questions still hadn't been resolved and, while at university, he sought out and became a student of Imakita Kosen. Kosen died within a year, and Suzuki continued his training with Soyen Shaku, who assigned him the koan Mu. For lay students like Suzuki, the week-long meditation retreats called sesshin were particularly important. During these, students spent the whole day engaged in zazen, meeting regularly with their teacher in formal interviews – sanzen – to be tested on their understanding of the koan on which they were working. Suzuki struggled with Mu for four years, unable to resolve it. At one point, he wondered if his difficulty was due to a lack of familiarity with Zen literature and so immersed himself in the books of the temple library. This would prove to be of great value later, when he began writing, but was of no help whatsoever in understanding Mu.

Suzuki was probably not one of Soyen's more promising students, and Soyen may not have given him much thought until he needed someone to help him in his correspondence with the organizing committee of the Parliament of Religions. Then, when Paul Carus asked Soyen to consider remaining in the United States to work on the translation project, he suggested that Teitaro Suzuki would be better suited for the position.

It was a great opportunity for a young man, but Suzuki realized that if he accepted the offer, he might not be able to partake in sesshin for many years. If he did not resolve Mu during the upcoming sesshin, he would not have another opportunity to do so until he returned to Japan, and he had no idea when that would be. As it happened, the next retreat was the December Rohatsu Sesshin marking the anniversary of the Buddha's awakening. Traditionally it's the most demanding sesshin of the year; the periods of zazen are extended, and the participants are spurred on by frequent blows from the *kyosaku* – or "encouragement" stick.[168]

Suzuki concentrated on Mu with all his might, synchronizing it with his breath. By the final days of the retreat, the koan was no longer something separate from him. He entered the deep state of concentration – samadhi – in which there was not the koan on the one hand and the person repeating it on the other; there was only Mu. In an article he prepared for the British Buddhist Society many years later, Suzuki described the condition this way:

> Up till then I had always been conscious that *Mu* was in my mind. But so long as I was conscious of *Mu* it meant that I was somehow separate from *Mu*, and that is not a true *samadhi*. But towards the end of that sesshin, about the fifth day, I ceased to be conscious of *Mu*. I was one with *Mu*, identified with *Mu*, so that there was no longer the separateness implied by being conscious of *Mu*. This is the real state of *samadhi*.[169]

Then, after one of the rounds of meditation, he was roused from this concentrated state by the sound of a bell being rung, and Mu was resolved. He achieved *satori*, the awakening to one's true nature – the *raison d'être* of Zen – about which he would write so tantalizingly in the future.

> Without the attainment of satori no one can enter into the mystery of Zen. It is the sudden flashing of a new truth hitherto altogether undreamed of. It is a sort of mental catastrophe taking place all at once after so much piling of matters intellectual and demonstrative.[170]

Suzuki rushed to sanzen and was able to answer all but one of the testing

---

168. A long stick flattened at one end, used by monitors during zazen to encourage (or wake up) meditators.
169. D.T. Suzuki, *The Field of Zen* (New York: Perennial Library, 1970), pp. 10.
170. D.T. Suzuki, *Essays in Zen Buddhism: First Series* (London: Rider and Company, 1973), p.261.

questions Soyen put to him; the next morning, he was able to answer that question as well. Soyen acknowledged the validity of his awakening and gave Suzuki the Buddhist name "Daisetz" meaning "Great Simplicity." Suzuki retained the name for the rest of his life, joking that it actually meant "Great Stupidity."

Suzuki joined Carus at his home in LaSalle, Illinois, in 1897. His first assignment was to assist with a translation of the *Dao De Jing*. Suzuki was not happy with the rendition that resulted, believing that Carus distorted the work by his use of Western terminology which did not adequately reflect the intention of the text. Suzuki took it upon himself to translate Ashvaghosha's *Awakening of Faith in the Mahayana*,[171] which would be the first of many books in English he would release under his own name. This was published in 1900, after which Suzuki began work on *Outlines of Mahayana Buddhism*, in which he sought to counter the perception of western scholars who viewed the Mahayana as a degenerate form of Buddhism compared to the older Theravada School.

Soyen Shaku's Second Visit to North America

Following the Parliament, there was growing academic and popular interest in Buddhism, although the number of Westerners who gave serious thought to adopting the Buddhist faith was miniscule. There were a few, however, some of whom even found their way to Engakuji and undertook Zen training under Soyen Shaku's tutelage. In 1905, one of these, a San Francisco resident named Ida Russell, invited Soyen to make a second visit to the United States as her guest.

Soyen accepted the invitation and stayed with the Russells long enough to introduce Ida to koan study, making her the first person in North America known to work on koans with an authorized teacher. Arrangements were made for Soyen to give a number of talks to the Japanese immigrant communities in San Francisco, Los Angeles, Sacramento and Oakland. Then in 1906, attended by Suzuki, he proceeded across the country by train. During that tour, Soyen met a range of political and academic figures, including President Theodore Roosevelt, and gave public lectures on Zen. Like Suzuki in his *Outline of Mahayana Buddhism*, Soyen sought to correct popular misconceptions. Christian critics had been vociferous in condemning Buddhism as a negative and

---

171. The document known as the *Daijōkishinron* – which Suzuki translates as "Awakening of Faith" – was attributed to the Indian Buddhist Ashvaghosa in the first century BCE; however, it is more likely a Chinese composition of the 6th century CE.

life-denying doctrine whose goal was the total extinction of the person in Nirvana. Soyen argued instead that Buddhism was life-affirming, and that through meditation practice the individual came into direct contact with

> – the most concrete and withal the most universal fact of life...
> It is the philosopher's business to deal with dry, lifeless, uninteresting generalizations. Buddhists are not concerned with things like that. They want to see the fact directly and not through the medium of philosophical abstractions. There may be a god who created heaven and earth, or there may not; we could be saved simply by believing in his goodness, or we could not...True Buddhists do not concern themselves with propositions such as these...Buddhists through [meditation] endeavor to reach the bottom of things and there to grasp with their own hands the very life of the universe, which makes the sun rise in the morning, makes the bird cheerfully sing in the balmy spring breeze, and also makes the biped called man hunger for love, righteousness, liberty, truth, and goodness.[172]

The Introduction of Zen to the West

Zen was the first Buddhist tradition to be established in North America outside of the ethnic communities,[173] and this was largely due to Suzuki's writing. In 1908, he left Carus's publishing house, undertook a tour of Europe, then returned to Japan, where he eventually married an American woman – Beatrice Erskine – whom he'd met in New York. They lived in a small cottage in the Engakuji compound until 1919, after which they moved to Kyoto where Suzuki taught at Otani University.

The couple founded the Eastern Buddhist Society and published an English language journal, *The Eastern Buddhist*, to which they both made frequent contributions. A number of Suzuki's articles were collected and published by the British company, Rider, in 1927 under the title, *Essays in Zen Buddhism*. The book related Tang dynasty koans and tales never before heard in the west and was surprisingly successful. More than any other work to that date, it would be responsible for promoting a popular interest in Zen outside of Asia.

Suzuki was 57 when *Essays in Zen Buddhism* was released; his output after its publication was prodigious. A second and third volume of *Essays*

---

172. Quoted in Peter Matthiessen, *Nine-Headed Dragon River* (Boston: Shambala, 1998), p. 14.
173. In Europe – particularly in Britain which had colonized Sri Lanka – the first inquiries into Buddhism focused on the Theravada tradition.

were brought out by Rider. He released a translation of the *Lankavatara Sutra* in 1932; *The Training of the Zen Buddhist Monk* was published in 1934; and *Zen Buddhism and Its Influence on Japanese Culture* came out in 1938, the same year that Beatrice published *Mahayana Buddhism*.

The appeal of Suzuki's books was due to the portrait he gave of a religion that stood in stark contrast to the Judeo-Christian heritage of the West – a religion without a deity, a religion that held that the practitioner could attain the same insight and awareness its founder had had. In response to those critics who viewed the Mahayana as a distortion of the Buddha's original teaching, Suzuki insisted that a vital religion must not be limited to its earliest expression but must demonstrate the ability to evolve. Zen, he argued, was Buddhism "shorn of its Indian garb," the cultural and historical trappings of the original teaching. What was central to Zen, after all, was not a "dependence on words and letters" but the transmission of the original awakening experience by which Siddhartha Gautama became the Buddha and which he passed onto his disciple, Mahakasyapa.

Later scholars would accuse Suzuki of providing a distorted description of Zen. He largely ignored the Soto school and even his presentation of Rinzai teaching and practice was very personal. Regardless of whether it was objective or not, it was a presentation that would resonate with a much larger audience than he – or anyone else – could have foreseen.

A talk he gave at Oxford in 1953 summarizes the themes to which he returned time and again in his writing.[174]

He started from the premise that Zen was "a combination of Chinese psychology and Indian philosophy" that provided a practical demonstration of "the highly abstract teachings" of Indian Buddhism. The goal of Zen Buddhism is not to understand the Buddha's teaching but to share his experience of awakening or satori. The Buddha was not – as was Jesus in Christianity – a being of a different order; he was an ordinary man. So, what he attained, others could attain as well.

The Buddha's understanding came from his quest to answer the great questions of life and death and all other forms of duality:

> – or, as we might say nowadays…the bifurcation of subject and object. When we are faced with this bifurcation, when subject and object oppose one another, the result is the anxiety and fear which troubles us all.

The Buddha first sought to resolve this issue through philosophical analysis, and, when that proved inadequate, "he turned to moral discipline

---

[174]. "Buddha and Zen" in Suzuki, *The Field of Zen*, pp. 13-20.

and ascetic practice" as undertaken by the yogic tradition of the time. This, too, proved futile. "Thus, neither intellectual discipline nor moral discipline availed to solve this problem."

> Now the religious or spiritual life is something which transcends an intellectual attempt to reach reality. Other religions emphasize moral discipline, but moral endeavor can never reach the realm of spirituality. When we have attained the spiritual plane, moral life emanates naturally, but moral discipline and intellection will never bring us to this spiritual life. We must transcend the subject-object aspect of existence.
>
> How are we to reach this transcendental realm? It is reached when the personality and the teaching, or the questioner and the question, are identified. So long as Buddha had his question before him; so long as he had it outside and separate from himself, as if it could be solved by external means, it could never be solved. The question comes out of the questioner. But when it is out, the questioner mistakenly thinks it is something outside himself. The question is answered only when it is identified with the questioner.

To analyze a problem philosophically is to separate oneself from the problem. "When the question goes out from the questioner and becomes separated from him, he cannot solve it." It is precisely the "bifurcation" of subject/object that is the root of the problem of life and death. Humankind, according to Suzuki, has

> – a persistent desire to return to the state of innocence prior, epistemologically speaking, to creation, to the state where there is no division, no knowledge – prior to the subject-object division, to the time when there was only God as He was before He created the world. The separation of God from the world is the source of all our troubles. We have an innate desire to be united with God.

After failing to do so through intellectual or moral effort, the Buddha sought to address the matter of duality by turning inward through meditation. He took his place beneath the Bodhi Tree and sat. At first his mind remained in "great turmoil," but eventually consciousness sank

> – back into itself. This is what is called samadhi, being absorbed in meditation, and when we come to this everything is lost. There is psychologically a complete state of unconsciousness.

But when this state is reached, even this is not final. There must be awakening, and this awakening usually takes place through sense-stimulation.

In Suzuki's case it had been the sound of the bell. For the Buddha, it was the sight of the morning star. When he saw the star on the horizon, he saw into his true nature and was awakened to that unity which precedes and underlies dualism. The full significance of this awareness can only be appreciated when one comes to awakening oneself. Buddhism, therefore, is the

> – religion of enlightenment. To understand it, we have to become enlightened ourselves. By being enlightened we attain *bodhi*[175] and become Buddha; it is by experiencing bodhi that we become real Buddhist followers.

"...and Never the Twain Shall Meet."

Zen is a Japanese interpretation of Chinese Chan, which in turn was a Daoist interpretation of Indian Buddhism, and differed so much from the earlier forms of the Buddhadharma that Soyen Shaku realized it would be hopeless to try to explain it to the monks he lived with in Ceylon. The Zen story maintains it is a practice that has been passed in unbroken succession from teacher to student since the Buddha's transmission to Mahakasyapa down to the present. In fact, while the focus on meditation may be a constant – at least after the tradition entered China – in all other aspects the teaching has been adopted and modified to accommodate particular circumstances. Korean "Soen" and Vietnamese "Thien" both claim common descent from Linji Chan but are distinguished from Japanese Zen by the unique characteristics of the cultures in which they arose. Further, those interpretations took place in environments in which the basic tenets of Mahayana Buddhism – and Daoism – were embedded in the culture, where the words of the *Heart Sutra* were as familiar as the formula of the Lord's Prayer is in the West. Inevitably what would come to be considered Zen in North America – where this is not the case – is very much a Western interpretation of an Asian spiritual tradition marked by its own distinctive non-Buddhist perspective.

The reason Suzuki objected to Paul Carus's translation of the *Dao De Jing* was because Carus used Western terms in an attempt to make the text

---

175. As Suzuki uses the term, "bodhi" is roughly to see things are they actually are rather than as one thinks of them. In this sense, a Bodhisattva is one who has attained such wisdom.

accessible to his readers. Translations of Asian spiritual writing not only needed to overcome the challenges of language but of those fundamental differences in point of view that had thwarted the first Jesuit missionaries in their conversations with Buddhist teachers in Japan.

Suzuki was just as guilty of floundering here as Carus had been. In spite of his insistence that the concept of "God" is foreign to Buddhism, he used the term in the Oxford lecture quoted above when referring to an ultimate reality behind existence similar to what the Chinese meant by Dao. The fact that he was using the term analogously rather than literally didn't prevent readers from misunderstanding and making an identification that he hadn't intended.

It could be argued that both "Dao" and "God" are metaphors for something that cannot be defined, but the terms are not equivalent. The idea of "God" implies volition, intention, and moral expectation, none of which are associated with the Dao. From early on in the transition of Buddhism and Zen from Asia to North America and Europe, a pattern emerged in which western readers "interpreted" Buddhism in a manner consistent with their own cultural heritage.

Suzuki was a prolific writer. Over his career, he composed more than one hundred books in Japanese and another thirty in English. Most of these were written before the outbreak of the War in the Pacific, but his popular success largely came after the war. His work was admired by figures as diverse as the pioneer psychotherapist, Carl Jung, and the Catholic monk, Thomas Merton, whose imprimaturs gave Zen – as Suzuki portrayed it – an intellectual credibility in the West denied to other non-Christian traditions. At the same time, his writing retained an aura of the exotic that attracted the attention of people who might have been drawn to spiritualism or Theosophy. Two successive but very different cultural movements – the Beats in the 1950s and the Hippies a decade later – were drawn to Zen and other Asian traditions in this way. It is notable, however, that when they began their exploration of Buddhism, they did not do so in the temples serving the Asian populations in the country, that they correctly recognized as devotional centers for lay people. What the early Western students were drawn to was the monastic practice of meditation – although not to the restraints of monastic discipline – and, ironically, they often viewed this not as a means of seeing through the illusion of the personal self but as a means of personal growth.

Throughout the '50s and '60s, much of the West's understanding of Zen was based on the writings of either Suzuki or Alan Watts, whose early books were largely a reworking of Suzuki. The vision presented in these books was one that many American and European readers found attractive, but like many allurements they were not without their distortions. Suzuki had limitations. He wrote as a scholar rather than as a teacher, and – as critics like Philip Kapleau would later complain – provided almost no attention to the how-to element, to the mechanics of meditation. Consequently, his Zen was literary and theoretical, rather than practical.

Other critics argued that his presentation was too narrow, focusing almost exclusively on Rinzai Zen. Although in later life he would write about the Pure Land School and about Western mystics such as Meister Eckhart, he wrote very little about Soto Zen and what he did write was often dismissive. Even his portrayal of the Rinzai School overlooked the devotional and ritual practices common in Rinzai temples. Other critics chastised him for separating Zen from its foundations in traditional Buddhism and presenting it as something fundamental to all spiritual traditions – as he put it, "the ultimate fact of all philosophy and religion."[176]

As I've written elsewhere, in many cases, these criticisms amounted to little more than complaints that Suzuki did not present Zen the way his critics would have. Suzuki was not an authorized Zen teacher, nor did he claim to be; however, it was through his writing that the concept of satori – no matter how misunderstood – was first presented to the west, raising the possibility of a way of perceiving reality outside the common dualistic framework of Western thought. His belief in the universality of Zen insight allowed Western readers, still attached to their own religious heritages, to investigate how those traditions could be enhanced or deepened through Zen. There have been more profound writers on Zen since Suzuki, and there have, no doubt, been many whose Zen insight was deeper than his. But no matter how flawed his presentation may have been, it was his exposition of Zen that introduced it to the West and inspired the first Western practitioners to seek out teachers.

And if some sought in Zen something that it didn't offer, there were others who would complete the transference to the west – including a man who spent all of the Second World War in a Japanese prisoner of war camp, a former soldier who had taken part in the American invasion of Okinawa, a missionary priest stationed in Hiroshima when the atom bomb fell, and a court reporter at the Nuremburg and Tokyo war crimes trials.

---

176. Suzuki, *Essays in Zen Buddhism: First Series*, p. 268.

In India during the time of Bodhidharma, Buddhism was in a state of decline. So Bodhidharma's teacher told him to take the Dharma to the East. Likewise in Japan, Buddhism is now dead. And so you, my Dharma heir, who know the true teachings of the Buddha, take them to the West so that Buddhism may again flourish.

Kodo Sawaki's instructions to Taisen Deshimaru

Out of Asia[177]

Nyogen Senzaki

WHEN SOYEN SHAKU accepted the invitation from the Russells to come to San Francisco, he brought a young attendant with him named Nyogen Senzaki.

Senzaki had been raised by his grandfather, an abbot in the Pure Land tradition. The grandfather was a devout man who lamented the degraded condition to which Buddhism had fallen in Japan. When he sensed that his grandson was drawn to religious life, he encouraged the boy to live by the Buddhist precepts but discouraged him from ordaining. "Corruption among Buddhist priests keeps getting worse," he told his grandson. "Although you have always wished to leave secular life and seek the great Dharma, entering monkhood may, ironically, hinder your goal. Beware of joining that pack of tigers and wolves called monks."[178]

Senzaki entered a pre-med program after his grandfather's death but continued his Buddhist studies as well. He first learned of Zen through the poetry of Matsuo Basho and, delving further into the literature, happened upon the story of Deshan Xuanjian (J: Tokuzan Senkan), a Tang dynasty monk and student of the *Diamond Sutra*. Deshan came to realize that his academic study was not furthering his spiritual development so one day he burned all the notes he had gathered on the sutra and began his formation anew under the direction of Zen Master Lungtan Chongzin. Inspired by this example, in 1896 Senzaki gave up his medical studies, ordained as a monk, and began study with Soyen Shaku.

At some point during training, he became disturbed by the disparity he saw between the Buddhist vow to "liberate" all creatures and the secluded, comfortable existence monks led far from the daily cares of lay

---

177. A fuller treatment of the material in this and the succeeding chapter can be found in my previous work, *The Third Step East* (Sumeru, 2015).

178. Nyogen Senzaki, *Eloquent Silence* (Boston: Wisdom Publications, 2008) p. 367.

life. He was also disillusioned by many of the priests he met who paid slack attention to the precepts. He never questioned Soyen's commitment to the Dharma nor the sincerity of his teacher's vows, but he saw little of that same zeal among the majority of priests in the Zen establishment. Recalling his grandfather's words, he found himself in sympathy with the criticisms common during the Meiji Restoration about the nature of the Buddhist clergy.

With Soyen's support, Senzaki returned to his home village and established a primary school that he called a "Mentorgarten." His envisioned an institution in which students and teachers would "mentor" one another; however, he didn't have the financial resources necessary to maintain the school, and, when Soyen invited him to be his attendant in San Francisco, he was grateful for the opportunity.

The Russells didn't understanding the relationship between the Zen master and his attendant and assumed Senzaki was a servant, so they took him on as a houseboy. His duties included doing laundry and general cleaning. Their housekeeper, however, decided the new houseboy's English wasn't adequate for his duties and dismissed him. Senzaki gathered his few possessions into a suitcase and set out on foot to find one of the hotels in San Francisco that catered to Japanese clientele. Soyen, who had not intervened on Senzaki's behalf, accompanied him, carrying the suitcase. When they came to Golden Gate Park, Soyen handed over the suitcase and told Senzaki: "This may be better for you than being hampered by being my attendant. Just face the great city and see what happens – whether it conquers you or you it." He instructed Senzaki to find work in the city that would help him learn as much as he could about the country and its people. "You must come to understand these Americans before you will be able to teach them. Find work, no matter how modest; work in anonymity for at least seventeen years. Then you will be ready." Then the two parted, and, although they maintained a correspondence until Soyen's death in 1919, they never again met in person.

During those seventeen years, Senzaki worked as a household servant, farm laborer, hotel manager, cook, and language tutor. When he had time, he also meditated in the Japanese Gardens of Golden Gate Park and spent long hours at the public library reading American and European philosophy. He also wrote a series of articles on Zen that he sent back to Japanese periodicals, but he made no effort to teach.

In 1919 – the year Soyen Shaku died – Senzaki found a publisher in Japan for a collection of short tales he entitled *101 Zen Stories*. The book would later be translated into English by Paul Reps and be included, along with their translation of the *Mumonkan*, in a small volume called *Zen Flesh, Zen Bones*, that would become one of the most influential books published in America on Zen in the 1950s.

Senzaki had not completed his Zen training in Japan, and he never received inka, or formal sanction to teach, but he understood Soyen's words in Golden Gate Park as authorization to do so after the specified time had passed. So, when the seventeen-year period of silence came to an end in 1922, he rented a hall and gave a public lecture on Zen. The subject was meditation although no meditation instruction was provided. From time to time after this initial lecture, as money became available, Senzaki would present another. He had no permanent temple to work from and called this series of talks a "Floating Zendo."

His first audiences were primarily Japanese, but eventually a small number of curious occidentals also began to attend. These were often people drawn to Zen as result of their interest in Theosophy and the occult. Robert Aitken wrote that many of them:

> – were dealing with confused concepts about past lives, guidance from angelic beings, astral walking, and the like. People would corner this kind, clear-eyed man [Senzaki] and talk on and on about the mysteries of the pyramids or transmissions from ageless beings in the Himalayas. He would smile gently and say, "Oh, really? I didn't know that."[179]

As the number of non-Asian participants increased, Senzaki began to hold separate sessions for them, and, when he felt the members of his audience were ready, he instructed them in meditation. If D.T. Suzuki introduced Zen theory to America, Senzaki was the first to introduce Zen practice.

In 1931, he moved to Los Angeles where he continued to hold separate lectures for Japanese and non-Japanese audiences. He called the Los Angeles zendo the Mentorgarten Meditation Hall. By now, periods of zazen were a regular part of the evening's activity.

Senzaki informed his students that the purpose of both Buddhism and zazen was to come to the realization that from "the very beginning we are all buddhas, for our minds as well as our bodies are nothing but Dharmakaya, the Buddha's true body, with infinite light and eternal life. It is our delusion to see ourselves in the small cells of individual egos."[180]

He stressed, however, that this was something each student had to discover on his own.

> I am a senior student to you all, but I have nothing to impart to you. Whatever I have is mine, and never will be yours. You may consider me stingy and unkind, but I do not wish you to produce

---

179. Robert Aitken, *The Gateless Gate* (New York: North Point Press, 1991), p. 110.
180. Ibid., p. 238.

something that will dissolve and perish. I want each of you to discover your own inner treasure.[181]

During meditation, Senzaki's students sat in chairs rather than on cushions. He assigned them koans and held sanzen interviews after the meditation periods. He used the cases of the Mumonkan but also at times assigned a passage from Meister Eckhart as a koan.

> Meister Eckhart, a Christian mystic, said, "The eye with which I see God is the very eye with which God sees me." We use these words as a koan to cut off all attempts at conceptualizing. When you work on this koan, you will see that there is no God, no "me," but just one eye, glaring eternally. You are at the gate of Zen at that moment. Don't be afraid, just keep on meditating, repeating the koan in silence: "The eye with which I see God is the very eye with which God sees me." There is no reality other than this one eye.[182]

In 1934, Senzaki's landlady showed him a magazine from Japan that had published some poems written by a young Japanese Zen monk named Soen Nakagawa. The poet was reported to be a hermit on Dai Bosatsu Mountain near Mount Fuji. Like Senzaki, Nakagawa was openly critical of the lax moral lives and careerism of Zen clerics as well the vain ritualism that preoccupied temple life. Recognizing a fellow soul, Senzaki wrote to Nakagawa, sending him a copy of the translation work he and Paul Reps were engaged in. As a result of this initial correspondence, Senzaki and Nakagawa began an enduring long-distance friendship. In 1940, the younger monk made preparations to visit Senzaki in Los Angeles, but the outbreak of war between the United States and Japan prevented those plans from being carried out.

After the 1941 attack on Pearl Harbor, public attitude towards Japanese living in America was highly charged. All persons of Japanese descent were excluded from California as well as parts of other west coast states. They were eventually relocated to internment camps set up inland. Senzaki was sent to Heart Mountain in the Wyoming desert.

After the war, when the displaced Japanese returned to what had been their homes, they often found that their properties had been confiscated or foreclosed; former neighborhoods where they had dwelt were now occupied by people of other ethnic backgrounds. Many found themselves homeless. In 1945, forty years after he had parted from Soyen Shaku in

---

181. Ibid., p. 41.
182. Ibid.

Golden Gate Park, Senzaki had as little as he'd had when he first arrived in North America. He described his situation in a poem he wrote on the anniversary of Shaku's death:

> For forty years I have not seen
> My teacher, So-yen Shaku, in person.
> I have carried his Zen in my empty fist,
> Wandering ever since in this strange land.
> Being a mere returnee from the evacuation
> I could establish no Zendo
> Where his followers should commemorate
> The twenty-sixth anniversary of his death.
> The cold rain purifies everything on the earth
> In the great city of Los Angeles, today.
> I open my fist and spread the fingers
> At the street corner in the evening rush hour.[183]

After years of correspondence, Senzaki and Soen Nakagawa met in 1949 when the younger man visited Los Angeles. He stayed almost six months. Senzaki had hoped to entice him to remain in America and become his heir, but Nakagawa felt obligated to return to Japan, where the following year he was appointed abbot at Ryutakuji.

In 1955, Senzaki made his only return visit to Japan after fifty years away. Nakagawa recognized that his friend was becoming feebler with the passing years and kept apprised of his condition after Senzaki returned to America. In 1958, Nakagawa asked one of his younger monks who spoke English, Tai Shimano, to go to America to act as Senzaki's attendant, but, before Shimano was able to leave, they received word that Senzaki had died.

His ashes were divided in two. Half were buried in Los Angeles. The other half were reserved and would eventually be mixed with a portion of Soen Nakagawa's ashes to be buried at the Dai Bosatsu Zendo established by Tai Shimano in the Catskill Mountains of New York.

Nyogen Senzaki compared himself to a mushroom – without a deep root, no branches, no flowers, and probably no seeds. He underestimated the legacy he was to leave behind. He never acquired the celebrity that D.T. Suzuki attained, but through his students – several of whom went to Japan to study with Soen Nakagawa – the practice of Rinzai Zen obtained its first firm foothold in North America.

---

183. Quoted in Louis Nordstrom, *Namu Dai Bosa* (New York: Theatre Arts Books, 1976), p. 107.

Sokei-an and Ruth Fuller Sasaki

D.T. Suzuki was a scholar. Nyogen Senzaki was an effective teacher but not a formally authorized one. The first officially transmitted Zen teacher in North America was Sokei-an Sasaki.

His introduction to Zen occurred while he was studying art at the Imperial Academy in Tokyo. Discussing how to paint the sea, one of his teachers instructed the students:

> – not to sketch the waves on the seashore or to copy the waves in the ancient masterpieces. "Without brush or palette," he said, "go alone to the seashore and sit down on the sands. Then practice this: forget yourself until even your own existence is forgotten and you are entirely absorbed in the motion of the waves."[184]

Sasaki's love of art and nature eventually led him to formal Zen practice with one of Soyen Shaku's disciples, Sokatsu Shaku. When Sasaki presented himself at the temple and asked to be accepted as a student, Sokatsu asked him, "What career do you follow?"

"I'm a wood-carver," Sasaki replied.

"And for how long have you practiced this craft?"

"Six years."

"Very well. Carve me a Buddha."

Sasaki returned to his studio and began a carving that, when completed, he presented to Sokatsu. The Zen master took the statue and demanded, "What is this?" Then he tossed it into a nearby pond. In that way, Sasaki's Zen training began.[185]

Sasaki was drafted during the Russo-Japanese War and was sent to Manchuria where he drove a dynamite wagon. Following the war, he joined Sokatsu and five others in an ill-fated attempt to establish a Zen community in America. Sokatsu wanted the members of the party to be married, so it was arranged for Sasaki to wed another student named Tomeko. In September of 1906, the group purchased a ten-acre farm in Hayward, California. It was not a well-thought-out endeavor. None of the Japanese had agricultural experience, and the land was poor. The enterprise failed after a single crop of strawberries was harvested. Sasaki and Tomeko left the farm to go to San Francisco where he enrolled at the California Institute of Art. While in San Francisco he met and was befriended by Nyogen

---

184. Michael Hotz (ed.), *Holding the Lotus to the Rock* (New York: Four Walls Eight Windows, 2003) e-edition, location 462.

185. Sasaki wasn't consistent in telling this story. At times he claimed it was Soyen Shaku who told him to "carve the Buddha."

Senzaki. The two would remain in contact throughout their lives although they did not always see eye to eye.

When Tomeko became pregnant, Sasaki had to earn a living. For a while, he repaired statues for an importer of Asian sculpture in California. Then he hiked north to Oregon where he was able to make use of his wartime experience by dynamiting tree stumps for a farmer. He also worked as a janitor in a bar and for a time as a professional dance partner at a roller rink. In the evenings, he sat in meditation on a rock by the river.

Eventually he and Tomeko came to Seattle, where he found work as a picture framer. He also took up writing and began a series of humorous reflections on American life for Japanese periodicals. Sasaki and Tomeko lived in humble circumstances. For a while, they stayed with the Salish people on an island in the Puget Sound. Like many Japanese, the couple had encountered a great deal of prejudice in America, and Tomeko felt more at ease with the Native Americans than she had anywhere else. When, in 1914, she became pregnant for the third time, she told Sasaki that she wanted her children to be raised in Japan. She left him and went to live with her mother-in-law.

Unencumbered by family obligations, Sasaki wandered about the United States for the next two years, arriving in New York City in 1916 at the age of 34. Because of his artistic leanings he gravitated to Greenwich Village. He was fascinated with the variety of lifestyles he'd come across during his travels, ranging from the conservative values of small-town America to the sophisticated charlatanism of the Bohemian community he fell in with in the Village. The essays Sasaki sent back to Japan became popular, and he acquired a literary reputation.

He was welcomed into the artistic milieu of the Village and led a comfortable life. Then on a hot and humid day in July 1919, he came upon the putrefying carcass of a horse lying in the street. The sight struck him so strongly that he immediately made arrangements to return to Japan in order to resume formal Zen practice with Sokatsu.

He tried reconciling with Tomeko but remained restless and soon returned to the US. For several years, he travelled back and forth by steamship between Japan and America, studying Zen with Sokatsu and working as an art restorer in New York. Eventually, during one of his return trips to Japan, he realized that if he were serious about Zen, he needed to commit to it until he achieved full awakening, and he threw his wood carving tools into the sea as a pledge to do so.

Sokatsu assigned Sasaki the koan based on the story of the Sixth Patriarch, who demanded of General Ming, "Show me your original face, your face before your parents were born." Sasaki had been looking into Western philosophy and tried to reply to the koan in the light of his reading. Often, however, he barely began to speak before Sokatsu rang the bell dismissing him. Finally, Sokatsu bellowed, "Before father and mother there were no words! Show me your face before their births without words!"

After that encounter, Sasaki said:

– I wiped out all the notions from my mind. I gave up all desire. I discarded all the words with which I thought and stayed in quietude. I felt a little queer – as if I were being carried into something, or as if I were touching some power unknown to me. I had been near it before; I had experienced it several times, but each time I had shaken my head and run away from it. This time I decided not to run, and Ztt! I entered. I lost the boundary of my physical body. I had my skin, of course, but I felt I was standing in the center of the cosmos. I spoke, but my words had lost their meaning. I saw people coming towards me, but all were the same man. All were myself! I had never known this world. I had believed that I was created, but now I must change my opinion: I was never created; I was the cosmos; no individual Mr. Sasaki existed.[186]

Sasaki was 47 years old when he completed his training. Sokatsu encouraged him to return to the United States, telling him that interest in Zen was diminishing in Japan; the tradition needed to be carried to North America if it were to survive. Because of his reservations about the Zen hierarchies in Japan, Sokatsu wanted Sokei-an to remain a lay teacher. Sasaki, however, felt that he would have more credibility in America if he were ordained.

In 1928, he returned to New York City, determining to be the first Zen Master to "bury his bones in America" and thus "mark this land with the seal of the Buddha's teaching."[187] He avoided his former haunts in Greenwich Village and found an apartment elsewhere in the city.

His first students were a group of eight Japanese businessmen who, in 1931, established the Buddhist Society of New York. As with Senzaki, gradually a handful of occidental students joined the group as well. One of his later students, Mary Farkas, described the format of their meetings. They took place in Sokei-an's apartment and began with a short period of meditation. Farkas suggested it was Sokei-an's silence that drew the participants into meditation. "It was as if, by creating a vacuum, he drew all into the One after him." Students working on koans were called into sanzen in an adjacent room. During sanzen there were

---

186. Sokei-an Sasaki, "The Transcendental World" in *Zen Notes*, I:5, First Zen Institute of America, New York, 1954 [http://www.firstzen.org/1954.php], p. 1.

187. Hotz, op. cit., location 1216.

– no psychological or philosophical discussions, no worldly advice or explanations, just the business of Zen. When I was in recent years asked if we were given "instruction" in Zen my considered answer had to be "no." To those of us who received Sokei-an's teaching, the word "instruction" must be a misnomer, for his way of transmitting the Dharma was on a completely different level, to which the word "instruction" could only clarify the state of ignorance of the questioner. If I were to say he "demonstrated" SILENCE, even that would be true but would give no indication of how he "got it across" or awakened it, or transmitted it.[188]

The group grew slowly but steadily. After seven years, there were thirty members. Sokei-an was not in a hurry. He reminded his students that it had taken hundreds of years for Zen to become established in China and Japan. What was required, he told them, was patience and perseverance.

In 1938, the Buddhist Society acquired an unlikely wealthy sponsor, Ruth Fuller Everett. Ruth was the wife of a prominent Chicago attorney, Edward Warren Everett, and their daughter, Eleanor, was married to Alan Watts. Ruth had only been eighteen years old when she married Everett, who was twenty years older than she. The marriage was not a happy one, and, in self-defense, Ruth developed a forceful personality in order to resist her husband's tendencies to bully her. Once she gained the self-confidence to stand up to him, Everett resigned himself to allowing her to pursue her own interests.

In 1923, Ruth took their five-year-old daughter with her to participate in a retreat at a country club outside New York City operated by Pierre Bernard, who called himself "Oom the Magnificent" and purported to be a master of yoga and a spiritual guide. Although Bernard was a fraud, the time Ruth spent with him fostered a genuine interest in Eastern Philosophy. When she returned to Chicago, she took up a study of Asian philosophy and languages at the University of Chicago.

In the '30s, she and Eleanor traveled to Japan where she introduced herself to D.T. Suzuki. He gave her some preliminary instruction in Zen but advised her that, if she were serious, she would need to practice with an accredited Zen master. He introduced her to Nanshinken Roshi, who, at first, was reluctant to accept her. He had no other female students and

---

188. Mary Farkas, "Zen Talks, II" in *Zen Notes*, XIII:6, First Zen Institute of America, New York, 1966, [http://www.firstzen.org/ZenNotes/1966/196606_Vol_13_No_06_June_1966.pdf], p. 4.

doubted that pampered Westerners would even been able to sit properly. Ruth persisted in seeking admission to the zendo, and finally Nanshinken arranged for a plush arm chair to be provided, which he said she could use for meditation on the zendo veranda; however, only cushions were permitted in the zendo itself. Ruth learned to sit cross-legged and in a short time was practicing with the men in the zendo.

In 1938, Warren Everett was confined to a nursing home, and Ruth moved to New York. She took an apartment in the city and arranged for her recently married daughter and son-in-law to occupy the one next to it. Learning there was an authorized Zen teacher in the city, she sought him out. She was not a passive student.

When Ruth met him, Sokei-an's students were still seated in chairs while meditating. From her experience in Japan, she knew that westerners were perfectly capable of adopting formal meditation postures, and she took on the responsibility of teaching them how to sit on cushions. Soon she was tightening up other aspects of the Buddhist Society program.

Despite Zen's claim not to be dependent upon words and letters, Sokei-an believed it was necessary to ensure there were adequate Buddhist texts available in English for serious students, so he began an extensive translation project with which Ruth assisted him.

In November 1941, just a few weeks before the attack on Pearl Harbor, Ruth arranged for the Buddhist Society to move into more spacious quarters on East 65th Street. With the outbreak of war, the institute drew the suspicion of government officials, and that July, Sokei-an – like Nyogen Senzaki – was arrested as an "enemy alien" and sent to an internment camp. Conditions were harsh, and he wasn't in good health. He lost so much weight during his time in the camp that he was able to tighten his belt four notches. Ruth used her social connections to intervene on his behalf and was successful in arranging for his release in August 1943. Warren Everett was dead by then, and in 1944 Ruth and Sokei-an were married in order to provide him protection from still suspicious authorities.

After his release, Sokei-an told the members of the Buddhist Society that it was probably still too early for Zen to take root in America.

> I came too soon to this country. These two civilizations [Japan and America] will meet in the future. Now they are fighting, but the fighting is a sign that there will be some contact later. Physical contact is fighting, but mental contact is exchanging minds. Buddhism came into China after the war between China and Central Asia. Buddhism came into Japan after the war between

Korea and Japan. War is always introducing Buddhism to the other country...

I love this country. I shall die here, clearing up debris to sow seed. It is not the time for Zen yet, but I am the first of the Zen school to come to New York and bring the teaching. I will not see the end.[189]

Sokei-an's physical condition continued to deteriorate after his release from internment. Recognizing he didn't have long to live, he became concerned that he had no heir and tasked Ruth with the responsibility of ensuring that a formally trained Rinzai teacher be found to work with the Buddhist Society. He also encouraged her to return to Japan after his death to complete her own training.

On May 17, 1945, after less than half a year of marriage, Sokei-an died. Afterwards, the Buddhist Society was renamed the First Zen Institute of America and committed itself to preserving Sokei-an's teachings.

As Sokei-an had hoped, Ruth returned to Japan to continue her training. She approached Zuigan Goto at Daitokuji who accepted her as a lay student and provided her a small house within the temple grounds, separate from the monks who were all male and Japanese.

In 1955, after six years at Daitokuji, Ruth was able to fulfill Sokei-an's wish that she identify a qualified teacher to take his place. She returned to New York with Isshu Miura Roshi, who gave a series of talks in New York on koans with Ruth acting as translator. These became the basis of a book they co-authored entitled *The Zen Koan: Its History and Use in Rinzai Zen*.

In 1957, Ruth returned to Daitokuji, where Goto allowed her to add a small zendo to the side of her house. This was the first zendo in Japan specifically intended to receive Western students. The following year, she became both the first woman and the first Westerner to be ordained in the Daitokuji temple system.

After Ruth's return to Japan, Miura stayed with the First Zen Institute for a while but was not comfortable with the predominantly female board of directors. In 1963, he resigned his position, although he stayed in New York and maintained a small number of private students with whom he worked until his death sixteen years later.

To the end, Ruth remained a formidable personality and often a generous one. Through her efforts, and those of the First Zen Institute, several Americans – including Walter Nowick and the poet, Gary Snyder – were able to travel to Japan in order to study Zen. She also gathered together a group of scholars in Kyoto to continue Sokei-an's work of making Chinese and Japanese texts available in English. Several of these – including Philip

---

189. Hotz, op. cit., locations 2010-16.

Yampolsky and Burton Watson – later became significant figures in the academic world.

In her own way, Ruth made as significant a contribution to the process of bringing Zen to North America as had Sokei-an.

Soen Nakagawa

Soen Nakagawa began his Zen studies with Keigaku Katsube but didn't feel at ease in the communal life of the monastery and, with the abbot's permission, chose to go into seclusion on Dai Bosatsu Mountain where he lived an ascetic life, foraging for wild food, practicing zazen, and writing poetry. He published a few poems in popular Japanese magazines – where Nyogen Senzaki's landlady in San Francisco came across them – and eventually became recognized as the most accomplished haiku composer of his generation.

While at Dai Bosatsu, Nakagawa developed a very personal practice. He composed an original mantra – *Namu Dai Bosa*, "unity with the great bodhisattva" – that he chanted with fervor for hours. Aware of current global tensions, he dreamed of establishing an International Dai Bosatsu Zendo where people from all nations could come to practice Zen.

Eventually he began working with Gempo Yamamoto at Ryutakuji and later accompanied him to Manchuria in 1937. The region had been occupied by the Japanese in 1931, and – following the example set by European colonizing powers – Buddhist missionaries followed in the wake of military forces.

Through their correspondence, Nakagawa and Nyogen Senzaki discovered they shared many opinions and values, and, although the political situation didn't permit Nakagawa to visit Senzaki, they determined that they would meet in spirit. In 1938, Nakagawa wrote to Senzaki from Manchuria proposing that they set aside the 21st day of each month for a shared practice to be known as Spiritual Interrelationship Day. He envisioned a time when Dharma practitioners all around the globe would sit for half an hour in zazen starting at 8:00 p.m. local time, then recite the twenty-fifth chapter of the *Lotus Sutra* followed by a period of chanting "Namu Dai Bosa."

During the war years, Nakagawa remained with Yamamoto, who was respected throughout Japan for his wisdom and sound judgment. When it became clear that the Japanese would not be able to prevail in the War, the Prime Minister – Admiral Kantaro Suzuki – sought Yamamoto's advice and was told that he needed to advocate surrender. According to Eido Shimano, Nakagawa's Dharma heir, the words that the Emperor of

Japan used in the radio broadcast announcing the end of the war were those Yamamoto had spoken to Admiral Suzuki: "we must endure the unendurable and suffer what is insufferable."

When the war was over, Nakagawa was finally able to travel to San Francisco and meet Senzaki after fifteen years of correspondence. He arrived on the 8th of April, the day recognized on the Japanese calendar as the Buddha's birthday. He was delighted by the form of Zen practice he found in America, shorn of the more archaic Japanese traditions. Senzaki's relationship with his students was free of stilted formality and even in sanzen there was a freer, franker, communication between teacher and student than common in Japan.

Nakagawa's first formal presentation in America was given at the Theosophical Society Library where a number of Senzaki's students, as well as members of the local Theosophical Community, gathered to welcome him. Nakagawa chose to speak on the traditional objectives of the Theosophical movement,[190] although his approach to the subject may have mystified the Theosophists in attendance. He slapped the top of the table behind which he was seated and demanded, "Who is it who hears this sound?" The Master of Hearing, he went on, the one who hears, is without race, gender, or creed. To be able to hear that sound is the nucleus of a Universal Brotherhood of Humanity. However, in order to understand this, one needed to ask

> – and ask until you reach the Bottom. All of a sudden, when the bottom is broken through, you will realize what "the unexplained laws of nature" really are, and you will be able to acquire an understanding of "the powers latent in man."[191]

In 1950, Yamamoto announced his retirement and appointed Nakagawa his successor. Inspired by Senzaki's example, Nakagawa relaxed many of the formalities associated with the abbot's position. He chose not to distinguish himself from other monks, wore the same robes they did, ate with them, and even shared the same bath house. While Nakagawa's unconventionality was not always admired by the Zen establishment in Japan – which saw it as a sign that he had not sufficiently matured into his responsibilities – it was a major factor in the spread of the Dharma to North America.

Although he had passed some 500 koans under Yamamoto's tutelage

---

190. Cf., p. 209 above.

191. Quoted in Louis Nordstrom, *Namu Dai Bosa* (New York: Theatre Arts Books, 1976), p. 129.

and was an abbot in his own right, Nakagawa felt the need to deepen his understanding of the Dharma and so undertook further training with Daiun Harada Roshi.

Harada was a priest in the Soto tradition who – dissatisfied with the level of understanding he had acquired through Soto practice – undertook koan study with a Rinzai teacher and came to awakening. He and his successor – Hakuun Yasutani – became advocates of koan practice. Although they were both monks, they also questioned whether monastic life was a necessary prerequisite for Zen practice. Their perspective grew increasingly distant from orthodox Soto, and Yasutani eventually broke ties with it and established an independent school of Zen that combined Soto and Rinzai elements. He called the new school Sanbo Kyodan, or the Fellowship of the Three Treasures.[192]

Nakagawa remained formally associated with the Rinzai school but completed his koan work with Yasutani after Harada's death and held those two teachers and their approach to Zen in high esteem throughout his life.

Nyogen Senzaki died in 1958; Gempo Yamamoto died three years later, and Nakagawa's mother in 1962. The deaths of so many people who had played important roles in his life sent Nakagawa into a depression he had difficulty dealing with. For a while he returned to his hermitage on Dai Bosatsu, but, by this time, his reputation was such that he received invitations from Zen communities around the world which he felt obligated to accept.

In 1967, he apparently climbed a tree on the grounds, possibly in order to gain a better view of the area. He slipped, fell, and lay on the ground, unconscious, for three days before he was found by the monks. He was rushed to hospital, where it was discovered that a sliver of bamboo had pierced his brain. Doctors advised surgery, but he refused it. The fall and his injuries had consequences on his health and personality for the remainder of his life.

Eido Tai Shimano

Eido Tai Shimano was a young monk at Heirinji in 1954 when Zen Masters and teachers from throughout Japan gathered for the funeral of a former abbot. When the dignitaries first met, Shimano was assigned to bring them tea. Most accepted their cups without acknowledging him. The youngest of the abbots, however, put his hands together in gassho, palm to palm, and bowed his thanks. Surprised to be recognized in this

---

192. In 2014, the school was renamed Sanbo Zen.

manner, Shimano returned the bow and, later, inquired who the polite master had been. He was informed it was the recently appointed abbot of Ryutakuji, Soen Nakagawa.

After the funeral, Shimano left Heirinji and sought acceptance at Ryutakuji. That October, he took part in his first sesshin with Nakagawa. During their initial face-to-face meeting Nakagawa appeared to ask him a series of personal questions:

"Where are you from?"

"Chichibu," Shimano replied.

"Where did you spend the last training period?"

"At Heirinji."

"When did you leave there?"

"Last summer."

At that point, Nakagawa rang his bell, signaling that the meeting was over, and Shimano left the sanzen room unclear about what had just occurred. It took him a while to realize that he had been assigned the koan that is the fifteenth case in the *Mumonkan*.

> Tozan came to study with Unmon. Unmon asked, "Where are you from?" "From Sato," Tozan replied. "Where were you during the summer?" "At Hozu, south of the lake." "When did you leave?" "August." "I spare you sixty blows," Unmon told him.

Shimano proved to be a committed and insightful practitioner, and, over time, master and disciple grew close. As he progressed in his training, Shimano was given a number of duties within the monastery. Because of his knowledge of English, he was assigned responsibility for explaining monastery procedures and etiquette to the European and American students who made their way there. He was known to them by his familiar name, Tai-san.[193] He later wrote that he liked the Westerners he met but recognized that their approach to Zen practice was very different from that of Japanese students. Americans demanded explanations and clarifications and posed questions their Asian counterparts would have considered inappropriate. He also seems to have been attracted to the way in which many of these Western students challenged and flaunted those traditional values and mores that seemed, to them, no longer relevant.

Recognizing Shimano's ability to interact smoothly with Americans, Nakagawa intended to send him to Los Angeles to act as attendant to the aging Senzaki. When Senzaki died, Nakagawa instead sent Shimano to Hawaii to assist Robert and Anne Aitken who had recently established

---

193. San is an honorific roughly equivalent to Mr.

the Koko-an Zen Center – also referred to as the Diamond Sangha – in Honolulu. The Aitkens had met Shimano in Japan and had liked him, so were happy to sponsor his immigration to the US. Shimano arrived at Koko-an in 1960; he was 27 years old. Four years later, he moved to New York City and began gathering his own students. Along the way, he assisted Hakuun Yasutani in leading sesshin in various US cities where one of his duties was to act as translator during dokusan.[194] The experience, he would later say, taught him how to work with American students.

The New York Zendo, as it was called, originally met in the living room of Shimano's small apartment. There were, as yet, no membership fees, and Shimano earned a small income by going through the Manhattan telephone directory culling Japanese names for a mailing list being compiled by the Bank of Tokyo.

As the number of students increased, programs and activities grew. At first there were only regular short sittings at the apartment; then day-long sits were added and even weekend sesshin. When the living room zendo was no longer adequate, the sangha discussed ways in which funds might be raised to purchase or rent a larger space. In order to do so, they needed to incorporate as a religious organization and acquire tax-exempt status. The expense associated with that process, however, was beyond their means. According to Shimano's account, it was for that reason that they approached the Zen Studies Society which had been established some years prior to promote the work of D.T. Suzuki. The society was currently inactive and owned no property although it still existed as a legal entity. The secretary of the society, George Yamaoka, assisted Shimano in becoming a board member, and the Society quietly merged with the New York Zendo.

After the merger, fund-raising began in earnest, and the group was able to move into new quarters on 81st Street, where Yasutani led their first sesshin in the summer of 1965. There was a growing interest in Zen practice throughout America, a surge never equaled since, and, before long, people were turned away because there was insufficient room for them.

Then, in 1968, Chester Carlson – the founder of Xerox – donated funds for them to move to more suitable quarters in a former carriage house on East 67th Street. Carlson's wife, Dorris, was interested in Eastern Spiritualities, and, through her intervention, Carlson anonymously assisted both Shimano and, later, Philip Kapleau in establishing their communities. That summer, Nakagawa came to New York and presided at a ceremony officially inaugurating the New York Zendo Shobo Ji (Temple of True Dharma). He was declared the zendo's abbot, and Shimano was the teacher-in-residence.

---

194. Yasutani used the Soto term "dokusan" rather than the Rinzai equivalent, "sanzen."

Post-War America

By the 1940s, information about Zen was plentiful and accessible outside of Asia. The number of actual practitioners in North America was small, but there were active communities on both coasts. It might have remained a minor religious and intellectual curiosity, however, had there not been a growing audience that found something compelling about this very foreign tradition. One of the factors that contributed to Zen becoming a cultural phenomenon in the United States began with an unlikely group of writers who met in New York in 1943.

Jack Kerouac coined the term "Beat" to refer to a small cadre of poets and prose writers including himself, Allen Ginsberg, Gregory Corso, and William Burroughs. He was inconsistent about what he meant by the term. At times, it referred to being "beat down" by the circumstances of their lives and the difficulties they had with contemporary culture; at others, it referred to the "beat" of jazz music and the spontaneous improvisations that the writers emulated in their own work; and at times he suggested it referred to "beatitude," to an effort to develop a spiritual basis in one's life.

By the 1950s, many of the Beats had relocated to San Francisco where Ginsberg was enrolled in classes at the Berkeley campus of the University of California. He also attended the poetry soirees of established poet, Kenneth Rexroth, who introduced him to a few young West Coast poets, including Gary Snyder. These writers were the harbingers of the counter-culture movement of the 60's, railing against contemporary mores and standards. They were deeply aware of the injustices they saw in America and the disenfranchisement of marginalized members of society – homosexuals, racial minorities, or people whose ideas were considered socially or politically suspect. They were sexually adventurous; they flaunted their use of alcohol and experimented with drugs like peyote. Their books and poems inspired a generation of young readers to question the structures of previous generations – institutionalized and legal racism, conservative Christian moral and religious values, assumptions about what it was proper for women to do or be engaged in, the belief that homosexuality was a psychological aberration, the unquestioning acceptance of what was generally referred to as the American Way of Life. It was a generation that would be receptive to new ideas from distant cultures.

Kerouac became interested in Buddhism by accident. He was tracking down a reference to Hinduism he had come upon while reading Thoreau, and, searching the library, he found a biography of the Buddha. He was struck by the first of the Noble Truths – that "life is suffering." This led him to peruse other Buddhist literature, including the works of D.T. Suzuki. He was especially impressed by Suzuki's descriptions of the Tang Dynasty

Zen Poets, Hanshan and Shide – Zen lunatics, as Kerouac would dub them, the original "Dharma Bums" who flaunted the conventions of their day and inscribed their poems on rock faces and the bark of trees.

In 1954, Ginsberg introduced Kerouac to Gary Snyder. In Snyder, Kerouac found an American Hanshan, someone who actually lived like a hermit and was familiar with the mountains of the Pacific Northwest. Snyder was also, at that time, preparing to go to Japan to study with an authentic Zen Master. He became the inspiration for the character Japhy Ryder in *The Dharma Bums*, the book Kerouac released after the success of *On the Road* and that he dedicated to Hanshan.

The portrait of Japhy Ryder is exuberant and appealing – a Zen practitioner, an outdoorsman and poet; a scholar, in addition to being both sexually accomplished and wise in the ways of the natural world. He did not look like a Bohemian at all, Ray Smith – the narrator of the book – noted; instead he was vigorous and athletic. It was a characterization that would intrigue and inspire many young readers.

Kerouac, Ginsberg and their friends had met in New York City and shared an urban East Coast perspective. Gary Snyder came from a very different background. He was twenty-five years old when he met Ginsberg and Kerouac, but he had already been a seaman, had worked as a timber scaler, had cleared forest trails, and had been a fire-lookout in deep isolation in the North Cascades.

He grew up in rural Washington State and Oregon, where he'd hiked and explored the countryside from an early age. He was an experienced mountaineer by the time he was twenty. He also had a great admiration for the way the native peoples of the Pacific Northwest related to the natural environment. From them, he developed the idea of a "sense of place" – a sense of belonging to a particular region and being a participant in a complex ecological pattern that included both the human and the nonhuman. It was a point of view similar to the Zen teaching that all things had Buddha-nature, all things had inherent value and were connected with all other things.

Snyder earned a scholarship to attend Indiana University to pursue a degree in linguistics and folklore. Before he set out to hitchhike to Bloomington, he picked up a couple of books by D.T. Suzuki, whom he had heard of but not yet read. During a lull between drives, he started to read the first volume of *Essays in Zen Buddhism* and, unexpectedly, found something to which he was deeply drawn. The Zen tradition, with its emphasis on personal realization and physical labor rather than academic study, made sense to him as did its inclusive view of nature not as something "fallen" – as in the Christian tradition – but as something with which humankind was ecologically bound. Snyder had been drawn to a similar perspective in the spiritual traditions of Native Americans but recognized that they were closed to him. One had to be born a Hopi, for example, in order to follow the Hopi way. But Zen, with its emphasis on personal experience, appeared to be open to anyone who was willing to undertake the training.

Suzuki's book redirected Snyder's life. He remained at Indiana University for a single semester, then returned to San Francisco in order, as he put it, to pursue the Dharma. He decided he needed to go to Japan to work with a Zen master, and, in order to prepare, he enrolled in courses on Asian languages and cultures at the University of California at Berkeley and attended seminars at the American Academy of Asian Studies. The director of the Academy at the time was Alan Watts.

When Ruth Fuller Sasaki visited San Francisco to speak at the Academy, Watts introduced her to Snyder, and she helped the young poet get to Japan in 1955. He wasn't there long before he realized that the portrait of Zen presented by Suzuki had been idealized; there was often a "snobbish aristocratic and insular self-esteem"[195] in the monks he met. Zen was no longer a popular pursuit in Japan; many contemporary Japanese youth viewed it as a remnant of feudalism and the militarism that had resulted in the war which had ended so disastrously. Snyder came to believe that one of Suzuki's most important contributions to Zen was to revitalize the tradition by bringing it away from Japan and presenting it to an American audience that had no knowledge of its political past.

Ruth Sasaki had arranged for Snyder to share quarters with another American student, Walter Nowick, and to be accepted as a lay student at Shokokuji where he would study with and serve as an English tutor for Isshu Miura, who was then preparing to move to New York. Snyder formally became a Buddhist by taking the refuge vows from Miura, and he began koan study. He was given a Dharma name, Chofu ("Listen to the Wind"), but remained a layman and knew that he would eventually return to America. He recognized that monastic life in Japan was elitist and that it removed monks from the mainstream life of the community. While monks dedicated themselves to their meditation practice, as Snyder put it, someone else had to grow the tomatoes.

Zen training turned out to be arduous. It was very different from the laissez-faire Buddhism imagined by Kerouac. In an article later published in the *Chicago Review*, Snyder noted: "Zen aims at freedom but its practice is disciplined."[196] He was, however, better prepared than many who followed him to Japan. In addition to having some knowledge of the language, he was inured to hardship and privation from his childhood and early work experiences.

---

195. Quoted in John Suiter, *Poets on the Peaks* (Washington D C: Counterpoint, 2002), p. 245.
196. Gary Snyder, "Spring Sesshin at Shokoku-ji" in *The Gary Snyder Reader* (Washington DC: Counterpoint, 2012), electronic version, location 513.

In spite of his friendship with Ginsberg and Kerouac, Snyder didn't consider himself a "Beat writer," and certainly his work went on to become more varied and successful than that of any of the other writers of that milieu. He would win the Pulitzer Prize, and his work would begin an unprecedented school of environmental writing. Throughout it all, however, there remains a profound Zen perspective.

In his writing and life, Snyder made Zen something less fantastic and exotic. Zen practice cultivates an awareness of the interrelatedness of things – interdependence – and thus fosters a respect for life in all its forms. In Japan, this awareness is cultivated in a monastic environment, but Snyder and others would demonstrate that it was a perspective that could be taken out of the cloister and made the basis for an effective politically and socially engaged lay life.

When Gary Snyder returned to California in 1964, he found a very different social environment than the one Kerouac had described in *The Dharma Bums*. The short-lived Beat movement was already passé; beatniks had been supplanted by hippies. Two years later, Ginsberg and Snyder both took part in the Human Be-In at Golden Gate Park that ushered in the "Summer of Love."

This new generation was more flamboyant than the dour Beats had been; they listened to a different type of music and were more politically engaged. And many were pursuing a "higher consciousness" through the use of drugs like psilocybin, mescaline, and LSD. The experiences these youths attained by using psychedelics seemed to make more sense in terms of Eastern rather than Western traditions, and suddenly young Americans were reading classical Asian texts such as the *Upanishads* and the *Bhagavad Gita*. They also read the books of an expatriate Englishman and former Episcopalian Priest and listened to his broadcasts about Zen and related topics on the radio.

Alan Watts

The lead article in the 1958 issue of the *Chicago Review* in which Gary Snyder's "Spring Sesshin at Shokoku-ji" appeared was Alan Watts' "Beat Zen, Square Zen, and Zen." Much to the amusement of his former mother-in-law, Watts had acquired the reputation of being an expert on Zen. Ruth Sasaki's opinion on the matter is probably best revealed in a remark she made about the "misinformation being spread about…by those professed exponents of Zen in the west" who had not actually undergone Zen training.¹⁹⁷

In the *Chicago Review* article, Watts contrasted the popular Beat use of Zen as justification for what he considered often mediocre art and a lifestyle flaunting traditional values with the Square Zen of those, like Ruth, who were trying to establish formal Japanese Zen training and discipline in America. Neither, in Watts' opinion, were true to the spirit of Zen as he understood it:

> For Zen is above all the liberation of the mind from conventional thought, and this is something utterly different from rebellion against convention, on the one hand, or adapting foreign conventions, on the other.¹⁹⁸

As Square Zen became more established in North America, Watts' credibility as an expert diminished, but – whether he intended it or not – his contribution to the development of American Zen was as significant as that of Suzuki or any of the early teachers who had come to the United States.

Watts was a fifteen-year-old student attending King's College, a public – that is to say, private – school in Canterbury, when he came upon a pamphlet published by the Buddhist Lodge in London. In the overview of the Buddhadharma it provided Watts found a view of life that struck him as more reasonable than Christianity, and he boldly announced to his classmates that he had become a Buddhist. He also initiated a correspondence with the president of the Lodge, a London barrister named Christmas Humphries. Watts expressed himself so maturely that Humphreys assumed the writer from King's College was a member of staff and was surprised to discover, when Watts attended his first Lodge meeting during the holidays, that his correspondent was in fact a sixth form student.

Although the expectations of his masters at King's College – and his parents – had been that Watts would earn a scholarship to Oxford, he didn't do well on the examinations and didn't attend university. He was largely self-educated but also received guidance from Humphreys, who was a theosophist. So in addition to reading the Hindu *Upanishads*, the *Diamond Sutra*, and the *Daodejing*, he also read Blavatsky. Watts and Humphrey's greatest shared interest, however, was the recently published work of D.T. Suzuki, and in 1935 – at the precocious age of 19 – Watts wrote

---

197. Isshu Miura and Ruth Fuller Sasaki, *Zen Dust* (New York: Harcourt, Brace & World), p. 4.
198. Alan Watts, "Beat Zen, Square Zen, and Zen" in *This Is It* (New York: Collier Books, 1967), p. 91.

and published his first book, *The Spirit of Zen*, with a foreword contributed by Humphreys. It was a small work, less than 40,000 words, that was essentially a reader's guide to Suzuki, but it already demonstrated a skill, that Watts would hone throughout his life, of being able to describe spiritual issues in a clear and intriguing manner. A second book, *The Legacy of Asia and Western Man*, was released in 1937.

The year after *The Spirit of Zen* came out, Watts met Suzuki, who was in London to attend the World Congress of Faith. As the guest of the Buddhist Lodge, Suzuki made a greater impression on his hosts than they had anticipated. Here, they found, was someone who not only understood Zen but embodied it; Suzuki struck Watts as a man wholly at home and at ease in whatever environment he found himself. His presence alone validated Zen.

In 1937, Ruth Fuller Everett was in London and showed up at a Buddhist Lodge meeting accompanied by her daughter, Eleanor. Watts was overwhelmed by the mother – who, after her time in a Japanese monastery, knew more about Zen than he – and was smitten with the daughter. She had an American vivaciousness and freedom of behavior unlike anything he had encountered in the few girls he had been with prior, and she enjoyed trying to tease him out of his British reserve. When Ruth returned to America, Eleanor stayed behind.

Eleanor was more relaxed about her Buddhism than her mother, but she proved to have more insight into Buddhist practice than Watts. As they walked home one evening after a meditation session, Watts mused aloud on the methods of concentrating on the present moment they were being taught. Eleanor asked,

> "Why try to concentrate on it? What else is there to be aware of? Your memories are all in the present, just as much as the trees over there. Your thoughts about the future are also in the present, and anyhow I just love to think about the future. The present is just a constant flow, like the [Dao], and there's simply no way of getting out of it." With that remark my whole sense of weight vanished. You could have knocked me down with a feather. I realized that when the Hindus said *Tat tvam asi*, "YOU ARE THAT," they meant just what they said.[199]

Looking back on that moment in his autobiography, he referred to it as a "premature *satori*" for which he remained "perpetually grateful to Eleanor":

---

199. Alan Watts, *In My Own Way* (Novato, CA: New World Library, 2007), pp. 152-53.

– I was unable to resist the temptation to write, think, and intellectualize about it. Yet when I am in my right mind I still know that this is the true way of life, at least for me. Conscious thoughts, reflections, analysis, cultivation, and intention are simply using the mind's radar or scanning beam for purposes which the mind as a whole can do of itself, and on its own, with far more intelligence and less effort.[200]

Eleanor and Watts were married in April 1938. He was 23, she 18 and pregnant. She was also wealthy. The young couple moved to New York where Ruth had arranged for them to have an apartment next door to hers.

Through Ruth, Watts met Sokei-an. He made an effort to work with the Zen master but discovered – as he would realize throughout his life – that he preferred being the teacher to being taught. After their brief formal relationship ended, Watts continued to observe Sokei-an in order to learn how a Zen master lived his life, something that became easier to do when Sokei-an began his unexpected courtship of Ruth after her husband's death.

Possibly because she was having difficulties as a young mother, possibly because she still lived closer to her own mother and her mother's influence than she would have liked, Eleanor didn't fare as well in New York as her husband. She became increasingly unhappy and depressed. Then one day she stopped at Saint Patrick's Cathedral, looking for a place to rest during a trying day, and there she had a vision of Jesus so vivid that she could describe in detail everything he was wearing.

This vision came to her around the same time that Watts had become interested in Christian mysticism and was wondering whether – as long as it shed its claim to be the only true religion – Christianity might also be an effective means to achieve that sense of union with God/Dao/Ultimate Reality that in his most recent book, *The Meaning of Happiness*, he had asserted was the purpose of religion and the route to happiness.

Ruth wasn't surprised when Eleanor and Watts suddenly dropped their purported Buddhism – apparently, she had not thought it very deep to begin with – and began attending services at St. Mary the Virgin Episcopalian Church. Not long after this, Watts approached the curate to inquire how he could become a priest.

In his autobiography, he struggles to rationalize this decision, explaining that if he were to help Western people understand the "perennial philosophy" underlying all genuine religious traditions, he could best do

---

200. Ibid.

so within the prevailing tradition of the West. His biographer, Monica Furlong, posits that it might have been simply a way to earn a living and become less dependent upon Eleanor's family; his daughter, Joan, speculated that, as the United States was drawn into the war, her father may have sought to become an ordained minister in order to avoid military conscription.

Whatever his motives, Watts and his family moved to Evanston, Illinois, where he entered Seabury-Western Theological Seminary. Six years later, the now Reverend Alan Watts served as a chaplain on the campus of Northwestern University. He published another book, *Behold the Spirit*, in which he compared Christian mysticism with Zen and other Asian traditions. It was well received in church circles.

His clerical career came to an end in 1950, when his marriage with Eleanor ended and he married Dorothy DeWitt, his children's sometime babysitter. Eleanor allowed him to retain custody of their children, but he no longer had the financial security her wealth had provided him. His income from writing was inadequate to support his new family, so he accepted an invitation to move to San Francisco to help Frederic Spiegelberg establish the American Academy of Asian Studies. He shed his nominal Christianity and returned to nominal Buddhism without compunction.

He still had a restrained British manner and dressed formally, and he had – what sounded to Americans – a cultured accent. He came across with authority, and it was natural for him to assume the position of Director of the Academy when Spiegelberg stepped down in order to teach at Stanford. Watts arranged for a number of interesting guest lecturers to visit the Academy including D.T. Suzuki and his former mother-in-law with whom he retained a civil relationship.

California had long attracted people with an interest in Asian philosophies. In addition to Vedantists, Yoga teachers, and Theosophists, a Soto Zen master – Shunryu Suzuki – had recently arrived and begun attracting Western students. Watts fit in easily. In addition to his work at the Academy, he became a frequent guest on educational radio and television. Then in 1956, he published the book for which he would become best known, *The Way of Zen*.

D.T. Suzuki's books had appealed to a broad but relatively small and well-educated readership. Watts was much easier to read than Suzuki, and his book introduced Zen to an even wider audience. To some extent it was a matter of timing; the book came out when interest in Zen, in part because of the Beats, was on the rise. In the Preface, Watts suggests this might be the case because people in the West had lost faith in traditions that no longer seemed viable in the light of advances in the physical sciences and psychology.

> Familiar concepts of space, time, and motion, of nature and natural law, of history and social change itself have dissolved, and we find ourselves adrift without landmarks in a universe which more and more resembles the Buddhist principle of the "Great Void."[201]

Under these circumstances, it was natural that some people would feel attracted to:

> – a culturally productive way of life which, for some fifteen hundred years, has felt thoroughly at home in "the Void," and which not only feels no terror for it but rather a positive delight.

Watts, however, warns that he is not in favor of importing Zen wholesale from Japan:

> – for it has become deeply involved with cultural institutions which are quite foreign to us. But there is no doubt there are things which we can learn, or unlearn, from it and apply in our own way.

He begins his analysis of Zen with a point to which he frequently returns throughout his work: that what one perceives as one's Self is an arbitrary social convention. It is not only that one tends to see oneself in light of the way in which others perceive and define one (one's social role, personality, even physical appearance); one also tends to view the Self as what he described elsewhere as "an ego encapsulated in a bag of skin" – a soul separate from and animating a physical body, both of which (soul and body) are cut off and distinct from the environment about one.

Zen is a "way of liberation" through which the individual can realize the restrictions and limitations of social conventions and come to identify the "self" as part of a larger ecological whole which is all of Being. This is not a matter of rejecting or rebelling against other perspectives. It is rather a matter of seeing through the illusion of separation or dualism. For Watts, this is something that must occur spontaneously; it can't be achieved by effort that inevitably only substitutes one set of conventions for another.

He presents Zen as a matter of cultivating a particular attitude towards life rather than as a training that brings about a change in one's manner of experiencing. Seated meditation, zazen, is just a natural way to sit and be; it had not been intended, he suggests, to become the strained and sustained practice it evolved into in Japanese monasteries. To support this

---

201. Alan W. Watts, *The Way of Zen* (New York: Vintage Books, 1957), p. ix-x.

contention, he quotes the story about Nanyue (J: Nangaku) polishing a broken tile to demonstrate to Mazu (J: Baso) the futility of doing zazen in order to become a Buddha.[202] Philip Kapleau and later Zen practitioners would complain that Watts distorted the intent of the story. To present it as a condemnation of zazen, Kapleau writes:

> – is to do violence to the whole spirit of the koan. Nangaku, far from implying that sitting in zazen is as useless as trying to polish a roof tile into a mirror – though it is easy for one who has never practiced Zen to come to such a conclusion – is in fact trying to teach Baso that Buddhahood does not exist outside himself as an object to strive for, since we are all Buddhas from the very first.[203]

The criticism was just, but, in fairness to Watts, he had specifically denied being a spokesperson for traditional Zen in his book and didn't intend it to be an instruction manual. What it did do was present the Zen perspective as an appealing orientation towards life from which Western readers could learn to develop a healthier relationship with their fellows and their environment than currently found in contemporary North American society.

The book became, as Watts put it, a "minor bestseller," and its publication allowed him to resign his position as Director of the Academy – that was in a hopeless financial situation – and earn his way as a writer and lecturer. His reputation was on the rise, and he received invitations from as far away as Zurich. Tens of thousands of people attended his seminars and read his books. Ironically, his personal life was a mess. He became a heavy drinker and proved to be no more capable of fidelity to Dorothy than he had been to Eleanor.

As his fame grew, so did the number of his detractors. Academics dismissed him as a popularizer, and some members of the growing Zen community dismissed him because of his lack of formal training. Shunryu Suzuki, however, when overhearing his students criticize Watts, told them that they should respect what he had accomplished and consider him a great Bodhisattva.

Young people flocked to him and sought to become his disciples; the fact that he did not accept any of them only increased his allure. At the Human Be-In of January 1967, Watts was present with Ginsberg and Snyder; Shunryu Suzuki was there as well. In the counter-culture, Watts had become mainstream.

The "Summer of Love," however, was short lived, and, as the original innocence of the first hippies dissipated, a few began serious spiritual

---

202. Pp. 145 above.
203. Philip Kapleau (*et al.*, eds.), *The Three Pillars of Zen* (Boston: Beacon Press, 1969), p. 22.

quests. Richard Alpert, who with Timothy Leary had introduced hundreds of Harvard students – and celebrities – to LSD and psilocybin, went to India and remade himself as a Hindu mystic now named Baba Ram Dass. Zen centers, located in places as unlikely as Minneapolis, were filling up. The total number of practitioners was not large compared to the general population, but it was large enough to have been unthinkable in 1958 when Kerouac, in *The Dharma Bums*, had predicted a generation of Zen practitioners across the land.

Europe

Zen was the first of three major forms of Buddhism to be established in North America; however, the other two – Vipassana (a modern version of Theravada) and Tibetan Buddhism – both found followers in Europe before Zen did. The first Buddhist Temple in Europe was established in Berlin in 1924 by a German physician who converted to Buddhism in Sri Lanka. Tibetan teachers, such as Chogyam Trungpa, fleeing their homeland after the Chinese takeover, made their way to India and from there to Britain and elsewhere on the continent.

D.T. Suzuki was as popular in England as he was in America. Christmas Humphrey's Buddhist Lodge – that began as an affiliate of the Theosophical Society – hosted him when he attended the World Congress of Faith in London in 1936 and were charmed by him. Humphreys declared that Zen was the "apotheosis" of Buddhism, but meetings of the Lodge focused more on discussion than practice. Alan Watts' mother, Emily, once remarked that Humphreys ran lodge meetings much like a Sunday School class.

There was plenty of material for lodge members to discuss. The three volumes of Suzuki's *Essays in Zen Buddhism* were published in England by Rider and Son before they were released in North America. A German professor of philosophy and student of archery, Eugen Herrigel, published a description of his training in the sport while teaching at Tohoku Imperial University in Japan. The book, entitled in English *Zen and the Art of Archery*, was released in German in 1948 and was soon translated into English as well as other languages. It became an international bestseller and the model for a number of later books purporting to demonstrate the Zen approach to golf, writing, happiness, motorcycle maintenance, and even stand-up comedy.

Then in the mid-'60s, as many Japanese teachers were traveling east to Hawaii and the mainland US, a Soto priest named Taisen Deshimaru came west to Paris at the instruction of his teacher, Kodo Sawaki, who told him:

> In India during the time of Bodhidharma, Buddhism was in a state of decline. So Bodhidharma's teacher told him to take the Dharma to the East. Likewise in Japan, Buddhism is now dead. And so you, my Dharma heir, who know the true teachings of the Buddha, take them to the West so that Buddhism may again flourish.[204]

Deshimaru had avoided conscription during the war because of poor eyesight and was sent, instead, to oversee a copper mine in Indonesia. While at sea, the ship he was on was sunk by Allied planes. He floated in the water, sustained by his life jacket, for a day and a half before being rescued, arrested, and eventually placed in a prisoner of war camp in Singapore. After his release, he traveled back to Japan and continued training with Sawaki until the latter's death in 1965. It was on his death bed that Sawaki entreated Deshimaru to carry the Dharma west.

Although he spoke no French, Deshimaru managed to gather a group of students in Paris and began instructing inquirers in zazen. His retreats became increasingly popular and by 1980 he was holding them at a chateau in the Loire Valley where they were attended by as many 1500 participants.

The most unexpected source to introduce Zen to Europeans, however, were Jesuit missionaries returning from their postings in Japan.

Once Japan had been re-opened to the west in the mid-19th century, the Jesuits returned to the mission fields. They did so, however, with a very different attitude than their predecessors had had. Their efforts in China had taught them the importance of understanding and respecting local culture and institutions. One of the priests sent to Japan was a German, Hugo Lassalle, who was appointed Mission Superior in 1935. Just before the outbreak of the Second World War, he relocated to Hiroshima. There, professors at the Bunrika University convinced him that to understand the character of the Japanese people he needed to understand Zen Buddhism, and he began what was at first a fairly superficial study. But by 1943 – as the War in the Pacific raged on and the toll it took on the people of Japan became increasingly more arduous – he recognized that Zen practice could be a means of deepening his own spirituality. That spring he took part in his first sesshin. It was in no way a conversion to Buddhism – Lassalle remained a committed Jesuit throughout his life – but a recognition on his part that Zen had potential application beyond Buddhism.

Lassalle was in Hiroshima when the atom bomb was dropped on August 6, 1945. That experience was one of the factors contributing to

---

204. Quoted in Stephen Batchelor, *The Awakening of the West* (Williamsville, VT: Echo Point Books, 2011), p. 122.

his decision to express solidarity with the Japanese people by becoming a naturalized citizen. He did so in 1948, taking the Japanese name Makibi Enomiya. For the remainder of his life, he signed his name "Hugo M. Enomiya-Lassalle."

After the war, Enomiya-Lassalle persisted in his Zen practice. He theoretically identified the kensho experience – that he had not yet had – with a "natural" rather than "supernatural" experience of God. The church didn't deny that genuine experiences of God – mystical experiences – were possible outside the faith, but it made a sharp distinction between these "natural religions" and the "supernatural religion" that is Christianity. Enomiya-Lassalle in his life and teaching presented Zen practice as a natural methodology capable of leading persons to supernatural achievement. While studying with Daiun Harada, Enomiya-Lassalle published a book – *Zen: A Way to Enlightenment* – in which he outlined what he believed Zen could contribute to Catholicism.

After Harada's death, the Jesuit continued working first with Hakuun Yasutani and then his heir, a childhood friend of Soen Nakagawa, Koun Yamada.

Nakagawa and Yamada had attended high school and university together, where they both read books on Zen, although neither began formal practice until later. Unlike Nakagawa, Yamada remained a layman even after becoming Yasutani's Dharma heir. Once authorized as a teacher, he built a small zendo in the yard of his home and began gathering students. He stressed the importance of both zazen and awakening, insisting that one needed to

> – know that subject and object are intrinsically one. This is the most fundamental point of Buddhist teaching. It is the true satori of Zen. To intuit, experience, and realize this fact is the main reason for doing zazen.[205]

It took Enomiya-Lassalle many years to attain awakening, but in 1973 he achieved a breakthrough experience that Yamada acknowledged as kensho. He then began a lengthy koan practice after which Yamada gave him full transmission, recognizing that the Jesuit was an awakened Zen teacher – a Zen Master – and a Dharma heir in the Sanbo Kyodan tradition.

Enomiya-Lassalle opened a zendo in Hiroshima – *Shinmeikutsu* or the "Cave of Divine Darkness" – for Christians and offered sesshin throughout Europe. He insisted in his retreats and his books that because "Zen is not bound to any particular ideology, it can have a liberating effect

---

205. Yamada, Koun, *The Gateless Gate* (Boston: Wisdom Publications, 2004), p. 109.

for anyone and be useful in all situations of daily life."[206] He frequently quoted Yamada Roshi, who said:

> I am often asked by Christians, especially by Catholics, whether it is possible to practice Zen and still remain true to their Christian faith. To this question I usually reply that Zen is not a religion in the sense that Christianity is religion. Therefore there is no reason why Zazen and Christianity should not coexist. The outer garment is of a different form and colour, but what is underneath, the heart, remains the same. And this heart, this experience is not embellished with any thoughts or philosophies. It is a pure fact, an experienced fact, in the same way that tasting tea is a fact. A cup of tea has no thoughts, no ideas, no philosophy. It tastes the same to Buddhists as it does to Christians. There is not the slightest difference there.[207]

Enomiya-Lassalle's retreats were popular enough that a permanent zendo was established at the Franciscan Abbey in Dietfurt, Germany, to host them. Following his example, several other Catholic religious studied with Yamada who gave Dharma transmission to twelve of them. Some of these – like Ruben Habito – would help establish Zen practice in North America, while others – like Willigis Jäger – had an equally significant impact on the development of European Zen.

Both Deshimaru and Enomiya-Lassalle contributed to a Zen Boom that took place during the '70s in Europe, but it was an only an echo of the much larger explosion that had occurred on the other side of the Atlantic Ocean. And the teachers who followed them in Europe were more likely to have trained in California or New York than in Asia.

---

206. Hugo M. Enomiya-Lassalle, *The Practice of Zen Meditation* (London: Thorsons, 1990), p. 8.
207. Ibid.

Part Three

A water buffalo passes through a latticed window. Head, horns, and four hoofs all cross through. Why can't the tail pass through?

38th Case in the Mumonkan

The Zen Boom

Shunryu Suzuki

WHEN SHUNRYU SUZUKI's children came from Japan to visit him in San Francisco during his final illness, they were astonished by what they found. They respected their father but had thought of him as little more than a small-town priest of no particular stature. They were surprised to discover that he led two thriving monastic communities in America with numerous disciples who obviously revered him. Likewise, when Suzuki's American students travelled to Japan, they were dismayed to find that their beloved teacher was quite an insignificant figure in Japanese Soto circles. Suzuki had been a relatively ordinary figure in Japan, but Zen training can mold individuals of impressive character, which made him an extraordinary figure in America.

In the 1950s, he had been the resident priest of a small, rural Soto temple where his duties included conducting funerals and memorial services, carrying out ritual activities, and chanting sutras on behalf of the community. His position was technically that of an abbot and students were occasionally sent to him for training, but few had any serious interest in the Buddhadharma; they were simply preparing to take responsibility for family-run temples, as Suzuki himself had. He came to feel that the Zen tradition had grown stale and was in need of revitalization.

While a student himself, Suzuki had boarded for a time with his English teacher, Nona Ransom, who had previously been a tutor in the imperial household in China. She didn't know much about Buddhism, which struck her as a primitive form of idol worship, and she was surprised that her boarder, who otherwise seemed a reasonable young man, paid so much reverence to a statue of the Buddha displayed in her home. The statue had been given to her by the imperial family and, as far as Miss Ransom was concerned, was merely decorative, but Suzuki treated it almost as if it were sentient. He bowed before it every morning and brought it tea and incense offerings. Eventually she asked him why he did so, and he explained that in honoring the image of the Buddha one was not offering it worship but was rather acknowledging one's own true – or Buddha – nature. She slowly acquired a greater respect for the tradition under Suzuki's tutelage and started sitting zazen with him.

Nona Ransom was the first Westerner to whom Suzuki tried to explain Buddhism, and he found it a rewarding experience. He believed it was precisely her unfamiliarity with the Buddhadharma that made her a receptive student. The experience led him to think about working with other westerners. There were, after all, Christian missionaries in Japan; could he not become a Buddhist missionary to the west?

In 1959 the opportunity arose to do just that. The International Division of Soto headquarters, Soto-shu Shumucho, had established a number of missions for the benefit of Japanese immigrants and their descendants in California. Suzuki was invited to take responsibility for the San Francisco mission, Sokoji. The temple served about sixty Japanese families and was the center of community life, a place where traditional Japanese values were retained and respected in an environment often hostile to them.

The building was a former synagogue. Nothing about its architecture looked Japanese, much less like a Zen Temple. Pews were set up in an auditorium before an altar as in a Christian church. There were regular Sunday services at which the temple priest – addressed as "Reverend" – was expected to preach a sermon. Although there was a shrine room, there was no zendo or meditation hall. Zen might be the "meditation school" of Buddhism, but, like most Japanese, the temple members considered zazen something that monks – not lay people – did. The membership tended to be middle-aged or elderly and traditional. They welcomed Suzuki graciously but expected him to carry out his duties without fuss.

While temple members probably did not listen to Alan Watts' local radio broadcasts about Zen, many others outside the Japanese community did, and some began to look for a teacher to introduce them to Zen practice. A few took courses at Watts' American Academy for Asian Studies in San Francisco where Suzuki was invited to speak. He mentioned, in passing, that he sat zazen in the shrine room of Sokoji every morning at 5:45. None of the temple members sat with him, but gradually a handful of non-Asians started to show up.

Suzuki responded warmly to the occidental students. They were more curious about Zen than the laity in Japan had been, and they had the quality that he had recognized in Nona Ransom. Because they knew little about Buddhism, they were clean slates. They had what he called "beginner's mind."

The new students included teachers and housewives, people who had attended programs at the American Academy for Asian Studies, artists, and beatniks, to be followed later by hippies and even some street people.

There were serious and intent youth who used terminology they had picked up from reading D.T. Suzuki and Alan Watts. They were searching for a "Zen Master" – someone who had attained "satori" and had achieved "enlightenment." Shunryu Suzuki used none of these terms. The Soto meditation practice he introduced them to was very different from D.T. Suzuki's Rinzai Zen. There was less emphasis on achievement. In Rinzai practice, the need to attain awakening – kensho – is stressed, after which there remains the specter of hundreds of koans that students are expected to resolve in order to deepen their insight and integrate it into their lives. The practice was difficult for Japanese; it was often brutal and frustrating for Western students. North American meditators could spend years working on Mu without resolving it; the few who did pass it continued to struggle with and be stymied by other koans that drew imagery from Chinese and Japanese folklore or literature with which they were unfamiliar. Instead of koan study, the Soto practice asks only for the meditator to sit with an alert mind not focused on anything in particular. It is not necessarily an easier practice than working with koans, but for many North Americans it proved to be a more accessible one.

The western students remained distinct from, and not always welcomed by, the temple congregation. Slowly the Shrine Room was transformed into a room for meditation practice, a zendo with tatami mats and cushions called zafus (Buddha seats). There was no talk of enlightenment, no koans or obscure remarks. Suzuki's instruction focused almost exclusively on how to sit, how to place the hands, how to focus the attention on the breath. Occasionally a student would come with questions about theory or philosophy, but Suzuki became deft at side-stepping these. Over and over, he directed people back to practice.

It was important to Suzuki that the expenses associated with the zazen group be kept apart from those of the temple itself. He didn't think that the donations of the congregation should support the American students; the students needed to cover their own costs. So in 1961, the sitting group was incorporated as Zen Center.

In August of 1962, Zen Center held its first seven-day sesshin, after which fifteen members received what Suzuki called "Lay Ordination." They accepted the precepts of Buddhism and were given Buddhist names. The ceremony was conducted in Japanese and made use of traditional Japanese forms. These were the forms Suzuki knew. He told his students that American forms might eventually evolve, but until then they should use the forms he could teach them.

With incorporation, Suzuki's vision for Zen Center underwent a major change. It was no longer just a place where people came to practice zazen as one element among many in their lives. He began to see it as a training center based on Japanese models – in effect, a monastery.

Trained priests from Japan were recruited to work with both the Sokoji congregation and the zazen students.

Senior students were ordained as priests and sent to Japan for formal training. They weren't always inspired by what they found there. The Japanese authorities made no accommodations for their foreign novices. Every activity – other than zazen that was done in a cross-legged posture – was done seated in seiza, the traditional Japanese form of sitting on one's heels. In Japan, this was the natural way to sit; for Western students, used to chairs, it could be excruciating. There was a lot of popular superstition still associated with Buddhism, hungry ghosts, for example, that needed to be propitiated. The behavior of Japanese novices was often petty. Careerism and rivalries were still common in the Soto training centers. Suzuki was well aware of the problems in Japan and even harbored the hope that his American students might eventually reform the stagnant Soto School in Japan. He didn't like his students to complain, however, and told them to persevere and to write letters home that focused on the positive elements of their time in Japan.

Certain students were given more responsibility at Zen Center than others; the student Suzuki expected the most of was Richard Baker, who became the center's second president. As Baker's status rose, there were jealousies and rivalries. Members who had been with Suzuki longer than Baker resented the preference he was shown, but Suzuki recognized and admired Baker's energy and capacity to get things done. On July 2, 1967, Baker was installed as head monk at the training center recently established at Tassajara Hot Springs.

As the membership of Zen Center expanded, the congregation at Sokoji came to feel that Suzuki was spending too much time with his zazen students. Eventually they pressured him into resigning his post at the temple, and Zen Center was forced to look for other quarters. The new location was a former women's residence on the corner of Page and Laguna Streets. It could house 75 students who, as in Japan, would live in a residential monastic Zen community. There were four periods of zazen every day, as well as chanting and ritual services, communal vegetarian meals, and work assignments. The training regime for new students was what it had been in Japan; instead of being told what to do, new members were expected to observe senior students and follow their example.

Where Senzaki and Sokei-an had sought to develop a lay Zen practice in America, Suzuki was establishing a highly disciplined and structured monastic practice – although without the traditional celibacy associated with monasticism. What made it truly astonishing was that more anti-authoritarian counter-culture hippies sought to reside at Zen Center than it had room for. Many of those not able to live in the residence found apartments and rooms nearby in order to be close to it.

A new generation of students was practicing on Page street. Some of Suzuki's original students fell away, finding the new Center too large and institutional. Tassajara was placed under the direction of a Japanese novice master, Sotan Tatsugami, who insisted upon a highly ritualized – and very Japanese – practice format.

With Tassajara and Zen Center filled to capacity, all that Suzuki needed to ensure his legacy was to identify a successor, to give "transmission" to a worthy heir. There is evidence that he had intended to give transmission to several students, all of whom would then have had equal authority. But in the end, only one student – Baker – received transmission, and it was a controversial choice.

Part of the difficulty that would arise was that Suzuki's students understood transmission differently than he may have. The students had no doubt that their teacher was a fully enlightened and officially transmitted Zen Master although Suzuki had not claimed to be either. For Suzuki – as was common in the Soto tradition – transmission was more a matter of authorizing another to teach. Often it was conferred as a matter of course to ensure that a son inherited his father's temple; Suzuki, for example, conferred transmission on the son of a friend during a visit to Japan even though the young man had not studied with him. Suzuki's students, on the other hand, saw transmission as an acknowledgement of achievement, a recognition that the recipient was also now a fully enlightened teacher. When Suzuki's chosen heir later exhibited what others considered unenlightened behavior, it became problematic.

The reason no other student received transmission was that Suzuki was dying. His heath had been poor during a visit to Japan in 1970, although he seemed to recover when back in San Francisco. In March of the following year he had an operation to remove his gall bladder, and a routine biopsy revealed that it was cancerous.

Suzuki's impact was felt far beyond San Francisco because of a book of "informal talks" that became one of the bestselling Buddhist books of all time – *Zen Mind, Beginner's Mind*. The talks were short, spontaneous discussions of whatever was on Suzuki's mind at the time. Edited by one of Suzuki's disciples, they continue to provide an overview of his teaching and methodology.

The book begins with the practice of zazen. Following the teachings of Dogen, Suzuki stressed the importance of having a proper sitting posture:

> To take this posture itself is the purpose of our practice. When you have this posture, you have the right state of mind, so there is no need to try to attain some special state. When you try to attain

something, your mind starts to wander about somewhere else. When you do not try to attain anything, you have your own body and mind right here.[208]

Unlike in the Rinzai tradition, enlightenment was not considered something to strive for: "Enlightenment is not some good feeling or some particular state of mind. The state of mind that exists when you sit in the right posture is, itself, enlightenment."

Therefore, one practices meditation without seeking anything from it:

> The most important thing is to forget all gaining ideas, all dualistic ideas. In other words, just practicing zazen in a certain posture. Do not think about anything. Just remain on your cushion without expecting anything. Then eventually you will resume your own true nature. That is to say, your own true nature resumes itself.

The attention follows the breath as it comes in and goes out like a "swinging door." If students complained that they did not feel enlightened while sitting and following their breaths, Suzuki told them that the problem wasn't with the practice but with their desire to get something from it, the expectation that there was some special feeling they were supposed to get from sitting zazen.

Elsie Mitchell, who founded the Cambridge Buddhist Association in Massachusetts, related a story that captures the quality of character Shunryu Suzuki had that made so many people – students or otherwise – come to love him deeply.

She had invited him to visit their Center in 1964, and he accepted, informing her that he would arrive at the airport on a Wednesday evening. On Tuesday morning, several members of the Association met at Mitchell's house and began to prepare the place for Suzuki's arrival.

> That evening the library cum meditation room was in the process of being scrubbed down when the doorbell rang. My husband climbed down a ladder and opened the front door. Suzuki Roshi was on our doorstep with a smile on his face. He was amused to find us amid preparations for his arrival. In spite of our protests, he immediately tied back his long kimono sleeves and insisted on joining in "all these preparations for the important day of my

---

208. Quotations from Shunryu Suzuki, *Zen Mind, Beginner's Mind* (New York: Weatherhill, 1994).

coming." The following morning, after breakfast and a meditation session, and after I had left the house for shopping, he found himself a tall ladder, sponges, and pails. He then set to work scrubbing Cambridge grease, grime, and general pollution from the outside of the windows in the meditation room. When I returned with the groceries, I discovered him on the ladder, polishing with such undivided attention that he did not even hear my approach. He had removed his black silk kimono and was dressed only in his Japanese union suit. This is quite acceptable attire in Japan. Nevertheless, I could not help wondering how the sedate Cambridge ladies in the adjoining apartment house would react to the sight of a shaven-headed man in long underwear at work just outside their windows.[209]

Shunryu Suzuki died on December 4, 1971, just two weeks after Richard Baker had been formally installed as his successor and abbot – for life – of Zen Center.

Taizan Maezumi

The Soto-shu Shumucho that sent Shunryu Suzuki to San Francisco in 1959 had sent Hakuyu Taizan Maezumi to Los Angeles three years earlier. Unlike Suzuki, this was Maezumi's first posting; he was 25 years old at the time and was chosen to go to California because he had some knowledge of English. His duties were much the same as those Shunryu Suzuki would have in San Francisco: to conduct traditional ceremonies and otherwise minister to the needs of the local Japanese congregation. The mission was not wealthy, and Maezumi had to take a series of part-time jobs in order to cover his living expenses. He worked as a gardener and, for a time, composed texts for Chinese fortune cookies.

The Los Angeles congregation was no more interested in zazen than the congregation at Sokoji in San Francisco would prove to be, but Maezumi was committed to deepening his own practice. He studied Dogen's *Shobogenzo* with the Soto bishop, Reirin Yamada, and undertook koan practice with Nyogen Senzaki. Maezumi was surprised to find that Senzaki had a number of non-Japanese students. It hadn't occurred to him that Americans, whom he assumed were all Christian, might be interested in Buddhism.

Eventually, Maezumi recognized that if he were going to remain in the United States, he needed to improve his spoken English, so he enrolled in

---

209. Elsie P. Mitchell, *Sun Buddhas, Moon Buddhas* (New York: Weatherhill, 1973), pp. 189-90.

courses at the San Francisco State College. While in that city, he occasionally attended ceremonies at Sokoji. He also met Hakuun Yasutani during one of Yasutani's visits to the United States and served as his translator on subsequent visits.

When he returned to Los Angeles, Maezumi initiated a weekly zazen gathering. As in San Francisco, the people who showed up were not of Japanese descent but were rather young Western readers of Watts and D.T. Suzuki. Maezumi was a younger man than Shunryu Suzuki and more social. His American students were drawn to him as much by his friendly, open manner as by their sense of his spiritual understanding. The members of his Japanese congregation, however, were not happy about having to share him with the zazen students, and, by 1967, Maezumi realized he needed to find separate quarters for his meditation group. He located a house in what had been a Hispanic area of the city but was gradually transitioning to a Korean neighborhood. Here he established the Los Angeles Zendo, later to be renamed the Zen Center of Los Angeles or ZCLA. Maezumi declared his father, Hakujun (White Plum) Kuroda, the honorary founder of the zendo, and it was officially registered with Soto-shu in Japan.

Although he was already an authorized teacher, Maezumi continued to feel the need to deepen his practice in order to better serve his students. So in 1969, he left his senior disciple, Bernie Glassman, in charge of the Zendo and returned to Japan to continue koan study with Yasutani. He received inka from Yasutani the following year, after which he resumed work with a Rinzai teacher, Koryu Osaka, who offered to come to Los Angeles to complete his training. Over a period of three years, Maezumi went through 400 koans with Osaka and received transmission from him in 1973.

With authorization in the Soto, Rinzai, and Sanbo Kyodan schools, Maezumi's credentials were unrivaled by those of any other teacher in America.

Zen practice at ZCLA followed orthodox Japanese Soto guidelines augmented by koan study. Maezumi's insistence on correct ritual behavior, including formal prostrations, was a sticking point for some students, and he knew and expected that the first generation of American-born Zen teachers would make changes to these structures. His principal dharma heir, Bernie Glassman, noted:

> Over and over he said to me that I should take whatever I can from him – in terms of Zen – and then spit out what I think won't work in this country. He said, "I'm not an American. I'm Japanese. And I can't present the American Zen." He said, "You've got

to do that."[210]

But before Glassman or others made those accommodations, Maezumi wanted to ensure they were grounded in the traditional forms.

In spite of its strictness, ZCLA went through a period of rapid growth in the 1970s. The communal atmosphere of the Center proved to be a draw; unexpected numbers of people were attracted by the idea of living in a community focused on a formal spiritual practice. When John and Joan Loori first came to the center there were 27 residents including Glassman and his wife. The Looris and their four-year-old son were given a single room. Soon the number of residents was approaching 200, and space needed to be found to accommodate people.

In addition to the hippies then swarming to California in search of spiritual guidance, ZCLA also attracted a number of well-educated professionals. Glassman was an aeronautical engineer; Jan Chozen Bays (then Jan Soulé) was a pediatrician; John Daido Loori, a professional photographer; Gerry Shishin Wick was an atomic physicist and oceanographer. Maezumi ordained nearly thirty priests from among his senior students to provide leadership to the inquirers who continued to show up at the door, and, by the 1980s, he had given transmission to twelve individuals, some of whom went on to become teachers in their own right.

Two hundred people living together inevitably presented challenges. There were families with young children for whom childcare needed to be provided. Parents were torn between family responsibilities and the desire to commit as much time as possible to their quest for Enlightenment. On top of which most also had to earn a living. It became easy to understand why Zen practice in Japan took place under monastic conditions.

The situation was exacerbated by the fact that the neighborhood was not a good one in which to raise children. People in the area had mixed feelings about the relatively well-off outsiders who came to the center, and participants could be harassed as they made their way to and from morning or evening sits. There were also tensions between resident and non-resident students. The non-residents recognized that the resident students had greater access to the teacher than they did; the residents felt that non-residents didn't contribute as much to the maintenance of the center as the residents did.

The Center purchased buildings and apartment complexes on their block as they became available; these were prudent investments but required initial funding. Glassman proved to be a natural entrepreneur and – as Richard Baker was doing in San Francisco – he established a number of businesses to help meet rising expenses. ZCLA ran landscaping, carpentry,

---

210. Interview with the author, July 15, 2013.

house-painting, and even plumbing operations. Partly to establish good will with the surrounding community, he encouraged Chozen Bays to open a medical clinic. Services at the clinic expanded as new students came to Zen Center bringing with them expertise in alternative therapies such as chiropractic, acupuncture, and homeopathy. Originally intended to serve the neighborhood, the clinic began to draw clients from other parts of the city as well.

Maezumi was committed to ensuring that the Zen tradition would continue in America after the initial Japanese teachers gave way to a new generation of American-born teachers. He saw himself as a "stepping stone" in a process by which Zen would become fully Americanized. He envisioned a network of associated centers led by his Dharma heirs. Charlotte Beck opened a Zendo in San Diego. Glassman founded the Zen Community of New York, and Daido Loori established Zen Mountain Monastery in the Catskill Mountains. Chozen Bays established the Zen Community of Oregon, Genpo Merzel established the Kanzeon Zen Center in Salt Lake City, and Shishin Wick, the Great Mountain Zen Center outside Denver. Other centers would be established in Mexico, New Zealand, Great Britain, Switzerland, Belgium, the Netherlands, France, Germany, and Poland. Each of the new centers was registered with Soto-shu. ZCLA and its associated centers was easily one of the most vibrant Zen programs in America.

Maezumi assumed that people were drawn to Zen by a desire to discover their true nature, to understand the significance of birth and death. Anton Tenkel Coppens edited several of Maezumi's formal talks – *teishos* – for publication and chose to present them in poetic form in order to capture the slow, careful cadence of Maezumi's manner of speaking:

> Who are you?
> How come you are there?
> That is the question.
> What is there?
> Where did you come from
> standing there?
> If I present anything in particular
> as the answer,
> it is not it.[211]

---

211. Taizan Maezumi, *Teaching of the Great Mountain* (Rutland, VT: Tuttle Publishing,

In orthodox Soto fashion, Maezumi asserted that all persons are endowed with Buddha-nature; however, without practice and realization this Buddha-nature cannot be perceived. The wisdom, or understanding, Zen students strive for is

> – our life itself. We not only have that wisdom; we are constantly using it. When it's cold, we put on more clothing. When it's hot, we take some clothes off. When hungry, we eat. When sad, we cry. Being happy, we laugh. That's perfect wisdom.
>
> And this perfect wisdom doesn't only pertain to humans, but to anything and everything. Birds chirp, dogs run, mountains are high, valleys low. It's all perfect wisdom! The seasons change, the stars shine in the heavens; it's perfect wisdom! Regardless of whether we realize it or not, we are always in the midst of the Way. Or, more strictly speaking, we are nothing but the Way itself.[212]

The basis of Zen practice is zazen, which Maezumi presented much as Dogen had in the *Fukanzazengi*:

> First we learn to bring our bodies into harmony – we learn how to physically sit in the proper fashion. Then, sitting properly, our breathing settles into a harmonious cycle on its own – we stop panting and gasping and start to breathe easily, smoothly, and naturally. And as body and breath begin to settle down, and no longer create disturbances for us, we find that the mind too is given the opportunity to settle into its own smooth and natural functioning. The racket and babble of our noisy minds give way to the clarity and naturalness of our true selves.

Central to his teaching was the need to appreciate one's life "just as it is" – rather than to seek it to be something different. This was, he said, the "essence of Zen practice."

> The point of our practice is not to become something other than what we already are, such as a buddha or enlightened person, but to realize or become aware of the fact that we are intrinsically, originally, the Way itself, free and complete. If we practice to become something else, we simply put another head on top of our own.

2001), p. 14.

212. Quotations from Taizan Maezumi and Bernie Glassman, *On Zen Practice* (Boston: Wisdom Publications, 2000).

THE STORY OF ZEN

What hampers this realization is our

> – limited, self-centered consciousness. With consciousness per se, there is nothing at all wrong. Consciousness is a plain, pure function of the body-mind, and not a matter of right or wrong, problematical or not problematical. But our trouble is that we give too much value, too much authority, to our conscious functioning. We think that we can figure out everything by our intelligence, by our thinking, by our ideas and thoughts and concepts. That's how we get into trouble.

So, in practicing zazen, set aside those ideas and preconceived notions. Just stop that entire process of analysis and idea formation.

Koan work, for Maezumi, was an aid in overcoming this self-centered consciousness. Koan study in itself was not the main thing:

> The main thing is always oneself.
> And when oneself and the koan become identical
> that's the moment of realization
> of koan.[213]

Quoting Dogen, Maezumi reiterated that the proper way to study Self was to forget self. This was also the way to approach Mu.

> Dogen Zenji says, "Forget the self."
> Mu-ji,
> the same, see?
> Dissolve yourself into Mu-ji!
> Don't hold on to yourself
> when you are dealing with Mu.

> – when you work on koan,
> the important thing is no I, my, me.
> How can you do that?
> Throw yourself into the koan.
> Be the koan yourself.
> So when we work on Mu-ji
> become Mu yourself.
> Either way it's okay –
> give yourself altogether away to Mu,
> or let Mu occupy yourself completely.

---

213. *Teaching of the Great Mountain*, op. cit.

> Nothing but Mu!
> Give up yourself
> and let Mu-ji take care of it.

When self-centered consciousness comes to an end, then "you recognize that you and the universe are one"[214] – that is enlightenment.

Dainin Katagiri

Dainin Katagiri was born in Osaka in 1928. His family were devout Pure Land Buddhists, who gathered every morning to chant in front of the family shrine before beginning their daily chores. He was drafted into military service at the age of 15. The war was going badly, and the government called up all males over the age of 12. According to one of his Dharma heirs, Dosho Port, Katagiri had just been "a normal kid who believed what his government told him."

"He trained to be a kamikaze pilot," Dosho Roshi told me, "but flunked out because he couldn't master the training glider. So, he became an air force groundsman. Somewhere in there he had been a national champion marathon runner, representing the Air Force, but he had an intestinal obstruction and then a botched surgery that he suffered from throughout his life. The scar on his abdomen looked like they'd opened him up with a hand saw. So, he couldn't run anymore. He was then assigned to a base on Kyushu where he reported having great patriotic fervor, screaming with others, 'Die for the Emperor,' but when the American planes approached, everyone would run for their lives and jump into the fox holes. He said he'd cover his head with his arms and scream to himself, 'Save me Amida Buddha.'"[215]

Although he never left Japan and never saw battle, he had firsthand experience of the devastation wrought when, after the war, his platoon was marched through Ground Zero at Hiroshima.

It would have been a sobering occurrence, but he was still as devastated by the surrender as were the rest of his countrymen. The young, in particular, felt betrayed by leaders who had demanded enormous sacrifices but whose policies culminated in defeat and occupation. Katagiri's family's business had been destroyed by Allied bombing, leaving them destitute. He was depressed and unsure what value or significance his life held.

Everything in Japan changed after the surrender. American soldiers patrolled the streets and were in control of all national activities. Every major city in the country – except Kyoto which Allied forces had spared

---

214. Maezumi and Glassman, op. cit., p. 25.
215. Correspondence with the author, January 2019.

because of its religious importance – had been devastated by bombing; the manufacturing industry was in shambles. Poverty was the norm even for families that had been well-off; food shortages would continue for years.

The only place where things seemed to continue as they had before the war were Buddhist temples like Eiheiji. There monks spent their days, as they always had, in meditation and labor, in chanting and performing rituals for the benefit of others. Here there was the illusion of something permanent and stable in a world that – as the Buddhadharma teaches – is characterized by impermanence. Katagiri was drawn to Zen as much out of a nostalgia for a lost way of life as from a hope that it would help him find peace and a sense of meaning.

At the age of 18, he sought out his first teacher, Daicho Hayashi, a temple priest in the small fishing village of Taizoin in Fukai Prefecture. Later Katagiri would explain that Hayashi didn't so much teach Zen as exemplify it in the way he served the needs of his community. Katagiri was trained to perform memorial rituals and to chant sutras; he also spent time grooming the grounds and the small cemetery attached to the temple.

After a time with Hayashi, Katagiri went to Eiheiji for more formal training. The novice master was Eko Hashimoto. At their first formal meeting, Hashimoto gave his new charges this simple instruction, "Sit. Become Buddha." Katagiri was not entirely certain what was being asked of him but threw himself into the practice of shikan taza with all his will. His commitment to practice was noticed, and not long after he was appointed Hashimoto's attendant, a post usually reserved for more experienced students. It was a demanding position. Without being told what to do, the attendant was required to anticipate each of his master's needs – when to bring out his slippers, when to take them away, when to provide tea, when to clean up. The attendant was reprimanded whenever he failed to act promptly; there was no praise for carrying out the duties as expected.

After three years at Eiheiji, Katagiri received transmission, then went to Tokyo where he earned a Master's Degree in Buddhist studies at Komazawa University. Following graduation, he worked in the International Division of the Soto-shu Shumucho where he had responsibility for the temples that had been established in the United States. One of his early duties was to see Shunryu Suzuki off at the airport when he left for San Francisco.

In 1963, Bishop Reirin Yamada of Zenshuji in Los Angeles requested a priest to assist him. Katagiri applied for the position and was accepted. There was a large Japanese congregation at Zenshuji and several priests, including Taizan Maezumi. The bishop wanted Katagiri to work with the English-speaking second and third generation members, so, at first, he had no contact with Western students.

During a visit to San Francisco, he was re-introduced to Shunryu Suzuki. Although Sokoji was not as large as Zenshuji there seemed to be more going on, and, when Suzuki invited Katagiri to be his assistant, the younger man accepted with alacrity. His first duties were to the Japanese congregation at Sokoji which was pleased to have him, but he saw that Suzuki's interest was in the young Western students who showed up at the door seeking instruction in meditation. These were unlike any Zen students with whom Katagiri was familiar. They were largely undisciplined, morally lax, used drugs, and often lacked even basic hygiene; he had difficulty believing they were serious.

The irony was that while in Japan Zen was increasingly seen as one of the archaic institutions that young people sought to shed in their quest to re-establish their nation as a modern industrial and intellectual power, in the United State youth were turning to Zen as a way of seeking release from what they perceived as stifling social conditions. Katagiri eventually overcame his distaste for the counter-culture members and began to work with them.

He assisted Shunryu Suzuki from 1963 until 1971. In 1969, when Suzuki left Sokoji to focus on his American students at their new facilities on Page Street, Katagiri went with him. Suzuki appointed him Master of Training and told the students that Katagiri was to be formally addressed as Roshi. Suzuki depended on Katagiri and trusted him but also took him for granted. When it became clear that Richard Baker was Suzuki's intended heir, Katagiri wondered what future he had at SFZC.

Then a guest teacher, Sotan Tatsugami, was brought from Japan in 1970 at Baker's invitation in order to lead the practice periods at Tassajara, and Katagiri was asked to serve as his translator. He resented it. He began to think about starting his own zendo. He had the idea of operating one where what he thought of as ordinary Americans could learn the Dharma. As much as he had come to respect the commitment of the hippies at SFZC, he recognized that they didn't represent mainstream America.

Katagiri's first attempt to establish a zendo was in his own home in Monterey. Then, in 1972, he received an invitation from a small group in Minneapolis that included Robert Pirsig, author of the bestselling *Zen and the Art of Motorcycle Maintenance*. There Katagiri would have an opportunity to be a trailblazer. He pictured a Sangha of working people coming to the center before or after they went to their jobs.

He specifically asked his former students in California not to follow him; a few ignored that request and came anyway. When other Midwest youth heard that a Zen master had moved to Minnesota, they sought him out. The numbers were never large nor were they the kind of students Katagiri had imagined, but they were committed. The first major influx was made up of members from Stephen Gaskin's commune in Tennessee. Gaskin, an activist and counter-culture leader, was one of the inspirations behind a number of communal efforts blossoming throughout the United States at the time.

Pirsig donated $20,000 for the purchase of a building to house the center and provide accommodations for the teacher and his family. A former half-way house for drug addicts was found on Lake Calhoun. It was in poor repair, but the Tennessee commune members had sufficient carpentry skills to put things in order. The Center was officially inaugurated on February 1, 1976.

Katagiri's Zen was demanding. It was the practice of clear seeing, of perceiving things as they are rather than as one wishes or imagines them to be. There was an emphasis on impermanence and the realization that nothing has a static identity. Katagiri, who had a facility with analogies, used the example of water:

> – all phenomena in the world are constantly appearing, disappearing, and changing based on the conditions functioning in the moment. If you study water according to Buddhism, you may say, "Well, as a human being I think it is water for me to drink, but if I were a fish I would think that it is my house, my world. To me it is water, but to a fish it is not water." There are a hundred different ways to understand water, because a moment of existence is really complicated.
>
> The understanding that water has no permanent identity is the difference between Buddhism and our usual sense of things.[216]

Suffering (the Buddha's First Noble Truth) is essentially the result of the human desire (Second Noble Truth) that things be other than they are, the desire for permanence and stability in a world where they do not exist. People generally respond to that suffering in one of two ways. The more common is to seek relief through the pursuit of pleasure and a futile quest for physical security. The other is to develop what Katagiri called "a way-seeking mind" and the quest for spiritual security (Fourth Noble Truth).

> Spiritual security means you are fully alive and comfortable in your life as it is, without expecting anything. With a calm, way-seeking mind, you can face the naked nature of time, whatever happens, without escaping into your own ideas of

---

216. Quotations from Dainin Katagiri, *Each Moment Is the Universe* (Boston: Shambhala, 2011).

progress or meaning, relief or satisfaction. This is the way to find real relief and satisfaction, but it's not so easy to do.

The route to spiritual security is through zazen.

> As a human being, you inherently have a great capability that enables you to realize...truth and to experience your life with deep joy.
> To know this joy we practice looking at ourselves with a calm mind. That is Zen meditation, called *zazen*.

But this "deep joy" can only come about if one undertakes zazen without expecting anything from it. If one takes up the practice with expectations, those expectations cloud the ability to see clearly. Like Shunryu Suzuki – and in contrast to the teachers who emphasized the importance of attaining kensho – Katagiri instructs the student not to strive for anything in particular. "When you do zazen, don't have any expectations. You don't know what will happen. Zen Masters always tell you, 'Don't expect enlightenment – just sit!'"

> Buddhism is really hard, particularly Dogen's teaching. He gives you a very hard practice: Keep your mouth shut and look directly at impermanence! This living practice is called zazen. Zazen is not a way to escape from life by being mindful of something that is apart from the human world; it is the practice of being present in the real stream of time and looking directly at life itself. Zazen enables you to plunge below the surface and leads you to touch the core of your life. It's not so easy. But even so, you have to do it, because spiritual life originates from the direct observation of impermanence.

By zazen, Katagiri meant shikan taza. "In Rinzai Zen," he asserted, "they sit with many questions, many koans. In Soto Zen, we have just one big koan, so called *shikan taza*."[217] Students sat shikan taza and adhered to the four vows. By doing so, they overcame their own desires and learned to live in service to others. Katagiri called this "Selfishnessless." It was a practice that required perseverance and promised, as Katagiri put it, "no sweet candy."

---

217. Dosho Mike Port, *Keep Me in Your Heart a While* (Boston: Wisdom Publications, 2009), p. 43.

In January of 1989, Katagiri was diagnosed with terminal cancer. Determined that his work continue after his death, he began formal ceremonies to give transmission to twelve of his students. He chose not to identify any of them as his principal heir; it was his intention that they remain peers, equally responsible for continuing the spread of the Dharma.

He died on March 1, 1990, at the age of sixty. A portion of his ashes was buried near those of Shunryu Suzuki at Tassajara; another was buried in Minnesota.

Robert Aitken

While Nyogen Senzaki and Sokei-an Sasaki were in internment camps in the United States, Robert Aitken was a prisoner-of-war in Japan. He had been working with a construction crew on Guam when the island was captured the day after the attack on Pearl Harbor. The crew members were classified as "Military-Civilian Prisoners of War." As such, they were kept separate from military prisoners and were spared the harsh treatment to which those prisoners were at times subjected. On the whole, Aitken had greater liberty than Senzaki and Sokei-an had in the United States.

There was a library to which the detainees had access; they were also allowed brief excursions into the town for medical appointments and to purchase books and other supplies. The book that redirected his life, however, did not come from the library or a bookstore but was loaned to him by one of the guards. It was *Zen in English Literature and Oriental Classics* by Reginald Horace Blyth, who had taught English at the high school the guard had attended. Blyth was not a Zen practitioner but valued Zen insight which he believed was universal. The book was an attempt to demonstrate that Zen themes – such as the quest for enlightenment – were common throughout world literature. It was an unorthodox approach but an ideal introduction for Aitken, who already admired the Zen poetry he had encountered.

Coincidentally, Blyth was not far away in another camp for civilian prisoners where he was detained as an "enemy alien." In 1944, the prison camps in the area were combined, and Blyth and Aitken were both housed in a complex that had previously been a reform school. They became friends and shared a common attitude to their imprisonment, turning it into something like a monastic opportunity for study. Blyth taught Aitken some rudimentary Japanese and introduced him to Suzuki's *Essays in Zen Buddhism*.

After the war, Aitken attended the University of Hawaii and graduated in 1947. From there, he and his wife, Mary, went to California where they met Nyogen Senzaki. Aitken enjoyed discussing philosophy and literature with Senzaki, as he had with Blyth, but eventually realized that what he wanted was not information but a way to develop the insights that animated Senzaki. So he and Mary joined Senzaki's meditation group. Instead of a traditional koan, Senzaki assigned Aitken Meister Eckhart's "the eye with which I see God is the same eye with which God sees me." "Show me that eye," Senzaki commanded him.

In 1950, the Aitkens returned to Hawaii where Robert completed a master's degree on the haiku of Matsuo Basho. He also helped organize the East-West Philosopher's Conference that D.T. Suzuki attended. When Robert expressed an interest in returning to Japan in order to pursue further Zen training, Suzuki helped him obtain a fellowship to do so. Mary had recently given birth to their son, Thomas, and chose to remain in Hawaii.

Back in Japan, Aitken renewed his acquaintance with Blyth, who arranged for him to take part in a week long sesshin at Engakuji in Kamakura under the direction of Asahina Sogen. This was Aitken's first experience of extended zazen. He was thirty-three years old and not very flexible but was expected to sit in traditional cross-legged posture for ten to twelve hours a day. The participants were given no formal instruction, although the monk seated beside Aitken was told to explain zendo protocols to him. When they were introduced, the monk said, "How do you do? The world is very broad, don't you think?" Aitken admitted later that he had no idea what the monk meant but was charmed, nonetheless.

Eagerly, Aitken took his place on the *tan* (platform) where the monks were seated. The atmosphere in the zendo was all he had imagined it would be – incense burning, black-robed monks steeling themselves for the ordeal ahead, the sounds of the various clackers, drums, and bells, even the staccato chanting of the opening ceremonies. Then the teacher prostrated himself before the altar with its image of Manjusri, the Bodhisattva who oversees sesshin. Not once, but a total of nine times, Asahina Roshi lowered himself to his knees, bent forward until his forehead touched the floor, then brought his hands beside his head palms up and made a lifting motion, as if receiving the feet of the Buddha. Aitken was appalled to realize that he, too, would be expected to prostrate himself before the statue. His western sense of dignity and a cultural aversion to idol worship rose up in protest. He had not fully comprehended until that moment that Zen was more than a psychological practice; it was a religion. He continued with the sesshin but with new reservations about Zen or what he had imagined Zen to be.

In sanzen, he informed Asahina that Senzaki had assigned him the Eckhart quotation as a koan, and Asahina told him to meditate on Huineng's "Original Face" instead, that, he explained, had the same intent. It was difficult to remain focused on the koan, however, as he struggled with the pain in his legs and rising doubts about the ritual elements of the sesshin. In spite of these challenges, he persisted and, in December, returned to Engakuji to take part in the Rohatsu sesshin.

Through Nyogen Senzaki, Aitken received an invitation to visit Soen Nakagawa at Ryutakuji. Nakagawa explained that it was not unusual for Zen students to attend sesshin at a number of temples and with different teachers before they found the one best suited to them. He suggested Aitken take part in their January sesshin.

The teacher at Ryutakuji, Gempo Yamamoto, felt that Aitken's approach to "Original Face" was too intellectual, so he assigned him Joshu's Mu, which allowed no room for rational analysis.

> I felt a little resistance to this change, but on returning to my cushions, I discovered what zazen really is. No longer was I aware that the cracks in the tile floor formed a weird pattern. I could sink at last beneath the surface of my mind.[218]

Aitken stayed at Ryutakuji for the remainder of his time in Japan, but the physical demands of monastic life were ruinous to his health. His knees and legs ached constantly, and the drafts in the zendo during winter exacerbated respiratory problems he'd had since his time in internment. Finally, after being hospitalized with dysentery, he returned to Hawaii disappointed by what he considered a lack of progress.

After his return, things didn't go well for him. He had difficulty finding appropriate work; his marriage unravelled. After his divorce, he returned to Los Angeles in order to train with Nyogen Senzaki. He found a job in a bookstore where he earned so little that all he could afford for housing was a room at the YMCA.

In 1956, another of Senzaki's students told Aitken that Krishnamurti's Happy Valley School in Ojai was in need of an English teacher. Jiddhu Krishnamurti was an Indian-born mystic who many Theosophists believed to be an incarnation of the Buddha.[219] Aitken applied for the position and was accepted. Within a year he was married to the school's assistant director, Anne Hopkins.

Their wedding trip to Japan wasn't what most newlyweds would have considered a honeymoon. The day after they arrived, Aitken abandoned the marriage bed to attend sesshin at Ryutakuji where Nakagawa was now abbot. Anne supported her new husband's desire to take part in the sesshin but had no intention herself of spending seven days sitting immobile with aching knees. Nakagawa made one of the monastery's guest rooms available to her. It had a fine view of the temple garden, and, while Aitken struggled with Mu, Anne passed the time reading the few English books available in the temple library. Nothing she read changed her mind about

---

218. Robert Aitken, *Taking the Path of Zen* (New York: North Point Press, 1982), p. 118.
219. Cf. p. 314 below.

the practice of zazen.

After the sesshin, Nakagawa served as a tour guide for the newlyweds, taking them, among other places, to Mount Fuji. He also introduced them to Tai-san Shimano. Then, in August, Robert went with Nakagawa to participate in sesshin with Hakuun Yasutani. Anne had not intended to take part in it; however, there was little else for her to do. Yasutani provided her a western-style easy chair on the verandah where she was free to sit if she chose; it was similar to the accommodation Nanshinken had made for Ruth Fuller years earlier. Anne didn't care where she sat; she was just filling time. Yasutani also told her she could attend dokusan if she wished. It was those private meetings with Yasutani that finally broke down her resistance to zazen, and before the sesshin was over she was making a serious effort.

By the end of the sesshin, two participants had attained kensho, and, while Aitken hadn't done so himself, he was convinced in a way he hadn't been before that awakening was achievable.

The Aitkens moved to Hawaii so Robert could be nearer his son, and in Honolulu, they opened a second-hand bookstore specializing in books on Asian spirituality. They kept a record of customers who purchased books on Buddhism and – when they received authorization from Nakagawa to organize a sitting group – invited those customers to join them for regular Zen practice at their home. Only two others joined them in their first sitting, but the number of attendees increased steadily. The group referred to itself as the Diamond Sangha, an allusion to both the *Diamond Sutra* and the nearby Diamond Head peak. Shimano was sent from Japan to assist them. Eventually, they needed to move to larger accommodations. When Soen Nakagawa visited the new house, he named it Koko An.

In 1961, Nakagawa led a sesshin at Koko An that Aitken approached with determination. He put as much vigor into his sitting as he was able to muster and continued late into the night after the formal meditation periods had ended. Then, on the fifth day of the sesshin,

> – Nakagawa Roshi gave a great "Katsu!"[220] in the zendo, and I found my voice uniting with his, "Aaaah!" In the next dokusan, he asked me…a checking question. I could not answer, and he simply terminated the interview. In a later dokusan, he said that I had experienced a little bit of light and that I should be very careful.[221]

---

220. A traditional but meaningless shout. Cf. Linji's "Ho!" p. 153 above.
221. Aitken, op. cit. 123.

In 1967, Aitken turned 50. Anne was 56. They began to think about their eventual retirement and purchased a former hotel rumored to have once been a geisha house on the island of Maui. It had previously been rented to a succession of young social drop-outs. Hippies had arrived in Hawaii, and Maui was a popular destination. The island was under-populated and had large public beaches. There was ample space to build make-shift shelters, fresh fruit in abundance, and a climate suitable for clothing-optional lifestyles. Drugs were also easily accessible. Before the Aitkens moved to their new property, they allowed young people to stay there in exchange for looking after the grounds. It turned out to be a one-sided arrangement.

People kept showing up even after the Aitkens were in residence, and Aitken recognized that some of them, at least, were genuinely engaged in a spiritual quest. The new inquirers were very different from the original membership of the Diamond Sangha who had belonged to the generation largely drawn to Buddhism through their interest in Theosophy and the occult. Many of the new, younger, members had been attracted to meditation as a result of their drug experiences. So, although they had not originally intended to do so, the Aitkens once more opened their home to people interested in practicing Zen. The response was even greater than it had been in the city, and the new Maui Zendo became an official center of the Sanbo Kyodan Zen School. Although it remained a center for lay practice, Aitken established a formal schedule centering around zazen and manual labor that was almost monastic; he decided that the young people with whom he was now working needed structure in their lives.

In Honolulu, meanwhile, the Koko An Sangha was firmly enough established to continue without the Aitkens' daily supervision, although Robert returned regularly to sit with the group. Shimano had moved to New York by this time, so Nakagawa arranged for one of his lay students, Katsuki Sekida, to move to Hawaii to assist the two communities.

Not all awakening experiences are dramatic, and, after a time with the Diamond Sangha, Sekida came to believe that Aitken had attained realization without being aware of it. He expressed his opinion to Yasutani who had come to conduct the first sesshin at the Maui Zendo in October 1969. Yasutani tested Aitken and agreed that he'd had kensho, although Aitken himself remained unsure.

After Yasutani retired, his successor – Yamada Koun – continued to lead sesshin in Hawaii, and it was Yamada Roshi who gave Aitken inka in 1974. Still doubtful of his qualifications, Aitken went to California to do further training with Taizan Maezumi. Afterwards, encouraged by Maezumi and Yamada, Aitken felt confident enough to take on the responsibilities of a teacher and became the first American to be given the title *Roshi*.[222]

Prior to transmission, Aitken also took part in a ceremony called jukai. Jukai refers to "taking the precepts" or agreeing to abide by the precepts. It has been described as "lay ordination" by some North American practitioners, but Aitken objected to that terminology. He thought of himself as a layman and, to his mind, ordination meant something else. In current Western usage, jukai is more frequently a formal way of declaring oneself to be a member of the Buddhist community.

Now that he was an authorized teacher within the sangha, Aitken felt that he needed to determine how that role should be defined in a lay western – as opposed to a monastic Japanese – context. His practice was intimately connected to social and political activism. That type of engagement was unknown in Japan nor would it be a priority for most of those who came to the Maui or Koko An Sanghas. Aitken was one of the founders of the Buddhist Peace Fellowship and was committed to environmental issues, pointing out that one of the fundamental teachings – and realizations – of the Zen school was the interconnectedness of all things. His spiritual practice wasn't a retreat from the world and its challenges, as it could be for persons entering monasteries whether Buddhist or otherwise; for him, practice included being deeply engaged in the world.

The Maui Center had been communal from its beginning but was not a monastery. The question of what shape that community should take was a complex one. With transmission, Aitken had gone from being a senior student (a first among peers, as it were) to being the teacher, and while he didn't view himself as an authority figure, others started to. He was aware that the traditional structures of Zen practice were cultural rather than intrinsic and over time it became clear that many of the forms could be moderated. Japanese behaviors fell away, although students still bowed – rather than prostrated – when presenting themselves at dokusan. Experiments were made in coming to community decisions through consensus.

There were things, however, about which Aitken was inflexible, such as prohibiting the use of marijuana which most of the students considered harmless. Some members drifted away, feeling the rules were too

---

222. Regarding the title "Roshi," see fnt. 36 above, p. 92. There are two ranks of "Zen Master" in the Sanbo Zen school. The first is *junshike*, roughly equivalent to "associate Zen Master." The second, *shoshike* – which Aitken received in 1985 – conveys full transmission. Aitken was the only American to receive full transmission from Yamada, and that was later questioned by Yamada's heirs. The issue eventually resulted in the Diamond Sangha separating from the Sanbo Kyodan School in what Aitken described as an "amicable divorce" in 1995.

strict; on the other hand, Yamada – a gentle and humble man by Japanese standards – was uncomfortable with what he considered the degree of informality he found at the Zendo.

The process of developing appropriate Zen structures and traditions for North Americans was going to be a long and difficult one played out over and over again in Maui, San Francisco, Los Angeles, Minneapolis, Rochester, and elsewhere.

Robert Aitken died in 2010 at the age of 93.

Joshu Sasaki

In his history of American Buddhism – *How the Swans Came to the Lake* – Rick Fields recounts the story of the time Rinzai master, Joshu Sasaki, gave a talk at the Berkeley campus of the University of California. One of the people in attendance asked if there were a place in the San Francisco area where one could get Zen training. Sasaki appeared to give the question a moment's thought then said he wasn't aware of any and suggested that if the inquirer were serious, he should arrange to visit Sasaki's center in Los Angeles.

> There was a surprised, audible reaction from the audience, many of whom were students and friends of Suzuki-roshi's San Francisco Zen Center, which by then had more than one branch in the Bay area, and Sasaki's translator, a Japanese-American doctor, hastened to add, "The roshi means that there is nowhere else where one can study his particular line of Zen."[223]

It is possible that Sasaki was making a distinction between Soto and Rinzai Zen; the Zen community in the United States, even in its earliest days, was divided along sectarian lines. It is also true, as Fields adds, that "it certainly appeared – to some at least – that the roshi had rather enjoyed the stir his blunt answer had caused."

Sasaki is sometimes identified as the fourth of four Japanese missionaries – following Shunryu Suzuki, Taizan Maezumi, and Eido Shimano – who established Zen practice in America. He was two decades older than Maezumi and Shimano, although they came to the US before him, and only a few years younger than Suzuki. He had been born in 1907, was ordained a monk at the age of fourteen, and became an osho – or priest – seven years later. He spent several years at Myoshinji in Kyoto, which remains one of the principal teaching centers for Rinzai Zen. In 1947, at the age of 40, he was given Dharma Transmission and became abbot of a

---

223. Rick Fields, *How the Swans Came to the Lake* (Boston: Shambhala, 1992), p. 247.

small temple in Nagano Prefecture.

According to an interview Sasaki gave in 1969, he'd had no idea of coming to the United States until two American aspirants, Dr. Robert Harmon and Gladys Weisberg, wrote to Myoshinji requesting that an authorized teacher be sent to Los Angeles.

> Up until that time, I had no dreams whatever of coming to the United States and furthermore the temple I belonged to was so poor that they couldn't entertain any such ideas. However, Myoshin-ji said that I would be very useful in the United States so suggested I come here.[224]

He arrived in America, reputedly, with only the robes he was wearing, a Japanese/English dictionary, a Bible, and a small valise. He didn't waste time but began receiving students almost at once in a one-bedroom house in a Los Angeles suburb. Within five years, the group moved to new quarters in what had once been a luxurious residence on the corner of Cimarron and 25th Streets. The neighborhood had deteriorated, and the building itself had been condemned by the city as unsafe for occupancy. Sasaki's students, however, refurbished it, and it was officially opened on April 21, 1968 – Sasaki's 61st birthday – as the Cimarron Zen Center. Later the name would be changed to Rinzai-ji. 200 students took part in the opening ceremonies.

Three years later the community had sufficient funds to purchase another property in the San Gabriel Mountains east of the city. This became the Mount Baldy Zen Center. A third center – the Bodhi Manda Zen Center in Jemez Springs, New Mexico – was established in 1973. The three centers quickly acquired reputations as rigorous and austere practice centers. In a talk given at Bodhi Manda, Sasaki said: "The standpoint of this Zen Center is our own practice of Dharma Activity. Therefore, we accept those who want to study Dharma Activity. Those who are not interested in Dharma Activity should leave immediately." The training provided wasn't easy nor for the faint of heart. Sasaki's type of Zen has been described as Samurai. Those who couldn't cut it were invited to "leave immediately."

Many did. More to the point, there were others who remained and flourished. Within a few years, senior students established affiliate centers elsewhere in the United States, Canada, and Europe. Sasaki received invitations to facilitate sesshin at locations throughout North America including St. Joseph's Roman Catholic Trappist Monastery in Spencer, Massachusetts.

---

224. sasakiarchive.com/PDFs/19691220_Sasaki_Interview.pdf.

His students worked with koans but instead of being chosen from classical collections these were often adapted to the condition of the particular student. One might be asked how he realized Buddha nature while driving an automobile. To the monks at St. Joseph's, he assigned the question, "How do you realize God when making the sign of the cross?"

Sasaki never acquired a very good command of English and had to make use of translators throughout his time in America, even so it was the impact of his personality that his admirers most frequently reference when talking about him. The Canadian song-writer, Leonard Cohen who spent a period of residency at Mount Baldy in the 1990s, said that Sasaki was such an inspiring figure that were he to have been a Heidelberg physicist, Cohen would have learned German and studied physics.[225]

Seiju Bob Mammoser was at one time thought to be in line to become abbot of Rinzai-ji after Sasaki retired, although this never came about. When I spoke with him in 2013, I was struck by how reserved and even cautious he was when speaking except when talking about Sasaki, whom he always described in superlatives. He was "amazing" and "an utterly remarkable, unique man." I asked in what way, and he told me, "You meet somebody who inspires you. Motivates you and moves you and demonstrates – in front of you, in his manifestation – exactly what he's talking about. I hadn't really met other teachers. I'd read books. I'd read *Zen Mind, Beginner's Mind*. That was a beautiful book. But he was the first living teacher I'd met. He was sufficient. I didn't have to go see somebody else. I knew what I was dealing with."

Father Kevin Hunt, a member of the Trappist Community at Spencer and an authorized Zen teacher, was equally fulsome in his praise of Sasaki. "We had him in choir, and he had a room in the monastery itself. So he participated; he ate in our dining room. He gave a couple of talks to the community. There was quite a lot of interest in what he said. Basically, he spoke of his experience in meditation and the Zen way of doing meditation. And, you know, a novice master had once said to me, 'If there's any rule in prayer it is that it will always become simpler. Less verbal.' And so, he addressed that aspect, that in Zen there's no talking. That to speak a word in Zen is already a betrayal. And that was something that we could identify with because we had a rule of silence, and silence is very, very important in our practice. And he loved it, so somebody said to him something about coming back sometime and giving a weekend sesshin. And so, he said, 'Yes. I come back next year.'"

---

225. Cohen also admitted that he and other Sasaki students "were gravitating to teachers who were quite flawed as human beings, but that's what we cherished. We wanted to see the dark side made bright." http://sasakiarchive.com/Video/JoshuSasakiPortrait.mov.

In fact, he came back ten years in succession to lead retreats at St. Joseph's.

He most definitely did not coddle his students. When I asked Zengetsu Myokyo Judith McLean of the Enpuku-ji center in Montreal what Sasaki Roshi was like as a teacher, her immediate answer surprised me:

"He was cruel. He was strong. He was…"

I interrupted to ask what she meant by "cruel" and why that was the first thing she said. She explained that she hadn't meant it as a criticism. "I was talking with a student here yesterday, and, it seems to me, it was a very effective tool for dissolving the ego."

"The strongest teaching he gave me," she went on a bit later, "was that he gave me a lot of responsibility." She had been head monk of Rinzai-ji in Los Angeles in 1992 during the Rodney King riots. Sasaki, himself, was away at the time. "That was a lot of responsibility, because we were hemmed in. There were fires all around us and so on. And never any comment about 'job well done' or how bad it was.

"And while I was at Rinzai-ji, there was a very, very difficult older nun. She was an alcoholic. Very difficult. She used to drive people away from the Zen Center. So I was in charge of her there, and I dealt with her in an okay way. Then the Roshi turned the tables on us, and he made her the head monk. And things went kind of crazy. Like really crazy. So that was a cruel situation. And he watched and watched and no comment. He watched to see how I dealt with that. So, at the time, that seemed cruel to me. But he's just cutting off any kind of attempt to grandify oneself or to even feel competent. Because we all had something more to learn in the sense of dissolving our self.

"His methods are very effective. I mean, when your whole world falls apart, then you learn from that. And if that keeps on happening, then you keep on learning. And so, if I had someone who was just kind and helped me along a little bit, that wasn't so interesting. So, I think it's a very particular kind of character that would study with a teacher like that. I was very stubborn, but there was never a doubt in my mind that this was the person I wanted to study with, that I was glad to be studying with. No doubt. Even when it was difficult and I felt he should really give me a break once in a while, still there was no doubt in my mind."

Others have described him as "playful," charming, and as having an infectious laugh. He advised his students – whom he accused at times of being too serious and humorless – to practice laughing as a spiritual practice.

> When you wake up tomorrow morning, first thing, stand up, put your hands on your hips, and laugh five or ten times, and that will cure you of much of your illness. This exercise is even better than a long period of meditative sitting. As a beginner in meditation,

instead of suffering a long period of cramped legs, it would be better for you every morning as soon as you get up to immediately stand in this position and laugh about ten times. This is really the best beginning of Zen. If during that time you are doing this exercise and laughing vigorously, I were to ask you "Where was God at that time?" "How would you answer? Then immediately your logic and your consciousness starts to work. That is what is bad. That is time and space learning. That is not Zen. Just simply laugh and you will begin to realize.[226]

Although Sasaki ordained individuals like Seiju and Myokyo as Oshos and assigned them their own centers, what he did not do is give any of his oshos "transmission." None of them would be his heir, and – without transmission – none would have authorization in the Rinzai system to identify their own heirs. Where other Japanese teachers were concerned to ensure that there would be an official line of succession after their deaths, Sasaki was not.

He died on July 27, 2014, at the age of 107, without having named a successor.

Walter Nowick

The first non-Asian to establish a zendo in the continental US did so not on the west coast or in the Metropolitan northeast, but in the woods of rural Maine. Students who wanted to work with Walter Nowick had to begin by finding him.

Nowick was the fourth of seven children born to Russian immigrants who had a potato farm on Long Island. It was a cultured family, and Nowick's mother insisted that her children take piano lessons. Walter showed the most talent and entered Juilliard while still in high school. His piano tutor there, Henriette Michelson, spent her summers in Maine teaching at the Kneisel Hall Chamber Music Program. Nowick was one of the students who regularly accompanied her, and, while in Maine, he lodged at the farmhouse of Leverett and Addie Morgan in the township of Surry. The Morgans and Nowick became friends, and he became fond of the area.

After graduating high school, Nowick enlisted in the army and was involved in the "mopping up" campaign on Okinawa. The brutality he witnessed there affected him profoundly and roused an unexpected sympathy for the suffering of the Japanese populace.

After demobilization, he returned to Juilliard, and, one day, while sitting in Henriette's waiting room, he saw a translation Sokei-an Sasaki had

---

226. https://terebess.hu/zen/mesterek/Joshu-Sasaki-Roshi-About-Zazen.pdf

made of a classic Zen text, the *Zenrin Kushu*. The sensibility expressed in one verse, in particular, struck Nowick:

> Bamboo shadows sweep the stairs, yet not a speck of dust is stirred;
> Moonlight penetrates the bottom of the lake, yet not a trace remains.

Michelson was a member of the First Zen Institute in New York, and Nowick began to accompany her to zazen sessions. His commitment to practice caught Ruth Sasaki's attention, and, after he completed his music degree, she suggested he go to Japan to study with Zuigan Goto at Daitokuji.

Although he would eventually become proficient in the language, Nowick spoke no Japanese when he arrived in Kyoto in 1950. Goto, however, had a smattering of English. During his first sanzen with Goto, Nowick – overwhelmed by the strangeness of everything around him and the formality of the occasion – stammered, "I may be a little slow."

"It doesn't matter," Goto told him. "Slow or fast. We will proceed."

Daitokuji was a training center for young men preparing to become temple priests. The training was rigorous. Depending on the time of year, the day began at either 3:00 or 4:00 a.m. with two hours of meditation and a chanting service; there was another four hours of meditation in the evening. During the day, the monks were engaged in various maintenance tasks. Once a day, each student met with Goto to report on his practice. During sesshin, the schedule was even more arduous.

When Sean Murphy asked Nowick if he hadn't found conditions at Daitokuji daunting, Nowick told him:

> If you want to play the piano in a certain style...you find the person who teaches that style best, and do what they say. If you want to do something else, you do something else. But if you want to learn what they have to teach, you follow their directions.[227]

After a period as a resident student at Daitokuji, Nowick moved out of the temple and continued as a lay student. He earned a living by providing music lessons to private students as well as teaching at the Kyoto Women's University and the Kyoto Music School. In all, Nowick spent sixteen years in Japan. He took the precepts from Goto and was given the Buddhist name Gessen, which translates as "Source of the Moon" or Moonspring. He remained a lay person, however. It had never been his, or Goto's, intention that he become a priest.

He didn't return to the US permanently until after Goto's death in 1965. The Morgans had died in the interim, and Nowick's family had

---

227. Sean Murphy, *One Bird, One Stone* (New York: Renaissance Books, 2002), p. 63.

bought their farm in Surry for him, perhaps as an incentive for him to return home. When he returned to Maine, he brought a third of Goto's ashes with him.

Nowick, then forty years old, moved into the Morgans' farm house and redesigned the second floor in Japanese style with tatami mats, shoji screens, and a Buddha altar. He maintained his personal practice but gave no thought to teaching Zen. Instead, he taught in the Music Department at the University of Maine at Orono and supported a number of music students from Japan who came to America to further their studies. These young people either lodged with Nowick or with one of the families in the area who were used to hosting students. The Morgans' barn proved to have unusually good acoustics and was converted into a concert hall where performances by the visiting students were given.

One of the Japanese youths who came to Surry was Masanobu Ikemiya, who had studied Zen with Soko Morinaga, Zuigan Goto's heir at Daitokuji. In 1967, Ikemiya was accepted at the Music Conservatory of Oberlin College in Ohio, and Morinaga arranged an introduction to Nowick. Nowick invited the young man to Morgan Bay for the Christmas break, and the two sat zazen together in the mornings. Slowly, other students seeking Zen instruction showed up.

Lenore Straus, a sculptor, had met Nowick while she had been supervising the installation of an exhibit in Japan. He gave her her first zazen instruction during that visit, and, when she returned to the US, she continued to attend sesshin with Hakuun Yasutani. She resolved the koan Mu during a retreat at Pendle Hill, Pennsylvania.[228] After achieving kensho, she wanted to maintain and deepen her practice. When she learned that Nowick was back in the United States, she made her way to Surry and asked him to be her teacher. Other students were referred to him by the First Zen Institute.

In 1968, with some reluctance, Nowick agreed to work with a small number of students he felt were sincere enough to commit themselves to practice. He established a board of directors, and they incorporated "Moonspring Hermitage." Nowick still considered himself to be primarily a musician, and many of the students who came to Moonspring were musicians as well. The statement of purpose declared that Moonspring Hermitage had been established to "maintain, and support a religious, philosophical and cultural center or centers dedicated to teaching in regular meetings between students and teachers, the spirit, precepts, and practice of Zen Buddhism and to encourage and teach the practice of the arts."

---

228. Lenore Straus's description of her kensho is included in Philip Kapleau et al., *The Three Pillars of Zen* (New York: Anchor, 1989), pp. 250-54.

Nowick tried to recreate something of the atmosphere of Daitokuji at Moonspring. There were two three-month training periods a year, run as formally as those in Japan. A woodshed was converted into a small zendo, and a sanzen room was improvised in Nowick's living quarters. Ever since the eighth century Chinese Zen Master, Baizhang Huaihai had declared that "a day of no work is a day of no food," manual labor has been a traditional part of formal Zen training. So Nowick revived the Morgan farm in order to provide work and income for the community developing there.

Nowick allowed students to call him by his first name, although those who preferred to be more formal addressed him as "Sensei." He didn't insist upon rituals, seldom gave formal talks, and refused to discuss theory. For him, Zen consisted of zazen, sanzen, and mindful labor. He insisted that students give their full attention to whatever activity they were engaged in, whether in the zendo or the fields.

He also stressed that Zen training wasn't automatic and that following a certain discipline doesn't necessarily guarantee a particular result. "What you are doing here isn't easy," he is reported to have told students taking part in a sesshin:

> Your body hurts and your mind creaks with stress. The trouble you are going to, and which you think will release you in the end, is nearly maximal.
>
> But…you must be aware that it is quite possible that this training may not give you any result whatever.[229]

In spite of the challenges, students continued to arrive, and by 1969 it was necessary to build a larger zendo to accommodate them. The lumber was milled on site from trees harvested on the property, and the community – under the supervision of a student who had worked as a set-designer for motion pictures – completed the construction of the new zendo in 1971. Soko Morinaga came to Maine to take part in the official inauguration.

Near the zendo, a short path – marked by a statue carved by Lenore Straus – led to a glacial rock known as the "Roshi Stone" where, three years prior, Nowick had interred the ashes of his teacher. A plaque, marking the spot, read:

> Here lie some of the ashes of the Japanese Zen Master Goto Zuigan, my teacher. They were placed here in October 1968, with hope that his teaching will continue.

---

229. Janwillen van de Wetering, *A Glimpse of Nothingness* (New York: St. Martin's Griffin, 1975), p. 132. Van de Wetering wrote three semi-fictional books on Nowick; in the first two (*The Empty Mirror* and *A Glimpse of Nothingness*), Nowick is called "Peter." In the third (*Afterzen*), he is called "Sensei."

Nowick had a complex personality. He could be friendly, humorous, and enormously generous and caring. He enjoyed preparing meals for people, and he loved music. When he sang Schubert, it was with an exuberance that affected even people unfamiliar with classical music. But he was a demanding Zen teacher. While it was not a role he had sought, it was one he took seriously. Unfamiliar with what was happening elsewhere in the United States in the still fledgling Zen movement, he developed his own style of teaching and working with students, bringing to it the single-minded, autocratic perspective of an orchestra conductor – or of the Japanese teachers with whom he was familiar.

Those who came to Moonspring did so because they were in search of something. The Vietnam War had polarized the generations, and there was general anxiety about a possible nuclear conflict. Young people throughout the western world were questioning the values and standards of their elders. They recognized the underlying racism and sexism of contemporary society and sought to address them. Many abandoned the religious traditions of their parents. Driven by what Buddhists term "suffering," they sought teachers who – they hoped – could show them a better way. They made sacrifices to come to Maine and put up with hardships their peers would have scorned. But by the early 1980s, some students began to question whether Nowick's heart was still in the teaching.

In 1984, while the Cold War between the US and the Soviet Union was still simmering, Nowick saw a television program about the probable after-effects of a nuclear war. The program stunned him. A student, who was with him at the time, reports: "He said, 'I actually realized everything could come to an end: Mozart, Beethoven, Zen, Buddhism, everybody could stop.'"

He told Sean Murphy:

> I just couldn't feel comfortable any longer...with sitting here pursuing our own practice while out there tensions were building that could destroy the planet. In former times Zen could afford to be apolitical, even during times of conflict, because whatever the damage, it was going to be limited. But when you have war machines out there that can destroy everything – well, at a certain point I just had to do something. What I knew how to do was music.[230]

Nowick performed all thirty-two Beethoven piano sonatas in Ellsworth, Maine, to raise funds for Ground Zero, an organization that sought to

---

230. Murphy, op. cit., 150-51.

reduce the threat of nuclear war. That same year, he formed the Surry Opera Company which sang Verdi's *Aida* and Mozart's *The Magic Flute* as choral performances in the barn. Launching the Opera Company with non-professional singers was just as improbable an endeavor as establishing a zendo in rural Maine, but within a year of its inception, the company was invited to perform at Wolf Trap near Washington DC. The following year the Opera Company performed Mussorgsky's *Boris Godunov* in Russian and, in 1986, made the first of several trips to the Soviet Union, inaugurating more than two decades of musical collaboration between Nowick's company and musicians from Russia, Japan, France, and elsewhere.

Several Moonspring students were members of the chorus, but others felt that Nowick was spending too much time with music and not enough time teaching. They wrote him a letter in which they expressed their concerns. He responded with a brief hand-written reply:

> It has become distinctly clear to me that I have fully involved myself in music and that it has taken me from my work with you as a teacher. Because of this situation, I wish to inform you without further delay of my decision to resign from Moonspring as teacher. I will help in any way I can to support its growth. I hope you will accept this decision along with me as the wisest one for all of us concerned.

A handful of former students established a board in order to maintain the zendo, and Nowick turned Moonspring Hermitage over to them in 1993 with the request that the name – which had been derived from his Dharma name – be changed. They reincorporated as the Morgan Bay Zendo and evolved into a center for meditation practice unaffiliated with any particular school of Buddhism.

Nowick continued to live in Surry. As Cold War tensions eased after the collapse of the Soviet Union, the Surry Opera Company gradually faded. For the remainder of his life, Nowick's energy was focused on music. He still gave piano recitals in the barn as well as in Russia and Japan. Russian musicians continued to come to the farm in Maine each summer.

Nowick maintained his personal Zen practice, but, although he visited occasionally, he remained separate from the operations of the zendo and didn't resume formal teaching. He died in February 2013 at the age of 87. That April, a memorial service was held at the zendo where friends and former student shared stories. The following November, a portion his ashes were buried at the Roshi Stone alongside those of Zuigan Goto. Another portion were flown to Japan and scattered near the plot where the remainder of Goto's ashes had been interred.

Philip Kapleau

Philip Kapleau was a Chief Allied Court Reporter during the war crimes trials at both Nuremburg and Tokyo. He later wrote that the testimony at the German trials – "a litany of Nazi betrayal and aggression, a chronicle of unbelievable cruelty and human degradation" – and "the apparent absence of contrition on the part of the mass of Germans, plunged me into the deepest gloom."[231] He expected to encounter something similar in Japan but instead found the atmosphere of the Tokyo trials very different. The Japanese, unlike the unrepentant Nazis, seemed to have accepted responsibility for their actions. Kapleau wondered what caused this difference in attitude and was told by acquaintances that it was the result of the Buddhist understanding of karma that held that the current sufferings of the people of Japan were the direct consequence of their behavior during the war.

This was Kapleau's introduction to Buddhist thought, and it intrigued him enough to accept the invitation of a friend to visit D.T. Suzuki at his cottage at Engakuji. Kapleau was impressed by the meeting, but the conversation didn't go beyond the theoretical. At this point he wasn't interested so much in Zen practice as in the influence of Buddhist philosophy on Japanese culture.

Back in the US, Kapleau continued to look into Buddhism casually and attended a series of lectures Suzuki gave. He was experiencing a lot of personal difficulties at the time and wondered if Zen might be a means of addressing them. Then a Japanese friend pointed out that Zen wasn't something that could be learned through books; if Kapleau were serious, he should go back to Japan and find a teacher. So in August of 1953, at the age of 41, Kapleau quit his business, gave up his apartment, and returned to Japan.

He began his studies with Soen Nakagawa at Ryutakuji. Nakagawa made allowances for Kapleau's lack of physical flexibility. He could use a chair if necessary, or sit on his heels in the traditional Japanese seiza style, but he was kept separate from the monks in the zendo. The only meditation instruction Nakagawa gave him was, "Put your mind in the bottom of your belly, there's a blind Buddha there, make him see!"[232]

Three weeks after arriving at Ryutakuji, Kapleau was introduced to Hakuun Yasutani, who was visiting Nakagawa accompanied by Nakagawa's friend – and the man who would later become Yasutani's chief disciple and heir – Koun Yamada. They talked about the upcoming Rohatsu Sesshin

---

231. Philip Kapleau, *Zen: Merging of East and West* (New York: Anchor Books, 1989), p. 261.
232. Unless otherwise noted, quotations are from Kapleau et al., *The Three Pillars of Zen*, op. cit.

that was to take place at Hossinji, in the city of Obama, under the direction of Yasutani's teacher, Daiun Harada. Kapleau asked Yasutani if he believed it were possible for an American to achieve satori in a seven-day retreat. Yasutani replied, "You can get it in one day of sesshin if you're genuinely determined to and you surrender all your conceptual thinking."

Harada was a more severe teacher than Nakagawa, and the rules governing the sesshin were strict. For seven days, the participants didn't speak, bathe, or shave. Kapleau was assigned the koan Mu and was told to forget all the theories he had about Buddhism and focus solely on Mu! "Put your mind in the hara, the pit of your stomach," Harada instructed, "and breathe only Mu! in and out."

The physical pain of sitting on cushions, even with frequent changes of posture, was agonizing. The blows of the kyosaku were more distracting than encouraging. And Harada's manner during dokusan was intimidating. But Kapleau persisted. On the fourth day, he was given a chair and, grateful for this concession, threw himself with renewed vigor into the practice, focusing with such energy that he passed out. When he came to, he was in bed, Nakagawa seated beside him. Nakagawa congratulated him, and Kapleau asked if that meant he had achieved satori. "No, but I congratulate you just the same," Nakagawa said.

The following April, he took part in a second sesshin at Hossinji following which, with Nakagawa's encouragement, he was accepted as a student by Harada and spent three years with him as a lay monk. In November of 1956, however, health problems forced him to leave and return to Ryutakuji.

That Rohatsu, Nakagawa arranged for Kapleau to participate in a sesshin presided over by Yasutani. Although the atmosphere of the sesshin was taut, it wasn't as severe as that at Hossinji, and Kapleau felt he had finally found his teacher. Between December 1956 and July 1958, Kapleau took part in nineteen sesshin under Yasutani's direction. The retreat that August was his twentieth, and he entered it with the conviction that he was close to a breakthrough. By the third day, he had attained such a degree of concentration that his responses to the Roshi's questions during dokusan came quickly and spontaneously.

The crisis came on day four. The previous evening, he had continued his practice late into the night, completely focused on Mu. At one point he stood up to go to bed and "staggered into a nearby fence. Suddenly I realized: the fence and I are one formless wood-and-flesh Mu." Energized, he continued sitting until the morning gong rang. When Kapleau next went into dokusan, Yasutani saw that he was on the verge of a deep realization. He asked a number of testing questions, many of which Kapleau responded to immediately. Yasutani smiled and pointed out that some roshis would accept Kapleau's replies as evidence of awakening. Kapleau told him, "I wouldn't accept sanction of such a picayune experience even if you wanted to grant it. Have I labored like a mountain these five years only to bring forth this mouse?"

Kapleau threw himself "into Mu for another nine hours with such utter absorption that I completely vanished." Kapleau didn't eat breakfast, Mu did; Kapleau didn't sweep the floor during the work period, Mu did. Then in the afternoon dokusan, Yasutani told him:

> "The universe is One…The moon of Truth –" All at once the roshi, the room, every single thing disappeared in a dazzling stream of illumination and I felt myself bathed in a delicious, unspeakable delight…For a fleeting eternity I was alone – I was alone…Then the roshi swam into view. Our eyes met and flowed into each other, and we burst out laughing…
>
> "I have it! I know! There is nothing, absolutely nothing. I am everything and everything is nothing!"

Years later, a student would ask Kapleau whether, relatively speaking, the koan Mu was easy or hard to solve. "Both," Kapleau answered. "Easy in this sense: When you resolve it, you realize that the 'answer' was there all the time. And hard because it takes longest to see what is closest to you."[233]

Kapleau remained with Yasutani for another six years, doing further koan work. Over time, his command of Japanese became proficient enough that he was able to act as translator for western students who came to study with Yasutani.

While at Hossinji, Kapleau had had the idea of writing a book about actual Zen practice to balance the idealized portraits of Zen more commonly available. He worked on it with the assistance two other of Yasutani's students, Koun Yamada and Akira Kubota.[234] The book was *The Three Pillars of Zen*. First published in Japan in 1965, it would become one of the most influential books ever written on Zen. When it first came out, it was unique in presenting Zen not as a theory or a philosophy but as a practice with a clearly defined goal. The content includes translations of a series of introductory lectures given by Yasutani, a teisho by Yasutani on the koan Mu, transcriptions of private interviews with students in dokusan – something that had never previously been available in any language – and

---

233. Kapleau, *Zen: Merging of East and West*, op. cit., p. 84.

234. Philip Kapleau is given title page credit for editing and "writing" *The Three Pillars of Zen*, but the issue remains a touchy one within the Sanbo Zen school, where it is widely believed that both Yamada and Kubota – who succeeded Yasutani as the second and third abbots of the Sanbo Zen school – should have received equal credit.

the personal accounts of eight lay practitioners, Japanese and American, who had achieved kensho.

In San Francisco, Shunryu Suzuki seldom talked about enlightenment and taught his students to sit without expectations. In contrast, kensho was all important to Kapleau's understanding of Zen, as it had been to Yasutani and Harada. Without enlightenment, Kapleau declared in his outspoken manner, Zen practice was meaningless, and he had little patience with students who worked with Soto teachers whom he dismissed as unenlightened. For many readers, the awakening narratives in *The Three Pillars* demonstrated that not only was kensho achievable, but that it was within the grasp of Western lay practitioners as well as Japanese monks. Unfortunately, the narratives also portrayed kensho as an overwhelming psychological incident with the consequence that later practitioners – seeking the kind of experiences described in *The Three Pillars* – could doubt validity of their own awakening if it lacked the drama and emotional catharsis of those in the book. Without intending to, Kapleau contributed to a continued desire among Zen inquirers for extraordinary personal experiences.

Both Kapleau and Yasutani had been careful to stress that kensho in itself is not the culmination of Zen practice. "Enlightenment," Kapleau explained in another book, "is not a static condition; it is capable of endless enlargement."[235]

In 1965, Kapleau – who by then had completed about half of the 800 koans used in the Harada-Yasutani school – was ordained a Zen priest and given permission to teach by Yasutani. He was not, however, given *inka*, the "formal acknowledgement on the part of the master that his disciple has fully completed his training…"[236] Considering the increasing numbers of westerners coming to Japan to study Zen, both Yasutani and Kapleau felt it appropriate that he should return to the United States and introduce authentic Zen practice there.

Before he left Japan, Kapleau received a visit from Ralph Chapin, an American who had heard that one of his countrymen was studying Zen and was curious meet him. When he came to Kapleau's apartment, the galley proofs for The *Three Pillars of Zen* were spread out on the floor. Chapin read a few paragraphs and asked Kapleau to send him twenty copies once it was in print. These he distributed to members of a Vedanta group to which he belonged in Rochester. Chester and Dorris Carlson – Eido Shimano's financial supporters – were also members of the group, and they were so impressed with the book that they distributed another 5000 copies to libraries throughout the country.

Kapleau accepted an invitation from the Carlsons to come to

---

235. Kapleau, *Zen: Merging of East and West*, op. cit., p. 69
236. *The Three Pillars of Zen*, p.333.

Rochester, that then became his home base in the United States. His first students were members of a group organized by Dorris – largely of women in their forties – that was exploring Vedanta and other religious traditions. Kapleau taught them how to sit zazen and set up a regular schedule of sittings. The group, however, didn't show up on Sunday mornings because most of them were also regular church attendees.

Then young readers of *The Three Pillars* began to make their way to Rochester. Some had begun to follow the instructions provided in it. In 1966, when the numbers were sufficient, Kapleau rented a larger house and converted one of the rooms into a zendo. Most of the members of the Vedanta studies group fell away, but the new people stayed and formed the nucleus of the Zen Meditation Center of Rochester. A residential program was initiated. Kapleau even attempted to establish a monastic community but was unsuccessful. Like Yasutani, his work would be with lay people.

And there were more than enough of these making their way to Rochester. They came expecting the training to be rigorous, and it was. In the early years of the Rochester Center, people talked of "boot-camp Zen." The kyosaku was used robustly. When the dokusan bell rang, meditators exploded off their cushions in order to get into line because there was never time for all of them to meet with the teacher. Sunyana Graef described the atmosphere:

> In the moments before dokusan began, the inspiring words of the monitors, followed by the vigorous whacking of the stick, created an intensity bordering on hysteria. The zendo filled with crackling energy, adrenaline surging, hearts pounding, as everyone waited for Roshi's handbell to signal the start of dokusan. The instant the bell rang, students flew off their mats to be first in the waiting line. Races to dokusan resulted in more than a few injuries over the years…
>
> The highly charged atmosphere of sesshin was often compared to a pressure cooker, an apt analogy. The pressure was so great that people occasionally broke under the strain. The sound of the kyosaku alone, even without feeling its stinging bite, was enough to dissuade some sitters from attending a second sesshin. All this was done for the purpose of helping students come to awakening. And it worked. It was a rare sesshin conducted by Roshi Kapleau when no one "broke through."[237]

Kapleau experimented with ritual forms, seeking adaptations that seemed appropriate for Americans. Instead of the traditional Japanese takahat-

---

237. Sunyana Graef, "Seeing the Ox: A Second Look" in Kenneth Kraft (ed.), *Zen Teaching,*

su begging rounds undertaken to foster humility, Zen Center students cleaned up sidewalks and street gutters in the blocks around the center. In addition to maintaining the area, the clean-up won the respect of the center's neighbors. He also arranged for English translations of the chants, in particular the *Heart Sutra*.

Yasutani wasn't happy with the changes, and Kapleau, on his part, stubbornly refused to make concessions. Yasutani took further offence when Kapleau suggested he shouldn't use Eido Shimano – about whom he had reservations – as a translator during a scheduled tour of the United States. The two became estranged, and Yasutani died not long after, precluding a chance for a reconciliation.

Later Kapleau would express regret over his intransigence, but the immediate question was his status within the traditional Zen establishment. Because he had not completed koan training or received transmission, he wasn't formally recognized by either the Soto or Sanbo Kyodan hierarchies. On the other hand, before Kapleau had returned to the United States, Yasutani had given him permission to teach and had presented him with a robe and bowl symbolic of that authorization. Kapleau decided that this was adequate endorsement to continue teaching. He was careful not to claim to be a transmitted Zen master although – after he learned that Richard Baker was using the term – he, too, adopted the title "roshi." He pointed out, however, that the word only meant "venerable teacher":

> – that is, one who commands respect and reverence by reason of age or great dignity. The abbot of a monastery, the chief priest of a temple, or a lay teacher beyond the age of, say, fifty could be addressed as roshi and the title would simply imply deep respect...– it is not a title signifying completion of a prescribed course of study or in recognition of high spiritual accomplishments.[238]

There were people in the emerging American Buddhist community for whom the formalities of transmission were of primary importance. They would question Kapleau's legitimacy, but most of his students remained loyal to him. He acknowledged several heirs who – regardless of the question of his transmission – have been recognized as significant and effective teachers in their own right.

He struggled with Parkinson's Disease in later life and died in May 2004 in the garden at the Rochester Zen Center surrounded by grateful students and disciples.

Zen Practice (New York: Weatherhill, 2000), p. 110.
238. Kapleau, *Zen Merging of East and West*, p. 30.

Jiyu Kennett

Although not in large numbers, there were women engaged in both Soto and Rinzai practice in Japan; there were even temples specifically dedicated to their training. Women were much more actively engaged in promoting Zen in North America. Many studied with the pioneer teachers in the United States and went on to become respected teachers: Joko Beck and Jan Chozen Bays received Dharma transmission from Taezan Maezumi; Mitra Bishop and Sunyana Graef were authorized to teach by Philip Kapleau; Melissa Blacker and Janet Sutherland are both heirs in the tradition that originated with Robert Aitken. The first female teacher to establish a Zen community in North America, however, was unlike these teachers and promoted a form of Zen that remains unique.

Peggy Kennett was born in Britain in 1924. She served in the Royal Navy during the Second World War then studied medieval ecclesiastical music at Trinity College. For several years, she was a church organist and admitted later in life that she'd felt drawn to the priesthood; unfortunately, that wasn't yet an option for women in the Anglican Church. That discrimination caused her to question gender roles both within the church and in society in general. It also provoked a growing dissatisfaction with Christianity as it was currently practiced.

Her father had belonged to Christmas Humphrey's London Buddhist Society when it was still associated with the Theosophical movement. Kennett joined as well in 1954 and began a correspondence course on Theravada Buddhism through the Young Men's Buddhist Association in Ceylon. Her interest in Zen began when she met D.T. Suzuki during one of his visits to London. Then, in 1960, the Society asked her to organize the visit of a Soto priest, Keido Chisan Koho. He was pleased with her work on his behalf and invited her to come back with him to Japan. She agreed although it took another two years before she was able to join him at the prestigious Sojiji in Yokohama.

Kennett didn't have an easy time at Sojiji. There hadn't been a female student there since the 14th century. More traditional members of the community resented her presence not only as a woman but as a foreigner, and they made her stay difficult. With Chisan Koho's support, however, she persisted and even achieved kensho. In her biography, she said it came about in part because of the frustration she felt with the way she was being treated. Once she let her sense of self drop, she achieved awakening and felt only gratitude for those who had tormented her.

Chisan Koho gave her Dharma transmission in 1963, and for a period she was appointed abbess of Unpukuji in Mie Prefecture where she worked with non-Japanese students. Koho expected that she would return to England and sent a letter to the Buddhist Society informing them that Kennett was to be the Soto bishop of London. Humphreys was surprised and wrote back, tactlessly, that they would prefer a "real Zen master." Koho was angered at having his authority questioned and ordered his secretary to "write to this man in England and tell him he obviously understands nothing whatsoever about true Zen."[239] Humphries didn't appreciate the tone of the letter, and Kennett was no longer welcome in the London Buddhist Society.

She left Japan after Koho's death in 1967. Her health wasn't strong at the time, and the animosity of the conservative Soto community continued. She may have hoped to establish a teaching center in England regardless of the Buddhist Society, but as it happened, she undertook a lecture tour in the United States that gave her an opportunity to visit the San Francisco Zen Center in 1969. Impressed by what she saw there, she was inspired to remain in the city. She found an apartment in the Potrero Hill district and began receiving students. Within a year, she and a number of disciples she'd gathered moved three hundred miles north of the city to the township of Mount Shasta.

Shasta Abbey – as her community became known – could house fifty monks, a term indiscriminately used for both males and females. At times Kennett referred to the members as "he-monks" and "she-monks." Her experience both with the Anglican Church and in Japan made her determined to ensure that men and women were equally respected in the community. Sandy Boucher, in her book, *Turning the Wheel: American Women Creating the New Buddhism*, wrote that in her personal experience – not just as a Buddhist but as an American woman – her visit to Shasta Abbey in 1981 was the first time she felt she was "in an environment where women were equally visible and equally responsible with men."[240]

Kennett's health remained poor, and she fell seriously ill in 1975. She consulted a traditional Asian healer who diagnosed her condition to be due to stress. He warned that she would be dead within three years if she didn't change her lifestyle. In 1976, she took leave of her position as abbess and went into solitary retreat. Over the next nine months, she claimed to have meditated both on her present and past lives and as a result had a series of forty-three visions – including one of a God-like figure she called the "Cosmic Buddha" – comprised of both Christian and Buddhist elements.

---

239. Quoted in Stephen Batchelor, *The Awakening of the West* (Williamsville, VT: Echo Point Books, 2011), p. 132.

240. Sandy Boucher, *Turning the Wheel* (Boston: Beacon Press, 1988), p. 133.

It isn't unusual for people engaged in prolonged meditation to have visions. During the sesshin in which he experienced his "little bit of light," Robert Aitken had a vision of himself seated on the stone floor of an ancient temple with tall monks circumambulating him and chanting sutras. The Japanese term for these is "makyo," which essentially means hallucination, and they are thought of as not being more or less significant than dreams. Kennett, however, called her visions a form of kensho and believed they were genuine revelations. The fact that she overcame her illness – and lived for almost another twenty years – was, to her mind, evidence of their validity.

In some ways – as the content of the visions demonstrated – Jiyu Kennett never wholly abandoned her emotional ties with the Anglican church. She claimed that Chisan Koho had told her to develop Western forms for Zen practice in order to make it more accessible to Americans and Europeans. Taizan Maezumi had said something similar to his heirs. The controversy with Kennett was the way in which she chose to carry those instructions out. In the early days, the clerics of her order wore Roman collars, were addressed as "Reverend," and resided in "abbeys" or "priories." The chants were translations of traditional Soto texts but were sung in Gregorian plainsong with organ accompaniment.

Unlike many Soto teachers, Kennett insisted on the importance of kensho, maintaining that it was fairly easily attained through committed zazen practice provided the student remained focused on the "intuitive understanding which the teacher is always exhibiting." Stephen Batchelor explained:

> All theories, ideas, concepts and beliefs have to be discarded. In their place one "must have absolute faith in the Buddhanature of the teacher." Therefore, she concludes, "Zen is an intuitive RELIGION and not a philosophy or way of life." She deplores how for centuries Buddhism has been denied as a religion: "this was because [people] feared saying the Truth lest they set up a god to be worshipped. The Lord is not a god and He is not not a god."[241]

Although the initial kensho experience, according to Kennett, was equally accessible to lay and monastic, if one wanted "to go further than that" a deeper commitment was required which was – she insisted – not consistent with an active sex life.

---

241. Batchelor. op. cit., p. 135, quoting Kennett's *Zen Is Eternal Life* (Shasta Abbey Press, 2000).

If you're married, the singleness of mind, the devotion, the oneness with [the] eternal can't take place, because you're dividing it off for a member of the opposite sex or a member of the same sex, or whatever.[242]

Most Soto priests in Japan were married.

As Kennett's methods and perspective moved further from traditional models, Soto authorities became less at ease with her. In the end, they chose not to acknowledge her order or the validity of the transmissions she authorized.

Jiyu Kennett made a recovery after the period of her visions and resumed teaching, although some of her early disciples withdrew from her and sought to follow more traditional Buddhist routes. She died in 1996 at the age of 72.

Infrastructure

Shasta Abbey was – and remains – a cluster of stone cottages connected by covered walkways circling a stand of pine trees and surrounded by 16 acres of forest property. In the background, Mount Shasta provides a majestic backdrop. Although it looks as if the buildings had always been intended to serve as a Zen retreat, in fact, they'd been constructed by an Italian stonemason in the 1930s for a motel. Whatever the original intent of the site, however, it now stands as a proclamation: This is sacred territory.

From the 1950s into the early '60s, if one spoke about "Buddhism" in North America one was almost certainly talking about Zen. By the mid-'70s, this was no longer the case. Tibetan Buddhists had established themselves in the US and were rapidly expanding. Three American Theravada teachers founded the Insight Meditation Center in Massachusetts in 1975 and began the "mindfulness" movement. Hindu teachers, yoga instructors, and popular innovations – like est training seminars – abounded. By the 1980s, there was competition not only between schools of Zen but between orthodox and non-orthodox expressions of these traditions, as well as competition between Buddhism and other forms of Asian spirituality.

There was something else as well. There were not only numerous authorized Zen teachers in North America, there had also been significant investments in infrastructure. Nyogen Senzaki's homeless floating zendo had been succeeded by some very substantial properties.

---

242. Sandy Boucher, *Turning the Wheel* (Boston: Beacon Press, 1988), p. 143.

Tassajara

In the 1960s, Shunryu Suzuki wanted to establish a practice center outside the city where American Zen students would be trained not only to spread the Dharma in America but eventually to revitalize the tradition in Japan. Richard Baker was charged with finding an appropriate site and chose an abandoned resort at Tassajara Hot Springs that he had first seen while on a camping trip. Suzuki loved the place, and Baker determined to raise the funds necessary to purchase it. The annual budget of Zen Center at that time was less than $5,500, and they had $2,304.24 in the bank; but Baker undertook to raise $150,000. In the end, the price was double that. It seemed an impossible task to many Zen Center members, but Baker had exceptional organizational skills and was able to get support for a fund-raising campaign from a number of prominent people friendly to the idea, including Alan Watts, Allen Ginsberg, and Gary Snyder. Rock groups like the Grateful Dead and Big Brother and the Holding Company held a "Zenefit Concert." Major donors – including the Carlsons – materialized. The impossible started to become probable, and the Tassajara Zen Mountain Center became the first Buddhist monastery ever to be established outside of Asia.

It was only the first of several property acquisitions the San Francisco Zen Center made. By the early '80s, these included a third practice center and organic farm – Green Gulch – numerous apartment buildings, a corner grocery store, a bookstore, and a vegetarian restaurant that won rave reviews even from committed carnivores.

Dai Bosatsu

In the 1970s, no sooner had Eido Shimano established Shobo Ji in New York than he and his board gave thought to opening an American Rinzai temple and training center with a residential program. Shimano imagined something much grander than the refurbished hot springs resort the San Francisco Zen Center had transformed. He envisioned an actual temple, and, because Zen temples in Asia were usually in the mountains, he hoped to find a suitable mountain setting. A 1400 acre estate in the Catskill Mountains including a fourteen room summer house was found. It would have been prohibitively expensive had it not been for another generous donation from Dorris Carlson.

When Soen Nakagawa came to New York that summer, Shimano took him to the site, and he was entranced. As they walked about the property, Nakagawa told his disciple of his youthful hope to establish an International Zendo on Mount Dai Bosatsu. Shimano suggested that this new site – in what Nakagawa liked to call the Cut-kill Mountains – be named the Dai Bosatsu Zendo. Nakagawa's dream would become a reality not in Japan but in America. A local architect, Davis Hamerstrom, was hired and traveled to Japan with Shimano to study temple architecture, and, in the spring of 1973, work began on what remains, arguably, the most significant Zen construction project to be undertaken in America. A Japanese-style temple of classic design was built. Its full formal name is Dai Bosatsu Zendo Kongo Ji (Diamond Temple), and it was officially inaugurated on America's bi-centennial – July 4, 1976. Rinzai dignitaries from Japan came for the occasion; teachers from throughout America were there as well, including Robert Aitken, Richard Baker, Taizan Maezumi, the Tibetan teacher, Chogyam Trungpa, and the Korean Zen Master, Seung Sahn.

Zen Mountain Monastery

In 1980, one of Taizan Maezumi's heirs, John Daido Loori, was invited by a friend to visit him at Mount Tremper, New York, not far from Woodstock. On a March afternoon, the friend took Loori, his wife and son, to look at a National Heritage building constructed by Norwegian Catholics as a retreat center in the 1930s. It was a spectacular and gracious structure with vaulted inner stairways and elaborate hand-crafted stone and ironwork surrounded by a 230-acre property. The Catholics were long gone and since the 1960s the site had been operating as a Lutheran children's camp. It so happened that the day Loori visited, the man who ran the camp was on the grounds thinking that he was too old to maintain the program another year. Loori went over to speak to him, then came back to his wife – Joan Yushin – and told her, "I think I just bought this place."[243]

"He was sparkling," she told me. "He was thrilled. He had twenty-five cents in his pocket."

Daido was able to borrow $10,000 from friends for a down payment and received further help from Peter Schlesinger of the Apeiron Photography School who was interested in developing the property with him. Between them they established the Zen Arts Center. Although the partnership seemed like a good idea at first, it didn't last.

"Peter and Daido were sort of like a two-headed dragon," Yushin told me. "Peter had concerts out here on the grass. People drinking, smoking, doing all the things that people did at that time, going home at 2:00 in the morning. And those of us who were going to be sitting…well, there would be like three of us in the zendo in the morning."

Eventually Loori forced the Apeiron people out and set about establishing a more formal training center. The Zen Arts Center was renamed Zen Mountain Monastery. Programs in the arts were still offered, but the atmosphere became far more formal with robed clergy who shaved their

---

243. Interview with the author, June 8, 2013. Cf. *Cypress Trees in the Garden*, Chapter 13.

heads, incense and altars, chants and scripture study, formal bowing and prostrations.

John Daido Loori died in 2009 and his remains were buried in the graveyard at ZMM. A stupa there commemorates Taizan Maezumi as the monastery's first abbot and Loori as its second. Graves are marked, Japanese style, with simple upright wooden planks. Loori's marker identifies him as the founder of the Mountains and Rivers Order.

When a community dedicates space for burying their dead it's a good indication that they intend to be there for the long run. There may have been competition from vying spiritual traditions by the early 1980s, but it also looked like North American Zen was stable, secure, and here to stay.

...right before everything fell apart...Baker Roshi came to ZCLA. And [Maezumi] Roshi and Genpo [Merzel] and Tetsugen [Glassman] and all the guys happened to be gone, and it was just us girls running the Zen Center. And I remember sitting down with him, with a couple of other women, and we had this very down to earth conversation in which he said the most interesting thing. Talking about the empire he had built and that we had built, he said something like, "You know, everything is impermanent, and it may all come crashing down one day." Well, in retrospect, he had left the San Francisco Zen Center and everything was coming crashing down. We didn't know that, but he said it with such poignancy and emotional depth that I realized, "Something's wrong here. He's not happy."

Jan Chozen Bays [244]

---

244. Interview with the author, March 26, 2013.

Things Fall Apart

1964

THE FAULT LINES were there almost from the beginning, but they were deliberately concealed.

When Eido Shimano moved from Honolulu to New York in 1964, he explained to Soen Nakagawa that "the Hawaiian climate is too good – it is a place for vacationers or retired people, but not for Zazen practice."[245] He also complained to others that while the Aitkens, who had sponsored his visa application to the United States and therefore had financial responsibility for him, provided him room and board, they were careful with money to the point of stinginess and allowed him only an allowance of $30 a month. Shimano was 27 years old when he came to Hawaii, and – as he told Mark Oppenheimer in 2012 – the Aitkens were "much older than me, so they ate, for example, in the evening, two pieces of biscuit and soup, and that's enough for them. But not for me."[246] He claimed that he only survived because a Zen priest in Honolulu provided him supplemental meals. Finally – according to this version of events – the combination of the ill treatment he received from the Aitkens and the inappropriateness of the Hawaiian climate for serious Zen work compelled him to leave the islands for New York.

Aitken didn't contradict Shimano's claims at the time and said nothing publicly about their separation; however, when his private papers – which had been entrusted to the University of Hawaii – were made public in 2008 a different tale emerged.

Over the four years Shimano resided with the Aitkens, relations between them became strained. The polite, deferential monk the Aitkens

---

245. Louis Nordstrom, Louis (ed.), *Namu Dai Bosa* (New York: Theatre Arts Books, 1976), p. 189.
246. Mark Oppenheimer, *The Zen Predator of the Upper East Side* (The Atlantic Books, 2013), location 169.

had met in Japan proved to be more problematic in Hawaii. While it was clear he was committed to Zen practice, he also insisted on little extravagances, like a motorcycle he claimed to need in order to get around. Aitken may not have been happy with these requests, but a case could be made that most of them were reasonable; it's also probable that the Aitkens had sparse funds with which to work.

Then, in 1963, Aitken and Shimano were invited by the director of the Queen's Medical Center to volunteer with patients suffering from mental illness. Coincidentally, two women associated with the Koko An Zendo had recently been hospitalized there because of "breakdowns." Their social worker, when reviewing their cases, was surprised to find that one of the new volunteers was named in the files. She informed the director that they had each reported having been involved in sexual affairs with Shimano. After the director confirmed the situation, he brought the information to Aitken's attention.

In an undated note included in the archived papers, Aitken wrote that once he determined the accusations were credible and that Shimano "had been ruthless in his exploitation of the women," he was unsure how to proceed. Shimano was popular with the members of Koko An. Aitken feared the if he accused Shimano of inappropriate sexual behavior the young Japanese would likely deny it, and, very probably, the sangha would believe him. Aitken also stated that he was concerned about protecting the two women and was reluctant to subject them to any further stress.

Aitken went to Japan to discuss the situation with Soen Nakagawa and Hakuun Yasutani. "Both teachers could believe that Tai San [Shimano] had been philandering, but could not accept the idea that he was pathologically compulsive."[247] Aitken discovered, as others would after him, that sexual affairs – even between teachers and students – did not carry the same weight in Japan as they did in North America as long as they are handled with discretion.

Aitken was unhappy with the situation but – heeding legal advice – decided to deal with the matter quietly in order to protect the still nascent Zen community. When Shimano learned that Aitken had gone to Japan, he left Koko An and moved to New York. After Shimano became associated with the Zen Studies Society, Aitken contacted them and requested they take on responsibility for Shimano's visa sponsorship. The Society wrote back that they weren't in a position to do so, and there the matter rested. Aitken didn't inform them about the women at the Medical Center.

---

247. A copy of the note, with handwritten emendations, is available at http://www.shimanoarchive.com/index.html#page1.

1981

Compared with what followed, the initial tremor was relatively mild, although it seemed catastrophic at the time.

During the twenty years between Shimano's arrival in Hawaii and 1981, Zen had undergone a massive transformation in the west. Practice centers could be found in cities throughout North America. The word itself had entered the English language, suggesting tranquility, arcane wisdom, and spiritual accomplishment. If Zen wasn't mainstream, it was at least credible and respected.

In Asia, where Buddhism was part of the culture, people were drawn to Zen practice for traditionally acceptable and understandable reasons. In fact, one of the reasons monasteries in Japan were failing to attract the numbers they had previously was that post-war youth considered Zen old-fashioned and archaic; it was identified as one of the institutions responsible for the nation's involvement in a war that had ended in a humiliating defeat.

In America during the 1960s and '70s, on the other hand, the young people who flocked to burgeoning Zen centers were questioning the values of their culture and era. They were largely disaffected with Judeo-Christian teachings and, often inspired by psychedelic drug experiences, sought alternative spiritual paths.

The two most influential centers in America in the early '80s were the San Francisco Zen Center and Philip Kapleau's Rochester Zen Center. These represented two very distinct approaches to Zen practice, and, as different as they were, their founders' books – *The Three Pillars of Zen* and *Zen Mind, Beginner's Mind* – inspired tens of thousands of persons to experiment with meditation even if they never took up formal practice or ever visited a center.

In Rochester, Kapleau emphasized the importance of kensho in a way that Shunryu Suzuki had not, and he maintained what was called a "Bootcamp" style in order to bring students to the awakening experience. While this worked for many of the members, it didn't for all, and in 1981 the community was riven when Kapleau's first ceremonially recognized disciple and designated successor, Toni Packer, left the Zen Center taking approximately half of the sangha's members with her.

Toni Eggert had been born in Berlin in 1927. Her parents both held Ph.D.'s in chemistry; her father was instrumental in the development of color photography. When Toni was six years old, the Nazis came to power, putting the family at risk because her mother was Jewish. While her father's position at IG Farben afforded them some protection, the family still needed to be circumspect. When she was eight years old, Toni copied some negative remarks she had heard about the Nazi Party in her journal. Her father found the passage and lectured her on the danger of putting such things in writing.

Although her parents weren't religious, the children were baptized and raised Lutheran. Toni had a naturally religious attitude and chose to be confirmed when she was fifteen. As she grew older and more aware of what was happening in Germany, however, her belief in the concept of a caring God faltered. The Nazi years also left her with a profound suspicion of all forms of external authority.

After the war, her family moved to Switzerland where she met and married an American university student – Kyle Packer – who eventually brought her to the United States. They settled in western New York, and she enrolled at the University of Buffalo. She acquired an interest in Zen from reading and began sitting on her own guided by the instructions provided in *The Three Pillars of Zen*. When Kapleau opened the Rochester Zen Center, only 75 miles from her home, she and Kyle became members.

Toni was older and more mature than most of the members of the center, and she was driven by more profound life experiences. She attended as many sesshin as she was able and progressed rapidly in koan work, gaining Kapleau's notice and respect. By 1975, he invited her to give Dharma talks at the center and even entrusted her with leading sesshin both in Rochester and in Europe.

When Kapleau began to think about retirement, he told Toni it was his intention that she become the resident teacher at the center in his place. He explained that he believed the community would respond well to a lay leader with family responsibilities. Toni was nonplussed by the suggestion, but, since Kapleau's retirement was still some years off, she didn't argue with him. Besides which, as she later admitted, she felt an obligation to do whatever her teacher asked of her.

Kyle wasn't comfortable with the ceremony and ritual at the Zen Center and withdrew from formal practice. Toni also came to question the necessity of certain structures such as the use of the kyosaku and the practice of prostrating before the teacher, especially when she was the one to whom the prostrations were being made. Then she and Kyle began reading Jiddhu Krishnamurti's books.

When he was still a child in 1929, Krishnamurti had been identified by the Theosophical movement as the incarnation of Maitreya, the Buddha of the future, and they groomed him to become the "World Teacher." When he reached the age of 34, however, he dissolved his association with the Theosophists, denied their claims for him, and advised would-be disciples and followers to question all forms of authority or religious formulae. Toni and Kyle attended several talks given by Krishnamurti, and his thinking began to impact the way Toni looked at both Buddhism and Zen.

In 1981, Kapleau left Toni in charge of the Rochester Zen Center and went to Santa Fe where he hoped to open a new center and eventually move. Toni struggled with the forms Kapleau expected her to maintain in his absence. In an interview she gave to Lenore Friedman just a few years after these events, Toni said:

> I myself was doing all these prostrations, and lighting incense, and bowing, and gassho-ing[248] and the whole thing. I realized that I was influencing people, just by the position I was in, the whole setup. I could see it, and I wasn't going to have any part in it anymore.

She believed that people could become dependent on the structures of Zen in an unproductive manner.

> The system is very supportive to not questioning some things. Even though it claims to question everything. You question everything and you "burn the Buddha," but then you put him back up!
>
> I examined it very carefully: did I have any division while I was bowing? It had always been said, "When you bow, you're not bowing to the Buddha, you're bowing to yourself. And when you're prostrating, everything disappears, you disappear, the Buddha disappears and there's nothing." I tried to look, and it wasn't completely clear. I could see there was often an image, of the bower, or of the person who "has nothing." Often there was a shadow of something, somebody there who was doing it. Or maybe the idea of being able to do it emptily![249]

She decided to loosen some of the structures and relax the atmosphere at the center, but her action caused a rift between members. Many supported and even welcomed her changes; others however – perhaps proving her point – believed the changes subverted the taut atmosphere they felt necessary for Zen practice. People wrote to Kapleau, and, under pressure, he returned to Rochester. A meeting was held in which the members who were unhappy with the way Toni was running things were allowed to voice their complaints. Some of the things said reminded Toni of the

---

248. In gassho, the palms of the hands are brought together often accompanied by a bow. It is a sign of respect and reverence.
249. Lenore Friedman, *Meetings with Remarkable Women* (Boston: Shambhala, 2000), pp. 52-53.

denouncements that had taken place in the Germany of her youth, and she found it hurtful. In the end, Kapleau expressed his support for her and gave her permission to bring about whatever changes she felt appropriate. It was too late, however. Toni had already begun to wonder if she could continue to view or present herself as a Buddhist.

Instead of returning to Santa Fe that June, Kapleau went to Mexico to work on a book. Two weeks before he was scheduled to return for a trustees' meeting, Toni flew there to inform him that she could no longer continue to work within the Buddhist tradition.

She left the Rochester Center and established the independent Genesee Valley Zen Center. Nearly half of the Rochester members went with her. Others, discouraged by the division in the community, fell away from practice altogether.

Toni explained that the term "Zen" in the title of her new center was not intended to imply affiliation but was rather a descriptor of the method of seated meditation used. The group continued to meet in Rochester until 1984, when they purchased 284 acres of undeveloped farmland in Livingston County. In an interview recorded with Joan Tollifson, Toni explained that she wanted a place where people could "be in close touch again with land and sky and running water."[250]

A period of stripping down followed the break from Kapleau's group. At first, Toni continued to have students work with koans, then she gradually ceased to do so. Rules – even those governing retreats – became flexible. Participants were free to attend scheduled sittings or not as they chose. Nothing was mandatory except a daily work assignment and silence in certain places at certain times.

Toni encouraged her students to examine and question their assumptions about practice, about the roles of student and teacher, and to challenge any concept that came between themselves and the direct perception of self, others, and the external environment. She may have questioned Buddhism as an institution, but, in a classic sense, her approach was that of the Buddha himself when he told his disciples: "The bhikkhus must not accept the words of the Tathagata out of respect. Nor should they believe the words of the Tathagata solely because others do. The bhikkhus must analyze the teachings of the Tathagata as a goldsmith analyzes gold by cutting, melting, scraping, and rubbing it."

There was, Toni pointed out, no "technique" for doing this. As a result, some people found the approach discouraging. They wanted direction, and she refused to define procedures. There were, she insisted, no "authorities" who could lead one to what she called "awareing" or the "work of the moment." One needed only to attend simply and directly to what was

---

250. https://www.youtube.com/watch?v=se9iyLdRtYE

happening moment to moment. She advised her students to maintain a "not knowing" mind. "Not knowing," she explained, "means putting aside what I already know and being curious to observe freshly, openly, what is actually taking place right now in the light of the question. Not knowing means putting up with the discomfort of no immediate answer."[251]

She went on to say that the "essence of meditative inquiry is not obtaining answers but wondering patiently without knowing."[252]

Toni Packer raised the question – already faced by Catholic inquirers like Hugo Enomiya-Lassalle – whether Zen insight necessarily needed to be cultivated within a Buddhist framework. Essentially, she was asking whether that insight was linked with a specific spiritual tradition or if it was universal.

The Rochester Zen Center was wounded by her departure but recovered and became, perhaps, stronger as a result. Many of the changes Toni made were retained. And although Kapleau was disappointed that his intended heir had chosen not to carry on his work, he eventually passed Dharma transmission onto several individuals who capably maintained the Rochester Center as well as affiliate centers elsewhere in the US and Canada.

1983

The Zen story as recounted in popular literature extolled the concept of working with enlightened teachers who could reveal how to live meaningful and fulfilled lives. These stories presented the image of small communities of sincere students – working in intimate contact with wise, probably Asian, spiritual masters – achieving wisdom, compassion, and a deep sense of satisfaction in life. And when the first inquirers in San Francisco sought out Shunryu Suzuki at Sokoji, that is – to some extent – what they found. But by the time the community had moved to the building on the corner of Page and Laguna Streets, the situation was fast changing. The number of students was too large for newcomers to have direct personal contact with Suzuki Roshi, and, after he became ill, his older disciples shielded him from unnecessary disturbance, making him even more remote. After Suzuki's death, what new students arriving in San Francisco found was less a small number of dedicated spiritual aspirants than a large community with a hierarchy of lay and ordained individuals seeking ways to remain financially solvent in their quest to establish Buddhism and Zen in America.

Suzuki's only American Dharma heir was Richard Baker, who became abbot-for-life of the San Francisco Zen Center two weeks before Suzuki's

---

251. Lenore Friedman, *Meetings with Remarkable Women* (Boston: Shambhala, 2000), pp. 52-53.

252. Toni Packer, *The Wonder of Presence* (Boston: Shambhala, 2002), pp. 5-6.

death. Under Baker's leadership, SFZC grew into a multi-million-dollar empire. In addition to their practice center at Tassajara and several buildings in the area around the Page Street zendo, they owned and operated the premier vegetarian restaurant in San Francisco (Greens), a bakery, a stitchery (zafus and zabutons[253]), and an organic farm (Green Gulch). SFZC easily had the largest membership of any Zen center in the country and was supported by numerous wealthy and celebrity donors.

Baker was a huge personality. In addition to being an often inspiring teacher, he was an astute businessman. But as SFZC grew and administrative issues preoccupied him, he had less time for direct contact with his students. Although he was married with two daughters, it was known that he had been engaged in a number of sexual affairs. In itself, this probably wasn't a problem for most Zen Center members. On the contrary, since part of what the youth of the '60s and '70s was questioning were traditional Christian sexual mores, it was refreshing to see a spiritual leader who didn't treat such matters as something to be ashamed of. It seemed apparent that Baker's wife was aware of these relationships, and if she tolerated them, why shouldn't the students?

The situation became more problematic when Baker entered into a relationship with the wife of a man whom he not only identified as his "best friend" but who was also a major financial donor to SFZC. In this case, Baker's affair not only caused the collapse of the woman's marriage, it also resulted in the threat of a lawsuit from the aggrieved husband. The board of Zen Center recognized that the matter had to be addressed directly, and they summoned Baker to the first of what would be several meetings.

It's even possible that Baker would have weathered the ensuing storm had the affair been the only issue. But as the meetings progressed, a range of other long-held grievances came to light. Whereas Shunryu Suzuki had washed Elsie Mitchell's windows, Baker maintained a lavish life-style, holding elaborate dinner parties at the abbot's residence for political figures and entertainment celebrities during which Zen Center students were expected to serve as silent wait-staff. Baker's management style was one that left senior members of SFZC feeling their contributions to the center and the related businesses were undervalued. He had a tendency to take personal credit for everything that occurred at the center and expected the students who did the actual work to fade into the background.

Whatever vision of Zen new aspirants had when they sought out SFZC, it probably didn't include being seconded to twelve hour shifts of unpaid "work practice" at the bakery or at Greens Restaurant, functioning

---

253. Cushions and the mats on which the cushions are placed.

as household servants to an abbot whose three residences were graced with antiques and modern art work purchased with Zen Center revenues, or standing in rows at Tassajara to bow as Baker's BMW – again purchased with Zen Center revenues – drove by.

The revelation of the sexual affair, according to Mel Weitsman – who would become a co-abbot of SFZC in 1988 – "was just the tip of it...Dick was using the community for his own ends. He was the king, and the community members were the vassals." What the affair did was to prompt "something unprecedented. Things had been building underneath for a long time, but that was the clincher."[254]

The unprecedented thing the San Francisco Zen Center did in 1983 – which some Zen Center members refer to as the "year of the apocalypse" – was to force the abbot-for-life to resign. Essentially, they fired him. The step was momentous. Zen authorities both in Asia and America questioned it. The traditional Buddhist approach was that if students found fault with their teacher, they left him and went elsewhere. But the population at SFZC still felt if not loyalty to their current abbot then to Shunryu Suzuki, whose legacy they were determined to maintain. Further, many of them had dedicated decades of their lives to helping Zen Center become the institution it was, and they were unwilling to abandon it.

Dainin Katagiri was invited to come from Minnesota to act as interim abbot for a year. He expected to be offered the position permanently once the year was up but wasn't – a decision that had its own consequences. Instead the board appointed Reb Anderson, Baker's Dharma heir, as the new abbot-for-life. Baker then remembered that he hadn't completed his investiture of Anderson and questioned his right to be abbot. The board ignored that bit of pettiness, but the situation became further complicated when Anderson was arrested for waving a gun about in a low-income housing project. He'd been robbed of $20 by a man with a knife just outside Zen Center and responded by fetching a gun he'd found in Golden Gate Park years earlier – under equally bizarre circumstances, taking it from beside a corpse he'd found but hadn't reported – and chasing after the thief. Some of his defenders later pointed out that the gun hadn't been loaded, although that wouldn't have been something the people in the neighborhood – seeing a skin-headed white man with a weapon in his hand – could have been expected to know.

The board chose not to dismiss Anderson, but they did set term limits to the abbot's position and brought in Mel Weitsman to act as co-abbot. There would be no more abbots-for-life at Zen Center.

---

254. Quoted in Michael Downing, *Shoes Outside the Door* (Washington D. C.: Counterpoint, 2001), p. 245.

1984

One year after the Apocalypse in San Francisco, a film crew arrived at the Zen Center of Los Angeles to do a documentary. The center's abbot and teacher, Taizan Maezumi, was just returning from participating in an alcoholic recovery program, and the membership of the center was still struggling with his drinking, revelations of his infidelity to his wife, and his sexual flirtations and involvements with female students. Arrangements for the filming had been made long before, but, when the crew arrived, many of the residents at ZCLA wanted to cancel the project. The community was in disarray; emotions were still raw. Maezumi, however, insisted that the film makers be allowed to do their work and that nothing should be concealed from them.

Although in both San Francisco and Los Angeles it was perceived sexual impropriety that initiated internal crises in the communities, in neither was sex the primary issue. The issue in San Francisco was Baker's lifestyle and mode of management. In Los Angeles, even though Maezumi's marriage ended because of his affairs, the primary issue was alcoholism. Maezumi's students had been aware of his fondness for drink and, to some extent, encouraged it because, when tipsy, he became quick witted and acted and spoke more like the Zen masters in the stories that D.T. Suzuki, Nyogen Senzaki, and others had made popular. Jan Chozen Bays – one of Maezumi's Dharma heirs – told me that he was

> – funny when he got drunk, which was unfortunate. People would encourage him to get drunk, because another side came out. The Japanese don't usually tell you the truth because they don't want people to lose face. It's a different culture. For example, if Maezumi Roshi had something he wanted to tell me that was difficult, he would tell one of my Dharma brothers, and then they were expected – it took a long time to learn this – to come tell me, so I wouldn't lose face by being confronted by Maezumi Roshi directly. So he would tell Genpo [Dennis Merzel] or Tetsugen [Bernie Glassman] something he didn't like that I was doing, and then they would tell me. And vice versa. He would tell me something that I had to tell them. That's the way it's done in Japan. But when he was drunk, he would be very honest. In Japan, it's looked at very differently; if you're drunk, you can be forthright, and it's all forgiven the next day. So you could say something rude to your boss and the next morning it would be totally forgiven. So, when he was drinking, he would tell you what he thought of you. And you wanted to hear that, and you didn't want to hear that. But the

temptation was very strong to hear that. So people would drink with him, or sit with him when he was drinking, just to find that out.[255]

At first, Maezumi's drinking hadn't seemed problematic. He didn't allow it, for example, to interfere with his commitment to practice. Peter Matthiessen relates an occasion, during a trip to Japan, when he and Bernie Glassman stayed up late into the night drinking with Maezumi. The next day, the Americans rose too late to attend morning zazen, and Maezumi reprimanded them.

> When I murmured that our sluggishness might be accounted for by all that drink, Maezumi snapped, "Saki is one thing, and zazen is another! They have nothing to do with each other!"[256]

On the other hand, when he had been drinking, he would flirt with female students even during dokusan. Joan Yushin was not only married to one of his senior students, their son had recently been diagnosed with a malignant brain tumor, so she was both surprised and angry when she realized what Maezumi was doing.

> I went into dokusan, and he [Maezumi] was particularly loving, and so sweet, and he tilted his head, and he was smiling at me, no matter what I was presenting to him. He was flirting with me! And I said, "Don't be flirting with me! I don't want to know anything about that!" And that was the end of that. He straightened his head up, and he never did that again.[257]

Then in 1983, when it became clear that Maezumi had done more than flirt with other students, his wife left him, taking their younger children with her. Joan Yushin pointed out:

> So there was a lot of craziness going on at that place, and I'm not really sure why. I think we American women are extremely selfish and very dominating, and we want what we want. Not just women; men too. But, for sure, the womanizing thing had two folds to it. There were women who propositioned him as much as he took advantage.

---

255. Interview with the author, March 26, 2013. Cf. *Cypress Trees in the Garden*, Chapter 14.
256. Peter Matthiessen, *Nine-Headed Dragon River* (Boston: Shambala, 1998), p. 240.
257. Interview with the author, June 8, 2013, cf. *Cypress Trees in the Garden*, Chapter 13.

It was natural for students to want to be closer to their teacher, and this was one way in which female students, at least, could get close. Although her own affair with Maezumi contributed to the break-up of her marriage, Chozen Bays believes that the sexual aspect of her relationship with Maezumi was minor.

> We had this very strange mix of hippie commune and monastery. And not a terribly clear understanding of our own psychology. I think there was some spiritual-by-passing that happens in Zen often. So what happened with me was that I fell in love with Roshi. But in retrospect, after doing a lot of study and reading, I would say I fell in love with the Dharma through Roshi, as embodied by Roshi. In a way, what you're falling in love with isn't the Dharma in that person but your own potential. So, it's like a mirror. You're falling in love with your own potential to become what this person embodies for you – or your own version of it. And then you want to become intimate with it. More and more intimate with it. But because our human understanding of intimacy is so limited and involves sexuality, then you think, "Oh, this must be sexual. That's a way to become more intimate."

Maezumi made a full confession after his wife left and admitted that the lack of judgment he had demonstrated was due, at least in part, to his drinking. He acknowledged that he was an alcoholic and voluntarily entered the Betty Ford Rehabilitation Clinic. His students were stunned. Outside counselors were called in, and the community confronted the fact that they had, to a large degree, been complicit in enabling Maezumi's behavior.

While Maezumi underwent treatment, much of what he had accomplished in Los Angeles began to unravel. Students reacted in a number of ways. Some insisted that, at least as far as the sexual affairs were concerned, his private life should be no one else's concern. Some even tried to argue that the behavior of enlightened individuals shouldn't be judged by ordinary standards. Others, however, questioned his credibility as a teacher, and many left the center. One of his most influential heirs, Joko Beck, renounced her affiliation with him and ZCLA. Even Chozen Bays eventually left ZCLA and dropped out of Zen practice for a while.

It was in the midst of this trauma that the film crew arrived.

Maezumi agreed to be interviewed, and, in the released film, he frankly discusses his alcoholism:

> I have been drinking for this past, oh, maybe thirty years. I am a kind of periodical drinker, not every day. Being a monk and

having my position, simply said, I shouldn't drink. But, somehow, I was raised in Japan and so familiar with the social custom in which we even encourage drinking. To some degree, I was just carrying on that rather poor habit, even though knowing it's not a desirable thing to do. I was so ignorant about it, see? And in the past few years, I started to notice my drinking started having an effect on me, on many things, such as hurt people and destruction to the Dharma, and even regarding personal issues like hurting my physical and mental and even spiritual condition, and hurting my family, and all kinds of defects are relating to my drinking. I am very much remorseful about it. Frankly speaking, I don't know how much I hurt the people and how much damage I did to the Dharma. And I don't know how much I can make it up. At least I am more than willing to try…

I think it's true being alcoholic, becoming loose about morals. I agree that the negative point should be closely observed and be aware of it. Like myself, being alcoholic, I did not know how many immoral things I did. It's really outrageous.[258]

Maezumi apologized for his behavior and took full responsibility for it. There was never any question about the community asking him to resign his position. ZCLA survived and a period of reconciliation followed. However, the reduced membership meant that it had to divest itself of many of the properties that had been purchased during the period of expansion.

1988

In 1988, one of Joshu Sasaki's students, the poet Chizuko Karen Joy Tasaka, composed a poem that was distributed privately among the students at Bodhi Manda in New Mexico.

>Roshi, you are a sexual abuser
>"Come" you say as you pull me from a handshake onto your lap
>"Open" you say as you push your hands between my knees, up
>my thighs
>fondle my breasts
>rub my genitals
>french kiss me
>you put my hand on your genitals
>stroke your penis

---

258. From *Zen Center*, a documentary film by Anne Cushman. https://archive.org/details/ZenCenter.

jack you off?
this is sanzen?
my friend – she was inji[259]
sex with roshi
she tried to say no
you demanded, demanded, demanded
demon demand the force of a tornado
sex with roshi
for whose best interest?
I told you I don't like it.
I asked you why you do this?
You said, "nonattachment, nonattachment, you nonattachment"
I told you as shoji, "women very angry, very upset"
I asked you why you do this.
You said: "Be good daughter to roshi, and good wife to G.[260]"
Roshi, that is incest. So many women trying to shake the shame
from their voices of
Sex with roshi
We came to you with the trust of a student
You were our teacher
You betrayed us
You violated our bodies
You rape our souls
You betrayed our previous student-teacher relationship
You abuse us as women
You emasculate our husbands and boyfriends
Roshi, you are a sexual abuser
Your nuns you make your sexual servants
Your monks and oshos are crippled with denial
Roshi, Sexual Abuser.

The poem didn't have much impact on the majority of Sasaki's senior students because there was nothing in it with which they weren't already familiar.

 The story Sasaki had told about coming to America at the request of two students in California left out a number of significant details.[261]
 In 1944, he had been the *fusu* – or business manager – of Zuiryuji in the Prefecture of Toyama. Eight years later, it came to light that during his

---

259. Personal attendant.

260. Her husband.

261. See page 287 above.

time in office he had embezzled funds intended for temple renovations in order to pay for what the judge trying the criminal case against him called "a pleasure spree inappropriate for a religious figure."[262] Sasaki took responsibility for his actions, telling police that no one else was involved. He also confessed that "with regard to women, this is my distress as a human being."[263] The guards who had charge of him during his detention before trial were impressed by his demeanor, particularly the way he sat for hours in full lotus posture on his hard bed. One even obtained a zafu for him to make the posture more comfortable. He was found guilty in 1954 and served an eight-month sentence.

When he returned to his monastery, his "distress" with women didn't abate, and it was later reported that he had fathered at least two children for whom he assumed no responsibility. When the request came from America for a Rinzai teacher, the officials at Myoshinji may well have viewed this as an opportunity to rid themselves of a monk who continued to be an embarrassment. In Sasaki's version of the story, he performed the ceremony for permanent departure from Japan because he intended to stay in America until he had brought Rinzai Zen to the country. Another interpretation of events is that he was sent into exile.

He was, however, an effective teacher, and students were drawn to him. Leonard Cohen and Seiju Mammoser were not alone in praising him. David Yoshin Radin of the Ithaca Zen Center in New York told me that he had "had an immediate and very powerful bond to Sasaki Roshi as my teacher. His silence and poise were majestic. And his ability to teach that the self – my 'self' – was not identical to my body was direct and powerful. I had never seen anything like that before. Of course, I'd studied the teachings, but it's different when you get it live than when you get it from a book. It has the power to break through your own mental states. And that's why all this kafuffle is of no interest to me. I mean, he gave me such a profound gift that everything else is dwarfed."[264]

By "kafuffle" he meant the controversies around Sasaki's treatment of women, which hadn't improved after his move to the US.

Complaints surfaced early and were dismissed on the grounds that Sasaki was an enlightened Zen Master and anything he did with his students was actually teaching. One of the chroniclers of Sasaki's exploits reported that when

---

262. Details of the court case as recorded in the Japanese press at the time can be found at: https://sites.google.com/site/zuiganjiaffair/home.

263. Quoted in Stuart Lachs, "Modernizing American Zen through Scandal," in Hanna Havnevik et. al., (eds), *Buddhist Modernities* (New York: Routledge, 2017), p. 285.

264. Interview with the author, January 15, 2014. Cf. *Cypress Trees in the Garden*, Chapter 2.

– a young woman who was Sasaki's assistant (*inji*) at the time complained about Sasaki's constant sexual advances, one monk replied that "sexualizing is teaching for particular women." The monk's theory, widespread in Sasaki's circle, was that such physicality could check a "woman's overly strong ego." Sasaki claimed his sexual advances were in fact teaching non-attachment and emptiness, core Zen values.[265]

When male students did try to intervene on behalf of the women, Sasaki threatened to stop teaching if they questioned his methods. He also noted that having sex with young women helped him remain youthful.

Sasaki's tendencies – although they were successfully concealed from the general public for a long while – became well known within Zen circles, and women who chose to study with him were often aware of the stories. The abbess of Enpuku-ji Zen Center in Montreal, Zengetsu Myokyo, told me that she had been aware of the situation before she began her practice, and it hadn't discouraged her from seeking to study with him.[266] Even women who later complained about his behavior often continued to admire him as a teacher. One of the women who wrote to the Witnessing Council established in response to the "Sasaki Affair" stated that she

– stayed with Roshi because my experience largely was that he was a great and gifted Zen and koan teacher, and I believe I received great benefit from the other sanzen meetings – those unburdened by his sexual interests. I had met with other Roshis and teachers, but I felt he was absolutely the deepest and best teacher.[267]

As the number of incidents grew, even some of Sasaki's most ardent supporters came to have doubts. In 1992, one of his senior students – Gentei Sandy Steward – disaffiliated his North Carolina Zen Center from Rinzai-ji specifically because "of my objection to the sexual behavior and sexual teaching techniques of the Head Abbot" and "my disapproval of the lack of action by the Head Abbot, board of directors or ordained persons of Rinzai-ji to help those who have suffered on account of this behavior."[268]

Things finally attracted attention outside the Zen community when in 2012 a former Rinzai-ji priest, Eshu Martin, published an open letter on

---

265. https://buddhism-controversy-blog.com/2017/07/16/ready-to-mine-zens-legitimating-mythology-and-cultish-behavior/#_ftnref16

266. Interview with the author April 29, 2013. Cf. *Cypress Trees in the Garden*, Chapter 2.

267. Letter from Myo On Susan Linnell to the Witnessing Council, January 19, 2011.

268. Letter to Joshu Sasaki and Board of Directors of Rinzai-ji dated July 6, 1992. http://www.sasakiarchive.com/PDFs/1992_Resignation_letter.pdf.

the *Sweeping Zen*[269] website that explicitly described the state of affairs in the community:

> Joshu Sasaki Roshi, the founder and Abbot of Rinzai-ji is now 105 years old, and he has engaged in many forms of inappropriate sexual relationship with those who have come to him as students since his arrival here more than 50 years ago. His career of misconduct has run the gamut from frequent and repeated non-consensual groping of female students during interview, to sexually coercive after hours "tea" meetings, to affairs and sexual interference in the marriages and relationships of his students. Many individuals that have confronted Sasaki and Rinzai-ji about this behavior have been alienated and eventually excommunicated, or have resigned in frustration when nothing changed; or worst of all, have simply fallen silent and capitulated. For decades, Joshu Roshi's behavior has been ignored, hushed up, downplayed, justified, and defended by the monks and students that remain loyal to him.
>
> Based on my own experience as a student and monk in Rinzai-ji from 1995-2008 and many conversations during that time and since, it seems to me that virtually every person who has done significant training with him, the Rinzai-ji board of Directors, and most senior members of the Western Zen community at large know about his misconduct. Yet no one to my knowledge has ever publicly spoken out. Certainly, as an organization, Rinzai-ji has never accepted the responsibility of putting a stop to this abuse, and has never taken any kind of remedial action.
>
> For many years, I have struggled with my own part in this calamity; I have known but have not spoken out. I have watched the situations with [other teachers] unfold, and I have been overwhelmed by the courage of those brave Zen folk who have stood up to speak the truth, knowing that it would be painful, and would have very real repercussions in their lives, and in the lives of those around them. I have been reminded of the strength and courage that is required to speak the truth when it calls into question an individual of such high standing.
>
> I have decided to come forward now because to allow this kind of abuse to go unacknowledged, when so many of us know it has been happening is, in my opinion, inexcusable. I will not be silent

---

269. Sweeping Zen was a web site available from 2009 until 2017. It promoted itself as "the definitive online who's who in Zen" and provided a wide range of information about Zen practice in America. It also hosted the blogs of several Zen teachers and was a vehicle for current news about Zen activity. In 2017, its founder, Adam Tebbe became a born-again Christian and ceased to maintain the site.

any more. I feel that to ignore the damage caused by Joshu Sasaki and the leaders of Rinzai-ji who allowed it to continue is both a huge disservice to those who have been abused, and a lost opportunity for all of us to learn from our mistakes. I feel obliged to speak the truth about this matter, insofar as I am able to know it. I believe that only by doing so is it possible for any healing to begin. I hope that I may be an example for others, so that they may find the courage to speak out about their experiences with Joshu Sasaki and Rinzai-ji. My hope is that by being accountable to each other, and working together, honestly and transparently, we will all be able to proceed more clearly into the future.

In February of 2011, I contacted several Rinzai-ji Oshos personally and expressed my hope that they would begin to address this issue. I received two responses; the first, from Eshin Godfrey Osho that said, "You ask that I make every effort to address the issue you see of 'inappropriate conduct of Joshu Sasaki Roshi with female students.' This is exceedingly presumptuous of you…not being in the family I do not see you are in a position to expect it." The second response was a brief reply from Koshin Cain Osho that promised a later response, that has never come.

My own personal relationship to Rinzai-ji has been rocky to say the least, and I am no longer a member of their organization. It would be easy to turn the spotlight onto my relationship with Rinzai-ji, and I fully expect that will happen. I am prepared to discuss openly what I know, and how I know it as we go forward. This article is an opening statement for what I hope will be a much broader conversation. I would like to keep the primary point in focus. Whatever conclusions are drawn about me, and my history with Rinzai-ji, it in no way changes the facts regarding Joshu Sasaki's sexual abuse of students these many years. I hope that other more well-established members of the North American Zen community, who have also long known about Sasaki Roshi's sexual misconduct, will step forward to voice their own concerns, so that I do not remain alone in speaking out.

It is my sincere hope that the Oshos and Directors of Rinzai-ji will talk about this issue publicly and accept responsibility for the personal and organizational shortcomings that have allowed this abuse to go on for so long. My hope is that the healing that has been denied to so many victims can finally begin.[270]

---

270. http://sweepingzen.com/everybody-knows-by-eshu-martin/ - November 2012.

The letter had an immediate impact. It was spread through the internet, and its content was discussed on hard news sources like CNN and the *New York Times*. Seiju Mammoser spoke on behalf of the Rinzai-ji Osho Council in the *New York Times* article, admitting that he had been aware of the allegations against Sasaki since the 1980s and that there had "been efforts in the past to address this with him. Basically, they haven't been able to go anywhere." Mammoser added:

> What's important and is overlooked is that, besides this aspect, Roshi was a commanding and inspiring figure using Buddhist practice to help thousands find more peace, clarity and happiness in their own lives. It seems to be the kind of thing that, you get the person as a whole, good and bad, just like you marry somebody and you get their strengths and wonderful qualities as well as their weaknesses.[271]

In November 2012, Rinzai-ji established – and cooperated with – an Independent Witnessing Council made up of Zen leaders not associated with Sasaki or his centers. The council collected information from 25 individuals, half of whom experienced actual or attempted sexual contact with Sasaki; the other thirteen presented second hand reports. In their summary of findings, the council wrote:

> There were consistent reports of sexual behavior by Joshu Sasaki, often initiated in the formal setting, privacy, and "face-to-face" encounters of the sanzen room.
> There were many accounts of Sasaki asking women to show him their breasts, as part of "answering" a koan or to demonstrate "non-attachment." Some women repelled these requests and further physical advances. Many could not because they were physically overwhelmed, and subsequently experienced sexual behavior including kissing, viewing of breasts or genitalia, fondling of breasts or genitalia, viewing or being asked to touch his genitalia, oral sex, and vaginal intercourse. Several women recounted that they were asked to sit on his lap, presumably to be comforted. This physical intimacy progressed to sexualized behaviors initiated by Sasaki.
> There were no accounts of Joshu Sasaki asking men to show their genitalia in the course of "koan work."
> There were accounts of forced sexual and physical assault (against women's protests) that resulted in one report to the Los

---

271. http://www.nytimes.com/2013/02/12/world/asia/zen-buddhists-roiled-by-accusations-against-teacher.html?_r=0.

Angeles District Attorney's office and one report to a rape crisis center. There was another report to a Child Welfare agency concerning Sasaki and a sexual encounter with an underage girl. One person had interviewed women Rinzai-ji students, and three people extrapolated the number of women victims as well over one hundred.[272]

1993

In October 1993, twelve of Eido Shimano's female students took part in a workshop held in the summer house – now a guest lodge – at Dai Bosatsu. Among the participants was Roko Sherry Chayat who would become Shimano's principal heir and successor as abbot of the Zen Studies Society. She would also be the person who, in 2011, would install a deadbolt lock on the front door of the New York Shobo-ji Zendo preventing Shimano from entering the premises without making prior arrangements.

The purpose of the 1993 gathering was to consider the on-going complaints primarily made by women about Shimano's behavior. A summary of the points raised, marked "confidential," was included in papers Aitken donated to the University of Hawaii and were eventually reproduced on the Shimano Archives website maintained by an ordained Rinzai priest, Kobutsu Malone, who had previously been the gatekeeper at Dai Bosatsu.[273] The document begins by listing, in point form, "views expressed by one or more attendees." The first item notes that although many women involved sexually with Shimano "have been traumatized by the experience" Shimano himself "doesn't seem to have been adversely affected by these relationships…" One wonders if the statement was intended ironically.

A range of opinions were expressed during the meeting. Once again, as with Joshu Sasaki, there was recognition that in spite of his sexual predation, Shimano was a skilled teacher, and some of the women present defended him on those grounds. The list isn't organized; it appears items were noted as they were raised in open discussion:

- Roshi is a human like everyone else but is being judged by a harsher standard than we are.
- The mass exodus of people in 1967, 1975, 1979, 1982, 1986 and 1993 has caused a loss of extremely talented people and very few senior students remain.
- Some of the people who left would like to come back but can't because they do not feel safe and/or can't practice at a ZSS facility as long as

---

272. http://sasakiarchive.com/PDFs/20130111_Summary_Findings.pdf.

273. http://www.shimanoarchive.com/ Malone maintained a similar archive on Joshu Sasaki: http://sasakiarchive.com/

teacher/student relationships are allowed to happen.
- Others feel that so much had happened that they are not sure a reconciliation is possible.
- People want Roshi to "stop it!" This wish is framed within the context of compassion and gratitude.
- The scandals have been destructive to the Sangha and to individuals.
- People are dismayed about Roshi's apparent view that members can easily be replaced and feel he does little to try to heal the wounds that have been created.
- Telling people to "get out" when they don't agree with him is arrogant and unacceptable.
- The scandals have hurt everyone – not just women.
- Roshi's advances toward women are indicative of emotional immaturity, thoughtlessness, and insecurity.
- Roshi has a compulsive addiction that needs to be cured.
- Perhaps Roshi displayed affection towards certain women because he felt they needed some warmth and or kindness in their lives.
- Roshi is an excellent koan teacher but he is not strong on the Precepts.
- Roshi's behavior and lifestyle do not epitomize that of a Buddhist priest.

...

- Roshi is a lonely person and his whole lifestyle (i.e.; traveling constantly etc.) is very hard on him.
- One can be enlightened yet not actualize certain behavior.
- Students (especially new ones) are vulnerable – many view a Zen master as a "godlike" being who would never consciously hurt anyone. They trust such an individual implicitly.

...

- Roshi is isolated from his students and has too much power.
- Roshi and Aiho-san [his wife] do not want students to talk to each other. They want a "veil of secrecy" to surround everything.

...

- Roshi and Aiho-san consider public discussions of the student-teacher issue as a loss of face.
- Japanese culture has a tremendous impact on the practice. American students consider this a problem but Roshi and Aiho-san don't.
- Americans are very forthright and expect total disclosure of all facts – the Japanese are more subtle.
- Sometimes Roshi feels victimized too. The whole Zen master mystique may be an attractant to some women. Some women do throw themselves at him.
- Even if a woman does try to initiate a liaison, it is still Roshi's responsibility to not allow it to happen.

- No one is aware of any instances where Roshi propositioned a women – was turned down and then refused to continue being her teacher.
- The student-teacher issue is just symptomatic of deeper problems.
- Roshi won't change his behavior to correct the problem. He refuses to take responsibility for his actions.
- Roshi doesn't perceive himself as having a problem.
...
- Regardless of what has happened some people still consider Roshi their teacher.
- Roshi has engaged in other behavioral patterns such as deception which have also caused tremendous hurt and pain.
...
- American Zen has a horrible reputation because of sex, drug and money scandals.

Given the severity of several of the issues raised, the suggested "list of action items" the group put forward seems timid and feeble:
1. Create a Big Sister/Brother mentoring program for new resident students.
2. Request the Board of Directors call an annual Sangha meeting.
3. Change the Bylaws to help the organization move towards a more democratic/American model.
4. Have "women only" and "old timer" sesshins in the guest house without Roshi present.
5. Role modeling of other Zen centers.[274]

As the findings of the 1993 gathering recognize, Shimano's sexual activities had been going on at least since 1967 – when the first mass exodus took place – just three years after his arrival in New York City.

In 1982 the journalist (and sexual advice columnist), Robin Westen wrote an article for *The Village Voice* describing her experience and that of other women with Shimano. The editors decided the piece was too incendiary to print, but it's now available in Kobutsu Malone's archive. She begins by describing a meeting she had with Shimano during which he held out his hand to help her get up from cushion she was seated upon on the floor. Then he pulled her towards him and grabbed her breast.

> [He] prodded my mouth with his tongue, and started to pull up my skirt and reach between my legs.

---

274. http://www.shimanoarchive.com/PDFs/19931022R_Womans_Workshop.pdf

> For a moment, I was too stunned to react. But then I pushed him away, and stood there, my arms distancing us. I looked straight at him. He stared right back. He acted as though nothing had happened. He was still smiling.[275]

Westen felt violated both physically and emotionally by the assault. She also knew from the confident way Shimano behaved that it couldn't have been the first time he had treated a student in this manner. That afternoon, she began an investigation which eventually identified dozens of women who had engaged, sometimes reluctantly, in sexual activity with Shimano.

Her article describes a series of events, referred to by insiders as the "Fuck Follies," that came to light in 1975 after an earlier group of women compared their experiences with Shimano. One described an occasion when Shimano invited her to his quarters for what she thought was going to be a meeting to discuss her spiritual progress. He stopped her as she began talking, telling her to be quiet.

> And almost before I knew it, he had pulled off his robe and was laying down on the bed stark naked. Well, I was in such a state then, I thought this must be some sort of test of detachment. It sounds ridiculous now, but when you're serious about your Zen practice, and when you have a lot of respect for someone, you think the best, no matter what. And I thought the best when he ordered me to go down on him and perform fellatio. He told me it would be a spiritual experience for me…it wasn't.

Another student, whom Westen calls "Barbara," told Shimano during dokusan that she wondered if she were lesbian. He replied suggestively that there was only one way to tell. She had a second meeting with him that evening. There was a box on the floor when she arrived, that Shimano opened and brought out a silk scarf.

> He told me it was for me it was my present, but he just sat and fondled it on his lap. Well, I was sitting across from him. I felt relaxed. My legs were apart in lotus position and I was watching him fondle this silk scarf, and he never said anything, and the next thing I knew his hand wasn't fondling the scarf, it was up my skirt. I screamed at him: "Eido Roshi! What are you doing. What do you think you're doing?" He took his hand away and all he would say was, "What do you mean? I wasn't doing anything.

---

275. http://www.shimanoarchive.com/19820400R_Zen_Seduction.html

What did you think I was doing?" And that was the end of it for me. Like you don't make a mistake like that. I know what he was doing, so why didn't he admit it?

Westen didn't doubt that Shimano suggested Barbara's reaction was to something she had only imagined. He had done the same to her.

At the beginning of my investigation, I had sent a letter to Eido reporting my intention to write an article about our incident at the New York Zen Studies Society. When he received it, he phoned me at my office at ABC Television.

"You have your viewpoint," Eido said. "Other people have their viewpoint. You cannot write except by your own viewpoint."

I agreed with him.

"That's why I at least want to say what is my viewpoint so when you write you can see it from different angles," he continued. "The first thing I want to say is about what you mentioned you experienced in the dokusan room, and your personal feelings at the time. Do you remember what happened?"

I assured him I did. Perfectly.

Eido said, "I was really in a sense surprised when you held my hand and put it on your chest."

"What!" I was furious.

"Cheek. Chhh--eeeekk." Eido corrected himself.

Then I corrected him. "That's not exactly what happened. You told me to come closer in the dokusan room. Then you took my hand..."

Eido interrupted, "Yes, and then you placed it on your ch–eeek."

It was getting silly. "I placed my own hand, on my own cheek?"

"No, No. You took my hand and placed it on your cheek."

"Well," I said, "that just never happened."

Eido continued, despite my objections. "And you said to me, 'I want to stay like this forever.'"

"That just never happened," I said. "I have an entirely different perception of what took place."

"*This* is exactly the problem you see," Eido said. "What you remember and what I remember are entirely different. Nobody was witnessing, so you can say it your own way, and I can say it my own way. That's really the problem. What you will write will be from your point of view. Your subjective reality."

Although Roko Chayat had great respect for Shimano as a teacher, she and her then husband, Lou Nordstrom, were among those who left after the 1975 Fuck Follies in an act of solidarity with the women who had been abused by Shimano. She didn't return to study with Shimano until 1990, by which time she had been assured his behavior had changed.

Chayat was a committed practitioner and had been ordained by another teacher before she came back to ZSS. She continued to work through a process of advanced training with Shimano that culminated in 2008 when he bestowed the title Roshi on her and gave her the Dharma name Shinge, meaning "Heart/Mind Flowering."

Then in 2010, another student announced that she had been in an affair with Shimano. It became clear that, in spite of his assurances, Shimano's behavior hadn't changed.

As news of this most recent revelation spread through the Zen community, letters from Zen teachers throughout North America came to the board at ZSS suggesting they ask for Shimano's resignation. Under duress, he resigned that December, and on January 1, 2011, Shinge Roko Sherry Chayat was installed as abbot in his stead.

The following year, an official statement was released by Myoshin-ji, the head temple of the Rinzai tradition in Japan:

> Myoshin-ji has received many inquiries regarding its relationship with the Zen Studies Society in New York ever since the publication on 20 August 2010 of an article in the *New York Times* regarding the behavior of the Society's former director, Eido Shimano. On the occasion of establishing the Zen Studies Society, Eido Shimano stipulated that the Society was to have no relation to Myoshin-ji or any other branch of Japanese Rinzai Zen Buddhism.

As far as Myoshin-ji is concerned, all along it has had no connection with Eido Shimano, his activities or organizations, including Dai Bosatsu Zendo and all affiliated Zen Studies Society institutions, nor is Eido Shimano or any of his successors certified as priests of the Myoshin-ji branch of Zen or recognized as qualified teachers by them.

Wildfire

The last item on the list from the 1993 meeting at Dai Bosatsu stated that "American Zen has a horrible reputation because of sex, drug and money scandals." There were, of course, many centers not affected by scandal, but it couldn't be overlooked that it wasn't only Sasaki and Shimano who found women a "distress." In the early years of the 21st century, Zen had its "Me too" movement, with numerous revelations of sexual relationships between teachers and students. The reactions of individual sanghas ranged from indifference – which appears to have largely been the case with the Kwan Um Zen School in Providence – to demands for the teacher's resignation, which occurred in Toronto.

These revelations weren't, of course, limited to Zen, and it could even be – and was – argued that there were more egregious violations committed in other communities. Stories of sexual, financial, and even criminal behavior throughout the later decades of the 20th century undermined the credibility of spiritual leaders and guides within the Hare Krishna movement, the Rajneesh community, the EST and Synanon movements, Shambhala Buddhism, and even the Roman Catholic church. None of which, of course, either excused or explained the prevalence of inappropriate behavior – sexual or otherwise – within Zen centers. Nor did this activity come to an end after its impact on both individuals and communities became glaringly obvious and well publicized.

In 2011 one of Taizan Maezumi's heirs, Dennis Genpo Merzel, publicly admitted "dishonest, hurtful behavior as well as sexual misconduct,"[276] as a result of which he intended to disrobe as a Zen priest, a decision he later decided to reverse.

In 2015, Gentei Sandy Stewart – who had withdrawn the North Carolina Zen Center from the Rinzai-ji fold because of Joshu Sasaki's behavior – was himself forced to resign his position. A public letter from his board noted that a "number of prominent members of the sangha questioned various aspects of Sandy's leadership, his teaching style, and his relationships with current and former students."[277]

That same year, Konrad Ryushin Marchaj, an heir of Daido Loori, was relieved of his duties as abbot of Zen Mountain Monastery because – as he confessed in an open letter to the membership – he had been engaged in "an intimate relationship with someone outside our sangha," betraying his partner and breaking their "spiritual union vows and ending our marriage." He also admitted that he had been exploring shamanic traditions and religions and that his inclusion of elements of these in his presentation of the Dharma "was irresponsible and might have caused some confusion, and may make people have doubt in the dharma."[278]

As interest in the history of Zen grew, biographical material emerged that cast shadows on the memory of some of the most revered founders of American Zen. Numerous Zen teachers in Japan – including both Harada and Yasutani – were discovered to have been fervent supporters of Japanese

---

276. From a open letter originally posted on Merzel's Big Mind web site, reprinted at: https://clearviewblog.org/2011/02/23/the-cloud-of-knowing-not-knowing-sex-power-and-sangha/

277. http://www.nczencenter.org/wp-content/uploads/2015/11/Letter-to-the-Membership-6-4-15.pdf

278. Statement posted by Ryushin Marchaj on the ZMM website, January 26, 2015.

militarism and the war against the United States. The Zen establishment as a whole was found to have supported Japan's expansionist ambitions in the early 20th century. Soyen Shaku – D.T. Suzuki's teacher – even boasted that the Japanese success in the Russo-Japanese War (1904-05) had been due to the strength the nation drew from Buddhist culture and specifically from Zen training which helped instill a "Samurai spirit" in the population.

A biography of Shunryu Suzuki published in 1999 noted that he had been married twice before coming to America. His first wife left him to return to her family when she was diagnosed with tuberculosis. His second wife was murdered by a mentally unstable monk whom Suzuki – against the objections of his family – brought into his household. The monk struck Suzuki's wife in the head with an ax seven times. Suzuki's daughter, Omi, never recovered from her mother's death, was institutionalized in a mental hospital, and eventually committed suicide.

When Taizan Maezumi died during a visit back to Japan in 1995, the members of the Zen Center of Los Angeles were originally told that he'd had a heart attack. It was only two years later, when ZCLA required a copy of his death certificate for insurance purposes, that the actual details of his death were revealed. Although Maezumi had apparently been successful in remaining sober in California since 1984, he allowed himself to relax and drink socially while in Japan where attitudes towards alcohol consumption were different. On May 14, 1995, he passed the evening with his brothers at the family temple in Otawara. He intended to spend the following day with another brother in Tokyo, and, although it was late and they had been drinking heavily, Maezumi took the train into the city. He fell asleep during the trip and missed his stop, so it was even later than he had planned when he finally arrived at his brother's house. He told the brother that he was going to take a bath in the large traditional Japanese tub and then retire; there was no need to wait up for him. The next morning, when the brother got up, he discovered Maezumi had drowned in the tub.

Then there were stories brought back to North America by youthful enthusiasts who travelled to Japan for training and discovered a harsh and inflexible system often brutal in its methods. Conditions were so harsh at Ryutaku-ji in Japan that when the American, Genjo Marinello, went there in the 1980s, his fellow novices couldn't understand why he would have chosen to subject himself to them. They were there, largely, not by personal choice, but "because that was their lot in life. And they couldn't at all understand that I came there voluntarily to train, because no one would do that. That was incomprehensible, truly incomprehensible. So when I settled on saying that I had been sent there by my teacher, they could understand that. But if I tried to say I wanted to train in Zen, they would just shake their head. 'No. That can't be the reason.'"[279]

The romantic image of an enlightened teacher transcending ordinary human frailties was shattered over and over again. Instead even the most acclaimed teachers, teachers with impeccable transmission credentials, often proved to be – as Leonard Cohen said of Joshu Sasaki – "quite flawed as human beings."[280]

In June 2013 – two and a half years after Eido Shimano stepped down as abbot of the Zen Studies Society – I traveled to the elegant Dai Bosatsu Kongo-ji in the Catskill Mountains. It's not an easy place to get to. One travels along a narrow county road and then up a gravel lane that was partially eroded by heavy rains at the time of my visit. After passing the expected New England farms, one comes upon a traditional Japanese gate with adjoining side buildings. The sign over the entrance consists of three white kanji characters against a brown background. The property is 1400 acres, and the monastery structures are still two miles further on. The first thing one sees is the Guest Lodge where the 1993 workshop had taken place. Across the lake, a large bronze Buddha seated on a boulder is tilting backwards slightly.

The temple itself is every bit as impressive and improbable as I had been led to believe. Shimano and his architect, Davis Hamerstrom, had modeled it after Tofukuji, the largest Rinzai temple in Japan, using imported craftsmen when necessary to ensure accuracy of detail. There are polished oak floors and tatami mats, sliding shoji screens, splendid calligraphy scrolls, and antique Asian treasures throughout. But during my visit, the halls are nearly empty. Shinge Roko Chayat tells me there are currently only eight residents although two are away because of illness. Of the remaining six, only four are American; the other two are from Japan. Before what she refers to as "the troubles," as many as sixty people could be expected to attend sesshin. The previous May there had been only fourteen. She admits that a number of women have withdrawn from practice entirely.

As I review my notes in the room provided me after my meeting with Shinge, I'm reminded of a visit I had paid a few weeks prior to James Ford. James is the founder of the Boundless Way Zen centers in New England and would later establish the Blue Cliff Zen Sangha. He was also, until his retirement shortly after I met him, a Unitarian minister. We met in his office at the First Unitarian Church of Providence, Rhode Island – located on the corner of Benefit and Benevolent Streets – and discussed the

---

279. Interview with the author, April 28, 2014. Cf., *Cypress Trees in the Garden*, Chapter 4.
280. Cf., fnt. 225 above, p. 288.

various scandals that were challenging Zen's credibility. In a wistful tone, he remarked, "I fear there's a real good chance that we'll simply attenuate into…and – you know – we'll simply be a historical blip."

I share his evident sense of how sad that would be, but, in my room at Dai Bosatsu, I wonder what it would take to fill these empty halls again.

When a group of students asked Dogen to tell them something about his life, he made this brief assessment: "Just one mistake after another."

Revisioning

Taking Stock

CLATSKANIE is a self-proclaimed Christian township of less than 2000 persons in Northwest Oregon. I had informed the motor inn where I was booked that I would arrive late, and the office is closed when I pull in. The key to my room, however, is taped – as promised – on the door of the unit I'd been assigned. It's that kind of community.

It's also the location of Great Vow Zen Monastery, now occupying what had been the local primary school. The monastery is a residential training center with a surprisingly young membership. One of the monastics had just turned 20 a few days prior to my visit in March 2013. I had come to speak with one of the co-abbots, Jan Chozen Bays – previously Jan Soulé. In the six years following this meeting, I would interview more than 100 Zen teachers and senior students. But, as it happens, this is only the third interview I'd conducted, and I was still finding my way in the process. I was particularly nervous because I knew that one of the topics I would have to discuss with her was her sexual relationship – thirty years prior – with Taizan Maezumi Roshi, and I was unsure how to broach the subject respectfully. To my relief, she brought it up before I had to.

"We had this very strange mix of hippie commune and monastery," she told me. "And not a terribly clear understanding of our own psychology."[281]

She can be disarmingly frank. What had come about both in Los Angeles and San Francisco – and elsewhere – was something very different from the formal unisexual Buddhist training centers of Asia. The combination of – as she put it – commune and monastery is "part of how Zen got established in North America, and, of course, that has its problems." In an open letter in which she apologized to Maezumi's daughter, Kirsten, for the harm she'd done to both their families, she wrote:

---

281. Cf. *Cypress Trees in the Garden*, Chapter 14.

This is not an excuse, but a framing of the times. Looking back 30 years, it was a strange thing to do, to try to combine a hippie commune with a Zen monastery. In matters of mores, the hippie commune won out. It was the age of Aquarius, of rebellion against the old, of free love, open marriages, of turn-on-and-drop-out. Jealousy was regarded as a character flaw, and the Happy Hooker books extolled the joy and virtues of prostitution. When your father's good friend and drinking companion Trungpa Rinpoche traveled to cities like LA, he was supplied with consorts, sometimes offered up by their husbands as gifts for their teacher. As someone said recently, "ZCLA in the old days was a highly sexually charged atmosphere." While I can understand that it could seem to you that I was the cause of many difficulties, I and others got caught up in something that had been going on for some time there. While this is no excuse, it was a reality.[282]

Asian temples and monasteries were, of course, disciplined facilities. American Zen Centers weren't necessarily. The members were overwhelming young, many used drugs routinely. They weren't celibate. Sex was common not only between students but between teachers and students. And while they weren't uneducated – at the time of her affair with Maezumi, Chozen was a licensed physician – they often had a naïve understanding of Zen. Many, like Robert Aitken during his first sesshin in Kamakura, were surprised to learn that Zen was a Buddhist sect with rituals and protocols and proclamations of belief.

One of the functions of Zen is to provide an environment in which the practitioner can begin the lengthy and often painful process of seeing through the delusions that cloud his or her clear perception – seeing through one's cultural conditioning, one's ambitions, rationalizations, and self-justifications, the stories one tells oneself. After the crises in Los Angeles and San Francisco, for people like Chozen this meant looking at the practice itself and the often highly romanticized concepts early American practitioners had about Buddhism and Zen.

From its earliest encounter, the West has viewed Buddhism, Zen, and the East in general through a series of distorting lenses. Early Christian critics found Buddhism to be such a bewilderingly nihilistic doctrine that it was difficult for them to understand how it could be anything other than the creation of the Devil. Post-Darwinian Victorians sought in it an alternative to Christianity, the veracity of which was being challenged by the emerging scientific perspective. For Theosophists and their

---

282. http://sweepingzen.com/response-to-kirsten-mitsuyo-maezumi. See fnt. 269 on p. 327 above about the Sweeping Zen website.

descendants, Buddhism was conflated with a thirst for spiritualism and the development of both physical and psychic superhuman powers. After D.T. Suzuki's books raised popular interest about Zen in the West, early enthusiasts included the Beat writers who saw in figures like Hanshan – to whom Kerouac dedicated *The Dharma Bums* – models of spontaneous creative energy. Although there were exceptions – such as Gary Snyder – the Beats in general had little genuine interest in Zen as a discipline or study. The youth culture of the '60s, the hippies, equated Suzuki's descriptions of enlightenment with the experiences that often resulted from the use of psychedelic drugs. They approached Zen shamanistically. LSD, mescaline, and psilocybin revealed alternate states of consciousness in which one felt more deeply engaged in reality and open to spiritual insight. For more than a few, Zen was viewed as a "natural way" of exploring psychedelic insights more deeply. Especially after the publication of *The Three Pillars of Zen* in 1965, a large percentage of the people who populated not only SFZC and ZCLA but other emerging centers across the country came seeking "enlightenment," although it wasn't always clear to them what enlightenment was, nor how enlightened teachers should behave or how they could be recognized.

The term "enlightenment" carried a number of misleading connotations for North Americans. In the liberal parlance of the '80s, "enlightened" was often associated with the term "progressive" as when one is said to have an enlightened attitude about certain social or environmental concerns. It was challenging to discover that teachers who were supposed to be "enlightened" did not always have the same commitment to social causes their students did; some even espoused conservative political perspectives.

In Buddhism, "enlightenment" has a narrow meaning. To be "enlightened" is to be enlightened about one's True Self. One can realize one's Buddha-nature and remain "unenlightened" about a whole range of other matters. Many enlightened Zen masters in Japan, for example, had supported the imperialist ambitions that led to their engagement in the Second World War. Throughout the history of Buddhism, as far back as the Buddha himself, enlightened individuals were no more capable of overcoming contemporary social prejudices or traditional attitudes towards gender than anyone else.

By the end of the 1980s, Zen students in San Francisco and Los Angeles and throughout North America struggled with the assumptions they had made about the men in whom they had put their trust. Did Maezumi's alcoholism or Baker's behavior cast doubt on their legitimacy as Zen teachers? How real was the process of transmission? Did students have unrealistic expectations about their teachers? What precisely had they sought from them, and to what extent had their own desire for acknowledgement from those teachers distorted their capacity to view them and their teachings objectively?

One Teacher's Journey

Taizan Maezumi's alcoholism and sexual affairs were revealed shortly after Richard Baker's fall from grace in San Francisco. But, unlike Baker, when Maezumi was confronted about his behavior, he took steps to deal with it. One of his attendants told him directly that he needed to seek treatment for his condition, and he agreed. I asked Chozen Bays if it had really been that simple.

"It was the right time," she tells me. "I guess it was the right constellation. I mean, Roshi had already gotten in trouble because he'd had an affair with me, then he had an affair with another woman; his wife had left him. So there was enough ruckus in the community that it was time for a turning point. And he admitted right away that he had a problem and went into residential treatment."

Chozen's marriage had also ended, and she felt the need to separate herself from the community for a time, even though she had been acknowledged as one of Maezumi's Dharma heirs.

"I thought about all of us," she tells me. "I thought, if this is enlightened behavior, I'm not interested in it. But I need to investigate it. You know, I'm a physician, so I like to say, 'Okay, here's the condition. I need to learn about it. Learn how to diagnose it early and intervene.' So, I read books about the Hare Krishna community and how it had gone awry. The EST community and how it's gone awry. And Synanon and how it went awry. And the Rajneesh Community and how it had gone awry. That was very relevant because he came here to Oregon from India. Bought a bunch of land. Ran into all kinds of problems with authorities. Tried to take over a whole town. Brought in bus-loads of homeless people to stack the voting rolls. Poisoned people. I mean it's unbelievable what happened here in Oregon. And so when we moved to Oregon, the whole state was still smarting from that experience. They're still distrustful of cults. So I read about all of those to see what went wrong, and I developed a list of signs of when things are starting to go wrong."

Not all of the elements were pertinent to ZCLA, but several were.

"First, the community starts to idolize the teacher and imitate the teacher in all aspects of life. So, if the teacher had affairs – and Maezumi Roshi had affairs – then there's a looseness around affairs. Or if the teacher's an alcoholic – in Japan, they call it 'Wisdom Water' – there's this looseness around alcohol. If the teacher divorces, then divorce becomes okay and so on. So, there's an idolization, putting the teacher on a pedestal and imitating his behavior.

"Then there's going to the teacher with questions about all aspects of your life, and the teacher trying to respond to that. The teacher begins to have too much power over your life. So, people would go to Roshi and say, 'I'm thinking of changing jobs. What do you think?' Or, 'I'm thinking of getting into a relationship. What do you think?' And he would try his best to answer because he wanted to be helpful. But that's not helpful. Then you have what one of my Dharma sisters called 'too numinous a presence' in the person's life. You have say over too many aspects of their life, rather than just being their spiritual teacher. That can lead to problems.

"Then the next step is usually the belief that we are in the know and it is in the outside world where the problem is. And we're not going to go into the outside world because it's too problematic. So, it becomes isolated. There's the inside and the outside, and we're the inside, and we're the best, and we know.

"The next is when the ends justify the means. So, the Rajneesh community – and so did the Hare Krishna's – had what they called 'sacred prostitutes.' They would send women out to New York or Tokyo to prostitute and bring money back to the community. So, any aspect of 'the ends justifies the means' is the beginning of a downward slide. We didn't have that at ZCLA, but one aspect I saw that made me uncomfortable was that people who were living in voluntary poverty at the Zen Center would go on welfare. And then they would have welfare medical coverage, so they could come to the clinic and we could bill welfare. But these were people who could work, young, strong people, intelligent people. So it was kind of living off the dole in an inappropriate way."

While Maezumi was in a residential treatment center in San Diego, the community was forced to confront its own culpability in the situation.

"We had an alcohol intervention for the whole community. So, a group came in and did an intervention like they usually do with a family. But there were, like, almost a hundred people there. And it was stunning to all of us, to me, too, because I grew up in a family that doesn't drink, and I don't drink. What stunned me were that the words people spoke on the film were the same words we had spoken in the community all the time. 'Well, he can't be an alcoholic because he doesn't drink during sesshin and so on.' And so, to hear a disease – the words of a disease – spoken, as we had spoken them, that was stunning to me. And it was clear we were an enabling community. We were a huge alcoholic family."

In 1984, Chozen moved to Oregon, where she had a sister who taught at the University of Oregon.

"I think there was a feeling of gathering back to family, back to a sense of support from family. And I wanted to get the kids out of LA and into a healthier environment. LA was not a healthy environment for them. There was a lot of bullying in school, and they went backwards academically. So that was a motive. I felt like the family had, to a certain extent, been neglected while we were at the Zen Center because we were so focused on getting enlightened. And I had divorced, too, so there was that trauma to the kids. And so I felt I needed to gather the family together and be closer to other family members.

"And then this thing of, 'Wow! If that's enlightened behavior, I don't want anything of it.' So, I reacted against practice for several years. I didn't sit at all. Got a job. 'Cause I had to support the kids now that I was divorced and left the Zen Center. Worked back in medicine again, including academic medicine. Just hunkered down and took care of family and lived an ordinary life. And I was intrigued by the realization that, 'Wow! There's a lot of ordinary people out there who never studied Zen who are pretty wonderful people.' Then I sort of dragged my new husband through exploring different religious traditions. Just like, 'I've only done Zen for so many years now. I'm so immersed in it I have no perspective.' So we went to a Christian church; we went to a Hindu ashram; we went to an old-fashioned spiritualist group that still existed here that channeled spirits. And we went to a couple of other religious groups, but none of them were satisfying. So gradually we began sitting again."

Her new husband, Hogen, had also been a student at ZCLA. At first the two of them just sat by themselves.

"Then there was a sitting group in Portland associated with ZCLA, and the teacher of it moved to Mexico City. So, the group was without a leader, and they asked would I be willing to lead the group. So, the way I would say it is, I built up the practice again step by step. I sat and sat, and, 'Oh, yeah, I can see how sitting is helpful.' I had to learn everything afresh. 'Yeah. Sitting is helpful, and I can understand now.' Then they wanted services, would we lead the services? So, I did some services. Then they wanted to know would I do a talk once a month? I did a talk once a month. It was only by request. I didn't move forward at all myself. Then would I do interviews? I started doing interviews. And each time, I was saying, 'Is this valuable? And on what basis does it need to be founded on?'

"And then they started meeting in our house. So, we had a living room that was pretty much devoted to sitting. It was cleaned out and had cushions, and the group came and sat once a week. That committed us. We had to be ready for the group and welcome the group. And then they started asking for things. They asked for a weekend retreat. And then people asked to have jukai.[283] So Maezumi Roshi came up and helped me with that first jukai ceremony, getting the papers ready and everything, and

---

283. "Jukai" is the ceremony during which an initiate pledges to abide by the "precepts"

doing the ceremony. So that was nice. And it just gradually built back up as it seemed appropriate and was requested."

She and Hogen also took part in workshops dealing with clergy abuse and offered training on the subject at conferences for Buddhist teachers and at specific Buddhist communities. In her letter to Kirsten Maezumi she admits: "Because of what happened at ZCLA, I know that my mind has a big capacity for delusion and rationalization. Therefore I've surrounded myself with safeguards, an empowered board, ethical guidelines that are posted, a standing committee that is available to work with any sensitive issues in the sangha, and Bylaws that allow a vote of the Board or sangha to remove me from teaching at any time. I study with a Zen teacher[284] to whom I am accountable."

A Question of Ethics

Directly addressing the matter of ethical standards in her letter to Kirsten Maezumi, Chozen wrote:

> Zen teaching is a profession. Professionals have an obligation not to betray the trust of their students/clients/patients, trust that is essential to the work of spiritual teaching or therapy. When we take on the profession, we take on the responsibility to maintain proper boundaries with those we are caring for. If a patient tries to kiss a doctor or a minister or a therapist, it is the professional's responsibility to stop the behavior.

Ethical guidelines, of course, deal with more than sexual conduct. The "Guidelines for Behavior" adopted by Chozen's Zen Community of Oregon, for example, are based on the Five Precepts,[285] (1) to refrain from killing or doing harm, (2) to refrain from stealing, (3) to refrain from sexual misconduct, (4) to refrain from false speech, and (5) to refrain from misusing drugs or alcohol. But sexual misconduct posed a particular problem for several reasons. As Chozen's letter to Kirsten Maezumi points out, the cultural environment of the time promoted a sexual freedom that hadn't been available to women until the first effective forms of contraception allowed them to explore their sexuality in manners that hadn't been available to their predecessors, but that also made them vulnerable to predatory sexual exploitation.

---

and thus formally becomes a member of the Buddhist sangha.
284. Shodo Harada Roshi of Sogen-ji in Japan who also maintains Tahoma Sogen-ji on Whidby Island in Washington State.
285. Page 62 above.

There was also the fact that in Asian countries monogamy – at least for males – doesn't always have the same importance as it does in North America. Maezumi's sexual indiscretions raised questions and concerns among his students as well as in the wider Zen community, but in some ways – as Robert Aitken had discovered when he'd met with Nakagawa and Yasutani in Japan to discuss Eido Shimano's behavior – it was more an American than an Asian problem. Even though Maezumi accepted responsibility for his failings and didn't try to excuse his behavior, the circumstances and the way in which students responded to them revealed a significant cultural chasm not only between Japanese and North American values but also between the fundamental metaphysical premises underlying the Judeo-Christian worldview and those of Buddhism.

Many who were disappointed by Maezumi's behavior had to face the fact that they may have had inflated expectations of how "enlightened" Zen masters should behave. One of the most celebrated and respected Japanese Zen Masters, Ikkyu Sojun of the 14th century, brazenly frequented wine shops and brothels. In one of his poems he wrote that while his awakening experience had been profound, a night spent with a particularly talented prostitute provided an even deeper wisdom.

In Buddhism, there isn't the same connection between religion and morality as there is in the West where, to a large extent, they are equated. The responsibility of a Christian is to know and obey the will of a Divine Creator. Sins are not just human weaknesses; they are offences against God. This Judeo-Christian concept of sin is absent from Buddhism. The purpose of spiritual activity in Zen isn't to fall into step with a divinely revealed game plan but rather to overcome the reality of suffering (the first Noble Truth) by becoming aware of (enlightened about) one's Buddha-nature or True Self – one's inherent connection with all of Being. There are still appropriate and inappropriate, honorable and dishonorable behaviors, but these don't carry the weight of being directives from the Creator of the Universe. Adultery and the use of intoxicants are both prohibited in the precepts not because they transgress the directives of God but rather because they are recognized as impediments that perpetuate desire, which (according to the second Noble Truth) is the root cause of suffering – one's own and that of others. It was also recognized in the Zen tradition that spiritual insight (kensho) doesn't in itself necessarily make one a better person; that's why Zen is seen as a life-long process, not one that ends with awakening. There is always the need to deepen the awakening experience, integrate it into one's life, and cultivate karuna (compassion) through continued practice.

The guidelines that Zen communities developed in North America during the revisioning process acknowledged the differences between Asian and Euro-centric cultures but also considered the growing body of information about the dangers of sexual relationships between persons in authority and their subordinates and the evidence that genuine consent was often absent in such situations.

Personal relationships are frowned upon in some professions but, as Chozen noted, forbidden in others. While affairs between university professors and students are discouraged, they do occur and sometimes result in stable long-term marriages. Affairs between psychiatrists and their patients, on the other hand, are prohibited and can be grounds for the loss of professional credentials. In the early days of Zen in America, the relationship between Zen teachers and their students were considered closer to the former. Today they are generally seen as being in the same category as the latter.

The Oregon guidelines "are meant to establish reasonable expectations and limitations for behavior and yet respect the need for flexibility in our lives."[286] The matter of flexibility is what distinguishes "guidelines" from "rules," and it's an important distinction. If, for example, a Zen teacher were to be in a relationship with a person who didn't practice Zen, would that necessarily prevent the partner from ever studying with the teacher? In the case of a therapist, the prohibition – the rule – would stay in place. The issue is less clear in Zen practice. Guidelines recognize that there are situations in which rules should not be enforced literally and situations where compassion takes priority over regulation.

The San Francisco Zen Center

In San Francisco ethics were obviously an issue, but the more immediate problems after Baker's dismissal had to do with leadership and administration. Like most religious institutions, temples and monasteries in Asia were not operated as democracies nor would anyone have considered trying to do so. But in ousting their "abbot for life," the membership of the San Francisco Zen Center effectively declared themselves a republic, and they were immediately confronted with profound questions about how to proceed.

After the revelation of Baker's affair with the donor's wife, a series of board and general meetings occurred that almost tore Zen Center to pieces. Sides and positions were taken; grievances were aired; accusations were made. There were members who wanted Baker to remain as abbot, some even argued that it was the board who should resign. Others, while open to the idea of Baker remaining, felt he should take a sabbatical to do some "inner work" and possibly take part in a public repentance ceremony. Still

---

286. https://www.zendust.org/about-zco/ethical-guidelines-and-conflict-process-sangha-harmony-committee

other members simply wanted him gone. Although Baker wrote a letter to the board apologizing for his betrayal of the friend whom he had cuckolded, the suffering he caused his own family and Zen Center members, and for endangering the stability of Zen Center, he showed no inclination to take part in any form of public penance and would later claim that the only scandal at SFZC was the way in which he had been treated.

In the end, Baker's critics outweighed his supporters, and he was compelled to resign. The issue then became a matter of who would replace him. Although it was without precedent in the Zen tradition, this was a decision the board felt it was their right to make. To deal with the immediate situation, they asked Dainin Katagiri to return to San Francisco for a year in the capacity of "Interim Abbot." Katagiri was proud of the community he had established Minnesota, but there was no doubt that the abbacy of the San Francisco Zen Center was the most prestigious position in North American Zen. He came fully expecting to be appointed permanent abbot; that is the way things would have gone in Japan. He even suggested to the board that he work with Reb Anderson, Baker's only transmitted Dharma heir – although Baker was casting doubt on the legitimacy of that transmission – in order to prepare him to take on the duties of abbot later on. Anderson was still relatively young, and Katagiri assumed it would be some time yet before he would be considered qualified. The board, however, was committed to maintaining Suzuki Roshi's heritage and lineage, so when the year was up, Katagiri was thanked but not asked to stay. Instead, in 1986 Reb Anderson was installed as abbot-for-life. As it turned out, he served only a year before he was compelled to accept a co-abbot and term-limits to his abbacy.

In some ways, Anderson's fall from grace was more problematic to Zen Center than the prolonged and messy disentanglement from Baker had been. Questions were raised that affected not only SFZC but North American Zen in general; questions about precisely what "transmission" meant; questions about what reasonable expectations could be made about transmitted teachers. Questions about authority and the role of a center's membership in its operations. Questions about oversight and ethical standards.

The board in San Francisco still insisted that traditional protocols be adhered to in the matter of transmission and still wanted to identify abbots through Shunryu Suzuki's legacy. In the case of Mel Weitsman – who served as Anderson's co-abbot until 1995 – this meant travelling to Japan to receive formal transmission from Suzuki Roshi's son, Hoitsu, although the two had never worked together.

An administrative structure evolved originally maintaining two co-abbots, and later three serving at the same time. Under the latter system, there is an abbot for both City Center and Green Gulch as well as a co-ordinating abbot, but no specific abbot for Tassajara. These appointments are for four years with an option for another three. In this way, senior Dharma teachers have an opportunity to serve as abbot for a period of time. It also means that there is a growing number of former-abbots who have their own "Council." In addition, there are a range of staff roles concerned with the maintenance of practice – directors, heads of practice – as a result of which newcomers may still have little direct contact with the abbot and senior teacher.

Abbots are no longer autonomous but report to a board of directors. Some board positions are chosen by election, others are appointed. In addition, there are board committees that at times include non-board participants, an Outside Financial Advisory Board made up of non-practitioners who have an interest in the Center's work, and a Ethics and Reconciliation Council, that – as one of the committee members responsible for reorganizing Zen Center after Baker's departure explained – is "not a grievance committee" but "can appoint a grievance committee."[287]

An even more basic question the community had to address was what, precisely, people undertaking Zen training were being "trained" to do. Suzuki had apparently considered Zen Center a North American Eiheiji. But the monks at Eiheiji were trained to take responsibility for a temple, to become – in effect – the ministers for a congregation; they were trained to leave and go elsewhere. Many of the students at SFZC, on the other hand, considered the center not just a training facility; it was their home. They had nowhere else to go. Unlike Maezumi Roshi's heirs who spread across the country – Chozen to Oregon, Daido Loori and Bernie Glassman to New York, others to Colorado, Maine, and Utah – when senior SFZC members, like Mel Weitsman, established sitting groups, they remained in the general region around San Francisco.

The restructuring didn't immediately staunch the bleed off of members, which resulted in new financial burdens to the Center. Property was sold; businesses – that had been largely dependent on unpaid student "work practice" – were found to be unsustainable and had to be closed, but the need for revenue continued. One new source of income became renting Zen Center facilities – Tassajara and Green Gulch in particular – to other roughly compatible traditions for workshops and retreats. People who weren't ready to make a commitment to long term practice in any one tradition were often open to the opportunity to do a weekend – or even a week-long – retreat in a variety of traditions. Americans can, at times, be suspicious about putting all their eggs in one basket, but they are open to storing some of those eggs in different baskets for a period of time. So, Zen Center rented facilities to alternative traditions – Tibetan,

---

287. Barbara Kohn, quoted in Michael Downing, *Shoes Outside the Door* (Washington D.C.: Counterpoint, 2002), p. 149.

Vipassana, yoga, even Christian – in addition to offering secular programs (such as bird watching or watercolor painting) with a spiritual component. A look at their Spring and Summer Calendar for 2018 reveals workshops and classes entitled: "Meeting Trauma and Finding Release: A Somatic Approach"; "Poetry, Practice and Plenitude"; "Releasing the Habit of Fear: Zen, Yoga, and the Alexander Technique"; "Unpacking Whiteness: Reflection and Action"; "Radical Dharma: Embodying Race, Love and Liberation"; "Thriving in Uncertainty: A Workshop in Sensory Awareness"; "The Spirit of Practice: Christian and Zen"; "The Writer's Journey: Crafting Personal Stories That Are Vivid, Compelling, and True"; and "Fundamentals of Bread Making."

This is a route that many centers with the space to host other organizations' workshops and classes would take. It is a pragmatic and very much an American approach. It definitely is not Japanese. It was also evidence of a significant change in the spiritual environment in North America.

Pluralism

Outside ethnic communities such as those that had invited Suzuki and Maezumi to San Francisco and Los Angeles, Zen was the earliest Buddhist practice available to North Americans. It wasn't the only Asian tradition, however; Chester and Dorris Carlson – who contributed to the establishment of both the Rochester Zen Center and Dai Bosatsu Kongo-ji – were originally students of the Hindu Vedanta. By the 1980s, there were numerous practice options available, such as Transcendental Meditation – in which, for a small fee, one could purchase a personal mantra that the Maharishi Mahesh Yogi assured his followers was a "jet plane" to enlightenment in contrast to slower and more tedious practices – as well as a number of alternative Buddhist teachers. Tibetan and Theravada centers blossomed across the continent. The controversial Chogyam Trungpa, who was recognized by his followers as a reincarnated lama, developed a westernized version of Tibetan Buddhism that he called Shambhala training and even established a university – Naropa – in Colorado that remains an accredited academic institution. Secularized mindfulness programs, loosely based on Buddhist teachings, were offered at hospitals, business retreats, local YMCAs, as part of psychological counseling, and in rented facilities at Zen Centers such as Tassajara.

Norman Fischer, who was abbot of Zen Center from 1995 to 2000, admitted to Michael Downing that one could consider the multiplicity of programs and workshops – sometimes not even tangentially associated with Zen – available at SFZA facilities as fostering spiritual dilettantism. He preferred, however, to look upon it as "a fundamental pluralism – something new, something we haven't seen yet. In the past, there was the idea that this is the truth; now, everyone's talking to everyone." On the one hand, people were free in a new way to cull bits and pieces from a variety of religious sources; on the other, the individual traditions from which this culling took place needed to be maintained as entities in their own right. "One of our roles at Zen Center," Fischer explained, "is to preserve the integrity of one particular tradition."[288]

In this new spiritual environment, Zen needed to be able to articulate what made it unique among the spiritual offerings available; it needed to demonstrate how what it provided differed from other options. The development of secularized programs, such as the Mindfulness movement, contributed to a widely accepted belief that Buddhism provided a healthy psychological perspective consistent with contemporary understandings of the evolution of the human species. Traditionally Zen had posited that it brought practitioners not to a theoretical understanding of the Dharma but to an experience of its teachings. One did not just grasp the concept of inter-dependence intellectually, one encountered it directly and decisively. But that assertion in itself was a postulate, a theory. Zen teachers didn't speak with a single voice; there was no external monitoring structure to insist upon an orthodox interpretation of the Dharma. Zen teachers were independent, and their presentations of the teaching varied widely. Shunryu Suzuki held that there was nothing to be gained through practice. Philip Kapleau, on the other hand, not only insisted that practice had the capacity to bring one to kensho, but that it was absolutely central to Zen that kensho be attained. Walter Nowick, while accepting that there might be something to be gained, also stressed that individuals had to accept that fact that they might not attain it.

Even if there were something to be attained, the Mindfulness movement, in particular, raised the issue of whether the techniques of Zen had to be practiced within a Buddhist context with its attendant rites and structures. Mystical experiences, "peak experiences," and "cosmic consciousness" all occur outside of Buddhism and to the neutral observer don't appear to differ significantly from the experience of satori. Toni Packer's Springwater Center for Meditative Inquiry eschewed all elements not only of Buddhism but of any overtly religious orientation.

John Daido Loori, on the other hand, took a very different approach. He recognized that Zen was not just a means of acquiring a particular insight or achieving a particular experience. In themselves, these were of limited significance; it was the way in which the insight was integrated into one's life that made it Buddhist.

---

288. Michael Downing, *Shoes Outside the Door* (Washington D.C.: Counterpoint, 2002), p. 317.

Zen Mountain Monastery

Loori was 53 when the crisis occurred at the Zen Center of Los Angeles. He was older than people like Chozen who had been caught up in the communal atmosphere; he had a wife and child. He had also had a wider life experience than many of Maezumi's other students. He had served in the Navy, had been a research scientist – had been responsible for developing the artificial lime flavoring used in Jell-O – and was an acclaimed photographer. When he entered Zen practice, he did so with a maturity that younger people didn't have, and, when he was authorized to teach, he insisted on a Zen practice that was also very much a Buddhist practice. He recognized that often individuals drawn to Zen training during the boom period, even after years of formal practice, still knew little or nothing about Buddhism.

> One of the problems we face with Zen in America is that it has no continuity of tradition or standards. The Zen that arrived in this country has come from several places and cultures: from China, Vietnam, Japan, Korea. It was been taught by scores of teachers, and out of this evolved a real mixture of what is called Zen training. Today the training is very different as you go from center to center. There are no agreed upon guidelines of practice, no standards of transmission. There are a number of authentic lineages and a large group of unsanctioned teachers. The distinction between monks and lay practitioners has almost completely dissolved, to the point that at most centers the idea of a Zen monk has become just that – only an idea. Lay practitioners are practicing and living precisely the same as the monks. Why call one group "monks" and the other group "lay students" when there is virtually no difference between them?
>
> ...
>
> In most instances, the thrust of what Zen in America was and continues to be is zazen and the teacher-student relationship, which is the basis of the mind-to-mind transmission, common to both the Rinzai and Soto Schools. Not a lot of attention is given to other aspects of practice, particularly to the area of moral and ethical teachings, the Precepts. People "take the Precepts," but how much real training goes on in living the Precepts? Are the Precepts actually read, understood, engaged, lived? Are they a spiritual status symbol or the very substance of this life? There seems to be a real danger of stylizing and diluting this ageless practice to fit our fleeting fancies, to remain

relatively comfortable, and miss the opportunity to realize our true nature.[289]

His way of responding to this situation was to develop what he called the Eight Gates, eight areas of training in which students who came to Zen Mountain Monastery were required to take part: 1) zazen, 2) the student-teacher relationship, 3) liturgy, 4) art practice, 5) body practice, 6) Buddhist studies, 7) work practice, 8) right action. "Grounded within a rigorous monastic matrix," a pamphlet for guests at the monastery explains, "the Eight Gates training emphasizes practice, realization, and actualization of our true nature."

There were other issues ZMM struggled with, as the current abbot – Shugen Arnold – explained to me:[290] "Part of the evolution of our monastic community had to deal with three areas of concern Daido Roshi identified – power, wealth, and sexuality – that he felt were the three main sources of problems within religious communities. So power was somewhat distributed, although he was definitely the person in charge. But we have different governing groups, different governing boards, to handle different kinds of training and policy decisions. So, there's a little bit of a check and balance there. And we've really increased that in the years since his death. As for wealth, the monastics don't have any. We take a vow to not accumulate wealth. We get a stipend and we're provided with clothing and all our needs are met, but if I received an inheritance, I can do whatever I want with it except keep it. So, we don't own any personal property. If a monastic owns a car, when they're ordained they have to give that up.

"And then in terms of sexuality, you know, in the decades since Buddhism has been in the West, I'm sure you're well aware about the past and current issues around teachers and sexuality, and coming from the Zen Center of Los Angeles – where there was a lot of that as well – Daido Roshi felt that the most destructive thing in this regard was deception. So he wanted to create a community in which there were very clear rules around sexuality that would foster truthfulness. When I first came here, there was no rule, so people were forming relationships and ending relationships every other week, and there was a lot of tumultuousness in the community, 'cause men and women were practicing together in very close quarters, and finally he said, 'No more.' He said, 'If you're going to be in training, you really need to focus on that exclusively.' So anybody who forms a relationship will be counseled to chill that and not bring it to fruition. And if they can't or won't abide by that, then they will have to leave. They could come back as a couple after a year, when that initial period of excitement had

---

289. John Daido Loori, *The Eight Gates of Zen* (Boston: Shambhala, 2002), pp. 6-8.
290. Interview with the author, August 14, 2018.

died down a little bit. And then in regards to monastics he basically had the same rule, where monastics could be in a committed relationship – not dating, but in a committed relationship – but no children because we don't have any personal wealth, and our lives are full-time committed to the life of the monastery and the sangha, and so there is a commitment to not have children. And if a monastic was to have a child, they would need to leave and support that child, because then the child becomes their first priority."

I point out that Loori himself had been married more than once and had a son.

"Formally married three times," Shugen admits. "He was in four significant relationships. So, yes, I think he was also making that rule for himself as well as the monastics. And it's a mixed bag. 'Cause we have some monastics who have been living that way. I've been in a relationship. My partner, for over 32 years, she was a monastic with me for almost 30 of those years. And then she decided to take off her robes, so we're still together but she's now living a lay life. So it's a mixed bag. We have monastics who are living a solitary life; so that's not perfect, that we're not all living more or less the same life. And also because – you know – historically to be a monastic in most traditions means to be celibate. So we would not be considered monastics by many people's standards. So I accept that. I understand that. And I wouldn't fight for it. You know, we live a monastic life to the best of our ability with this..." (he laughs briefly) "...somewhat significant...um...shift."

Compassion

The pioneers who brought Zen practice to North America were basically all male.[291] One of the most notable changes that took place in the Zen landscape as a second generation of teachers emerged was the significant number of women it included: Joko Beck, Joan Halifax, Wendy Nakao, Joan Sutherland, Mitra Bishop, Blanche Hartman, and many others became as well known and as respected as their male colleagues as transmitters of the Buddhadharma.

Perhaps as a consequence, there simultaneously emerged a growing emphasis not only on insight/wisdom (prajna) but on the manifestation of that wisdom in compassionate action (karuna). Zen practice, it was beginning to be understood, wasn't undertaken for one's personal satisfaction alone but rather for the benefit of all "sentient beings everywhere," as is asserted in the first of the vows that Zen practitioners chant almost daily.[292]

---

291. Although there were women who played a significant role in the transference of Zen to the West – such as Ruth Fuller – they were not accredited teachers.

292. Cf. p. 89 above.

Sunyana Graef is an heir of Philip Kapleau. She founded the Vermont Zen Center and is the principal teacher at Zen Centers in Canada and Costa Rica. When I met her in Vermont, she drew my attention to the fact that the first room one enters when coming into the Center is a living room with stuffed furniture and a big fireplace. She explains that she wanted the members to form a community, to get to know one another. If they went straight into the Zendo or the Buddha Hall, they might not do so. With the intervening room, however, they have an opportunity to take a moment to sit and chat before proceeding into the formal areas of the center.[293]

The Rochester Zen Center when Sunyana first went there in 1969 wasn't very forward thinking about gender roles. "The women did women's jobs, and the men did men's jobs. So the women were the cooks, the cleaners, the receptionists. The men attended the meetings and made all the decisions. But at least I could practice. At least the roshi didn't say, 'Oh, you're inferior because you're a woman.'"

She laughs easily as she describes practice conditions in Rochester, but it's the laughter of someone who has survived something extraordinary. The first sitting in the morning was scheduled for 6:00. "But it was an *extremely* competitive atmosphere back then." It was also a very masculine atmosphere. "You wanted to prove you were *the* Zen student of the world. So, if the sitting started at 6:00, you had to be in the zendo by 5:00. You gotta be the first one in the zendo; you gotta be the first one in the dokusan line. And I bought into that completely."

She is an animated speaker, stressing words in variety of ways as she talks, sometimes emphasizing them sharply, sometimes whispering them, sometimes slowing down and pronouncing each distinctly and separately.

"Roshi Kapleau had spent thirteen years in Japan, and the *interesting* thing about him is that when he was at Harada Roshi's monastery, it was very strict, very samurai. The stick, the shouts, the blows; that whole style of Zen. And he didn't penetrate his koan when he was there. Finally, he went to Yasutani Roshi's monastery, where the monitor was a little old lady. It was very small, very lay oriented, *completely* different atmosphere, and it was *there* that he had his break-through. When he came to the US, what style did he bring? Harada Roshi's style! The stick was used *fiercely*. It was used – I think – inappropriately. So, it was a pressure-cooker; it was *incredibly* intense. Women, myself included, often stopped menstruating for months and months at a time. You were just pushing constantly. It wasn't…it wasn't entirely healthy. It was just too much. I don't think that it was a good way to practice for most people. Because it *pushed* people to a point in their practice artificially. That's my objection to the stick.

---

293. Cf. *Cypress Trees in the Garden*, Chapter 18.

Roshi Kapleau was once hit all night long with a stick. And he kind of *relished* that story and how his shoulders were *bleeding*, and I always thought, '*Why?*' Why would somebody think that was a good thing? If you don't have, within yourself, the desire, the need, the energy, the conviction, the perseverance for this practice, why do you think that being hit is gonna develop that in you, is gonna rouse that? It won't! It will temporarily, maybe, because you don't have a choice. But this is not natural. This is not healthy."

She received Dharma transmission from Kapleau in 1987, and, the following year, she and her family moved to Vermont. They bought a house in the middle of an alfalfa field that had a single pine tree in it. When I visited her in 2013, the center was marking its 25th anniversary. Proceeding up the driveway, I am struck by how lovingly the grounds were cared for. The Magnolia trees are in full bloom, their bases littered with large white petals. The rhododendron is in flower, and there are several beds of colorful annuals.

Sunyana retains great respect for Kapleau. "I was so *grateful* to my teacher – and still am so *grateful* to him – that he was willing to put up with this immature, really, really selfish person. I don't think I could have put up with me, but he did. He must have seen something, for whatever reason. You know?"

Still, much of our conversation focuses on the differences between her center and Rochester. "I have a much stronger emphasis on the Bodhisattva of Compassion, Kannon, because her presence in my life was so important, always has been since the day I met her. And so, Kannon is everywhere in the center. Another huge difference is the fact that we don't have staff. And that affects all aspects of life here, because everyone takes responsibility. So our practice is our life. Our life is our practice. And I hope I never hear from *anyone*, 'I don't know what this has to do with my life.' And I did hear that in Rochester. 'We're doin' this, but what effect does it have on my life?' And it doesn't. It takes a while for it to affect your life, but you need to make that connection from the beginning. So that's what I hope people see. That this is everything we do. It's the way we brush our teeth; it's the way we drive our car; it's the way we talk to our loved ones and strangers; it's the way we walk outdoors and smell the flowers. There's nothing that isn't practice. Nothing. So I hope people will get that. We didn't exactly get that in Rochester. That wasn't the focus that I knew about then."

"Where was the focus then?"

"Wisdom. Enlightenment. That was it."

"And here there's more focus on compassion?"

"I hope so. Well, not necessarily more but more evident? My teacher actually actively discouraged us from social outreach. And that's definitely not the case now in Rochester. But at that time, it was. And, of course, this was the '60s, the '70s, when there was so much activism going on, and he thought we needed to focus our attention within to develop ourselves. We were so immature and so scattered and so undisciplined and so drug-hazed that I think he was probably right about that. It's just that there were repercussions to that. And the repercussion was that we thought there was nothing more important in the world than enlightenment, and the more deeply enlightened you were, the better you were. Somehow you were more Buddha-ish or something. So that had its effect necessarily. It was not a good one. We were conceited as all get-out.

"So I began teaching Loving Kindness to my students. At every sesshin, there would be half an hour where we would do Loving Kindness, sending it to yourself, to a friend, so on and so forth. And then I started giving classes outside sesshin." Eventually one of her senior students took responsibility for offering the Loving Kindness classes. "There are people who sign up for those classes and don't do anything else, but they often come back. And it's been a very important part of our community, teaching that. Teaching that way of loving acceptance."

The teacher in 2013 was Dharman Rice, who tells me that he feels grateful to have a female rather than a male Zen teacher. "I'm glad I haven't practiced 'Samurai Zen.' The Zen that we practice here is the practice of Kannon, the compassionate heart. And Roshi starting to do metta practice here is a function of that. And it's not that metta practice hasn't been a part of the history of Zen, but it's not been an explicit part of it, really. And it certainly hasn't been in the West until recently.

"I knew a lot of people who practiced at Rochester in the old days, and I'm not sure it would have suited me. I'm not sure I would have been happy there. I mean, it was too samurai. I don't know what else to say about it. But Roshi has gradually – but very deliberately – changed that here. I mean, we don't use the kyosaku. I don't know if you saw the kyosakus we use. They're sort of little mini-kyosakus that are just symbolic kyosakus. And that's all. I usually monitor sesshins, and it's gotten to the place now where – other than the sweep before dokusan – we don't use the kyosaku at all. Roshi is of the opinion that Zen practice is very difficult, and, ultimately, if you don't find the energy to do it inside yourself, where are you going to find it? You know, you can't be beaten into enlightenment.

"One of the wonderful serendipitous things about the *Mettabhavana* [Loving Kindness] course was realizing that it goes hand-in-glove with our zazen, with our mindfulness practice. They're mutually reinforcing. There are many practices in Zen. Zazen is the main one, seated meditation, that is mindfulness or concentration meditation, usually involving a breath practice or a koan practice. Or it can involve chanting practice. The Metta practice is a practice of Loving Kindness, that is the six stages of sending metta to yourself, to a benefactor, to a dear friend, and so on.

"One of the things I learned about metta practice is that it's the Buddhist practice in which I think beginners can make the most progress. It's the quickest. And it's essentially learning how to be friends with ourselves and with others. And this practice of learning how to be happy and extend our feelings of loving kindness to others is one that goes hand-in-glove with the concentration meditation. I mean, it's just a fact that the more we pay attention, the friendlier we feel. Paying attention is an act of love. It's something every teacher, every parent knows; we all know that. And it just is a fact, too, that the friendlier we are, the easier it is to pay attention. So in a way, our paying attention and our being friendly and happy and extending loving-kindness to others – opening our compassionate heart – are practices that go hand-in-glove."

Zen Peacemakers and Bearing Witness

The stages of Zen maturation are portrayed in a series of illustrations called the Ten Bulls. These portray a young man searching for a lost bull. First, he has the desire to find it, then he discovers its footprints. He gets his first glimpse of the bull in the third picture and captures it in the fourth. The implicit point is that this is still early in the process of integrating Zen insight in one's life, the subject of the following portraits. The final image shows him as a mature man returning to his village and interacting with the citizenry. No better example of the Tenth Bull can be found in North America Zen than in the work of Bernie Glassman.

He was born in 1939 in the Brighton Beach area of Brooklyn, the fifth child and only son of parents who'd come to the United States from Eastern Europe. Most of his mother's family died in Poland during the Holocaust. Her sisters, who came to the US with her, were all members of the Communist Party. "My father wasn't really socially involved, but he had three sisters, and they were all in the Communist Party. I was brought up in that kind of environment. My cousin was the head of the Communist Youth Movement.[294]

"As far as I'm concerned," he tells me, "the function of Zen is to help people experience the interconnectedness of life. The oneness of life. So, there have been many upayas throughout the years of how to do that, and it's not strictly relegated to Zen. So, Zen – as you know – means 'meditation.' And that's been a major upaya. But even in Zen, all kinds of techniques and tricks have been used to help people have that experience. In '76, I had an experience that changed my venue of teaching from the zendo – the meditation hall or the temple – to society. I had an experience of what I call the 'Hungry Ghosts' – which is a term in Buddhism – but

---

294. Cf. *Cypress Trees in the Garden*, Chapter 12.

an experience of the thirsts and the hungers of everything around. And simultaneously I experienced it as myself, as that these were all aspects of myself. And a vow came up to try to satisfy those hungers. Those were hungers for food. Hungers for power. Hungers for love. Hungers for greed, status, acknowledgement. All kinds of hungers. So, my work really moved into whole different spheres.

"The enlightenment experience is an awakening to the interconnectedness of life, but it keeps deepening. So, at first, it's really awakening to the oneness of oneself. And then of the family. And then of the group. And then of the society. And then of the world. Then of the universe. Almost any Zen workshop I'm in, I'll start by defining what I mean by enlightenment – the experience of the interconnectedness of life – and I'll quote Kobo Daishi who's the founder of the Japanese tantric sect, Shingon, and he said that you can tell the depth of a person's enlightenment by how they serve others."

In December 1979, Taizan Maezumi asked Bernie to establish a center in New York. "For me, a very key thing was that over and over he said to me that I should take whatever I can from him – in terms of Zen – and then spit out what I think won't work in this country. He said, 'I'm not an American. I'm Japanese. And I can't present the American Zen. You've got to do that.' That was key. And when I went to start the Zen community in New York, he said, 'I'm gonna stay away for a year so you won't be influenced by me or want to do things that please me. You're on your own.' That's very rare. 'Cause most Zen teachers I've met want their students to replicate them. And he made that very clear that that was not the point."

At first the Zen Community of New York was organized very traditionally, with a primary focus on zazen and ritual activity. "In 1980, I started to emphasize the five Buddha families. That's done more in Tibetan practice. There's the mandala – the circle of life – and it's normally broken into five energies. They're called Buddha energies. And one is spirituality. That's the center of the mandala. And one is *ratna*, which I translate as the 'livelihood' family. One is *karma*, which I've translated as 'social action' family. One is *padma*, which I translate as 'relationship,' the world of relationships. And one is *vajra*, which is the world of steady training. And so when you see Tibetan mandalas, they're full of all these images – these are creatures within the five families – and they do a lot of studies in that way.

"So even before I came to New York, I had a meeting with the people who were going to be on my board in '79, and I said, 'We're going to develop our community in the light of the five Buddha families.' The meditation retreats were in the spiritual family – in the middle. But it also meant we were going to do things in terms of livelihood, in terms of social action, in terms of relationship. And that's what I did. I started to develop techniques within those fields. We developed strong meditation practice and training practice first. Some of the people who were closest to me wanted me to get immediately into social action. I said, 'No. First it's the meditation and training. And after that I want to develop work in the ratna – the livelihood world – 'cause that's where the resources come from. And then it's social action.'"

His first Livelihood enterprise in New York was the Greyston Bakery, that evolved into Greyston Social Enterprise. It provides opportunities and training to individuals facing barriers to employment as well as supporting local community projects, such as housing.

In 1991, Bernie turned responsibility for Greyston over to its board and changed direction again, holding the first of the Street Retreats in which participants, instead of sitting zazen for a week, lived on the streets with the homeless. "I didn't allow people to bring money. I did insist on people begging. We slept and ate at different places so that people would get an experience of different venues. In New York, I did not sleep in shelters. I never wanted to take a bed from anybody who needed a bed. So we slept in the streets, on trains, bus terminals. Different venues.

"Fifteen to twenty people would be average. We would meet, and I would give the initial orientation for the retreat. And then I'd break us into packs of three. And there's a pack leader, somebody that's got experience being on the streets. We'd sleep together. And we'd gather together usually twice but at least once a day to do what's called 'council,' sit in a circle and discuss what's happening to us. I liked to do it twice a day, but it didn't always work. Things would happen in the streets.

"We ask that for a week before you come you don't shower and you don't shave. That's about the only preparation we ask. Because our first tenet is 'not knowing.' Come completely open. No fixed ideas. What's much more important to me – but impossible – is to ask you to let go of any ideas of what it might be like. But everybody comes with some ideas of what it's going to be like.

"I did an orientation the first day. We'd gather somewhere. But my orientation was pretty damn simple. Don't take off your shoes and leave them so somebody can steal them. If you're going to go on your own – everybody was in a pack of three – but if you want to go on your own, you can do that, but you got to make sure that your pack leader knows that you are going to do that and where you're going to be. And, as I said, we sleep together in trains, in bus terminals. Wherever. But in those indoor places, we were getting kicked out all the time. Police would come and move us along. We'd have to catch the next train, stuff like that, but, during the evening, you can't go on your own. That's a rule.

"The other rule is always tell the truth when somebody asks. You don't have to volunteer but tell the truth. And to mix with people. So I encouraged people to tell people, 'This is my first time I'm here.'"

I ask how students used to more traditional Zen practice respond to this.

"You know what I'd tell a traditional Zen student? Or anybody? Anybody. How're you filling your time? Being here now. When you're on the streets," he says, chuckling, "there's nothing to plan. You're not thinking about your business. I mean, you are the first half day you're there or whatever. But after a while, all you're worried about is, 'I gotta pee. Where am I gonna pee? I'm hungry. Where am I gonna get food?' I call it a 'plunge.' My Bearing Witness retreats, generally they start off with 'plunges.' It's a way of getting you to deal just with what's coming up."

The Bearing Witness retreats came out of the Zen Peacemaker Order which he founded with his then wife, Sandra Jishu Holmes, who died in 1998. Gradually it developed into an interfaith network known as the Peacemaker Community that emphasized the integration of spiritual practice and social action through three tenets: 1) Not knowing, 2) Bearing witness, 3) Loving action. One of the most effective upayas associated with the Zen Peacemaker Order were the Bearing Witness retreats held in places like the Nazi death camps in Poland.

"I created these plunges as a way of helping you experience 'not knowing,' bringing you into a situation where your rational mind can't fathom it. The experience of 'not knowing' is hopefully to not be attached to your ideas. Have lots of ideas, that's fine. Have lots of knowledge, that's fine. But to not be attached. And not thinking that this idea or this process is going to take care of the situation. Go in completely 'not knowing.' And the plunge is helping you to do that because it's bringing you to a place where your mind, your ideas don't work. Your mind doesn't know how to rationalize this, and that's sort of an instantaneous sensation.

"'Bearing witness' – to me – means to stay in that situation. So it takes time. So it's not enough for me to say, 'Go into the streets and meet with a homeless person.' You have to live there to be in that. And if we create the environment right, then people will experience 'bearing witness.' Being in that state of non-duality. So it's getting you into a state of non-duality.

"Auschwitz, same thing. I do an annual retreat at Auschwitz. In any of the Bearing Witness retreats, there's no teaching. What I'm doing is setting an environment. So the environment at Auschwitz is I bring in as many different kinds of people as possible because the Auschwitz retreat – for me – is around diversity and the 'other.' It's an icon for a place that killed everybody who was an 'other.' In our daily life, the main way we deal with the 'other' is to ignore them. We don't invite them to dinner. We won't listen to them on TV. You know? We don't read those books. I mean, we all have our own club that we feel comfortable in. Everyone else is the 'other.' So Auschwitz was an extreme case where you kill everybody who's not an Aryan. It's a place where you kill the gays. You kill handicapped. You kill the gypsies. You kill the Jews. You kill Catholics. You kill Polish intellectuals. Because they all didn't fit Hitler's club model. But – you know – we did lynchings of blacks. We do bashing of gays. So, it's a common thing. So Auschwitz, for me, is an icon.

"So in our retreats, we have representatives from different groups. We always have gypsies. We have survivors. We have the children of survivors. We have children and grandchildren of SS people that ran the camps."

In many of the photos I'd seen of Bernie on the internet, he's wearing a bright, red clown's nose. When I visited him at his home in Montague, Massachusetts, I asked about it.

"In 1997, I decided that it was time for my wife at that time – she's passed away; her name was Jishu; she was the co-founder of the Zen Peacemakers – it was time for her to take over the Zen Community of New York, and I was not going to be formally involved in teaching any more. But what I wanted to do was go around to my Dharma successors that had places and make sure that they weren't being too arrogant or thinking they knew too much. And the best way to do that would be to pop-up unexpected as a clown and disrupt what was going on. So, I went to a friend of mine, Wavy-Gravy, and told him what I wanted to do and how do I get trained? And he assigned a trainer to me, Mr. Yoo-hoo. So Yoo-hoo and I did a lot of workshops on 'Clowning Your Zen.' Now, 'clown' is not the best word. In Native American, its Coyote. In Europe it's the *nar*, that we translate as jester. He can say things to the king that nobody else can say.

"So that was my idea. And then it turned out that the guy who was training me was a coordinator for Clowns Without Borders – *Payasos sin Fronteras* – and they work in refugee camps around the world. So I've been with him in refugee camps in places like Chiapas. And I found that to Bear Witness in a refugee camp is fantastic. Because you go there, you don't know the culture at all. And you don't know what the refugees have been through. So you have to be in a place of 'not-knowing.' You can't assume that anything you know is going to be funny, and you got to bear witness to the kids, 'cause you're doing things. And part of our training is how do you present something very lightly and then make it heavier, whether it's anger or love or hate or whatever. And that's what you've got to do. Do something very lively. See whether a smile appears or fear appears. And back away if it's fear, and if it's a smile, make it heavier. And then bear witness to the mothers. Are they feeling comfortable? And eventually to the fathers. Usually the kids are up front. Mothers are a little further back, and we've been in places where mothers never saw their kids smile. So I carry my nose with me everywhere I go" – he takes it out of his pocket – "and I'm always ready to make sure that if a situation seems too heavy or too 'knowing'" – he puts the nose on – "I'll put my nose on and shake it up. It's another upaya," he says, laughing.

Returning to Dai Bosatsu

The elegant Japanese furnishings and halls of Dai Bosatsu seem a world away from the refugee camps of Chiapas, but even there the vision of what Zen practice is or should be is undergoing change.

Five years after I had sat in the nearly empty zendo and wondered if the halls would ever be filled again, Shinge Chayat Roshi assures me that things have turned around. "As you recall, when you came we had just been through the throes of a very difficult crisis, and we were still trying to pull ourselves out of that. The numbers have gone way up. We have a full, packed zendo every sesshin these days. The resident numbers, right now I think we have ten. Yeah, I think we're probably up to fifteen, but that includes interns. In 2014 we began an internship program that's been very successful. Students from colleges all over the continent – including Canada – come for a period of time each summer, working, and sitting alongside us, going to sesshin with us. They seem to feel it's a very valuable experience. And some of them have come back, in fact, as residents. So we're seeing a very nice upsurge in membership and attendance, and in New York City as well. We're celebrating the 50th anniversary of the New York Zendo this fall. A lot's going on there."

This conversation took place in June 2018. Eido Shimano had died the previous February. Not all of his former students returned to study with Shinge; some left Zen practice altogether; and there were those who questioned whether she – as Shimano's chosen successor – was appropriate for the position; there also remained questions about the nature of her relationship with Shimano, that had been exacerbated by a gratuitous bit of vindictiveness when he chose to identify her as one of the students with whom he'd been involved, although she'd previously denied this – including to me during the interview in 2013. There seemed little reason for him to make this revelation other than to cast doubt on her credibility, but she persevered and oversaw the process of establishing a complex set of ethical guidelines for both the Zen Studies Society and Dai Bosatsu.[295] The document, found on the Zen Studies webpage, consists of a list of behaviors "not permissible for any teacher, guest lecturer, monastic, Sangha member, program attendee, or visitor at either Dai Bosatsu Zendo or New York Zendo." They include things such as "Failure to conform to zendo or monastery rules" or "Threatening, abusive or obscene behavior." There are also two prohibitions directly addressing sexual matters:

---

295. http://zenstudies.org/about/ethical-guidelines/

Sexual harassment, defined as any single act or multiple persistent acts of physical or verbal conduct that is/are sexual in nature; unwelcome or offensive behavior in the view of the receiver of such attentions.

Sexual intimacy between teachers and students; casual and/or serial sexual relationships among students; sexual advances on the part of residents toward visiting students at Dai Bosatsu Zendo. Students come to train in Rinzai Zen Buddhism. When people are living and working closely together, attractions may occur, but the monastery is not the appropriate place for developing an intimate relationship. If such a relationship is forming, it must be discussed with the Abbot and the Shika.[296]

Shinge tells me that new students who present themselves at Dai Bosatsu are often motivated by different concerns than those the Zen seekers of the '60s and '70s had. "There seems to be a lot more...what I would call desperation among the generation under 30 these days. They feel abandoned by those to whom they would have looked for leadership and guidance in their lives. There are no assurances that jobs will be available once they get out of college. They're not sure it's worth going to college. There's a lot of very deep soul-searching going on, and – from what I understand – they're looking for something that will bring them meaning. That will bring their lives a sense of purpose. So volunteer work is important, social justice work is important, and we feel that too."

I wonder if this means those coming to Dai Bosatsu no longer view awakening as a primary consideration. "There were those stories," I remind her, "like the enlightenment stories in *The Three Pillars of Zen*; stories about the retreats led by Yasutani Roshi where it was rare that at least one person didn't achieve kensho."

"I'm not into that," Shinge says, shaking her head. "That was actually a very negative approach. You know, people were beaten into kensho, and then what happened? It didn't really do much for their lives. They still had the same problems. In fact, some of the kensho experiences were more like psychotic breaks. So I'm very careful about that. I go more slowly, and I don't make people feel frightened."

I admit that I had known people who had had kensho and yet remained miserably unhappy persons.

"Exactly! Exactly! What are we talking about here? You could call it something. Yes, you can have an opening experience, but to really speak

---

296. The Shika is the "guest master" of a monastery.

of true insight is very different from an immediate flash of something. It's not that uncommon to have a wonderful opening experience in sesshin. But whether one calls it a bona fide kensho or not is something the teacher has to be very sensitive about."

This means that her attitude to sesshin is different from that of the teachers who preceded her who emphasized the importance of attainment.

"I don't expect anything, but I try to be aware of the spiritual maturation that may be going on and to encourage that. And not to make people feel that they should…perform, and that if they haven't had kensho that there's something wrong with them, if they've been doing Mu for ten years there's something wrong with them. So I'm actually trying to reverse some of that…"

She searches for the correct word, and I suggest "competition."

"Competition," she agrees but adds: "It's difficult to talk about because we use the word 'urgency.' It's urgent to wake up. And I will say that. But I don't want it to be the kind of thing where people are angry with themselves or despairing of themselves if they haven't had some huge experience. You know? I think that sesshin after sesshin you can't help but ripen. And when your path is ripened, something happens. And when that something happens, it may be very subtle. It doesn't always come as a great crashing breakthrough, but it changes your life in ways that are significant and that are felt by everyone. So when you see some of the older practitioners, you feel that you're in the presence of someone who has something of stability, of the receptivity and sensitivity to others, and that there is some kind of equanimity there."

She considers Yasutani, whom she met in 1967, to be her first Zen teacher, although, she admits, "I didn't really train with him. I trained with Soen Nakagawa Roshi, and his attitude was so different. It was so loving and so giving and so relaxed and so playful. And, of course, I had Eido Roshi who in a way combined both his teachers in his approach but never did that competitive thing. And then I studied with Maurine Stuart who was definitely not into that sense of…psychotic acquisition…"

We both laugh, and I ask, "Can I quote that?"

"Sure."

I remark that Philip Kapleau's heirs have tended to take a much less strenuous approach to Zen training than he had.

"There's a danger," she remarks. "It can become abusive and cult-like. When students are gathering around a very powerful person who demands a certain kind of allegiance and a certain kind of behavior and rewards that behavior, then people who do not fall into that naturally, but have a very different approach, can feel shut out."

One thing that characterizes Zen is its use of Japanese cultural forms. Yoga centers may have brightly colored portraits of Krishna and Ganesha, the Sanskrit script for the sacred syllable "Om" – looking pretty much like the number 30 – and images of Shiva dancing in a circle of flames. Tibetan Buddhist centers have prayer flags, statues of Bodhisattvas and their consorts sexually united in lotus posture, and an endless array of ritual paraphernalia including daggers, dorje scepters, and prayer wheels. In comparison, Zen Centers are usually very staid affairs, but this minimalist décor is no more North American than the others. The black ink calligraphy scrolls, reproductions of sumi-e paintings by artists like Hakuin and Sengai, even the highly formalized and restrained flower arrangements are very much Japanese.

It's something I wonder about when in places like Dai Bosatsu – certainly the most Japanese of the centers I've visited. When a young American man wearing robes and zoris responds to me with a sharp, "Hai!" I wonder if this isn't playacting to some extent. I ask Shinge if it's important to retain those elements of Japanese culture and am surprised when she tells me that – in her opinion – it is.

"I think so. I've been told that by people. There are people who come to Dai Bosatsu, for example, because of their love of Japanese culture as well as how it is manifesting in the path of Zen."

It's an aesthetic I admire as well, but can't help thinking must necessarily marginalize Zen, keeping it something "foreign." From time to time, I even wonder – as Toni Packer did – if Zen technique is necessarily Buddhist, and how valid Zen insight is if it only comes out of a particular ethnic tradition. D.T. Suzuki had insisted on the universality of the Zen experience of awakening.

I put the question to Shinge: "A lot of people practice yoga today without any connection to Hinduism. Can one practice Rinzai Zen without having any connection to Buddhism? Can Zen be separated from its Buddhist matrix?"

"What's Buddhist?" she asks. "The -ist and the -ism have very little to do with the awakening process. That awakening is Buddha. You *become* Buddha." She doesn't like the word "goal," but concedes that if one were to use that word – "which, of course, we don't" – then the goal of Zen practice "is to awaken, but not just to have some experience. To awaken in a way that then you are following the Buddha's path. You are following a path of caring for all beings, really looking at the unbelievable number of delusions you have that make you self-absorbed so that you cannot care for others. That you are investigating the Dharma deeply; you're investigating what those teachings are from your own awakened mind. I'm talking about the vows. And the fourth, which is to walk the Buddha's path. These four vows are primary whether you consider yourself a Buddhist or not."

As at Zen Mountain Monastery – on the other side of the Catskills – the teachings here are expressed within a Buddhist perspective in a way that they haven't always been in North America.

"We put the precepts in the context of Buddhism," Shinge tells me, "of what the teachings of Buddha are, and following them, following those precepts, would make you a 'Buddhist.' But, again, the -ist is not important. The -ism is not important. Become a Buddha. Become fully awake. Live that awakened life. The Buddha gave good teachings about how to do that. The eightfold path really works. We don't want Buddha to become an ideology. We want awakened mind and compassionate action to define you. If you want to call that Buddhist, okay."

Passing the Torch

Bernie Glassman Roshi died in November 2018. My primary teacher, Albert Low, died two years earlier. Abbot Steve Stuckey of the San Francisco Zen Center died nine months after I interviewed him for *Cypress Trees in the Garden* in 2013. Another abbot of SFZC, Blanche Hartman – whom I'd interviewed at the same time as Steve – died a few months after Albert. Toni Packer died only two months after my first visit to the Springwater Center. Eido Shimano, Walter Nowick, and Joshu Sasaki all died during the period in which I was doing my research.

The majority of Zen teachers in North America remain members of the Boomer Generation, but they are aging, and they are passing. The direct connections with both the Japanese pioneers who first brought Zen to the west and their immediate disciples is fading, and a new generation of teachers – upon whom the tradition will depend if it is to continue – is rising up to take their place. The significant factor is that there is a new generation of teachers.

Five years after he expressed concern about the possibility that Zen might be an "historical blip" in America, James Ford tells me he is slightly more optimistic than he had been. "There will be – without a doubt – the great die-off. The sheer number of boomers interested in and active in Zen – you know, actually giving our lives to it – is coming to an end. And there was a period where it looked like it just wasn't going to continue. But now what I believe is going to happen – my prediction – is there will be a major shrinkage. I suspect Zen twenty years from now will probably be half to a third the size that it currently is. But the difference is that these will be much better trained people."

James agrees with Shinge that what draws new students to Zen is often very different from what had drawn their predecessors. "I think they're most commonly looking for relaxation. I think the mindfulness/relaxation thing has been a tsunami that has changed many things and who comes. There's always a little bit of a thread because of the koan, because we emphasize the koans, and koans are aligned with awakening experiences. So there's the occasional person looking for awakening, but mostly people are not coming for that."

"But people still achieve kensho?"

"Well, koan people do. But it is a more mature approach. I think there are fewer people who are in the kensho-factory kind of mode. You see that with some of the Sanbo Zen people, but even there it's shifted. It's a life-practice; it's not about a momentary experience so much – although the momentary experiences are important – but they are more healthily contextualized, I think."

"So, if they're coming for mindfulness or relaxation, why come to a Zen Center rather than doing a Vipassana retreat or taking up yoga or Tai Chi? What is it that draws them to Zen?"

"I think that for many of them, they don't realize there's a difference. So it's a little bait-and-switch. 'Sure! We'll help you with mindfulness.' And others – an interesting sub-set – are people who've done mindfulness training and think it's too attenuated…"

"Too shallow?"

"Well, I think…well, yeah, I think it often is shallow. It often is. I want to hesitate because I think the mindfulness community can lead to depth, but it usually doesn't. I mean, if you're looking for relaxation, you'll find relaxation. And some people intuit that there's more to be had, and they drift over to the Zen community, and the next thing they know they're being encouraged to do retreats." And, at retreats, they're introduced to koan work.

"So koans are one thing that distinguish some Zen teachers from other spiritual traditions. What about Soto? Koans aren't part of that tradition. Is there anything that distinguishes Soto Zen from the other meditation offerings out there?"

"I think there will be many Soto people for whom there is very little distinction, except their saving grace (in some ways) is also a deep problem with their structure – our structure – with the emphasis on monastic training and the expectation of extensive meditation retreats. The ango, the ninety-day retreat. There's a pretty hard requirement that there be some experience of that in the normative training of a North American Soto priest.

"I think our generation, the boomers, were 'seekers' in a sense that the Gen-X were not. Although I have this kind of fascination with the Millennials, because they appear to have a seeker element as well, although it's somewhat different, and they have different access. When you and I were looking for Zen teachers, we had *Three Pillars of Zen* and – what? – five teachers on the continent? I mean, it was really hard. And Japan, you know, wasn't anything. But I know at least five Millennials who they graduated college and they went to Japan. You know, they spend three, four, five years, and come back ordained Soto Zen priests. In fact, it's kind of ironic; the Millennials tend to be more conservative around their spiritual stuff – not socially but religiously – than we were. Of course, we were mitigated by a lot of drugs and that kind of thing. They are really true believers, and that can be rather graceful and beautiful and totally authentic."

James and I and Shinge are approximately the same age; Shugen is only slightly younger. We are reflecting on a practice in which we've been involved for between forty and fifty years, which necessarily involves comparing previous generations of Zen practitioners with more recent inquirers. I wonder, however, if younger teachers – those who will be tasked with carrying the tradition forward when the boomer generation finally departs the stage – assess the state of North American Zen the same way we do.

We shall not cease from exploration
And the end of all our exploring
Will be to arrive where we started
And know the place for the first time.

T.S. Eliot, "Little Gidding"

Contemporary Voices

North American Zen doesn't speak with a single voice. There is nothing equivalent to the Vatican either on this continent or in Asia, although some lineages have chosen to defer to home temples in Japan. There are North American associations such as the Soto Zen Buddhist Association (SZBA), the American Zen Teachers Association (AZTA), and the Association of Soto Zen Buddhists (ASZB). There is even a Lay Zen Teachers Association (LZTA) that defines itself as "a sangha specifically for lay teachers…who have been formally entrusted to teach in their respective Zen lineages and who have chosen to teach not as priests but as lay people." In contrast, the ASZB consists solely of priests recognized by the Sotoshu in Japan. The association with the broadest membership, the AZTA, deliberately chooses not to present itself as a credentialing body. And none have very effective ways of imposing even the most basic oversight over their members. In the Sanbo Zen tradition, new teachers are appointed by the head abbot in Japan, but, once appointed, those teachers retain the same freedom to develop their own styles as do members of the Rinzai or Soto schools.

Individual teachers and lineages differ on a variety of issues, including the value of liturgy, lay teaching, and whether or not ordained persons should have "day jobs." Some centers have elaborate ritual services, others offer only a bare-bones opportunity to sit in silence. Some teachers don't work in centers or temples at all. The variations seem endless.

Jay Rinsen Weik

Rinsen Weik – in addition to being the abbot of the Great Heartland Buddhist Temple of Toledo – is an aikido instructor, a jazz guitarist, and a Dungeons and Dragons enthusiast. His head is shaved, but he has a ZZ Top beard that he frequently sweeps with his hand. He laughs easily and heartily and has the right build to remind one of the Santa Claus-like bodhisattva, Hotei, sometimes referred to as the Laughing Buddha. "These are things I've been interested in for a really long time," he tells me.

"So I'm just a kid who took martial arts and music lessons and was an altar boy when I was seven and just never quit."

The interest in martial arts led to his first encounter with Zen. "There was this great bookstore in Toledo named Thackeray's, and so I was seven, and I picked up this book, *Zen in the Martial Arts* by Jim Hyams, because it had a cool looking black belt on the cover. And so my mom's a school teacher, and I said, 'Hey, Mom, I wanna buy a book.' And she's like, 'You wanna to buy a book; we're buyin' a book.' And so we got this book, and it's a bunch of just cute little eastern martial arts teaching stories, but it mentions aikido as this very evolved spiritual form of martial arts. And it also mentioned meditation and Zen. So I heard all this stuff at once. So the next time we were in that bookstore, I got *Zen Mind, Beginner's Mind*. It had that same word in it, and it had the cool calligraphy, and on the back – you know – is Suzuki Roshi's face. And my mom is, 'Well, I don't know what that is, but if you wanna read it, let's do it.' So I can remember her being downstairs in the laundry room reading it to me, and us having no idea what the hell it's talking about and just laughing. But, in fact, there were seeds goin' in there."

His interest in music led him to the Berklee College of Music in Boston. "That's when I thought, 'I wonder if there's an aikido dojo here?' And I found Shobu Aikido of Boston with Bill Gleason Sensei."

Gleason Sensei was a student of Daido Loori at Zen Mountain Monastery, and soon Rinsen was attending sesshin at ZMM. "Daido Roshi was the first person that I met as a spiritual director who understood this experience I'd had. And not only did he understand my experience, he could help me deepen it and live in it and not pretend it wasn't real."

The experience he refers to occurred when he was a child. "I was so young that my feet couldn't hit the floor when I sat in the chair at the dining room table. I was obviously misbehaving or something, and I was in a time-out. My mom put me in a chair, facing the wall for me to have some quiet time, and I just sat there facing the wall. And I can still remember it. I mean, I literally started doing zazen right there, very spontaneously. And I had a dissolution of self, kensho, whatever you want to call it. But it was a real thing in my head, in my heart, and I just went with it. And my mom suddenly realized that I had been really quiet for like an hour, and she kind of swooped back to the room, 'Oh, Jay!' You know? I was just, like, in the zone. And so we got some ice cream and went on with life. But I still remembered that experience as a teenager and really was trying to find out 'what the hell was that?' I was very young when that happened. That was well before the martial arts classes or the book I got or anything like that. I've always had a very strong contemplative leaning. I didn't come to the Dharma because of great tragedy and trying to fix my life or anything like that. A lot of people do, and I get that, but that wasn't me."

From the first, he tells me, Zen just seemed to make a lot of sense. "There's a teacher. You practice. You meet with the teacher in dokusan. You get guidance. You work on this stuff. It gets better. That just fits in with my musical and martial arts experience perfectly, and it addressed this 'awakening/kensho' thing that I really couldn't find guidance with otherwise."

He remained in Boston from 1987 through 2001, attending sesshin as often as he could. "I never lived in Japan or in the forests of Thailand or in the foothills of the Himalayas or anything like that. It's been live in the city, be a professional jazz musician and educator, train in Aikido, and then travel and do a ton of sesshin. So I'm a sesshin junkie."

Eventually he returned to Ohio. The Great Heartland Buddhist Temple of Toledo (Daishin Koku-Ji) began as a small sitting group associated with the Aikido dojo he established in 2001. One of Daido Loori's Dharma heirs, Bonnie Myotai Treace, led the group until her health prevented her from continuing to do so. After that, Rinsen and his wife – Do'on – "fizzed around" for a time until they met James Ford. "That was just a clean fit. James and I just got along well. So we started travelling back and forth to Worcester, Massachusetts, to do sesshin all the time. And then ordination came, and once Do'on and I ordained, it started to really take off here in Toledo."

The community has about 150 members, which is large for most centers. Rinsen even has five students preparing for ordination.

He tells me there are a variety of reasons people come to Great Heartland for the first time. "A lot of people come to Buddhism because they've read some books, and they've thought about it for a while, and it seems like a good thing. And they've usually had some frustration or pain with other organized religious practices. So there's a certain group of people in my community that have been abused or just not well met, let's say, in a Christian tradition of some kind or other – the faith tradition of their family – then they start reading some Zen books. The books make sense, and, after a while, they kind of poke a toe in the door, kinda sheepishly. What they're looking for is something that's not patriarchal, something that's not oppressive, something that's not so rigid. But they also have this meditation thing going they want to explore and so there is a real need for deep lineage informed guidance and a healthy structure.

"I think the ones that stick it out are coming because they really want to alleviate suffering for themselves and, then, broadly for others." Suffering, he's careful to point out, isn't the same thing as pain. "Pain is kinda inevitable. But suffering really has to do – this is the way I would say it – with the fact that we live in a world-view that is in contradiction with the way the world actually is. You bump up against things all the time. And what that view is is that I'm an exclusively separate self. So I would say that this encounter with the non-dual and integrating it with compassion in daily life is what folks are goin' for, although they wouldn't articulate it that way in the beginning of their training.

"One thing people really want is they want a teacher who can help and be a guide. That's one of the big features. Another feature is they want a community of folks they can connect with. And so I think that's what people really end up relating to. Teacher. Having a strong teacher who can actually teach. And then this community thing is really important."

Two functions are scheduled at the Great Heartland Temple every week. The Sunday Sutra Service is family oriented and surprisingly similar to other services held on Sunday mornings in Toledo. After an initial social period, Rinsen and Do'on – who is a co-teacher at the Temple – process in wearing formal Soto garb accompanied by bells and incense. There are prostrations, liturgical readings, and what amounts to a sermon. The *Heart Sutra* is chanted, and dedications are invoked. The only zazen period on Sundays is fifteen minutes long. During it and the Dharma Talk, the children of the congregation leave the Zendo to take part in "Dharma School."

On Wednesdays the emphasis is on zazen. Participants sit for three thirty-minute periods linked by walking meditation (kinhin) while Rinsen and Do'on receive students in dokusan. This is followed by a teisho, that Rinsen points out, is different from the Dharma talks given on Sunday. "Those Sunday morning Sutra Service Dharma talks are like a point for the day, the week, that makes sense, that's very easy to understand. Wednesday is a Teisho. So I'll talk about a classic koan case, and it's much more just a straight up presentation of the Buddhadharma in a way that is generally dark to the mind but radiant to the dharma eye. There's a difference."

Some of the people who attend the Temple are passive participants, who come either for the talks or the opportunity to sit in meditation with a group. Any of them can attend dokusan – or sesshin for that matter – but there's a further step required before Rinsen will consider accepting them as a formal Zen students. They need to receive the precepts; they need to take jukai.

"And I'll tell you our thinking on this. For me, you can visit forever, that's great. But I don't want to go into deep-end wisdom training with someone if they don't have a moral and ethical base to build off of. So for us, the jukai process is very intense. I only offer it once a year. There's a very extensive series of formation retreats people go through, and I know that if they've done that program with me, they're bonded to each other, and I'm satisfied they have some good grounding in moral and ethical and compassionate mind and heart. And now I feel like, 'Okay, if we want to go and dance in the deep-end of the pool, we've got that compassionate and stable community base to do it with.'"

The stages of meditative practice Rinsen guides students through come from the Harada/Yasutani tradition, in which students generally are not introduced to shikan taza until they have first gone through a series of preliminary exercises and then completed the koan curriculum.

"In general I'm very specific about the process when you go from counting the in and the out of the breath, then just the cycle of the breath, and then you drop the numbers and just follow the breath. And those are very specific, and I tell them not to mess around with that. Like, if the teacher says this is your practice, you practice this. Right? You don't graze around and do a bunch of random practices. And then once there's a level of samadhi or concentration that's really kinda baked in there, typically what I'll get 'em to do is start following Mu. I'll read them the story. 'A monk went to Master Joshu and said, "What the hell?" And Joshu said, "Mu."' Then I say, 'Okay, what I'd like you to do now is just practice what we call "following Mu."'"

"And if someone asks what Mu means?"

"I tell 'em, 'Don't worry about that right now.' Meaning is just a bunch of weeds you don't want to get into. What I want you to do now is just follow the thing. Okay? Then, bring me what you find. If they start reading a bunch of commentaries on Mu, I'll say, 'That's too bad. Just don't bother yourself with it.' And see, there's a shift that is actually empirically verifiable to me when a student clicks into the samadhi of just being Mu. There's a thing that happens when they're chanting or following Mu, and there's another thing altogether when they become Mu. How exactly do you know? I don't know, but I do. And when that moment happens – and this can happen really quick or it can take a couple of years – but when the person slips into that place, then I'll spontaneously spring a checking question on 'em. And if they misfire, I'll say, 'Oh, forget about it. I was kiddin'.' And then just go back to following, and they just keep baking like that. The other complementary practice is called 'washing through with Mu.'"

"Washing through" requires greater focus, and he reserves it for sesshin practice. "So, they're a sesshin person, and we started to have 'em follow Mu, and then I'll have them 'washing through,' which is where you visualize – it's a visualization practice – it's where you mentally imagine that you take Mu and you wash any solid object through with it. So for example…" He holds up a plastic cup and passes his hand by it, as if passing through it. "And it goes, 'Whooo!' So I train the students in this visualization, and to be able to see any object, and to just wash it through with Mu very gently. So they're kinda getting nudged in this way of shifting perception. And then what ends up happening – and it works great, honestly – at a certain moment in dokusan, I'll ask them a checking question, and they'll just respond spontaneously. They don't think about it in advance, which is the way it oughta be. And then we start dancing the Mu checking questions together."

After experiencing an initial insight into Mu, students can begin the koan curriculum.

"So, for me, koan work's about actualizing the Dharma, the Buddhadharma. It's a way of really realizing the truth of the Buddhadharma and living from it. It's very expedient for a certain kind of person. Now there are some people who are wired in such a way that it's not a useful means, and so they don't benefit by wrestling with koan study. But for a lot of people – in fact, most people – koans work great.

"And honestly, I just love it. It's a ton of fun, and it works. The thing that just raises the hair on my beard," he says, grabbing his beard and pulling it to the side, "is when people who have no access to this from any other thing other than their own zazen, their own Dharma eyes, have the same response to these koans. And there's an intelligence behind it that I can see because I can look at the whole thing and look at it from a pedagogical point of view that I couldn't see as a student going through the curriculum. When you're a student going through it, you don't know what's going on. You're just on the stand, and the leader of the jam sesshin is calling tunes, and you're doing your best. But as the band leader, I can see the intelligence behind how this thing is set up. And it works. And what I mean by 'works' is, it actually does get people to a kensho that's meaningful and that actually shows up in their day."

The concept of koan systems "working" in some fashion, however, is one that I will find challenged elsewhere.[297]

Koun Franz

Koun Franz is a Montana-born Japanese-trained Soto priest living in Halifax, Nova Scotia. He is a deputy editor at *Buddhadharma* magazine and is the teacher at Zen Nova Scotia. His head is shaved, and he wears Japanese monastic garb – *samugi* – even when not officiating as a priest. His personal mannerisms are formal; for example, he uses both hands and bows slightly as he receives or passes things. At an event held at the Theravada Temple in Halifax – borrowed for the day by Zen Nova Scotia – as he approaches the huge white plaster Buddha at the head of the room he steps to the left slightly and then returns right after a few steps; he's stepping around a bowing mat that isn't there. "The officiant's movements

---

297. At the end of 2018, James Ford offered Rinsen *inka shomei* and warranted him to the use the title "Roshi."

are always in relationship to that mat," he explains, "either approaching it, stepping away from it, or walking around it to approach the altar and return." But he behaves this way and dresses as he does with an easy smile and such a light touch that it almost seems play. Regardless of whether or not one shares his views about Zen practice, one can't help but feel here is the genuine article.

I ask how important it is to retain the Japanese formalities he has chosen to adapt.

"It's not," he admits. "What is important is that we don't design it ourselves. Right? A spiritual practice of our own making is designed to make us comfortable. There's no way around that. This is a spiritual practice that makes us uncomfortable. That's good. It could easily be any one of a million different permutations of that, except that in order for me to do that, I have to make it, and then I'm making it so that I can be comfortable even if I'm making it so that my students can be uncomfortable. So to me it's just a matter of here's a practice that, I think, in its bones has a lot of integrity. And I think that it bothers people in the right ways.

"A huge number of Zen priests in North America are completely undercover. They have hair. They wear ordinary clothes then dress up when it's time. Some of them don't even do that. I'm interested in the idea of lay teachers, interested in the idea of other ways of doing that, but if you're going to pursue the path of an ordained priest, part of it is that it's a path of renunciation. And part of that is you don't get to choose what's in your closet anymore."

Problems, however, can arise. "I work above a sushi restaurant; two times now, people have stopped me on the street to ask me what the hours are because they think I work there. Or people think I'm a martial artist. It's a failing, and I stick to it because I'm determined to see it through to the other side."

Koun grew up in Helena which he describes as "disproportionately Catholic and disproportionately Mormon." His family was Catholic. One of his earliest encounters with Zen came when a friend of his father gave him a copy of *The Three Pillars of Zen*. "He has this karmic burden on him now that he did that," Koun says chuckling.

It also happened that a teacher at his High School was Buddhist and introduced him to like-minded people. It was a small group, but his involvement with it deepened his interest, and, after graduating from college, he decided to go to Japan. He found work at a private school but when he inquired about Zen temples, "What I got was this confusing message that there were Zen temples, but nothing that I could participate in at all. That was not what I expected. But most Japanese Zen temples don't have any zazen component at all." He shrugs. "So I came back to the US and went to graduate school."

It wasn't long before he realized he was "kind of hooked on Japan, even though it had been a failure according to all the metrics I had assigned to it. So throughout the time I was in grad school I was figuring out how to go back to Japan." But not alone this time. A young woman he met in graduate school, Tracy Terrell, came with him. "Our relationship kind of developed in Japan. It wasn't clear what we were doing by both going to the same place at the same time. But I was the guy who knew the area, and I had a car now. So on the weekends, I'd drive her around, and we kind of realized, 'Oh, we're a couple.'"

How far they could take that relationship, however, was tested both by the fact that they lived an hour away from each other and that this time around Koun did find a Zen teacher. "I was in a little tiny town, Takamori, inside the caldera of a volcano in Kyushu. And the first day I was there, I was determined. I said, 'Is there a Zen temple in this town?' They said, 'Yes. There is one. It's over there.' And I heard a temple bell coming from over there. So the next morning I got up, and I had a bicycle, and I waited. And when I heard the temple bells, I just started going in that direction. Found a temple; it had a bell. There was a little guy in back wearing overalls, but he had a bald head. My Japanese wasn't great, so the best I could do was ask, 'Is this a Zen temple?' He said, 'Yes.' I said, 'Do you do zazen here?' He said, 'Of course we do zazen.' I said, 'Great! Can I come do zazen here?' He said, 'Okay. Sure. Come tomorrow.' So I went the next day, and he was there, and he was wearing really fancy robes and the incense was going, and he set me up. And I sat there in front of the altar, and he walked around with the kyosaku and hit me a couple of times. And when it was done, they kind of rolled in this fancy table, and there was a meal, and his wife served me breakfast. Then they saw me to the gate, and I said, 'This is great. Can I come tomorrow?' And that was not what they expected. They thought they were giving me a kind of tourist experience. They had really done their best at it. And he said, 'Ohhhh...okay.' So I went back the next day, and the next day it was a little less of a show, and the next day it was less of a show, and eventually it wasn't certain whether he was going to be there or not. But I just went every day for two years. And eventually I just kind of had a key to the place, and I would sit, and I would clean the grounds, and then I would go into their kitchen and have breakfast with the family. As my Japanese got better, I asked more and more questions, and I asked about ordination. Not necessarily asking if I could be ordained, but just asking how does that work? But I think they kind took that to mean that that was what I was probing, so that became a conversation too."

"I'm guessing this was just a community temple," I say.

"Yeah, it's community service, a community center. One of the things

I've enjoyed since coming back to the US – one of the ways I can tell that someone is just full of it – is if they ask me who my teacher is and I tell them, and they nod, and they say, 'Oh, yeah. Yeah. I know who that is.' 'No, you don't. Because even the people in the next town over don't know who he is.'"

The priest's name was Kosoku Honda. "So he became my teacher; he became my ordination teacher. I was ordained at the end of those two years."

Over the next fourteen years, Koun and Tracy alternated between living in Japan and the US. In addition to his practice with Honda, Koun took part in lengthy monastic training periods – angos – although during the first of these he became so ill he had to leave before it was over.

"It was terrible. A huge eye-opener. It's very ceremonial; it's not that much about zazen, and when it is about zazen it's not about this kind of comfortable, nesty way that we tend to do in the west, where we're really concerned about it being a positive experience. It was kind of ironman zazen coupled with a lot of hard labor and very little sleep and no food, and I got really sick. I think I had lost 35 or 40 pounds in those two months." During a visit, Kosoku Honda's wife saw his condition and insisted he leave the temple at once. "Which was a huge failure."

"Didn't the experience make you wonder about the practice?"

"Absolutely! But, I think I'm an optimist by nature, and I figured there was something else. I was just in the wrong place. I ended up back there later, but I didn't see that coming."

I remind him that he had once told me that life at the temple was so regulated that the only choice one could make was either to stay or to leave.

"Yeah. That's exactly right. Which I now see as a virtue. And that was what I did. At that time, I made the choice to leave. But there is no room for anything. No individual expression; there's nothing."

He didn't give up and not only learned to survive the conditions at the monasteries, he even became a facilitator for other western students struggling with those challenges.

"My role was to keep the Japanese monks and the western monks from killing each other." The "cultural gap" – as he puts it – could not have been larger. "The two sides don't understand each other. Very simple illustration: Westerners, when they screw up, they laugh. They're trying to break the tension. They smile. They say, 'Ahhh, man!' In Japan, that means you don't care that you screwed up. So if somebody dropped an instrument or made a mistake serving tea or whatever, they'd do a little nervous laugh, and the Japanese monks would think, 'Not only are you a failure, you're an apathetic failure. You're rubbing our faces in it.' And I would have to explain this sort of thing to the Japanese side, and then I'd have to go back to the western side and say, 'Hey guys! Keep it together! Right? You have to look ashamed. You have to play this differently.'"

During a visit to her family home in Alaska, Tracy met Tozen Akiyama of the Anchorage Zen Center. When Akiyama learned that Koun was going through formal Soto training in Japan, he arranged for Koun to take responsibility for the Anchorage Group after his retirement. Four years later, however, the Franzes were back in Japan. "That had to do with me. Now I was integrated into the larger Zen community in the west, I could see that I was one of the youngest, by far, of the people who were attending teacher meetings in America. And one of the things I kept hearing older teachers say was, 'Oh, I wish I were young enough to go back to Japan and learn some of the stuff that didn't really happen for me.' And I thought, 'I actually could. I could go back to Japan.'" So Tracy got another university job in Japan, and they returned. After the birth of their second child, however, they decided they didn't want to raise their family in Japan. When he learned about the position at *Buddhadharma* magazine, he applied for it. "Had to look up where Halifax was. Now I live in a time zone I didn't know anyone lived in."

In many ways, Koun is representative of changes I see taking place in North American Zen. As he told me, his introduction had been through Kapleau's *The Three Pillars of Zen*, which describes an approach to practice very different from the training he went through. One of the reasons the book had so much influence in the early days of North American practice is that it posited that the experience of awakening was not only real but achievable.

"And," Koun admits, "that was very exciting. But at this point in my life, I really don't have any interest in enlightenment. That was such a driving force for so long, but to me, now, it doesn't hold up. The people I've met, by and large, who claim to have had some sort of enlightenment experience are no more mature – by any measure – than anyone else that I know. What I'm really interested in is maturity. I think Zen offers a vehicle by which people can grow up in a profound way.

"I tell this story a lot: When I was in my senior year in high school, I was about to graduate, I went to a Hallmark store in my town, and they had the graduation gifts – you know they always had the shelf for the season. And one was this little framed thing, and it said something to the effect of, 'Being an adult means taking responsibility for your actions.' And for me – I was 17 or something – that was a tiny 'falling away of body and mind.'[298] I looked at it, and it was absolutely true. And I knew it, and I

---

298. *Shinjin Datsurakuh*, a central element in Dogen's presentation of Zen.

didn't want to hear it. I wished I hadn't seen the sign. But I knew that was right. And I think what the Zen path does is it offers – through the model of the Bodhisattva – a way to take responsibility for your actions that goes beyond what we usually think that is into a much, much broader vision of adulthood. That's inspiring to me."

Of the teachers I have interviewed, Koun is the most articulate in questioning the koan system. When I say that, for me, koans seem to work, it's the word "work" he takes to task.

"From a Soto Zen perspective, there's nothing that works. Because there's no outcome. There's nothing that can be a means to an end. If there's an end, then what is that end? Right? That, to me, suggests that there's a metric by which we can measure practice. Even if the 'enlightened teacher' is not stuck in that, it's almost impossible that the student is not stuck in some question of success, some question of a measurement by which practice is succeeding or failing. Because 'I passed!'"

"I suspect," I tell him, "most people working with koans wouldn't think 'passing' meant any more than an ephemeral insight that is capable of deepening or changing over time."

"But in the moment that you pass, in the moment that a person passes Mu, have they not just been told that they've literally passed through a barrier? To me that feels problematic. Or at least something that I don't resonate with at all. And it's exactly the kind of thing that I would try to push back against in my own community. Any time that you're trying to measure what you're doing, I would say, 'Take that away.'"

"What, then," I ask, "is kensho?"

"It's an experience. It's like…. The first thing I wanted to say is that it's like a burp of the mind. I mean, it's a good experience. No one would say it's not. I think it's positive when people have those experiences. It's not a negative. It's not like, 'Go put it back.' But it is as temporary as anything. It doesn't mean anything. It means you had a good experience. It's like a drug experience. If someone takes mushrooms, and it inspires them to look more deeply into their mind, to think in a more universal way about something, great. If they take mushrooms and the first thing they do is want to go back and take more mushrooms, they blew it, as far as I'm concerned. They missed the opportunity. For me, Zen practice is about a kind of honesty and about a kind of maturity. And that doesn't require some kind of mind-blowing episode. This isn't about koan practice per se – people I respect do that practice and do it with great integrity, with real awareness of all the things I'm talking about. It's about how much of the practice is about building scaffolding, and how much is about knocking it down and doing without it. Kensho happens without koan practice, too, and when it does, the same issues arise."

He's also conscious of the potential problems associated with private interviews, dokusan or sanzen. "It's a relationship that largely takes place in private behind closed doors. And history has shown that that's very bad model for a lot of people. A lot of bad things happen behind closed doors, especially when one person has an incredible amount of authority and is seen to be holding the keys to something and the other person is not. That's just a huge danger. That's not to say that everyone is succumbing to that danger. But there is abuse of power. There's sexual abuse. There's coercion. And even when there isn't any of that, there are all sorts of projection that come from the other side. It's such a fraught space. And I think that really there aren't that many people who are good at holding that space in a really mature way. And then the second part of that is that it creates a teacher/student dynamic in which the teacher has something the student wants. Because the teacher gets to say, 'Yes' or 'No.' The teacher gets to say, 'You pass; you fail.' And that makes me nervous because I don't have that. I don't have something that my students don't have. I have an experience with this tradition that they don't have. But I don't have a key. Period. And I'm not the person who magically makes someone unstuck. That would be great. I'd love to be that, that person of legend who always says the right thing and breaks someone's mind open. But I'm not that guy."

"Aren't we all 'that guy' for one another at one time or other?"

"Yes. That opportunity is there. But the assumption in dokusan is that the teacher is going to do that. Right? And then everything that he says becomes magic. And I know myself, even though I'm not selling that, that I have said something in passing to someone that ended up being their practice for the next six months because they thought that I was saying something from this other place, and I wasn't. And it devastated them." He pauses for a while before continuing. "It's so delicate. And my confidence in people's maturity is not very high."

"You said you were an optimist."

"I am an optimist about things. But part of my professional job now is to know what people are doing in the Buddhist world. And it's a lot of bad news. And it's all the people that we expect to be the best. And the fact is that dokusan is extremely rare in Japan. My teachers have never done dokusan with anybody. I've never done dokusan with my teacher ever."

He does do dokusan with his students, on the other hand, because they expect it. "And I see real value in having that conversation, but with me it's not the conversation that people are necessarily expecting. It's certainly not the conversation you get in the koan world. And it's really the only personal thing that happens in the community between me and anyone. We don't have a center; we don't have a lot of schedule. There aren't lot of opportunities to check in. And what I find is that people have questions that build over time, and sometimes arise in a very intellectual way, but sometimes arise in a very raw way. And I think it's good that there's an avenue for that. But what I do when I'm sitting down there, before I hit the bell, before people come downstairs to see me, what I tell myself, over and over again, is to remember that I don't know. 'I don't know. I don't know. I don't know. I don't know. I don't know.'"

"You said – and I assume you were talking about your position at *Buddhadharma* – you said that it was part of your job to know what's happening, and what's happening is that things are a mess in many places. So, what is there in Zen that makes it worth preserving?"

He sits silent for a long while, then speaks softly. "I think that Zen offers a particular vision of responsibility that's very much in line with the kind of humanistic direction of the world. It doesn't rely on anything. You can take away all of the different Jenga pieces and it's fine. It doesn't rely upon any particular mythology. I'm speaking about this through my own lenses obviously. My teachers would speak about this differently because they would incorporate more of the mythology, and they would incorporate a more specific world view than what I'm presenting to anybody. But I think Zen has space for this. There's a way of examining your role in the universe that does not impose upon it a description of what the universe is. That, to me, feels really useful. It doesn't require you to believe something new. It just requires you to look at something that's present. Temperamentally, obviously, there are people who want that, and other people who will find that either boring or absurd or repellent. That's fine."

Michael Fieleke and Robert Waldinger

Mike Fieleke and Bob Waldinger both began their Zen studies with James Ford and later received the first stage of Dharma Transmission – *denkai* – under the tutelage of Melissa Myozen Blacker and David Dae An Rynick of the Boundless Way Temple in Massachusetts. As Bob explains it, having denkai "means I can have my own *shoken*[299] students. The next step is denbo, which authorizes me to give dharma transmission." Shortly after I interviewed them, both Mike and Bob received denbo, but at the time I spoke with them, they were essentially journeymen Zen Masters in the Boundless Way lineage. They both lead sanghas in Newton. Bob is the resident teacher at the Henry David Thoreau Sangha ("affectionately known as 'Hank'"), and Mike is the resident teacher of the Morning Star Zen Sangha.

---

299. "Shoken" is a formal meeting with a teacher – dokusan or sanzen.

Bob came to Zen relatively late in life. He was in his 50s before he began formal practice. "I had been interested in meditation since I was in my 30s because someone I did my psychological training with casually said one day that she and her partner had spent a weekend doing a silent retreat. And I said, 'You mean, you didn't say anything?' I couldn't imagine spending time with my girlfriend being quiet. So I think she recommended *Wherever You Go, There You Are*, the Jon Kabat-Zinn book, and I read it and was really drawn to basic Buddhist philosophy. The idea of impermanence resonated so much because since I was a teenager at least, reading some of the poets like Yeats, I realized that I was worried about all this stuff that didn't matter, and that all these ideas about what we were supposed to achieve and what people were supposed to accomplish had this kind of absurdity about it because it was all going to pass away. And that really struck me deeply as an adolescent, but I didn't have any way to talk about it, and nobody else was seeming to think that way. So I did all these very achievement-oriented things, but all the while kept thinking, 'There's a part of this that's completely made up and absurd.' Traditional religion hadn't worked for me. I was raised Jewish, and – like – I would be in services with my family and wanted to stop the action and go up front and say, 'Okay, raise your hands. How many of you really believe this stuff?' Of course I could never do that."

He dabbled in various meditation traditions for a while before meeting Ford. "My son's friend in middle school had a coming of age ceremony at the Unitarian Church where James was the minister. And I sat next to the friend's mom, and she knew I'd been interested in meditation; she pointed to James and said, 'You know, he's a Zen master.' So I emailed him and asked if I could come see him, and he said, 'Sure.' So one weekday morning I went to his office, and it was just a total mess, and he came in with his shirt-buttons wrong and – you know – was just James. And was very down to Earth. And I thought, 'Oh, I could probably learn from this guy.' One of the first things James said to me was, 'We do scruffy Zen.'" Bob accepted an invitation to try sitting with the group that James was running at his church. "And I went up to him afterwards, and I said, 'You know, I was really uncomfortable with all the bowing and the chanting.' And, of course, being James, he said, 'Good!' And that was sort of a dare to come back, so I came back, and..." He shrugs. "I drank the Kool-Aid."

"As long as you recognized it's Kool-Aid."

"Well, that was actually one of the most helpful things. The Zen I know doesn't present itself as anything but Kool-Aid that eventually you'll put down."

"I was raised Protestant," Mike tells me, "and that actually planted the seeds of practice, because I felt as a child – I bet many children do – a kind of sacred presence that was a mystery to me that I gave the name God. But I felt a sense of connectedness and vastness at a very young age. And when I was an adolescent, my parents were divorced, and I became very lonely and lost in my own religious practice. I think in rejecting my parents – out of anger – I also rejected their religious teachings and traditions and felt quite lost. So that's part of how Zen made its way into my life. I was looking for something different."

"And your students at Morning Star, what brings them to your door? What are they looking for?"

Mike considers the question a moment before replying. "I would say often what they're looking for is stress reduction. That's probably one of the most common things that brings people through the door. They just want to feel better, because they're suffering, and, often, they feel quite alone."

When I ask Bob what draws people to his sangha, he tells me he doesn't know. "Because I don't ask. I mean, I do sometimes. Sometimes we do little orientations and ask what they're looking for, and if they say they're looking for relaxation, we say, 'Well, that's a perfectly good thing to look for. That's not what you'll find here. But there are a lot of other places you can find it. In fact, we can even point you to some of those places.' So we do that, and usually most people come visit us once and don't come back."

"And the ones who do come back? What are they looking for?"

Once again, he says he isn't sure. "I think they're looking for something that feels authentic. You know, nobody's telling them what to believe. We're saying, 'Try this on. See if it resonates.' Many people feel that there's something wrong, there's something missing. And then it's" – using the same analogy James Ford had – "the old bait-and-switch. They're coming because, 'I want to get over this grief; I'm coming because my relationship failed; I'm coming because dot, dot, dot.' And the promise – we don't promise it – but the promise that they seem to see is, 'This is going to help me manage this.' And then the bait-and-switch is, 'Now we're going to ask you to face toward it.' But usually the people who stay are the people who find, 'Yes, facing toward is difficult and yet at the same time nourishing in some way.' I think the people who stay are people who find that it calls to them in ways they don't fully understand. You know, sort of this 'opaque to the mind and radiant to the heart.' I don't always know why."

I had asked James Ford why, if people were looking for stress-reduction, they take up Zen rather than go to a yoga studio or a mindfulness seminar. It's a question I come back to with Mike and Bob."

Mike reflects a moment, then says, "I guess it's what do we do different. Right? I guess the best way for me to put it is the lack of agenda. The idea that we aren't there primarily as a self-improvement project, and the goal is not to be different from what we are, but to see what we are. And there is a faith that that – in and of itself – is liberating. I took a mindfulness-based stressed reduction course many years ago, and I think there's good in these practices. You can really bring people into the moment through a kind of connectedness to their body and their breath and an awareness of what's unfolding. And I think the notion that it makes you feel better in some way, that it will relieve your stress, is sometimes true and great marketing, and it gets a lot of people in the door. In Zen, while there is a grain of truth that stress can fall away, still I worry that there's a little bit of a disservice in that goal too. I think that for me what has been most liberating about Zen and what I think it offers is that, of course, we can make changes in our lives and in our thoughts and behaviors, but that we don't necessarily have to. We can simply see, and everything unfolds, everything goes its own way, and we have the capacity to have faith in this unfolding. And that whatever is alive in the given moment is the Dharma, is exactly what we're seeking."

"Do people still seek awakening?"

"Yeah, that's a good question. In our group at least, we do acknowledge the importance of these moments but don't necessarily set them up as a goal. We're very careful about acknowledging it in any personal way. Like, 'Oh! That's kensho!' We're very careful about that because it can set somebody up for years of problems, where they're trying to aim for the same thing again and get attached to some previous experience and trapped in it."

"The early teachers in America often gave the impression that kensho was essential to Zen practice," I point out. "It was argued that the only suitable response to Mu, for example, was kensho."

"I think we have a certain level of expectation around, particularly, the source of Mu. I would say we are looking for a kensho experience in that. But I guess I would say that we allow for a different intensity of that experience, that we aren't looking for 'great kensho,' per se. And I think that – to go back to what people are looking for when they come in – I think you're right, fewer people come into practice thinking, 'I'm going to get enlightenment.' More people are coming in, like I said, saying, 'I just want to feel less stressed.' And so the way that we meet people maybe has shifted based on peoples' hopes.

"I wonder if part of our de-emphasizing awakening – although it is the heart of the matter – aligns a bit with the Soto tradition. And I think that's really woven into the fabric of who we are, to acknowledge that it's already true, that there's nothing to attain, and we just need to realize that. But I think another aspect of it might be that we are meeting people where they are when they come through the door. And if we suddenly say, 'I know you want less stress, but *what you really need is...*'" He laughs. "Then they'll just turn and run.

"You know, it's interesting; teachers can have different views of kensho. I've known some who really de-emphasize it and talk about it as makyo.[300] There are others who think, 'No, this is actually compass-setting. This actually matters. This is an important part of our practice.' For me, it depends. Kensho can become makyo when conceptualized, but the experience in and of itself is not. It's true waking up to the way things are."

"This awakening thing wasn't something I expected to encounter or was hankering after," Bob tells me. "And then I just got more and more involved and started to do koan study and – you know – kinda the whole nine yards."

"If someone had asked you – perhaps one of your colleagues who was wondering if you were going off the deep end..." He nods his head, grinning broadly. "Oh!" I say. "That's already happened has it?"

"Yeah, so I worked at Harvard Medical School, which is one of the most conservative institutions on the planet, and some of my friends were quite interested. Actually some of my psychoanalyst friends were really interested, because psychoanalysis is about watching the mind as well in a different way, with different frames. So they were interested. Other people were kind of polite. You know there's that, 'Oh?' And my wife was worried that it was a cult perhaps. And I said to her, 'If I never went back to this Monday night sitting group, no one would even call, no one would know. That's not what it is.'"

His office, he tells me, is now decorated with Buddha figures, photos of his teachers, and a picture of Guanyin. "So now I'm really out." And when he returns after taking time off work to attend sesshin, his colleagues will inquire how it went. "They'll ask, 'Was it really relaxing?' And I say, 'No, it was intense. Good. But not relaxing.' I tell them it's not about relaxation. It's not about self-improvement. It's about a radical understanding of the self in the world and what it means to be alive. That's the elevator speech."

Earlier he had told me, "The structure of Zen works for me, these frequent interviews with teachers are important because I tend to get discouraged. Doubt is a big part of my experience. So I would sit there and

---

300. *Makyo* are hallucinations experienced during meditation.

think, 'What the hell am I doing? I might just as well be phoning this meditation in.' And so it's really helpful to have another human being working to remind me what this is. So I found that structure helpful. And when Zen talks about 'already Buddha' – you know? – what the hell is that? And that seemed to me to be really important and much more…um… both surprising and real than what I understand from some of my friends in other traditions. Well, they eventually deconstruct all these levels. But most of us never get to that point. Most people don't get far enough along the path to deconstruct the various levels. What I like about Zen is it keeps knocking you back down and saying, 'We're going to deconstruct it moment to moment.'"

Boundless Way maintains formal ties with the Soto tradition but also makes use of the Sanbo Zen koan curriculum. In that regard, both Mike and Bob are sensitive to the potential value of koan work but also understand the reservations of teachers like Koun Franz.

"I think Koun would argue that koan study necessarily creates a mind of attainment," I say, "that you're trying to attain something, if only the approval of your teacher that you've got the right response. And the Soto line, as you pointed out, is that there is nothing to attain."

"I guess I would honor that critique," Mike tells me. "I think that is an actual risk. I guess it kind of depends on how we approach them and how we use them in our teaching. So, for me, koans were a big part of my own practice for many years, but I also appreciated very much the years of practice when I was not doing koans. I think what the students who do use them encounter is precisely this mind of wanting to attain something and imagining that if they can give the right answer to a koan that they're attaining enlightenment." Then he adds, with a laugh, "And so often answering a koan correctly can result in a feeling of, 'That was it?' Because koans affirm that it's really just this. And that can be disappointing."

"Koans don't bring about insights," Bob tells me. "I mean, I've had some insights when I do koans, but not that much. It's more like they confirm them. For me, it's so helpful to see that 400 years ago these guys were struggling with the same things. And it's that experience of humanness that koans illustrate that I find helpful. And sometimes the answer to the koan will reinforce something that's been arising on the cushion or just in my life."

In the end for Bob – as befits a psychoanalyst – it all comes down to how the practice affects one's life. "The analogy I've heard people use is that all of this practice – koan practice, sitting, even the experience of kensho – these are all part of what you might consider going to a batting-cage for batting practice. The bottom line is how we live our lives. The bottom line is what we do out there. And so even if you had the biggest kensho imaginable, you still have to do the laundry. You still have to get in the car and drive to work, you still have to figure out how you're going to deal with your annoying colleague. So, in some ways, let's get real about this. Let's put this into the bigger picture – right? – of what difference does it make? So in some ways it doesn't matter. Big kensho. Little kensho. No kensho. How are you living your life?"

Seiho Morris

Seiho Morris is an ordained Zen priest in the Rinzai tradition who works in an addictions treatment center. I first met him in Seattle but when I interviewed him, he was preparing to lead a retreat in Cincinnati for people engaged in 12-Step programs. I assumed the retreat was related to his work at the treatment center, but he tells me it isn't.

"No, this is Zen. Because the way I intersect with people in my day-to-day Zen practice as a monk is it's always meeting people where they're at. And so one of the things I'm experimenting with is not necessarily focusing on practice in a particular place, a temple." He describes himself as something like an itinerant monk, offering retreats where they are needed. That isn't, however, the way he had originally pictured his service as a priest.

"When I became ordained, I had this vision of what my practice would look like. Which is you marry, you bury, hospice, that kind of thing. Like monks, priests, yogis are part of a mental health system – physical, mental, emotional, spiritual system – to help individuals who come to them. So that's how I envisioned it. But what emerged – and it happened after the Trump election – was Zen Buddhism and people of color. And that surprised me. And actually that's been quite challenging for me because when you get into person of color issues, racism, social justice, equity, that's the stuff people don't want to do. It's not the pretty side of Zen or Buddhism as a whole. There's not very many African American practitioners out there, much less ordained.

"So it was really strange being confronted with this. I haven't really had to deal with these issues so directly. You know? But what happened was there's this thing in Seattle called Festival Sundiata, which is an African American cultural festival, but everyone can attend. It doesn't matter if you're a person of color, black, Hispanic, white, whatever. And I led two days of practice just around POC issues. And it was challenging because I hadn't actively practiced with this issue in this way. 'Cause, honestly, even though I'm black, I'm usually around people who are white or Asian. Because it's Zen. So I don't encounter a lot of African American people. I know that might sound strange, but it's true. At any rate, I was sitting there and attempting to learn more about this deeply. And one of the things I recognized that had never occurred to me is that if you're under a lot of pressure culturally, like the way American society is set up essentially it's a white, western kind of culture, and you're the minority of that culture, there's a lot of pressure. And I was sitting in a group at one of these person of color events, and I listened to all these people, not just African Americans. There were indigenous tribal people, people who were Asian, and what I heard in their story is there's a lot of mental health issues, anxieties, stress, depression – just profoundly so – that interferes with their inward stability, their inward harmony, and so I began practicing with people based on that. The first noble truth – which is dukkha – life, ego is the part of the wheel that's out of balance. So working on concentration, presence, and mindfulness, and different Buddhist practices from the Eightfold Path, to help them to find an inward stability. When you're like in a boat on the ocean how to essentially not capsize when the water's choppy. And Zen is good for that. Buddhism is good for that. How to not run away from your outward circumstances, but how do you turn into it and meet the moment with equanimity, harmony, and a sense of presence?"

Those same qualities are what makes Zen practice valuable to people recovering from addiction. They were also what brought Seiho to practice. He has been, as his puts it, in recovery for 31 years. He is currently 52, so I do the math in my head. "Since you were 21?"

"Yes."

"Does one ever come a point where one can say, 'I've recovered'?"

"No, it's very much like having diabetes. I'm not recovered. There's always more healing, there's always more integration to do."

"What was your addiction?"

"It didn't really matter. Alcohol was a very big thing. Marijuana. LSD. Cocaine. I was an equal opportunity addict."

"And what made you quit it all?"

He sighs deeply, then speaks very slowly. "I was tired of hurting my mother's feelings. I was reckless; I was impulsive. I was not inclined to hurt other people per se, but I could do things that hurt other people. I was not emotionally available, I wasn't really physically available."

"And that's when you first entered a 12-Step program? At 21!"

"Yeah, basically I say I was abducted by people in Narcotics Anonymous. That's a joke, but these people took me under their wing. And I went to a program. Got stabilized. Got out. Got a sponsor. I use this expression a lot, but it is true: these people – in 12-Step programs – essentially raised me. So if you ask me, 'Culturally where do you really come from?' It would be a more honest answer to say, '12-Step programs.' So I tend to look at things through that perspective, that lens."

For Seiho, the 12-Steps are "the perfect Zen deal. Which is, we admit that we're powerless over ego, self-rejecting thought, and, when we follow those thoughts, our life becomes unmanageable. Step two is – the way it's actually worded is – 'we came to believe that a power greater than ourselves could restore us to sanity.' I've reframed that for myself as, 'It's the power of love, which is greater than ego, which allows us to be restored to – as Trungpa Rinpoche says – "basic sanity" or "basic soundness of mind."' And then step three, is to make a decision to turn our will or life over to God – I say 'the care of love' – as I understand it in this moment. So, for me, that is Zen."

After he started the 12-Step work, he also began taking courses at Salisbury University where his mother taught social work and psychology. "There was this gentleman, Dr. Jamie Campbell, who was from the Rochester Institute of Technology, and he was a Zen practitioner. And I asked him, 'What happens when you die?' And his response was, 'Sit, and you'll find out.' And I said, 'Couldn't you just tell me?' And he's like, 'No. Come up and have a sit with us. Come for an Introduction to Zen weekend. It's not intellectual; it's experiential.' And he also told me to read *The Three Pillars of Zen*, which I did. And I went to an Introduction to Zen weekend. And after getting through that weekend, I went and got hold of a book called *Journey of Awakening* by Ram Dass, and in the back there was all these practice centers in the United States. So I decided wherever my finger landed, that's where I was gonna go, and I'd practice there until I got enlightened. So I stick my finger there and it lands – thank God! 'cause it was on the east coast – on Dai Bosatsu Zendo. So I wrote them a letter. Turns out that the vice abbot there was in recovery – his name is Jun Po Denis Kelly – and I told him who I was and what I wanted to do, and he invited me to come there. And that's where my training and my practice got catapulted into the reality of Zen, not the theory of Zen," he says, laughing heartily.

Even in the colorful history of North American Zen, Jun Po Kelly sticks out. He had been a major distributor and promoter of LSD as a means of spiritual enhancement who, after a period in prison, became a student of Eido Shimano and eventually received Dharma Transmission.

After Seiho had been at Dai Bosatsu for about a year, information about Shimano's sexual activity came to light which Seiho found seriously disturbing. "'Cause I'm this kid. I still had a major idolization, like once you become enlightened, it's like going from a 1.0 version to a 2.0 version. So I figured all that negative stuff, like depression, it just got cleared up, and then you lived differently as a person. So the news was a shock when it came, and the sangha just exploded."

"But you remained committed to the practice?"

"Right. I practiced on my own. So I got back into my job; I maintained a practice. And then I started hitting a bunch of different groups."

"Why?" I ask. "What does Zen do?"

"It gives us the opportunity to have conscious contact with reality, our values, and the distance in the relationship between them. So, what are my values? Am I following them, and am I in harmony with reality? Or do I have these values, and I can't see or maybe I'm oblivious, so I'm not really listening to reality, and I'm living in disharmony with it. And in that way there's suffering, unmanageability, confusion, some version of what I call an 'Unhappy Meal' which has the opportunity to get super-sized."

"Unmanageability?"

"Yeah. When we're not following our values, when we're not following reality, when we're not being honest about what's happening, we create unmanageability for ourselves. And so Zen has the opportunity – it's not a guarantee – because Zen is so fixated on meeting the reality of present moment circumstances, that when . . ." He pauses a moment, then remarks that he wants to be careful how he expresses the point he's trying to make. "When we're doing real Zen versus what I call Blank Zen – this kind of yoga/health version of Zen where people just want to be a little bit calmer or something – but Daijo Zen[301] is about affecting significant change and really meeting the reality of our circumstances." For Seiho there is an important and inevitable social dimension to that work.

"Zen – the way I translate it – means 'unification.' So that's physical, mental, emotional, and spiritual. Everything is moving maybe not perfectly but at least in the same direction, or, if there's a misalignment, we have the opportunity to come back to harmony as an individual. So that's Hinayana practice. In Mahayana practice we work together with others, attempting to have positive regard for each other. This is the Eightfold Path. We have Sincere Concentration, Sincere Mindfulness and Presence, Sincere Effort – which means ethics to me – Sincere Livelihood, Sincere Intentions, Sincere Actions, Sincere Communication, and all of that, and what it culminates in is – 'cause I believe in doing the Eightfold Path in reverse – is the natural resolve which is Sincere Understanding. So, for example, through this practice, through turning down the volume level on ego and allowing for conscious contact with our intuitive nature, our awareness, we realize that taking care of the environment is important. Taking care of each other is important."

In contrast to the type of compassionate relationships Seiho sees Zen practice leading to, contemporary society is alienating. It is the resulting

---

301. "Great Practice Zen," contrasted with other forms of Zen practice undertaken for reasons of health, etc.

"societal suffering," he believes, that draws people to Zen. "We are a society which is generating basically nothing more than wage-slaves. It's insane. People are literally working to get property to pass on to someone when they die. It's like if you ask people, 'Are you connected to yourself? Are you connected to your heart?' Of course not. They're spending their time at one, two, three, and, in certain instances, four jobs! There's so much suffering in the society that this drives people to ask, 'There's got to be something more than this, 'cause this sucks.' So the premise I work with – especially as a monk – is that nobody gets to a zendo by accident. They realize that something has gone wrong or is going wrong, and that brings them there. They come because they're being compressed, and they're looking for relief. And, I mean, people are really suffering. 'Cause once you get past the shiny, happy D.T. Suzuki version of Zen where there's enlightenment and this and that, what you're left with is the reality. You're left with the mud, and then that's where it's time to get real. Like when I'm interacting with people what I'm attempting to discern is kind of what you're asking: What's the motivation? Are they looking to the Zen Center as a kind of feel-better thing, or is what's going on with them that they're troubled."

Kensho he says, isn't that difficult to achieve, nor, perhaps – in itself – is it all that important. What matters is what one does with awakening. "How do we manifest it? And to me, I really believe that needs to be with authenticity and integrity supported by kindness. If you asked me the definition of kensho I would say 'completeness' in terms of my head, my heart, my feet, my spirit, my presence are moving in the same direction. Then what I'm talking about is also what I'm doing."

For Seiho the characteristic that distinguishes Zen from other spiritual traditions – including other Buddhist traditions – is its minimalism. "It's lean. Lean. Zen has minimal gimmicks. It's your back. It's your breath. It is essentially the practice of the Buddha. There's a lot of stuff on the Tibetan side that's beautiful, that's elegant. I understand one hundred percent what's happening, but the fundamental deal is embodying your body, being-awareness, meeting the wave. . . Because the wave of ego is always working under the assumption that it's actually the entire ocean. So the wave is attempting to control the ocean, awareness, which is us. And so Zen in a very lean, minimalist way, removes all the things, pulls all the furniture out, and says, 'Here's a cushion. Just sit on the cushion and see what comes.' And whatever comes, don't hold onto it, don't add, don't turn it into something else. Just notice it but remain right in here in your practice."

"You also use koans," I point out.

"I'm a big believer in koan practice. Koans are a very good tool for putting a crowbar into the way ego processes experience so that we notice the reality."

"How do they do that?"

"They place the ego in a position where it goes into a state of exhaustion. It comes to a point where it really can't answer. It becomes like a crowbar in the gear of the intellectual process, and then you just notice. It's a kind of listening. So a quick example would be that my mother died in 2005 about six months after I was ordained. And I was sitting there on my zafu, wondering, 'Why? Why did she have to die?' She was a big part of my compass. And the answer came back, 'Because she died.' It wasn't glorious. It wasn't terrible. It wasn't, 'Oh, this is a great awesome answer.' It was just the truth. Why did she die? Because she died. And what about this grief that I'm carrying? 'Cause then people would tell me, 'You'll get through your grief. You'll get through this. You'll get through that.' And then one day sitting on the cushion what came through was I noticed that grief was not something to get through. Grief is our way of saying we miss someone's or something's physical presence in our life, and we're sorry they're not here." He pauses a moment, as if reflecting back on the experience. "That was the koan of the moment. Other koans, like one that I've been working on recently, Nansen kills the cat. Have you ever done that koan?"

It's the fourteenth case in the *Mumonkan*. Nansen finds the monks in his temple arguing over a cat. He takes the animal away from them then tells the monks to say "turning word" or he will kill the cat. The monks don't know how to respond, and Nansen cuts its head off.

"I have."

"What did you notice?" Seiho asks me. "What did you come to?"

"I snatched the cat away from him."

Seiho claps his hands as if applauding. "That's it! Speak a turning word or I'll kill this cat! You know, these highfalutin Zen practitioners, sure their sit looks good, full lotus, all that. And they couldn't respond to the simple reality of what was happening. They were worthless. And that is my fear about Zen. These people that join us, they want ego-death, they want this, they want that. I mean, to me, they're insane. Zen is so we can respond with completeness to our present moment experience. It's being physically non-emotional and spiritually available to our self and other people. That is what it's for. So Nansen kills the cat, it points me to people who are in a situation, and they don't know how to respond to the reality. That's the point of the koan. Snatch the cat away. If someone falls down, you just help them up. You don't philosophize about it."

Tenku Ruff

Tenku Ruff is concerned about the way in which Zen is presented in the west. Too often, she feels, it is from the perspective of white boomer males. In 2017 she chaired the Generation X Dharma Teachers steering committee. Currently she is board president of the Soto Zen Buddhist Association – the youngest person to have held that position – and is engaged, she tells me, in leading the association through "a generational shift." I am a white boomer male.

She was raised in Northern Florida. "Very Southern culture. My family are evangelical Christians. I had no idea about Buddhism until I went to college." She took a course entitled "The Sacred Quest" that included an introduction to Buddhism. "It made sense to me in a way that nothing else had. We were required to keep a journal in that class, which I recently found when I was cleaning out my mother's house. Zen's teachings on emptiness drew me in. Re-reading that journal, I expected my 19-year-old ideas about emptiness to be very naïve, but they were actually pretty spot-on. This tells me that there are things we all already know on a deep level. Zen Buddhism isn't something that can be taught conceptually, but rather our practice helps us to understand what we already know."

After college, she went to Japan through a program that brought English-speaking graduates to the country as assistant language teachers. She was drawn both by a desire to visit the country and a desire to learn to meditate.

"There was no place in America where you could learn to meditate?" I ask.

"I wanted to go to Japan," she says with a laugh. "I might have guessed there were places in America, but these were two separate goals that overlapped over there, not over here."

She had hoped to be sent to Kyoto, "Because I'd read somewhere that that's where all the Zen temples were." But, being from the southern US, she also requested to be sent someplace that wasn't cold. "So basically, they sent me to the Alabama of Japan, very southern Japan, really far from Kyoto. But down there just happened to be the only Zen temple in Japan that had a western abbot, and he would hold sesshin in English for foreigners, structured around our holidays."

The teacher was Tesshin Paul Silverman. After an initial visit to his temple, she signed up for a five-day sesshin. It was the first time she received zazen instruction or folded her legs. "And I've never stopped since. It felt like a real home for me."

"Why?"

"I think, again, it circles back to that there was something already in me that was reaching out for something that it already knew. It was very hard, and certainly my mind was very active during that first sesshin, and yet in that stillness there was something that felt true. That, for me, was the point of connection, the stillness arising."

"I'm still not clear what prompted you to go to the temple in the first place. Was it just curiosity? Or was it that you felt something was lacking? Were you looking for something? Were you dissatisfied?"

"Definitely!" she says, laughing. "Dukkha! I mean, why do we all come to practice? Dukkha. Yeah, I was dissatisfied in life. I'd struggled with depression and not knowing my place, not understanding where I fit. I don't think zazen gave me an answer, but it gave me a way to work with it."

In 1998, she met Tessai Yamamoto. "We're a Soto Zen practice with a koan tradition, and, in our tradition, when a person understands their first koan – which is also known as kensho – it has to be confirmed by somebody who's more senior than the person teaching. It's usually a senior Dharma brother or sister. So in 1998 Tesshin had invited his Dharma brother, Tessai Yamamoto, down to lead sesshin and confirm the kensho of one other person and me." Yamamoto was a second-generation Dharma descendent of Daiun Harada from whose teaching the Sanbo Zen lineage is derived.

Tenku regularly attended sesshin with Silverman until he decided to return to North America, which coincided with the end of her teaching contract. She then spent a year visiting temples and monasteries throughout Asia before also coming back to the States. "Somebody told me that there was a temple in San Francisco where you could pay for room and board and practice Zen. So I applied to the San Francisco Zen Center and went there."

Initially she went for a practice period at Green Gulch Farm, after which she took up residency at the City Center temple on the corner of Page and Laguna Streets.

"It was culture shock. Or reverse culture shock. By that time I'd lived overseas for eight or nine years, and the San Francisco Zen Center was so different from anywhere I practiced before. I was greeted by the guest manager, who had on big earrings and had hair down to her butt. People were wearing sundresses with their shoulders showing. People had a lot of opinions about things and would argue!" She laughs at the memory. "This was all very different for me. It was strange. I couldn't figure out who was in charge. In Japan, it's important to know who is in charge, and there didn't seem to be anybody in charge in San Francisco. So that was really confusing to me. People my age were practicing there, but they made a lot of cultural references that I didn't understand. Not only because I'd been abroad for nearly ten years, but I hadn't grown up in California. So all of it…yeah…It was a big shock."

She was given a job in the front office but left in 2003 to go to Great Vow Monastery in Oregon, where she organized a visit to Hiroshima and Nagasaki for the 60th anniversary of the bombing of those cities. It had been five years since she was last in Japan, and she took the opportunity to visit Tessai Yamamoto.

"When I went back, I decided pretty instantly to ordain with him." She had thought they might resume koan work. "But he was very adamant in saying, 'You must understand that there is absolutely no difference between shikan taza and koan practice!' He told me, 'You're too attached to the idea of koans.' So for the first year, we practiced shikan taza together. At the time, I thought he was full of shit," she says laughing, "and that he just didn't want to do dokusan because the dokusan room was so cold. He lives in a very cold place. But finally, after about a year, I convinced him to do dokusan with me again during Rohatsu sesshin. I set up the dokusan room for him; I had everything ready to go. And I found that he was exactly right. Fundamentally, there is absolutely no difference. We started over with the koans. I'd already done quite a few back in the '90s, but we started over from scratch. My teacher sent me to Soto Zen monasteries for training where there's just shikan taza with occasional exceptions. Afterwards, I had to come back to his temple to complete the koans."

"Did you find the training hard?"

"I was pretty ecstatic to do it. I mean, my teacher gave me a list of things I had to do. When we talked about ordination, he said, 'You'll have to go to the training monastery.' And I said, 'Yay!' And then he said, 'Yeah, okay, but then you're going have to do the Shikoku Pilgrimage.'[302] And I said, 'Yay! I've always wanted to do that!' My novice training was very challenging, but I was ecstatic about doing it. So, for me it wasn't a hell realm; I was quite pleased to be there."

During the time she was traveling between Japan and the US to complete her formal training, she and her husband lived in Oregon. When he was offered a job in New York City, they moved east, and she became a chaplain at New York University Medical Center. "I focus on end of life care – usually I work in hospice or palliative care – and my responsibility is to meet each patient according to their own spirituality and help them identify coping resources for meeting the challenges they're facing, particularly from a spiritual point of view."

She wears traditional Buddhist robes and shaves her head. I ask her how important these choices are. The specific robes aren't, she admits, but adds, "I do think it's important for us to be recognized as monks. I know

---

302. A pilgrimage to 88 temples on Shikoku Island.

that a lot of Westerners choose not to keep their head shaved, choose not to wear identifiable clothing, but I made a decision when I was a novice to dress like my teacher and not to let my personal choice come into it. When I entered chaplaincy training, my supervisor asked, 'Why do you need to wear this?' And I said, 'Well, you know, it's an experiment for me. So let me try my first unit of chaplaincy training, and I'll make good notes and report back to you what I experienced.' What I found is it makes me identifiable as a source of help. People recognize that on the street. I do get questions. People approach me. I don't mind. In the airport I sit next to somebody who needs to tell their story or ask questions. When people need help, they know to come to me, and that's what I'm here for. On the flip side of that, I can't turn it off. I see that as my vow, that we are in this for a lifetime. I don't want to be a part-time monk. I can't say, 'Oh, I don't feel like being a monk today. I'm going to wear lay clothes and a baseball cap.' I don't think being a monk is something we should turn off, because the vows that we take… they're very heavy, and they require a lot of responsibility. Being visible as a monk holds us to those vows and that level of responsibility."

"The foreignness of it, the fact that it's Japanese, is that ever a problem?"

"It could be, but I don't allow it to be. I have an open question policy that acknowledges, 'Hey, I look different.' And anyone is welcome to ask me things. If the question is inappropriate, I just tell them, 'That's an inappropriate question.' But 99.9 percent of the questions do not come from a mean place. People want to connect. At the hospital, as a chaplain, we come from different faith traditions, but we're trained to be available to the patients according to their spiritual practice, not ours. I learned that I have one chance for that first connection with them, and that's the moment I walk through their door. Maybe that won't be the only chance, but that's the most valuable one. I've learned not to waste my time worrying about how I look but to walk through the door and immediately meet the Buddha in front of me. I've had very few people reject my help because of the way I look. That's the same attitude I take out in the world. It's our job as priests to be available, to not accept people's projections, and to just genuinely connect."

At her Zen Center in North Westchester, she maintains the Soto forms as she had been taught them but notes, "I'm probably not as strict as my teacher, especially with beginners. I try to adapt to the situation. In my zendo, we keep the forms, but when I go out and teach somewhere else, I'm a little lighter on them. When people come to my zendo, they know what to do. I try not to get rigid about it, and I don't scold laypeople for not keeping the forms properly. I don't believe in that."

The forms, after all, are only useful if they help the practice. In the end, what's important is that the people who come "feel at home in the world, and that they feel connection and love for the people and the world around them in a way that is genuine and real."

Rinzan Pechovnik

Rinzan Pechovnik is a Rinzai priest – or "osho" – in Portland, Oregon.[303] Like Koun and Tenku, of the Soto tradition, he chooses to wear Japanese garb as a matter of course, in his case, even when meeting with patients in his psychotherapy practice. "They think it's pretty cool that their psychotherapist is also a Zen Buddhist priest," he tells me. He also has had people on the street ask what martial art he practices. "None, I tell them. I can sit still for a very long time. I can probably sit still for longer than you. But you could probably beat me up." He dresses in this manner for much the same reasons as the Soto teachers. "I'm actually quite shy about wearing this. I don't love it. But it's to model that my whole life is this religion. My whole life is. It's a life practice. And I'm willing to share it."

He grew up in Sacramento in the 1970s, a time and place where drugs were readily available to school children. "You go to the park, and you look for a circle of dudes, and you go up, and you could buy from them. It was all over the place." He says he was smoking a lot of pot by the time he was 14. "And when I say, 'a lot,' I mean a lot. I was smoking it morning, noon, night, almost every day." He was in eighth grade.

"I had a brother who was four years older than me. The summer after he graduated from high school, he died in a car wreck, and the same night that he died was the night I first got caught smoking pot. I don't know how my pot smoking went below the radar until then, but my mother caught me. So the next day, given this confluence of events, I thought, 'I can't do this to my parents. I need to stop.'

"My brother died because he was racing his car. It was traumatic and shocking. The most profound experience that came from his death was, 'This can't be wasted.' Or to put it in blunt terms, 'Don't fuck around. Life is precious so don't fuck around with it.'

"After my brother died, when I was trying not to smoke so much pot, my aunt and uncle, who were your typical '70s spiritual seekers, unloaded a couple of meditation books on me. None of them were profound. There was one supposed 'Zen' book that was just awful in terms of what it was pointing to, but all of them did point to something beyond my current suffering even if not all that clearly, and I started to meditate, because if I can't smoke pot any more, I have to do something. So I decided I'm gonna try meditation. I just sat on my own in my room. I followed my

---

303. He was scheduled to receive full Dharma transmission eight months after I spoke with him.

breath. I also did some visualization exercises, sitting and watching my thoughts float up like bubbles for a while, but mostly it was just following my breath."

He tells me that the seeds of a later practice were planted but that, at fourteen, he wasn't able to maintain the discipline. "All my friends were smoking pot and getting laid and having fun, so after a month, I started smoking pot again for about another year. Then quit smoking pot and, after some time, started to drink."

He drank alcoholically for the next seventeen years. "I tried to cut back when my children were born. Again it was something – and I'm quite clear on this – something that woke up in me that said, 'There's something really important here, and you can't just follow your fancies and your addictions and your triggers. There's something that really needs to be tended to.' A tenderness and a softness woke up in me, an awareness of the importance of raising these kids, but sadly it didn't maintain. That's the problem with addiction and alcoholism. There was the tension between wanting to be a good father, a good husband, and the craving. And the craving was winning."

In 2003, he and his family were living in Portland. He had been underemployed for years, which caused tensions in his marriage. "And I was confronted with the very real possibility that my wife was going to leave me, and my family would fall apart, this thing that was so important and that I loved. And it was immediate. It was clear. I knew I was an alcoholic, and I knew I needed to stop. And I stopped. Poured all my liquor down the drain; I haven't had a drink since."

He consulted a therapist. "My relationship was extremely fragile, and my mind was spinning. Racing thoughts. And the therapist told me, 'The first thing you need to do is you need to get a grip on your nervous system. I suggest meditation.' She gave me a book, and while I was reading it, I realized that this was something I knew about. Incredibly, I had forgotten, but it came back to me that I used to do this. So I sat, and I found that seed planted when I was fourteen years old, and it continued to open in me.

"I started consuming books, getting as much understanding of what this seed was as I could, and every book said, 'If you're going to do this, you need to find a community.'" The community he found was the Zen Community of Oregon and Great Vow Monastery. "I immediately became very devoted and very committed. I think I did my first sesshin within three months of starting to meditate. My relationship repaired, and my wife agreed to come and check out Zen Buddhism with me, and we both became very involved."

"What was it that called you to the practice?"

"It was what I had tasted when I was fourteen. I tapped into – and words will fail here – but I tapped into something that was so present, so immediate, and so shining that I knew I was home. But I couldn't stay there very well. I kept spinning out. So I decided, I'm going do the work to cultivate and develop my relationship to this…this 'just this.'"

At the same time, he began his training to become a psychotherapist. Not long after that, he was working with the homeless. "I felt a kindred spirit with them because I felt that if I hadn't had the opportunities that I'd had, given my addiction, I would have been on the streets as well."

He practiced with the Zen Community of Oregon for nine years and became a senior student. It was his only exposure to Zen, however, and he felt a need to explore what else was out there. "I looked at a couple of upcoming retreats, and I saw there was this one at Chobo-ji in Seattle." A friend knew the abbot, Genjo Marinello, and recommended him. And in Genjo, Rinzan found the teacher he needed.

"What I love about Genjo is he's so absolutely ordinary. I was almost late arriving because I couldn't find my way around Seattle. I came in, and there was the abbot. He was just sitting there as announcements were being made, no airs about him. Then he gave his Dharma talk and something shifted. He had a different presence for the Dharma talk. There were not that many people in the room, but he might have been talking to a hundred. When we were doing samu,[304] he was just this guy mowing the yard, doing samu like all the rest of us. When I went in for Dharma interview, he was very bright, friendly and connecting, and I had this wonderful feeling. I thought, 'He's pointing exactly at what I'm wanting to see. He's pointing exactly to what I know already.'

"When I came into that first interview with him, he said, 'Are you a priest?' I had a shaved head. It's because there's nothing much going on here," he says, rubbing his scalp. "So I wasn't putting on Buddhist airs. I said, 'No. I'm not a priest.' He said, 'You seem like a priest to me. Why aren't you a priest?' I said, 'I'm not willing to abandon my vows. I have vows that are real and alive, and to leave those would harm people. I won't do that.' 'I get that,' he said. 'In this community, you ordain and still live your life. You don't leave your wife. You don't leave anything. You carry the Dharma into the world. Anyway, I see a priest in you. So, welcome. One monk to another, welcome to Chobo-ji.'"

Rinzan hadn't given any thought to ordination until them, but when he talked about it with Dharma friends, "They all said, 'Yeah. I've always wondered why you're not a priest.'"

He progressed rapidly through the koan curriculum and when the time was appropriate, he ordained. His situation, however, was untraditional in Rinzai terms. "Not only am I not in a residential setting, but I'm also not close to my mother temple. So I'm not serving daily functions.

---

304. Work practice, usually maintenance activities.

Genjo wasn't concerned about it, but I wondered, 'How am I going to express this?' I sat with other communities, and none of them seemed to be the right place, so finally I decided I would rent a place, and that I was just going to hold space. If I'm there by myself, so be it. I've always admired the abbots in Japan who hold temples and continue the rituals even though they're not populated. What they're saying is, 'This is important. No matter what, I'm honoring this. This bright shining presence. I'm honoring it. I'm giving it attention. And I'll hold space, and we'll just see what happens.' I called my center No-Rank Zendo, and I've never had to sit alone."

I ask what he means by "bright shining presence," and he tells it can't be put into words. When I press him, he says, "What can you say beyond 'bright shining presence'? You know, in preparation for this interview, I asked myself, 'What's the use of Zen? Why are we doing Zen?' And I will tell you, in all honesty, there's one part of my mind that wants to help relieve suffering and give people the opportunity to practice and train in the way I've practiced and trained. There's another part of my mind that has no idea. It has absolutely no agenda for it. None whatsoever.

"From that place of 'I don't know,' all words poison it. Even 'unification' misses it. But I'll stumble around them. In the pit of the belly – what the Japanese call the 'hara' – there's a deep knowing in this 'not knowing.' Everything is shining and sparkling and speaking to us. Always. And we forget it. We are held by it continually, and we always forget. I forget; everyone forgets. So what is going to bring us back, what is going remind us and bring us back to this place? Many times, when I tap very deeply into it, it's just like, 'Oh! I remember. This is where you are! This is where you're supposed to be.' To say that the trees, and the rocks, and the earth all speak to me is true but it's also a distortion because there's a division that takes place. To say 'I'm held' doesn't feel quite right, yet it has that quality of being in relationship. But whatever it is, it is beyond us. It is so beyond us, that I don't have an agenda for it. All I'm trying to do is connect with it and give it the regard it deserves. And in the end of my days, I'll disappear, and probably in no more than half a generation no one will remember me. Then I'll be completely obliterated from this earth, never to be seen, never to be heard of again. And it doesn't even matter. It doesn't matter in quite a lovely way. There are other places where I connect with the Dharma that have to do with it bringing me peace, making me more caring, opening a tender heart. All these are part of it. But from this core part, it's simply that I don't matter, and it's completely all right. It's completely all right."

"How is your work as a psychotherapist different from what you do as a Zen teacher?"

"Maybe I need to say something more about Zen first. I think it's part of the Rinzai flavor that we're playful and earthy. We're very direct, but there's a sense of play about it. There's a sense of delight. And yet we hold these forms with dignity. It's like a dance. We're dancing through this artifice. As a psychotherapist, what we do is completely protected by four walls, and the amount of myself that I disclose is protected by that fact. And because we have a whole hour, I have an opportunity to really hear and get to know somebody and give them the opportunity to unwind. And then I find out what they need and find a way to help align them. They all know I'm a Zen Buddhist priest, but I don't introduce them to Zen or Buddhism unless they're interested. I look for what is going to help. Of course, my Zen practice and my sense of presence, my ability to be clear, all that feeds into the psychotherapeutic practice. But I'm using modalities and techniques and going to different kinds of mysteries than I would ever go to in the dokusan room."

"Would you hope for something different for your Zen students than for your patients?"

"What I want for everyone is to feel free. And by that, I don't mean 'do whatever you want,' but to be unrestrained by the burdens of their tortured minds – by dukkha. I want everyone to feel free, I don't really care how. So I don't want anything different for my Zen students and psychotherapy clients. Zen just seems to be an approach that's helpful for some."

There are students who come to Zen – much as they would to a psychotherapist – looking to be "fixed." That isn't Rinzan's approach. "If you want somebody who's going to treat you like he's a guru, and he's going to bestow wisdom on you, you're not going to get that from me. If you want that, go somewhere else. There's nothing to be given. You have it already. You might just need some help seeing it. And there are students who want this practice to bring them something specific, who say, 'I want to be enlightened so that I no longer hurt. I want to feel only love or feel only bliss. I'm not interested in any of this. I want people to be free – free to be sad and full of grief as well as to be happy and full of joy. In psychotherapy, people also want to be fixed – in terms of no longer feeling or facing what they have to face – but there's more variance in terms of what people are asking for. They might want help with their relationship or work or to deal with their traumatic past. That's something I wouldn't address as a priest, but, as a therapist, I'll tell them, 'Okay, let's get into this and figure out what's going on and see if we can create some room.' I utilize different tools, but I'm not going to help people be a certain way except in that I want to help them to be free to face this life that is full of everything exactly as they are experiencing it and being okay with that. I want both my students and clients to feel free and be able to be spontaneous, authentic, unfettered in their relationship, at work, in their life. But we use different tools in Zen than we do in psychotherapy.

"But I will add this. In all my years as a psychotherapist and in Zen training, I see a difference with regard to the depth of freedom one can experience through psychological work and through spiritual work. You could say that psychotherapy helps us to function freely as mature adults, but it doesn't necessarily get to that fundamental freedom where it is truly okay that I don't matter at all and that I will lose everything – eventually even my own life – that my life is just a dust mote, and it's beautiful and wonderful as just that. In my experience, only spiritual work leads to that."

Valerie Forstman

Valerie Forstman is one of those interviewees who needs little coaxing. No sooner have I turned on the recorder than she sets a sprinter's pace. She's one of Ruben Habito's Dharma heirs in the Sanbo Zen tradition. Currently Valerie is the Associate Dean for Admissions and Common Life at Brite, a Protestant graduate theological school on the campus of Texas Christian University, but, for many years prior, she had been a professional orchestral flutist. "Finding Zen," she tells me, "came out of my life of music."

She was living in Dallas where her husband was the principal second violinist in the Dallas Symphony. The city provided a lot of opportunity for musicians. "I was a principal flutist in a chamber orchestra and a Bach society; soon also the first-call extra with the Dallas Symphony." In 1994, she was preparing for an audition that she found particularly – her emphasis – enticing. "Preparing for an audition is rather like Olympic training. For about three months, I did all the things that I knew to do to prepare. Yet as the time came nearer, I found myself waking up in the night visited by past failures. Disappointments. And during the day, I was practicing and training in order to play a certain way at a future time. It was all oriented to that. In the process, what you might call the present moment – I'm not such a fan of that language now – became increasingly elusive. It felt like the space where the present would be was opening up like a chasm between the past and the future, and I was losing my love for playing. The week before the audition, I subbed with the Dallas Symphony and a friend said, 'Hey! How are you?' I said, 'Well, something needs to change.' I told him briefly about this sense of a gap in time and of having lost the joy of playing here and now. He said, 'I've got just the thing. Come and sit.' Just six months earlier, he had found his way to Ruben's Maria Kannon Zen Center in Dallas. I had no idea it existed.

"The audition was on that Saturday. The next Monday I was at the Zen Center for the orientation talk, and the next Wednesday for the second orientation talk. I had done spiritual practices; had had some taste of that experience, but somehow – entirely new to this practice – it felt like coming home."

That October, she attended her first sesshin. "When I arrived and saw the schedule, I thought, 'Whoa! I can't do that,' but there was no turning back. It was just wonderful, potentiating naiveté. It can be so helpful not to have a clue what you're getting into." The venue had, as she puts it, "no particular symbols. Just a small altar with a photograph of Yamada Koun Roshi, Ruben's teacher, and Yasutani Roshi, Yamada Koun's teacher, and a candle, a flower. In kinhin, we walk by this altar and might glance at it, just notice. Otherwise, it was a concrete block room that had been turned into a zendo."

On the third day of the sesshin she had an unexpected experience. "I grew up in a progressive Protestant environment. My father was a theologian, but I had not been in a church for a very long time. And I'm sitting zazen and suddenly..." – she laughs softly as if a little reluctant to proceed – "...there appears a figure before me. It's white. The sense was that this is Christ. And I heard the words, 'This is my body.'" She pauses again, then resumes, speaking much more slowly. "For a few moments, I was riveted, utterly transfixed. Then came the thought, 'That's blasphemy. This is my body?' And, of course, it all went away. I came back to breathing, following the breath. Soon the bell rang and the clackers, and we began walking kinhin. And as I passed by that altar, my eye happened to fall on the photograph, the image, of Yamada Koun Roshi, this person I knew was my teacher's teacher, a person of great respect and obviously loved by Ruben, but for me, an inscrutable Japanese face. Right? In that moment of walking by, of the eye just chancing to glance at the face, suddenly that face was flooded with an outpouring of compassion, and I knew why. Not discursively, 'Oh, I can explain this to you.' It was just compassion – boundless – just pouring out, as I was walking back to the seat. Fairly soon I was tapped for dokusan. You know, forty people, next in line. Fortunately, there were four people waiting ahead of me and one person in the dokusan room. So I sat down, sitting with the koan Mu. Just sitting there, not reflecting, but with tears coming down. By the time I got to the seat right before the door, my lap was wet. I wasn't sobbing, it was just…quiet tears. The last thought I had was, 'I'll never get this.' The bell rang, I went in, and Ruben said, 'What's happening?' And I, 'Nothing.' Then, somehow, this experience came, and I simply told him, 'Well, I was sitting and this appeared and….' He began to ask checking questions, guiding questions. And suddenly they were just answered. It just came. Just so. Right here, this world where I had been knocking on the door, with just practicing Mu, just living Mu. Early on I had run into the, 'Your discursive mind's not going to get you anywhere but a headache.' So that had fallen off. Through Ruben's skillful guidance, the world opened up, easily, freely."

She takes a deep breath, almost a sigh. "And that was just a beginning. But oh my goodness! What a relief! Of course, for each one it's so different, but there are clear characteristics that are common. This sense of walking and no one walking, or of creation coming up here and here, here, here! Totally new. Nothing at all and yet this! In some sense, it feels like a baby being born, and the protective film on the eyes falling away, things coming into view. Just getting used to that amount of light. In the beginning, it's blinding. Gradually you focus, and you see this world as it is, this world in which we can practice." She smiles and shrugs.

"I think being a musician was very helpful. There's a traditional way of laying out, in typical Asian formality, the four reasons – or initial inspirations – for coming to Zen practice. These are curiosity, peace of mind or well-being, seeking a spiritual path or practice, and 'hair on fire.' I happened to come with 'hair on fire.' I'm not sure I'd have realized this without that audition, in which I ended up as runner-up. Had that not happened, it's likely life would have still been full of Zen, but it was a glorious failure. I'm really grateful as it happened."

"What do you mean by 'hair on fire'?"

"It's asking this fundamental question – and I think this is a point where Sanbo Zen differs from many of the practices that are finding roots and flourishing in the west – asking this fundamental question, 'Who am I? What is this life? What is it to be human? What is of ultimate value?' Again, with Ruben, because of the timing, I hadn't had the last introductory talk, so I didn't know what to expect when I went to dokusan. I just sat down and said my name. He asked, 'Why are you here?' And it just leapt out without a moment to figure out what to say, 'I want to be my true self.' It was the heartfelt, honest, naked truth. You can imagine the kind of suffering expressed in that longing, and yet how crazy is that? To want to be who you are? In a sense, it's Dogen's question: 'If from the beginning all beings are awakened...' – you know, if that's our nature – '...why do we have to practice?' Why can't we see it?"

Valerie's teacher, Ruben Habito, is a former Jesuit who remains a practicing Catholic as well as a Zen Teacher. Valerie is identified as one of the teachers at his Maria Kannon Zen Center in Dallas. When I interviewed Ruben for another book, he explained the significance of the Maria Kannon image to me.

"The image of compassion in Buddhism is Kannon, of course, and, in the West, it's Maria. Also Maria Kannon is a figure from the period in Japanese history when the Christians were persecuted, and they could no longer profess their faith openly, so they had to destroy or hide all their images of Jesus or the Holy Family or of the Virgin Mother that were of Western origin. So they found this feminine image of compassion in the Buddhist figure of Kannon, and they put it up on their altar and would recite the rosary before it. For them, it was Mary, the Mother of Jesus, but it was Kannon in public understanding.

"It's really Mary who stood at the foot of the cross of Jesus. The Stabat Mater is the image of Mary's compassion, bearing the wounds of her own son who bears the wounds of the world. So that compassion, of bearing the wounds of the world, is what is seen as the place of intersection with Kannon in the Buddhist tradition. And so there is the hope that we have that those who sit in Zen are able to activate that seed of compassion in them symbolized by Mary and by Kannon."

And then there are the facts that Valerie's father is a theologian and that she had had a vision of Christ during her first sesshin, so I ask if she still considers herself a Christian.

"I am reluctant to use those labels, but when asked, I would say Buddhist-Christian."

"The Dalai Lama once said that that amounted to trying to put a sheep's head on a yak's body."

"Yeah," she says, trying to find a way to express herself. "It's a construct. It doesn't really speak to my experience. Some time ago, I heard a lovely teacher, Susan Postal, speak to this in a more living way. She said, 'It's like being transfused by these two traditions.' So it's not one head and another body, it's just that the bloodstream is fed, is nurtured. If somebody said to me, 'You must pick a path,' and if Zen counted as one of the choices, there's no question for me that this is where I will go. At the same time, I work here, at Brite, with my whole heart. I love these students. I appreciate the chance to sort of swim around in Christian language and to practice and explore the connections between traditions. Thankfully we don't have to choose. Each tradition is replete, whole."

Chimyo Atkinson

Great Tree Zen Temple in North Carolina is specifically intended to be a women's residential center. The teacher is Teijo Munnich, a former Roman Catholic nun who became a disciple and, later, an heir of Dainin Katagiri. In 2018 there were several guests at the temple but only two permanent residents, Teijo and Chimyo Atkinson. Chimyo tells me that her official position is Head of Practice. When I ask what that means, she says, "I'm basically the…well…everything. Ino [manager], chiden [caretaker], tenzo [cook], tanto [assistant to the teacher], everything, because there's only two of us living here. So I basically do stuff that needs to be done, and she does stuff that needs to be done as teacher."

She grew up in New York City and attended Barnard College where she took a course on comparative religions that included an introduction to meditation. She tells me it was "stillness" that interested her in the practice. "Which can be misinterpreted as some kind of peace or whatever. The idea of just stopping and being still. To be able to stop the whirlwind for a second felt good, and that drew me to it. It was not necessarily a religious experience at that point, it was more a way of self-preservation in the environment I was in, to be able to stop and relax a little, just stop the noise."

It was a stressful time in her life. In addition to attending classes, she was working at the New York Public Library. "I was an 18-year-old and not really prepared for the responsibilities of being on my own. Running from class to class, running to work, dealing with money on my own for the first time. Those kinds of things. You know? Growing up. It was tough. Although academically I might have been ready, I was not mature enough or socially prepared."

She tried to follow the instructions she'd received in the course. "I did what I thought was meditation. It helped. It was a mental health kind of exercise, and it did help. Until it didn't."

She eventually left college to work full time. "At the library and later at a trucking company, doing secretarial work, that kind of thing." At the same time she attended events at the New York Open Center. "It was a New-Agey sort of place where they had a little meditation room. They did some meditation classes and things around meditation. Not exactly Buddhism. So little things like that."

In 1989, Chimyo moved from New York to be with her grandmother in North Carolina. "She was Baptist, and I did attend church with her a little bit when I first came down, but it just really wasn't my thing. It was a very conservative kind of church. The men were all in charge and said things like, 'Women should be obedient.'" She laughs at the memory. "And young people weren't attending anymore."

As it turned out, there were a number of Buddhist communities in North Carolina, and Chimyo eventually learned about Sandy Gentei Stewart's Squirrel Mountain Zendo. "I went to one of his weekends and met some folks that were starting a sitting group in Charlotte, near where I lived and worked. They introduced me to the Charlotte Zen Meditation Society. It was an eclectic group. There was one Maezumi person, one Katagiri person, one person who'd been to India. It was just everybody. And it was all guys." She laughs again; she laughs easily throughout our conversation. "It was all guys at that time."

Teijo was invited to give a talk to the group in 1991. "It was the first time I saw her, and she had this aura about her, a quiet sort of calm, which attracted me. She spoke very humbly about her experience. She spoke about what had happened to her and her interpretation of it. It was a very human sort of thing. It wasn't as if it was some person who had come to hand something down to you. It wasn't cerebral; it wasn't anything bookish. It was very authentic, is how it felt. And she was friendly. She smiled a lot. She was not what I expected. She was different, and it felt real, and it felt like something that I could connect with."

Teijo became the teacher for the Charlotte Zen Meditation Society. The community was – and remains – small. Chimyo estimates there is a core group of about twelve. "There were other people who were kind of satellites, but it was a large enough group that we could set up our own sesshins and have weekend events and things." And when the Society offered participants an opportunity to take jukai and formally enter the Buddhist community, Chimyo took advantage of it.

"Why?" I ask.

"Why? No clear idea. It was kind of a group thing. As a group, we had been practicing together since the beginning, for three or four years. We had done some study together, and it felt like the thing to do. It was sort of like a community congealing around that jukai."

"If someone asked you, at the time, 'Are you a Buddhist?' What would you have said?"

"Well, I recall being somewhat reluctant to commit to a religion at that time. So I probably would have said, 'I don't know.' And I didn't. I didn't know."

"And if your Baptist Grandmother had asked you what you were doing with this group of people?"

"I would have said these are my friends. They're nice people. We talk about philosophy, and we talk about Buddhism, and we talk about – how did I put it one time? – 'walking with clarity.' Being clear. Trying to be clear about where you stand in the world, how you act in the world. And what I probably meant at that time was 'being right.' Doing the right thing."

Her decision to ordain came in 2007.

"So somewhere along the line you decided you were a Buddhist after all," I suggest.

"Yeah. I think so." Then she chuckles. "I remember at one point, Teijo was giving dokusan at Harmony House where the Charlotte Zen people meet, sitting on this old porch, and I remember asking her about ordination and asking her about being a monk, and not knowing at all what that meant. I'd maybe seen a film about monastic life and probably had some romantic ideas. And I probably wanted to escape a lifestyle that wasn't working for me."

"In what way?"

She considers a moment before answering. "North Carolina's very conservative. You do certain things, and your life is supposed to look a certain way. You're supposed to have a car, and you're supposed to have certain type of clothing. You're supposed to want to buy a house. Because at that time there was all this language about entrepreneurship and home-ownership and the rising middle class, particularly in the black community. The move from poverty to the middle class and all of that. And none of it seemed to apply to me. I tried to do it. You know? I had a couple of cars. And I had a car payment, and I had school loan payments, and I had all these things that I was paying for but getting no satisfaction out of." She smiles. "And nobody that I was living around or working around was seeming to get any satisfaction out of it either. I was supposed to want all of these things that were not really attractive to me at all, and thinking something was wrong. You know, you think something's wrong with you when everybody else is going in this direction, and you're just kind of looking and not wanting it. There's nothing wrong in wanting any of those things. That's not what I'm saying, but basically it didn't fit what my heart wanted. So this idea of becoming a monk was very attractive, and I talked to her about it. And, of course, nothing came of it, because she probably didn't take me seriously at that time." She laughs heartily. "Thank God! Because I wouldn't have been ready for that either. So the idea of ordaining was around for a long time before I actually did it."

"What did you understand that step to mean when you did take it?"

"Didn't understand it at all. I'm still working it out."

Around the turn of the millennium, Teijo had the idea of establishing a Zen Temple for women. She had male students, and men would be welcome to attend sesshin and workshops at the new temple, but her vision was of a center dedicated to women's practice. In an interview given in 2002, she explained that the focus on women was not as the result of a feminist perspective per se – "I don't have that particular bent" – but arose from a recognition that women and men often approached practice differently. "Shikan taza is the purest spiritual practice that I've found because it helps one really look deeply at what life is. And this is what I have pursued over the last 27 years, so I have kind of an idea of what it's about. But one of the things I have discovered in the course of my pursuit is that the traditional style of Dogen's Zen appeals very much to men, and has been developed by men, and so has a very male quality about it. And I've felt for a long time that somehow the feminine expression of Zen practice has not been embodied within the practice itself. I like the simplicity of Zen practice, and I don't want to approach it by saying, 'Okay now, what is the feminine?' I don't want to approach it in that way. The way I want to approach it is by putting women together, doing zazen and seeing what happens – doing zazen, studying and working together, which are the three components that Dogen Zenji suggests, and see what happens."[305]

When the Great Tree Zen Women's Temple was established in Asheville – 120 miles west of Charlotte – Chimyo joined Teijo in residence there.

"Our mission at Great Tree Zen Women's Temple," Chimyo tells me, "states that it's a way of allowing the feminine to manifest itself in this practice in a way some may not have been allowed to in the past – ancient and recent – simply because, as in anything in society, it's kind of dominated by men. And so the feminine aspect of what Zen could look like hasn't – maybe – been nurtured as much as it needed to be or celebrated as much as it needed to be. So here's a place where, because it is centered on women and women's practice, you see what comes up, what it looks like, and how is it different – if at all – from the way men's practice manifests itself. That doesn't mean that it's going to be different, but we're trying to give it a chance to develop and be what it can be. Nobody knows what that is yet."

"And the women who come there," I ask, "what are they looking for?"

"I think they're looking for compassion and empathy. I think they're looking for a place where they feel comfortable and safe in doing their spiritual practice, whatever that is. They have a sort of a sense of community with us and in a non-intellectual way. We do our study groups and so on, and we can get heady in those study groups, but I think – mostly because of Teijo – I think they feel a warmth and a nurturing here that is maybe unusual at some American Zen centers. People tell us that we are warm and welcoming. That comes from Teijo's personality. She's very outgoing, very personable, a very enthusiastic, optimistic person. It's not harsh, this sort of standoffishness that a lot of Zen people look like they're doing.

"People have this incomplete idea of what Zen is, and I think they come sometimes looking for that. The sort of peace, bliss, kind of thing. I think the people that stick around are looking for community and looking for a place to be that is open, where they don't feel judged, and can just have a conversation about anything, really, with people who care.

"We do emphasize the sitting," she adds. "Our main practice is shikan taza, but it's also being able to be with each other and comfort each other when we need to."

"Is there a connection between shikan taza and the capacity to develop compassion and empathy?" I ask.

"Well, the whole point of doing this practice is to develop compassion, to develop that sense of interconnectedness and empathy for each other. That's where the clarity comes from, so that you can act

---

305. https://www.greattreetemple.org/about-gtzt/our-teacher/original-vision/

from that compassion, so that you can act from that understanding of connectedness."

"Suppose someone showed up for the first time," I say, "maybe a little timid, feeling a little cautious about something that she hasn't encountered before, and when you introduce her to meditation practice, she asks, 'What's this going to do? How is this going to make me more compassionate?' How do you respond?" Chimyo doesn't immediately answer, so I go on: "Maybe she just needs some kind of assurance, needs her anxieties assuaged a little bit before she can commit to trying this."

"I can't give you that assurance. Because it is your experience that will bring that about. And maybe this is or is not the practice for you, or maybe this is or is not the practice for you at this time. Everybody has a door. You know? We are here to help you find that door. There is no guarantee. There is no goal here and no instruction that we can give you other than sit down and experience the world. You know, how do you tell someone how to 'go in and go through' in Zen practice?" She laughs. "That's all I can say. You sit down, and you sit with your fears and you sit with your discomfort and you sit with your dukkha and all that and you work with it. Well, first you recognize it, and then you work with it. What you're doing on that cushion, I cannot say. All I can say to a person who comes to Great Tree is to sit down and try it. We're here with you. We're here trying to do the same thing as you are, whether we are wearing robes or not, whether we've been sitting for twenty years or since yesterday, this is it. Just put in the effort and that's it."

When I try to push the point by asking what, in that case, the Temple has to offer that can't be found at a dozen alternate places, she laughs again and says, "Not a thing. What do we offer? We offer you a cushion and a room to sit in. That's it. I mean, what else can we say? We offer you a cushion in a room and our support in doing this, our support and empathy in doing this practice. We offer the guidance that comes from our experience, which is just our experience. Nothing that is magical or scientific or any of those things. Just our experience. And a little faith in the Buddha's word that there is a way beyond suffering."

"And where would you hope that led? What is your hope for the women who come here?"

"I hope that they are able to find their way to a lifelong practice in this tradition or any other. I'm hoping that they find a refuge with us. I'm hoping that they find a way to share their own wisdom in the world, because that's part of it. A lot of times in a de facto male-dominated situation, women are reluctant or not encouraged or outright prevented from sharing the wisdom that they have. And I hope that I myself can learn from whoever walks in that door, because everybody brings something. Whether they practice forever or whether they're just discovering it."

"A lifelong practice to what end?"

"To what end? To relieving their suffering and the suffering in the world."

"Not awakening or kensho or whatever you want to call it?"

"You can find those things, but compassion and benefit to the world, what else is there? What else is there?"

The practice master of East Mountain said, "Shakyamuni and Maitreya are both the servants of another. Just say, who is this other?"

45th Case in the Mumonkan

Epilogue at Springwater

BUDDHIST SCRIPTURES emphasize that birth in the human sphere is rare and even more so is the opportunity to encounter the Dharma. The arising of Buddhas is rarer yet, and their teachings must inevitably fade with the passing of time. In the Mahayana tradition, however, Shakyamuni Buddha predicted that although his teachings would eventually be forgotten, a future Buddha – Maitreya – would arise to restore them to humankind. Perhaps in some sense, that prediction has already been realized.

North American Zen is as little like the Zen of Japan as Japanese Zen and Chinese Chan are like early Indian Buddhism. The Buddhadharma has been evolving not just for centuries but for millennia, fading in one region to find new life and strength in another. Almost extinguished in the land of its birth, it was revived and re-energized by contact with Daoism in China; so too, today, as it is on the wane in Japan, it appears to have discovered new vigor and form in the West.

Jeff Shore is the sole non-Japanese full-time professor at Hanazono University in Kyoto, the only Rinzai University in the world. He teaches what he calls "Blue-eyed Zen." Formal Zen training in Japan is arduous, and many of the students at the university are bewildered by why Americans and Europeans have any interest in it. "Westerners look at Zen in a very peculiar way," he tells me. "For the average Japanese priest, who – for the last hundred years could be married and have a son, and then his son would enter the monastery whether he wanted to or not – it's a very different system. A lot of those sons don't want to be priests, but they have to be. And then here's people like us coming half way around the world. We're not even going to become priests; we're not going to have a temple. And yet we're putting ourselves through this. And they wonder, 'Why?'"

"So you're teaching Japanese students how westerners view Zen?"

"More or less, yes. What do we see that they don't?"

What Westerners have seen in Buddhism and Zen has often been distorted by their personal interests. Sixteenth century Jesuits, 19th century Theosophists, the Beats, and the Counter Culture of the '60s and '70s each imagined Zen to be something very different from what Americans like Robert Aitken, Philip Kapleau, and Koun Franz encountered in Japan. Actual Zen practice in North America is still less than 100 years old. The first authorized teacher to make his home here was Sokei-an Sasaki who didn't begin teaching until 1928. So, as I noted in an earlier book, it is fair to say that Zen is still finding its way on this continent. It's also fair to say that so far it has not been a smooth ride.

The efforts of pioneers like Kapleau, Shunryu Suzuki, and Taizan Maezumi did establish Zen in North America, but it's a Zen which Jeff Shore's students have reason to find bewildering. In his 2002 study, *The New Buddhism*, James William Coleman described the situation this way:

> When Asian Buddhists visit the West, they are often confused by Western practitioners they meet. Not really monks but far more involved and dedicated than most laypeople, Western practitioners are hard to classify with the categories their teachers imported from the East.... All in all, the distinction between the monk and the layperson in [Western] Buddhism is a fuzzy one. Monks are not set off by an aura of holiness and reverence as they are in Asia. Although their practice is usually more highly focused, they are not really doing anything that isn't common among the laity as well. In one sense everyone is a kind of monk, and in another no one is.[306]

Zen was the first Buddhist tradition, outside ethnic communities, to establish itself in North America. It has since been followed by Theravada Buddhism, Vipassana Buddhism, and several Tibetan variants. What all of these have in common, as Coleman points out, is their commitment to meditation, which is largely a monastic – rather than a lay – practice in traditionally Buddhist countries. The youth who flocked to centers during the Zen boom of the '70s and '80s were driven not by an interest in Buddhist theory but in the potential of spiritual insight through meditation that had been promised by writers like D. T. Suzuki, Alan Watts, and Philip Kapleau. Because their practice was often disconnected from the philosophical and ethical framework of Buddhism, the atmosphere of places like ZCLA in the early days was – as Chozen Bays put it – as much that of a hippie-commune as a Buddhist monastery.

---

306. James William Coleman. *The New Buddhism* (New York: Oxford University Press, 2002), pp. 13-14.

Over time the numbers diminished; centers became smaller, but they also proliferated. The word Zen was accepted into the English language, with connotations suggesting a wide range of things which often had little to do with actual Zen practice. In a curious way, meditation, Buddhism, and Zen became mainstream.

But while the concept of Zen has entered western consciousness, the number of individuals who have ever practiced Zen, even briefly, remains small. I pointed out in *Cypress Trees in the Garden* that far more people have read about Zen than have spent any time at a Zen Center. Thomas Tweed of the University of Notre Dame refers to these as "night-stand Buddhists." "A few may practice on their own without the aid of a teacher," I wrote; "some might even claim to be 'Zennists.' The number of North Americans, however, who actually profess to be Buddhists, let alone Zen Buddhists, remains miniscule; 0.7 percent of the population in the United States, according to 2007 census data; the figure is slightly higher (1.1 percent) in Canada. But those percentages include all forms of Buddhism. The total number of 'Zen Buddhists' in North America can probably be described as 'statistically inconsequential.'"

I could have also added that it is not a particularly diverse community. From its beginnings on this continent, Zen has primarily appealed to college-educated whites. There are Asian practitioners, although not as many as one would expect for a tradition that originated in China and Japan. There are also black and Latino practitioners, some of whom – like Seiho and Chimyo – have ordained. Still, it was striking, while visiting some fifty Zen Centers and Temples throughout the US and Canada, how seldom I saw persons of color.

A number of factors contribute to this situation. Valerie Forstman identified "privilege (it takes time to sit and transportation to sit together), disparities in education, and cultural norms." Mike Fieleke and Bob Waldinger both mentioned center location. "Newton," Mike points out, "is a primarily white, wealthy city. So we now also sit monthly in Waltham, which is more diverse, in part in hopes of offering access to a wider population." But, he adds, that effort has just begun, "so we've yet to see whether this will work."

"I think often of how few newcomers we get at Zen Nova Scotia," Koun Franz reflects, "and of those, how many stick around. Of those who do, how many might realistically ordain – possibly none? If one does, what are the chances of that person actually training all the way through to full ordination, where they can teach autonomously? Chances of getting to that point are close to zero. Then go back and do the same math, but factor in that it's a person of color. And the problem of racial diversity won't be meaningfully addressed until more people of color are not just in sanghas but in leadership and teaching positions. There are lots of people now who are sincere about trying to address that gap, but it's really hard to do. And, of course, there are also a lot of people who aren't serious about it at all, who believe that they, as Buddhists, don't see color, or who believe that Buddhism is, at its roots, supposed to be elitist, so it will just naturally mirror other elitist/exclusionary institutions."

"My feeling is that convert white Zen communities should practice becoming aware of our own privilege and internalized racism," Mike goes on to say, "and we can make an effort to address these issues in ourselves and in our communities. But facing the problem can feel quite overwhelming at first, so we need lots of support and incremental paths to engage. So we are taking steps to address the issue, but we have a lot more to do both in my sangha and in the larger sangha of Zen practitioners in America, in recognizing systemic racism in America as a huge cause of suffering, strengthening outreach to diverse communities, bringing along more teachers of color, and maybe even opening up our forms so that they appeal to people of color. It is not exactly clear to me what role white folks can play in each of these goals, but for me now, listening deeply and engaging in affinity groups seems like a good start."

Mike also believes that there are other issues about which contemporary Buddhists need to be concerned. "I think our environmental crisis is an essential thing for us to address. How can we vow to save all beings and ignore the trauma of racism in America and the mass extinction of species? Only if we practice with our heads in the sand."

In most Zen Centers and temples, there are rituals associated with entering and leaving the meditation hall, or zendo. Generally, one bows, as a sign of respect, before entering. In some places, one also bows to one's cushions – the zafu (Buddha-seat) on which one seeks enlightenment – and perhaps to the other persons in the hall, in order to thank them for their support. Likewise it is traditional, when leaving the zendo, to turn and face back into the hall and bow in gratitude. At the Montreal Zen Center – where I did much of my formal Zen study – there is a variation. Instead of facing the zendo when leaving, one faces out. The idea is that whatever insight one achieves in the meditation hall needs to be taken into the wider world where one lives and acts.

Awakening – kensho – is at least in part a direct experience of one's interdependence not only with other persons but with all of being. Bowing out when leaving the zendo recognizes that that insight has consequences. In it effect, it asserts that awakening is not an end in itself; it asserts that it's pointless to achieve awareness if that awareness doesn't impact the way in which we live.

Epilogue at Springwater

From its beginnings in North America, Zen has called upon practitioners not only to be aware of their oneness with the rest of being but to behave accordingly. The recognition that humans are part a complex ecological pattern including both the sentient and non-sentient worlds has been a recurrent theme in the work of early Zen explorers like Gary Snyder and Robert Aitken, who wrote, "If our zazen has no application in daily life, then we are simply indulging in cultist tricks."[307]

The Rochester Zen Center holds "Earth Vigils," similar to Bernie Glassman's "Bearing Witness" activities, in which members publicly sit in zazen to give witness to environmental concerns. The current abbot, Bodhin Kjolhede Roshi, explains that one of the natural functions of zazen is "to see through the dualistic concepts that give rise to racism, environmental harm, and the many forms of tribalism that plague the world today. It's all in Sengcan's *Xinxin Ming*,[308] which we chant every day and try live up to: 'Not two!'"

The Vietnamese Zen[309] teacher, Thich Nhat Hanh, is one of the most widely known and celebrated Buddhist leaders in the world. At the center of his teaching is an awareness of what he calls "inter-being." He challenges his followers to examine the consequences of the consumer-based lifestyle common in west and to contrast it with the possibility of living mindfully in harmony with both one another and the physical environment. He tells his students that they need to face the very real possibility that a failure to address environmental issues honestly and directly could result in a human-caused mass extinction event.

"Civilisations have been destroyed many times and this civilisation is no different. It can be destroyed. We can think of time in terms of millions of years and life will resume little by little. The cosmos operates for us very urgently, but geological time is different. If you meditate on that, you will not go crazy. You accept that this civilisation could be abolished and life will begin later on after a few thousand years because that is something that has happened in the history of this planet. When you have peace in yourself and accept, then you are calm enough to do something, but if you are carried by despair there is no hope."[310]

One of the attractions of Zen is that it is a well-established practice which has proven, over the course of centuries, capable of leading people to awakening. The thing that – as Rinsen Weik puts it – raises the hair

---

307. Robert Aitken, *The Gateless Barrier* (New York: North Point Press, 1997), p. 223.
308. Pages 135-36, above.
309. *Thien* in Vietnamese.
310. https://www.theguardian.com/sustainability/environment-zen-buddhism-sustain-

on his beard "is when people who have no access to this from any other thing other than their own zazen, their own Dharma eyes, have the same response to these koans" as students of previous ages. The student who today successfully resolves Hakuin's "one hand clapping" will give the same reply as Hakuin's students 250 years ago.

Zen, however, is not static. It has had to adapt itself to expectations of different generations and cultures, and – one hopes – will continue to do so. Today, as Koun Franz tells me, questions surrounding issues such as diversity and environmental awareness are huge, and, if younger people are to be attracted to the practice, these are matters that will need to be addressed credibly.

I don't doubt that this will occur. The process of self-assessment and adjustment which has taken place just in the first two decades of this century demonstrate Zen's continuing capacity to evolve. When I began the series of interviews which were the basis of *Cypress Trees in the Garden*, teachers throughout North America were undertaking a deep and honest re-evaluation of Zen, and almost all the centers I visited either had or were in the midst of having a series of reflections which brought about new administrative structures and guidelines.

There was a change in focus when Buddhism moved from India to China. Originally Buddhism was a practice designed to overcome suffering. That was the goal that Shakyamuni sought when he abandoned his wife and newborn son. He ultimately found the way to the alleviation of suffering after his great awakening, and his followers committed themselves to following the path that he defined for that purpose. The Chinese Daoists who first encountered the Buddhadharma found the teaching intriguing didn't buy the first noble truth, so in China – and later Japan – Chan and Zen focused less on the philosophy which was derived from the Buddha's awakening than on that awakening itself. The goal was not so much to understand and follow the Buddha's teachings as it was to attain the same insight he'd had that led to his formulation of the Four Noble Truths and the Eightfold Path.

The teachers who brought Zen practice to North America emphasized the priority of kensho. Many of the students who filled Zen Centers during what I have referred to as the Zen Boom were drawn by the possibility of awakening, although only a few were driven – "hair on fire" – by the burden of suffering. But as kensho proved elusive for many, or

---

ability. If one identifies not just with one's species – much less one's race, nation, or community – but with all of being, that practice isn't as morbid as it may seem on first encounter.

the effort to attain it too strenuous, lesser attainments became sufficient. Philip Kapleau was particularly critical of this type of student, one who settled for less than what the practice was capable of achieving. He told them, "you won't open your Mind's eye no matter how often you do zazen or how many sesshins you attend. All you will gain is a certain calmness of body and clarity of mind, and while these qualities are not inconsequential, they are as different from enlightenment as chalk is from cheese. The ultimate aim of Zen training is full awakening, not serenity or high-energy states which are only by-products of zazen."[311]

Today, contemporary teachers tell me it is precisely for things like stress reduction that people now come to Zen. They add, however, that kensho still occurs even when it isn't the immediate goal of the student. In a curious way, Zen practice in the West is once more directly focused on the Buddha's path for alleviating suffering.

When I was a high school student in Indiana during the early 1960s, the only reference to meditation I remember encountering was a warning posted in the glass case in front of a Baptist Church – where the subject of the coming Sunday's sermon was announced – to the effect that meditation clears the mind so that the Devil can come in and take it over. Today, the benefits of meditation are touted by psychologists, medical professionals, and even Protestant ministers. Businesses provide stipends for their employees to attend mindfulness seminars, confident that it will enhance productivity.

The teachers I spoke with for this book – chosen in part because they were younger than me and so could be assumed to represent those who will carry the teaching forward – were largely advocates of a more conservative Zen than the one I'd been introduced to. The meditation they teach is not just a stand-alone technique but an element of a wider Buddhist practice. They often insist on ritual and appropriate dress, on a designated and dedicated clergy. They still have a reverence for Japanese structures which may have as much to do with aesthetics as with spirituality. I find it odd that they still – when they take a Dharma name – take Japanese names. The Japanese don't take Chinese names, nor did the Chinese take Indian names.[312]

There are ways in which Zen can be more formal than other meditative traditions in the west. And there is the danger that that can lead to a type of institutionalism wherein the preservation of the integrity of the in-

---

311. Quoted in John Daido Loori (ed.), *Sitting with Koans* (Boston: Wisdom Publications, 2006), p. 306.

312. When he first came to Nebraska, Dosho Port – whose Dharma name means "Identity

stitution becomes at least as important as what that institution is doing. In the course of writing this book, I encountered representatives from both Rinzai and Soto Zen who wanted to have some say over the content of the work as a whole before agreeing to participate.

In the history of Zen, there have been many notable reformers – from Hakuin to Harada and Yasutani – whose challenges to orthodox institutionalism have revitalized the tradition. So while I suspect that the formal institutions are the most likely vehicle by which Zen teaching and practice will be carried into the future, it is worth keeping in mind that there are other, less orthodox, routes the teaching could potentially follow.

Wayne Coger is the administrator of the Springwater Center for Meditative Inquiry. The post, he explains, deals primarily with physical operations. He's not the equivalent of an abbot – if the center had such a position – but is rather the person to whom an abbot would delegate matters such as making certain that insurance information is up to date, that bills are paid on time, and that the septic system is operating properly.

Springwater isn't affiliated with any formal teaching lineage. Wayne describes it as, "Zen without all of the trappings." It is one of the most extreme Zen experiments I am aware of.

There hasn't been a principal teacher at Springwater since Toni Packer's death, but there is a Teaching Committee to which Wayne belongs. Its members, he tells me, "are all equals among equals. We still are taking our cue from Toni who did not consider herself to be a teacher. So we're working together, and we're working with the people who come to retreat. And there's a presumption that the person giving the talks at the retreat is a person who has something to say, speaking not from an attempt to enhance themselves or for personal gain, but has a feeling for the work and is able to communicate that." The core members of that group are still individuals whom Toni had identified as being able to carry on the work. To that extent, one can consider them – although they wouldn't necessarily view themselves in these terms – her Dharma Heirs.

The elements Rinsen Weik described as basic to Zen structure are all here: "There's a teacher. You practice. You meet with the teacher in dokusan. You get guidance. You work on this stuff. It gets better." The interviews aren't called "dokusan" at Springwater, and the issue of "getting better" would probably be regarded with suspicion here – as it would at other centers – but I know what he means.

---

with Life" – tried for a while to use the Anglicized version, but it didn't catch on. On one occasion when a student was looking for him, she kept repeating in a sweet voice, "I've lost my Identity."

Epilogue at Springwater

When I first visited Springwater, in 2013, it struck me that the majority of the participants were people roughly in my age group (in their 60s and 70s) who appeared to know one another fairly well, as if they had been attending retreats together for a long time. According to Wayne, six years later that demographic has begun to change.

"We're seeing a new generation of people who are coming back. People quickly go from being the person who's new to someone who's coming back fairly frequently. The majority are under 45, which I consider young."

He tells me that "the majority of people who come for the first time do so because they were looking on-line for a retreat or a silent retreat or someplace to meditate or to learn about meditation."

Wayne was one of the students who had followed Toni Packer when she left Rochester. I ask him what had originally led him to Kapleau's Zen Center. He chuckles and says, "It's hard to answer that question without some kind of hindsight enhancement, but I had serious questions about, we'll say, the meaning of life, and I thought that Zen might be the place to explore those questions."

"Were you looking for enlightenment?"

"Yes. The presumption was that 'enlightenment' was what would answer those questions."

"And the new people who find you on Google, what are they looking for?"

As I remember from our previous conversations, Wayne is a cautious speaker. "It would be hard to speak for anyone or everyone, but I will say that a lot of us don't really know what we're looking for. One thing I do hear people talking about is wanting 'peace of mind' or less anxiety, less stress, or a way to be with stress that is actually helpful. Maybe that is a little different, because I think when I came to the Rochester Zen Center people were either postponing or throwing off their careers and were really throwing themselves whole-heartedly into this meditative work. I see a little – and, again, this is very speculative – but I see people often suffering from their careers, from the stresses, and from the stress of trying to make a living, and wanting a breather. And maybe having space to re-examine how they're relating to the world, and how they're relating with their friends, their family. But I think in some ways the essence is the same."

"And why come to you rather than attend a local mindfulness seminar or go to a yoga studio? If they're Googling, they didn't just come up with you; they came up with 95 other options as well."

"A lot of times people will say that they like the idea that they're not committing to a religious system – to a hierarchy – where someone will tell them what to do. They like that freedom to explore for themselves. And we get people here who also go to the mindfulness group or the yoga center, but they're looking for a place where they can go for a week and deepen and quiet. I have had people tell me they're intrigued by something that they read on the website – since we do provide a lot of content – and that what they read really made sense to them. I think in some ways it's what attracted me when I had read some of what Toni had written, that there is interest in looking for oneself and seeing how we are and seeing how we relate with others. And I am amazed that people who do find their way here often feel that they've found the right place. So, however we filter this or however we phrase it, it's interesting that they find we are offering something that they might not have gotten out of a more traditional or structured environment."

"You don't think you're providing an environment?"

"I would say that rather than an environment, we're providing an invitation to discover oneself. To discover. There was a woman who came to the May retreat, and she used a word that I hadn't heard people use before. She said she liked to explore. So I believe that's what we're offering; the opportunity to explore . . . I started to say 'to explore oneself,' but just to explore and 'to aware,' to be aware."

"But you provide that opportunity in a particular environment. One isn't doing this alone in one's apartment somewhere. You provide a set and setting."

"Right. We're providing support and the presence of others who have a similar interest. And not just that. We have a facility; we have land that is conducive to what we are doing here."

"So, an environment."

He concedes the point with a smile. "There's something about a place that's well cared for," he admits, "about people that are attentive and friendly – for the most part – that is supportive. And there's something about that first night of a retreat, when you're sitting with someone else – like you say, as opposed to sitting in your apartment or in your house, in your basement where your family won't find you, sneaking off somewhere – that's very supportive. So I'll go with that word, 'environment'; that it's a supportive environment and a shared energy. It's palpable. I couldn't prove it, but it's something one can feel."

"And what happens in that environment?"

He gives the question some thought. "I can't speak for anyone else, or in the most basic way of what brings them to this work, but for me it's an opportunity to work with oneself and to work with others, to be with oneself and to be with others, to explore, to question, and to quieten. And to see what arises. And this seeing, to me, is really the heart of this work. To see how we are in a kind of unvarnished way. Untainted, as far as possible, by our memories, by our desires, the way we want to appear, the way we want to be seen by others. Just to sit quietly, and to be with others, and see what comes up. And in that seeing, it's noticed here, that there's a quieting.

And I think that quieting is part of the environment that you're speaking of. It's a very tangible thing. And in the talks, and in the meetings, and in the quiet sittings, we can begin to clarify, to let some of the extraneous and the superficial stuff we live with most of the time fall away. And I think this is a very rare and precious thing in this world. I'll put it that way. That there is this invitation, there is this opportunity, and nobody's forcing you to do it, nobody's really telling you how to do it, how to clarify, how to sit, how to be. It's really up to one to discover this for oneself. And I think that's both the difficulty and the opportunity of a place like this."

There is no Buddhist or other religious iconography at Springwater. There are, however, elements familiar from more traditional zendos. Zafus and zabutons are available for those who wish them, but there are people who choose to spend the scheduled sitting period sitting in lounge chairs and looking through the windows at the grounds, where I once spent a sitting watching deer graze in the fields. The atmosphere at a week-long retreat is more relaxed than sesshin. People can change position during the periods. No one chides them for having a bottle of water on the mat beside them. The traditional formalities, Wayne tells me, aren't necessary. "And that's not to be critical of someone who finds that necessary. What we are doing here has been an on-going experiment. Can this be done? Or can it evolve, can it unfold without the formal trappings of a religious organization? Can there be religion without religion?"

"Human beings, of course, are enormously capable of self-deception," I point out. "So how do people initiate this reflection you're describing without some formal structure?

"Do formal structures keep us from self-deception?"

"Fair enough. So let's look at it this way. I'm someone who's found you on Google. And because I'm suspicious of Buddhists, and I gave up on Christianity a long time ago, I'd like to find out what you have to offer, so I come out for a day. And it would probably be natural for me to ask you, 'What do I do?' And what do you tell me?"

"Do nothing."

I can't help laughing. "And, of courses, that just pisses me off."

"Yeah," Wayne says, laughing with me.

"So, what do you mean, 'Do nothing'?"

"To see that all the manipulations, all the efforting, all of the self-deception, doesn't bring us any closer to the presence of this moment; to see that when we are busy doing things, we're not really listening, we're not really here. So, we're looking at the possibility that this doing is a kind of a trap. That it kind of lets us feel that we're going somewhere, that we're creating an illusion of kind of a goal, but, in reality, we're here. And what is calling for attention is here. So I wouldn't say that we're free of that tendency 'to do.' I was just answering you that that would be the response. But we're looking at looking; we're looking at seeing; we're looking at looking at the doing, at this incredibly agitated and nervous tendency to always want to have something on the fire, always to have a goal, always to have a yardstick, some way of measuring what kind of progress we're making. And part of this experiment is to see if it's possible to be without that. Even if only for a moment, just to be."

"So, if you drop the trappings, as you call them, then the energy has to come from oneself?"

Wayne nods. "Yes. Where else can it come from? The teacher can't see for you. The teacher can talk about what they're seeing, what's present for them. But the seeing has to be here. It's difficult. And it really can be very frustrating, I think, if one's looking for someone to take one by the hand, and say, 'Just do this, and everything will be okay.' But that to me . . ." He pauses to reflect on how he's expressing himself. "I don't know if that's self-deception, but it involves both of us – if we're making that kind of contract – in a very precarious situation." He takes another moment before continuing. "I think there's much more danger for the person doing the leading, but it's dangerous for both people. We can really get a sense of inflated worth. A lot of mischief can come out of that if we're the one who's going to show people the truth, so to speak. That's quite a heavy responsibility. So the approach here is to see if we can work together, look together. In this kind of together-working, can there be – I'll use the word again – a clarifying, a clarity that emerges, and I'm not saying that as a question, but I do see it happen. I don't want to be too equivocal out there."

"So people do – or can – achieve these moments of clarity by taking part in retreats here?"

"I wouldn't say that as a promise, but the experience here is that it does happen. I have seen it for myself."

"And would you equate that with awakening?"

"Yes. People are infinitely capable of waking up. The coming to is not dependent on the tradition. It manifests in human beings when there isn't the kind of entanglement with our beliefs, with our sense of oneself or one's separation or one's fantasies about one's self, one's idea. If there is a break in the continuity of that story, there can be an opening, a freshness, a seeing."

"I remember when I did a retreat here that that was an issue which came up a couple of times during the discussion periods, participants questioning whether or not awakening was actually possible. And, as I remember the discussion, there seemed to be doubt about that. My feeling was – and I remember saying this – that I think people often have an inflated idea of what awakening is which can get in the way of actually experiencing awakening."

Wayne nods his head. "That the feeling or idea of what awakening consists of gets in the way of a spontaneous or a free opening? Yes, I would agree with that. I'll put it the way it happens here. We read about something – enlightenment stories or awakening stories – or we hear somebody talking about this awakening, and not surprisingly, with a lot of ideas flowing, a lot of images, and hopes and dreams. And I think within or without traditions, within the Zen tradition or other meditative traditions, when there is a genuine coming to, waking up, it's discovered it's not what we imagined or wanted or thought it was. It's none of that. It's not thought. It's not imagination. And maybe that's part of the discovery, that we're living our lives in the imagination, in the realm of thought, in the realm of ideas. Not that there's anything wrong with thought, we just think that our thought is reality, that it's all there is in some ways. And we also think that because I've thought something it's invariably true. Again, this work is beginning to look at thought in a more open, unbiased way. To see thought as thought."

From my perspective, what is happening at Springwater is still within the Zen tradition. Wayne admitted as much when I first wrote asking for an interview. In that letter I mentioned that I was aware the center was no longer directly affiliated with Zen. Wayne wrote back: "While we are not a Buddhist Center we are incorporated as a Zen Center. The late Roshi Kapleau once wrote that the 'spirit of Zen is all pervading.' So legally, and perhaps in spirit, we are in the Zen tradition."

The concept of upayas – skillful means appropriate to the needs of the student – is basic to Mahayana Buddhism. Perhaps Springwater, then, is an upaya for people – as Wayne describes them – "who like the idea that they're not committing to a religious system – to a hierarchy – where someone will tell them what to do."

It strikes me that one reason why there can be Christian Zen practitioners like Hugo Lassalle and Valerie Forstman is because the insights Zen helps people attain are universal. There are individuals like Rinsen Weik – and the author – who had experiences long before they knew anything about Buddhism which were later confirmed as kensho. As Tenku put it, "There are things we all already know on a deep level. Zen Buddhism isn't something that can be taught conceptually, but rather our practice helps us to understand what we already know."

The structures within which the work of Zen takes place in North America still retain a predominantly Asian flavor. But it doesn't need to, as Koun Franz – who maintains those structures himself – admitted. "What is important," he told me, "is that we don't design it ourselves." And that is also certainly true. The history of religion is filled with cautionary tales of self-proclaimed prophets who caused enormous harm to others.

One of the important roles the institutional structure plays is in identifying persons who are the heirs of a long and continually evolving spiritual tradition with a proven track record, teachers whom prospective students can turn to with some confidence. That is the reasoning behind the emphasis put on the importance of formal transmission in Zen.

It is something I ask Wayne about: "In more traditional communities, if the primary teacher dies or retires, if he hasn't left a Dharma heir, one can be recruited from the same lineage or a related lineage. What about Springwater? Do you have an anxiety about what will happen when the current teachers – who, you've admitted, were largely chosen by Toni – have passed on? What is your level of confidence that Springwater will survive Wayne Coger and kin?"

"Springwater can easily survive Wayne Coger," he says, laughing softly. He sits silent for a moment. "Toni used to say, whenever I brought up a question like that, that this work is vital; that it's important, and that it's worthwhile. I'm not quoting exactly. And that the work itself, because it's vital, because it's worthwhile, she had no worries about the continuity of that work. In that spirit, I don't know what will survive. I don't know if Springwater itself will survive as an institution, but the work is not dependent on Springwater, or me, or the group."

"You mean this type of reflection has always been a way in which human beings respond to being alive."

"Yeah."

"And that's not likely to go away?" I say, pushing him.

"That's a way of putting, although I didn't exactly get there. Let's see if I can find another way to put it: That this what we're calling awakening is our natural state. It is not something outside of us, and this expression of dissatisfaction with how we're living, how we're living in conflict, how we're hurting each other, discovering how much suffering there is in the world, I don't think that's going away either. Maybe it's a germ within us, the desire to really see if there's a different way of living, a different way of being. I think, with confidence, that that won't go away either."

My conversation with Rinzan Pechovnik took place several months later. His was the last I conducted for this book, and, when we were wrapping up, I asked if there'd been anything we hadn't covered that he'd like to discuss. He reflected a moment, then said there was. I turned the recorder back on.

"I often ask myself, 'Where is Zen going?' Here's Zen in America, and we still maintain – I still maintain – the artifice of a Japanese system. And there are people who ask, 'What does Zen in America need? What do we need to do to accommodate it for America?' And I don't think that's necessary. I don't think that it needs to be guided. We're entering a third or fourth generation, and it has already morphed on its own and will continue to do so. I don't think we need to rush the river in order to make it American. I think we run the risk – whatever form of Buddhism you're bringing over – we run the risk of our ego getting involved, and our agendas getting involved in the sense of what we think would be good or helpful, as opposed to just letting drift happen. We try things and see if they fit. But not so much laying out a plan for it. Because it is alive. I feel that in my own life, that this practice and this lineage is alive. It's here alive in me. Does it look the same way it would have with Hakuin? Absolutely not. Not even with my teacher's teachers would it have looked the same. So just giving it attention, letting it grow, and being open, while at the same time respecting what has been. I think it's going to do what it needs to do. And if it survives for another hundred years, it'll look different and maybe people will have more western clothing and won't be confused with sushi chefs or martial artists. But I think that will simply happen, and, until then, we play with this strange artifice. We let it express itself."

They were the last words of the last interview I conducted. There really was nothing more to add.

Afterword

by Dosho Port Roshi
Nebraska Zen Center

Become a Buddha. Become fully awake. Live that awakened life. The Buddha gave good teachings about how to do that. The Eightfold path really works. We don't want Buddha to become an ideology. We want awakened mind and compassionate action to define you. If you want to call that Buddhist, okay.[313]

Shinge Roshi says it clearly. That's the point of the Zen story – become a Buddha.

To realize the same heart mind as the Buddha has been the guiding inspiration for many thousands of people through the many generations since Shakyamuni Buddha walked on this little planet. Since then, we've taken 2,500 trips around the sun and our ancestors have finagled many innovations, often in difficult times. What a story it's been! Even in some 400 pages, Rick has chronicled just a bit of it here.

Where is the Zen movement at in North America now? Let me add to the story with some numbers. There are ethnic Buddhist centers with their own statistics, but just looking at the convert communities – Buddhist Modernist centers – my best guess is that currently fewer than 10,000 people are members of Zen Centers, although – because we are too small to have any central organization – that is an estimate only. There may be about five times that number that identify as "Zen" but are not now affiliated with an organized group. That would bring us to about 60,000 people. Of those, and despite "the monastery" being the central metaphor of the tradition, I estimate that there are only about 500 practitioners now living in monasteries, or about one percent.

---

313. Shinge Roko Sherry Chayat Roshi, pp. 371 above.

THE STORY OF ZEN

As Rick pointed out, the Zen boom in the '60s and '70s involved rapid growth but in only a handful of places. The monastic centers founded by the first or second generation of teachers have continued, (i.e., Tassajara, Zen Mountain Monastery, Dai Bosatsu, Hokyoji, etc.), but few new monasteries have been established in the last several decades. One notable exception is the Korinji Rinzai Zen Monastery in Reedsburg, Wisconsin, led by the relatively young teacher (meaning in his 50s) Meido Moore Roshi.

The first wave of growth in the few original groups (San Francisco, Los Angeles, New York, Rochester, etc.), has leveled off and most of the growth in the last few decades has been in a proliferation of small centers with thirty-fifty or fewer members, as a result of which most small-to-medium sized cities in the US and Canada have a Zen Center.

James Myoun Ford Roshi recently asked on Facebook for the names of groups that owned a building. He has an extensive network of Zen friends and gathered about seventy-five groups, but I assume he doesn't yet know quite everyone, so perhaps there are one-hundred groups that own a building. By the way, one-third were on the West Coast and two-thirds were widely distributed with no other clear pattern (including New York).

In the latest data available – about a decade old – the average birth year for a fully authorized Soto Zen priests was 1948 (71 years old as I write this). That may have changed a bit in the interim, but it is still clear that most teachers and most groups are in their 50s and 60s, mostly white, about two-thirds male, and mostly over educated. We may now be entering the "Great Die Off" period that James Ford spoke to Rick about.

So, after fifty years or so of zazen in North America, Zen is still a small denomination. And yet, for a group of this size, there seems to be a heightened sense of something of particular significance happening in the American religious experience that it represents. For example, there are thousands of books about Zen, perhaps as many books as there are Zen students! Given that Zen is largely about sitting down and shutting up, that's saying something.

And now what? Jeff Shore told Rick about Rinzai students seeking to learn why westerners are interested in Zen. Young Japanese Soto Zen priests are also looking to the West to see what's working, hoping to find inspiration and approaches that will save their dying religion. Meanwhile, a good share of the younger American Soto Zen teachers, look to Japan and align themselves with the styles of practice and organization they encountered in their Japanese Soto Zen training. It is a peculiar time!

In addition to the aging out of the Zen teacher and student groups, Zen in North America faces many challenges and opportunities. Let's look at the challenges first. Recently, I invited my "friends" on Facebook to offer their thoughts about the challenges and opportunities we face. In short order, about one hundred comments were made, many focused just on the challenges. That negative self-evaluation seems to me to be one of our challenges.

Another way of looking at our present situation is that we have come far in a short period of time. Even Zen master Yoda recognized, "Hard to see the future is – always in motion."

There are a couple of baskets of challenges. The first are challenges due to our culture and the pace of technological change. There are so many choices now for everything, including for spiritual practice. Zen works best for those inclined to depth work, and, even though awakening is sudden, it can take years for it to open and many more years to ripen sufficiently to help others. People today may be looking for much more of a quick, pharmacologically-driven fix than what Zen has to offer.

Our culture of "selfism," supported by the shallow intimacies of social media, support the disease now reaching epidemic proportions – extreme self-involvement, maintained with a very short attention span.

The secular mindfulness movement, with its focus on well-being, has framed how many people see Zen practice, instead of the deeper ground of being ("Become a Buddha") realization that is Zen's touchstone. It seems unlikely to me that the message of Zen will soon rise above this din and roar. In addition, among younger people, Zen is often seen as a relic of new-age hippyism. And the very accommodations that gentle Zen training provides for aging Boomers takes the rigor and challenge from the work for younger folks.

Another basket of challenges is in North American Zen itself. For a long time there has been a lack of diversity in Zen communities, not only in generation and gender but in terms of sexual orientation, gender identity, and ethnicity. This challenge seems to be now, finally, to be getting the focus in deserves. The last conference of the Soto Zen Buddhist Association, for example, focused on this issue.

Another area of challenge, as Rick describes, has been ethical issues, mainly of a sexual nature and reflective of an over-idealization of teachers. Strides have been made in awareness and in action in this area, and most teachers and centers now have actionable ethics policies.

And there are more challenges. We have yet to develop a financial model that works well so that the buildings and grounds can be cared for and staff – including teachers – compensated at a livable wage. In North America, progressive people tend to give considerably less to their church than more conservative folks. And given that most people who are members at Zen centers are left-leaning, the average give is small – I would estimate less than 1 percent of their annual income – where the average American gives about 3 percent. Partially as a result of this chronic underfunding, we are now looking at more and more poorly trained teachers entering the field.

To summarize the challenges, I'll share a comment that came up when we discussed the challenges and opportunities facing Zen in North America in one of my teaching venues, the "Vine of Obstacles: Online Support for Zen Training." An old Zen hand said, "Challenge: To take a system that has been overwhelmingly monastic for hundreds of years and transform it into something different without losing its essence."

He went on to say, "Opportunity: To take a system that has been overwhelmingly monastic for hundreds of years and transform it into something different without losing its essence."

Indeed.

Although the challenges may seem daunting, the opportunities are many and, in my view, much more powerful. As with the challenges, let's first look at those opportunities that are more cultural in nature. First, there is a growing number of "nones" and "unchurch." These are often young people who are keen to doubt. Great doubt is a foundation of Zen and so there is a natural bridge for nones and the unchurched. Further, there is a generational hunger among young people who often feel betrayed by earlier generations. For example, the climate crisis has left them with the feeling of being on the Titanic, and, instead of rearranging deck chairs, many young people are looking directly at their predicament: "We're doomed, now what?" Zen practice offers a path of wisdom and compassion to do what we can do and to face difficult times directly.

Second, there is the internet. As I pointed out above, the number of people interested in pursuing Zen deeply is small and widely dispersed. The internet is a tool that can connect practitioners who might be living in far-flung places, like Fredericton, New Brunswick, with teachers in equally far-flung places like Omaha, Nebraska. I sense that we are just beginning to tap the potential of the internet to support people doing dharma practice. Many of the present efforts are like pouring old wine into a new bottle instead of brewing up something new and especially suited to this technology.

What opportunities are specific to North American Zen? First, we have, by and large, well-trained teachers. A survey on a teacher listserve found that the average teacher had trained for twenty-five years before authorization. Contrast that with the standard in the secular mindfulness or yoga worlds – where you might be qualified to teach after a single weekend – and I think most people would agree.

We are also in what may be the beginning of a very rich hybridization of the Soto and Rinzai schools. The majority of the teachers Rick interviewed for the last chapter of this book have roots in both traditions. This mixing represents the best of the Japanese tradition as expressed by both Dogen and Hakuin.

But the primary opportunity is that the Buddhadharma is an incredible process for living a deeply meaningful life with minimal resources in whatever situation you may be in. If you give yourself the opportunity to go deeply into the tradition, you give yourself to something bigger, a different paradigm than just "me, myself, and I." Isn't that what so many people are hungry for? Giving yourself deeply to the Buddhadharma involves intimacy with a community and support in changing – and maybe even catastrophic – times. It involves the close mentorship that comes from a teacher-student relationship, seeing and being seen through. It includes the deeply settled heart of samadhi and awakening through and through. Finally, I promise you, if you give yourself to the Buddhadharma, you will be taken by surprise.

A student on the "Vine of Obstacles" wrote": "It is true that Zen is not for all, but I also believe Zen too is radically unfinished/empty and there is more possibility."

Acknowledgments

My thanks to everyone who agreed to be interviewed for this and my previous books. You were all gracious and patient with me.

- Nikki Abraham (Oak Tree in the Garden)
- Hadrian Abbot (Tahoma Sogenji)
- Helen Amerongen (Picture Rocks Retreat Center)
- Andy Anderson (Springwater Center)
- Geoffrey Shugen Arnold (Mountains and Rivers Order)
- Chimyo Atkinson (Great Tree Zen Temple)
- Josh Barton (Greater Boston Zen Center)
- Jan Chozen Bays (Great Vow Zen Monastery)
- Sarah Bender (Springs Mountain Sangha)
- Frances Mitra Bishop (Mountain Gate)
- Melissa Myozen Blacker (Worcester Zen Community)
- Bruce Blackman (Zen Community of Baltimore)
- Fr. Roger Brennan (Oak Tree in the Garden)
- Louis Bricault (Montreal Zen Center)
- Roger Brouillette (Montreal Zen Center)
- Ti'an Callery (Vermont Zen Center)
- Shinge Roko Sherry Chayat (Dai Bosatsu Zendo)
- Wayne Coger (Springwater Center)
- Brother Contemplation [Quan Chieu/Taylor Rentz] (Blue Cliff Monastery)
- Hugh and Susan Curran (Morgan Bay Zendo).
- Dr. Ann Cutcher (Enso House)
- Shawn Daley (Abbaye Notre-Dame du Calvaire)
- Sister Dang Nghiem [Huong Huynh] (Blue Cliff Monastery).
- Lodru Dawa (Great Vow Zen Monastery)
- Roch Denis (Montreal Zen Center)
- Joan Yushin Derrick (Zen Mountain Monastery)
- Monique Dumont (Montreal Zen Center)
- Bonnie Durland (Springwater Center)
- Garrett Evans (Great Vow Zen Monastery)

- Christopher Ezzell (Puget Sound Zen Center)
- Carole Ferrari (Toronto Zen Center)
- Michael Fieleke (Morning Star Zen Sangha)
- Katherine Foo (Worcester Zen Community)
- James Myoun Ford (Blue Cliff Sangha)
- Valerie Forstman (Maria Kannon Zen Center)
- Koun Franz (Zen Nova Scotia)
- Brother Fulfillment [Phap Man/Aaron Solomon] (Blue Cliff Monastery)
- Patrick Gallagher (Oak Tree in the Garden)
- Gerardo Gally (Casa Zen – Mexico City)
- Tetsugen Bernie Glassman (Zen Peacemakers)
- Sandra González (Springwater Center)
- Sunyana Graef (Vermont Zen Center)
- Jodo Tina Grant (Dai Bosatsu Zendo)
- Kelly Anne Graves (Great Vow Zen Monastery)
- Malcolm Griffin (Montreal Zen Center)
- Susan and Charles Guilford (Morgan Bay Zendo)
- Maria Reis Habito (Museum of World Religions)
- Ruben Habito (Maria Kannon Center)
- Zenshin Michael Haederle (Albuquerque Insight Meditation Center)
- Blanche Hartman (San Francisco Zen Center)
- Nancy Hathaway (Morgan Bay Zendo)
- Taigen Henderson (Toronto Zen Center)
- Father Kevin Hunt (Day Star Zendo)
- Dokuro Jaeckel (Charles River Zen)
- Father Robert Kennedy (Morning Star Zendo)
- Jody Hojin Kimmel (Zen Mountain Monastery)
- Bodhin Kjolhede (Rochester Zen Center)
- MyoO Renate Krämer (Enso House)
- Dairin Larry Larrick (Tahoma Sogenji)
- Myo On Susan Linnell (Albuquerque Zero Zen Center)
- Albert Low (Montreal Zen Center)
- Sister Elaine MacInnes (Freeing the Human Spirit)
- Seiju Mammoser (Albuquerque Zen Center)
- Konrad Ryushin Marchaj (Zen Mountain Monastery)
- Genjo Marinello (Chobo-ji, Seattle)
- Eshu Martin (Zenwest)
- Levi McGovern (Great Vow Zen Monastery)
- Gary Morgan (Great Vow Zen Monastery)
- Fr. Greg Mayers (Mercy Center)
- Seiho Morris (Chobo-ji, Seattle)
- Zengetsū Myōkyō (Enpuku-ji)
- Tenney Nathanson (Desert Rain Zen)

Acknowledgments

- Rinzan Pechovnik (No Rank Zendo)
- Jeffrey Onjin Plant (Zen Mountain Monastery)
- Mihaela Poca (Toronto Zen Center)
- Dosho Port (Great Tides Zen)
- John Pulleyn (Rochester Zen Center)
- David Yoshin Radin (Ithaca Zen Center)
- Marcia Khadija Radin (Body Mind Restoration Retreats)
- Bobby Rhodes (Kwan Um School)
- Robert Moshin Ricci (Zen Mountain Monastery)
- Dharman Rice (Vermont Zen Center)
- Sr. Janet Richardson (Clare Sangha)
- Tenku Ruff (Northern Westchester Zen Center)
- Kaijo Matthew Russell (Dai Bosatsu Zendo)
- David Dae An Ryneck (Worcester Zen Community)
- Stephen Zenki Salad (Great Tides Zen)
- Shea Ikusei Settimi (Zen Mountain Monastery)
- Jeff Shore (Hanazono University)
- Richard Shrobe (Kwan Um School)
- Henry Shukman (Mountain Cloud Zen Center)
- Stephen Slottow (Picture Rocks Retreat Center)
- Myoki Stewart (San Francisco Zen Center)
- Myogen Steve Stucky (San Francisco Zen Center)
- Joan Sutherland (Awakened Life)
- John Tarrant (Pacific Zen Institute)
- Peter Torma (Enso House)
- Cynthia Trowbridge (Enso House)
- Edie Tsong (Awakened Life)
- Brother Phap Vu [Clifford Brown] (Blue Cliff Monastery)
- Robert Waldinger (Henry David Thoreau Zen Sangha)
- Michael Waldron (Mountain Cloud Zen Center)
- David Weinstein (Pacific Zen Institute)
- Mel Weitsman (San Francisco Zen Center)
- Jean Ann Wertz (Zen Mountain Monastery)
- Gerry Shishin Wick (Great Mountain Zen Center at Maitreya Abbey)
- Jay Rinsen Weik (Buddhist Temple of Toledo)
- Lisa Tetsugan Zummach (Nebraska Zen Center)

Bibliography

Abe, Masao (ed.), *A Zen Life: D.T. Suzuki Remembered*. New York: Weatherhill, 1986

Addiss, Stephen and Stanley Lombardo and Judith Roitman (eds.), *Zen Sourcebook*. Indianapolis: Hackett Publishing Company, 2008.

Aitken, Robert. *Encouraging Words*. New York: Pantheon, 1993.

Aitken, Robert. *The Gateless Gate*. New York: North Point Press, 1991.

Aitken, Robert, *Taking the Path of Zen*. New York: North Point Press, 1982.

Baroni, Helen J. *Love, Roshi*. Albany: State University of New York Press, 2012.

Batchelor, Stephen, *The Awakening of the West*. Williamsville, VT: Echo Point Books, 2011.

Benoit, Hubert, *The Supreme Doctrine*. Eastbourne: Sussex Academic Press, 1998.

Berg, Stephen (trans.), *Crow with No Mouth*. Port Townsend, WA: Copper Canyon Press, 2000.

Blyth, R. H. *Zen in English Literature and Oriental Classics*. Mineola, NY: Dover Publications, 2003.

Boucher, Sandy. *Turning the Wheel*. Boston: Beacon Press, 1988.

Braverman, Arthur (ed. and trans.), *Warrior of Zen*. New York: Kodansha International, 1994.

Campbell, Joseph, *The Masks of God: Oriental Mythology*. New York: Viking Press, 1962.

Chadwick, David. *Crooked Cucumber*. New York: Broadway Books, 1999.

Cleary, Thomas (trans.), *Shobogenzo: Zen Essays by Dogen*. Honolulu: University of Hawaii Press, 1986.

Cleary, Thomas, *Timeless Spring*. Rutland, VT: Tuttle Publishing, 1980.

Cleary, Thomas, *The Undying Lamp of Zen*. Boston: Shambhala, 1993.

Cleary, Thomas [trans. and edit], *Zen Antics*. Boston: Shambala, 1993.

Coleman, James William. *The New Buddhism*. New York: Oxford University Press, 2002.

Cook, Francis Dojun Cook [trans.], *How to Raise an Ox*. Boston: Wisdom Publications, 2002.

Coomaraswamy, Ananda. *Buddha and the Gospel of Buddhism.* Secaucus, NJ: Citadel Press, 1988.
Downing, Michael. *Shoes Outside the Door.* Washington DC: Counterpoint, 2002.
Dumoulin, Heinrich. *Zen Buddhism: A History – India and China.* Bloomington: World Wisdom, 2005.
Dumoulin, Heinrich. *Zen Buddhism: A History – Japan.* Bloomington: World Wisdom, 1990.
Durant, Will. *Our Oriental Heritage.* New York: MFJ Books, 1993.
Enomiya-Lassalle, Hugo M. *The Practice of Zen Meditation.* London: Thorsons, 1990.
Ferguson, Andy. *Zen's Chinese Heritage.* Boston: Wisdom Publications, 2000.
Fields, Rick. *How the Swans Came to the Lake.* Boston: Shambhala, 1992.
Ford, James Ismael. *In This Very Moment.* Newburyport, MA: Red Wheel, 2004.
Ford, James Ishmael. *Zen Master Who?* Boston: Wisdom Publications, 2006.
Franz, Tracy. *My Year of Dirt and Water.* Berkeley: Stone Bridge Press, 2018.
Friedman, Lenore. *Meetings with Remarkable Women.* Boston: Shambhala, 2000.
Furlong, Monica. *Zen Effects.* Woodstock, VT: Skylight Paths Publishing, 2001.
Furuta, Shoken. *Sengai: Master Zen Painter.* New York: Kodansha International, 2000.
Goddard, Dwight (ed.). *A Buddhist Bible.* Guildford, UK: Whitecrow Press, 2010.
Goldberg, Natalie. *The Great Failure.* New York: HarperOne, 2005.
Goldberg, Natalie. *Long Quiet Highway.* New York: Bantam, 1994.
Halper, Jon (ed.). *Gary Snyder; Dimensions of a Life.* San Francisco: Sierra Club Books, 1991.
Havnevik, Hanna, et. al., (eds). *Buddhist Modernities.* New York: Routledge, 2017.
Heine, Steven and Dale S. Wright (eds). *Zen Masters.* New York: Oxford University Press, 2010.
Hoover, Thomas. *The Zen Experience.* New York: New American Library, 1980.
Hotz, Michael (ed.). *Holding the Lotus to the Rock.* New York: Four Walls Eight Windows, 2003.
Kapleau, Philip. *Straight to the Heart of Zen.* Boston: Shambhala, 2001.
Kapleau, Philip (et al., eds), *The Three Pillars of Zen.* New York: Anchor, 1989.

Kapleau, Philip. *Zen: Merging of East and West*. New York: Anchor, 1989.
Katagiri, Dainin. *Each Moment Is the Universe*. Boston: Shambhala, 2011.
Katagiri, Dainin. *Returning to Silence*. Boston: Shambhala, 1988.
Kennett, Jiyu. *Zen Is Eternal Life*. Shasta Abbey Press, 2000.
Kerouac, Jack. *The Dharma Bums*. New York: Signet Books, 1959.
Kornfield, Jack. *After the Ecstasy, the Laundry*. New York: Bantam, 2001.
Kraft, Kenneth (ed.). *Zen Teaching, Zen Practice*. Boston: Weatherhill, 2000.
Kraft, Kenneth (ed.). *Zen: Tradition and Transition*. New York: Grove/Atlantic, 1988.
LeVine, Sarah. *A Brief History of Moonspring Hermitage*. Surry, ME: Morgan Bay Zendo, 2008.
Lin Yutang (tr. ed.). *The Wisdom of Laotse*. New York: The Modern Library, 1948.
Long, Philomene. *American Zen Bones*. Los Angeles: Beyond Baroque Books, 1999.
Loori, John Daido (ed.). *Sitting with Koans*. Boston: Wisdom Publications, 2006
Low, Albert. *Hakuin on Kensho*. Boston: Shambhala, 2006.
Low, Albert. *What More Do You Want*. Rutland, VT: Tuttle Publishing, 2013.
Low, Albert. *The World: A Gateway*. Rutland, VT: Tuttle Publishing, 1995.
Low, Albert. *Zen and the Sutras*. Rutland, VT: Tuttle, 1999.
Low, Albert. *Zen Meditation Plain and Simple*. Rutland, VT: Tuttle Publishing, 2000.
Maezumi, Taizan. *Teaching of the Great Mountain*. Rutland, VT: Tuttle Publishing, 2001.
Maezumi, Taizan, and Glassman, Bernie. *On Zen Practice*. Boston: Wisdom Publications, 2002.
Martin, Andrea. *Ceaseless Effort: The Life of Dainin Katagiri*. Published by the Minnesota Zen Meditation Center: http://mnzencenter.org/katagiri/bio_pdf/katagiri_biography.pdf.
Martin-Smith, Keith. *A Heart Blown Open*. Studio City, CA: Divine Arts, 2011.
Matthiessen, Peter. *Nine-Headed Dragon River*. Boston: Shambhala, 1998.
McDaniel, Richard Bryan. *Catholicism and Zen*. Richmond Hill, ON: Sumeru, 2017.
McDaniel, Richard Bryan. *Cypress Trees in the Garden*. Richmond Hill, ON: Sumeru, 2015.
McDaniel, Richard Bryan. *The Third Step East: Zen Masters of America*. Richmond Hill, ON: Sumeru, 2015.
McDaniel, Richard Bryan. *Zen Masters of China: The First Step East*. Rutland, VT: Tuttle Publishing, 2012.

McDaniel, Richard Bryan. *Zen Masters of Japan: The Second Step East.* Rutland, VT: Tuttle Publishing, 2013.
Merton, Thomas. *The Way of Chuang Tzu.* New York: New Directions, 1965.
Mitchell, Elsie P. *Sun Buddhas Moon Buddhas.* New York: Weatherhill, 1973.
Miura, Isshu, and Sasaki, Ruth Fuller. *Zen Dust.* New York: Harcourt, Brace & World, 1966.
Morgan, Bill. *The Typewriter Is Holy.* Berkeley: Counterpoint, 2010.
Murphy, Sean. *One Bird, One Stone.* New York: Renaissance Books, 2002.
Nordstrom, Louis (ed.). *Namu Dai Bosa.* New York: Theatre Arts Books, 1976.
Nukariya, Kaiten. *The Religion of the Samurai.* New York: Taylor and Francis, 2005.
Olivelle, Patrick (trans.). *Upanishads.* Oxford World's Classics, 2008.
Omori Sogen. *An Introduction to Zen Training.* Rutland, VT: Tuttle Publishing, 2001.
Oppenheimer, Mark. *The Zen Predator of the Upper East Side.* The Atlantic Books, 2013.
Port, Dosho Mike. *Keep Me in Your Heart a While.* Boston: Wisdom Publications, 2009.
Prabhavananda, Swami, and Isherwood, Christopher, (trans.). *The Song of God: Bhagavad-Gita.* (New York: New American Library, 1951.
Red Pine (tr.). *Lao Tsu's Teaching.* Port Townsend, WA: Copper Canyon Press, 2009.
Reps, Paul and Nyogen Senzaki. *Zen Flesh, Zen Bones.* Rutland, VT: Tuttle Publishing, 1998.
Rochester Zen Center. *Chants and Recitations.* Rochester, NY: Rochester Zen Center, 2005.
Ryokan. *One Robe, One Bowl: The Zen Poetry of Ryokan.* Boston: Weatherhill, 2006.
Schlütter, Morten. *How Zen Became Zen.* Honolulu: University of Hawai'i Press, 2008.
Schneider, David. *Street Zen.* Boston: Shambhala, 1993.
Sekida, Katsuki. *Two Zen Classics.* Boston: Shambhala, 2005.
Senzaki, Nyogen. *Eloquent Silence* (ed. Sherry Chayat). Boston: Wisdom Publications, 2008.
Senzaki, Nyogen. *Like a Dream, Like a Fantasy.* Boston: Wisdom Publications, 2005
Shodo Harada. *The Path to Bodhidharma.* Rutland, VT: Tuttle Publishing, 2000.
Snyder, Gary and Jim Harrison and Paul Ebenkamp (ed.). *The Etiquette of Freedom.* Berkeley: Counterpoint, 2010.

Snyder, Gary. *The Gary Snyder Reader*. Washington D C: Counterpoint, 2012.

Snyder, Gary. *Riprap and Cold Mountain Poems*. Berkeley: Counterpoint, 2010.

Suiter, John. *Poets on the Peaks*. Washington D C: Counterpoint, 2002.

Suzuki, D.T. *Essays in Zen Buddhism: First Series*. New York: Grove Press, 1994.

Suzuki, D.T. *Essays in Zen Buddhism: Third Series*. Newburyport, MA: Samuel Weiser, 1971.

Suzuki, D.T. *The Field of Zen*. New York: Perennial Library, 1970.

Suzuki, D.T. *Manual of Zen Buddhism*. New York: Grove Press, 1960. Digital edition: http://www.buddhanet.net/pdf_file/manual_zen.pdf

Suzuki, D.T. *Sengai: The Zen of Ink and Paper*. Boston: Shambhala, 1999.

Suzuki, D.T. *Zen and Japanese Culture*. Princeton: Princeton University Press, 2010.

Suzuki, D.T. *The Zen Doctrine of No-Mind*. Newburyport, MA: Samuel Weiser, 1991.

Suzuki, Shunryu. *Zen Mind, Beginner's Mind*. Boston: Shambhala, 2011.

Tames, Richard. *A Traveller's History of Japan*. New York: Interlink Books, 2008.

Tanahashi, Kasuaki (ed. and trans). *Endless Vow: The Zen Path of Soen Nakagawa*. Boston: Shambala, 1996.

Tarrant, John. *Bring Me the Rhinoceros*. Boston: Shambhala, 2008.

Tarrant, John. *The Light Inside the Dark*. New York: Harper, 1998.

Tetsu, Tim. *Touching Ground*. Somerville, MA: Wisdom, 2018.

Tworkov, Helen. *Zen in America*. New York: Kodansha USA, 1994.

Ueda, Makoto. *The Master Haiku Poet Matsuo Basho*. Tokyo: Kodansha International, 1982.

Van de Wetering, Janwillem. *Afterzen*. New York: St. Martin's, 2001.

Van de Wetering, Janwillem. *The Empty Mirror*. New York: St. Martin's, 1999.

Van de Wetering, Janwillem. *A Glimpse of Nothingness*. New York: St. Martin's, 1999.

Victoria, Brian Daizen. *Zen at War*. Oxford: Rowman and Littlefield, 2006.

Waddell, Norman. *The Unborn: The Life and Teachings of Zen Master Bankei*. New York: North Point Press, 1984.

Watson, Burton (trans.). *The Complete Works of Chuang Tzu*. New York: Columbia University Press, 1968.

Watts, Alan. *In My Own Way*. Novato, CA: New World Library, 2007.

Watts, Alan. *This Is It*. New York: Vintage, 1973.

Watts, Alan, *Tao: The Watercourse Way*. New York: Pantheon, 1975.

Watts, Alan. *The Way of Zen*. New York: Vintage, 1999.
Wright, Robert. *Why Buddhism Is True*. New York: Simon & Schuster, 2017.
Yamada, Koun. *The Gateless Gate*. Boston: Wisdom Publications, 2004.
Yampolsky, Philip B. (trans. and ed.). *The Platform Sutra of the Sixth Patriarch*. New York: Columbia University Press, 1967.
Zen Notes published by the First Zen Institute of America, http://www.firstzen.org/ZenNotesOnLine.php

Glossary

Anatman (Anatta in Pali) – One of the Three Characteristics of Existence, which see.

Ango – 90 day intensive training period.

Annica – One of the Three Characteristics of Existence, which see.

Arhat – In early Buddhism, one who achieves liberation from false perception

Arhatta – In early Buddhism, the state of being free from false perception; roughly equivalent to enlightenment.

Atman – The individual "self" subject to rebirth. In pre-Buddhist Indian thought, the Atman was assumed to be of the same or like substance with Brahman, the underlying reality of the Universe.

Awakening – One of several terms referring to achieving insight into the basic interconnectedness of all of Being.

AZTA – American Zen Teachers Association.

Bhikkhu (Bhikshu in Sanskrit) – Early Buddhist term for a monk. Literally, it refers to one who begs for his sustenance.

Bodhidharma – Legendary Indian figure who brought Zen to China. Bodhidharma is considered the 28th patriarch of India Buddhism and the first patriarch of Chinese Zen.

Bodhisattva – An enlightened (Bodhi) being (sattva). Certain historical or legendary Bodhisattvas function much the same as Saints in the Christian tradition.

Brahman – In Vedantic thought, the underlying reality of the Universe. Cf. Atman.

Buddha – Literally, "The Awakened One." When used with a capital B, it usually refers to the historic Buddha, Siddhartha Gautama. With a lower-case b, it refers to any enlightened being.

Buddha Hall – In temples, the hall where devotional activities such as chanting are carried out. The hall normally contains an image of the Buddha.

Buddhahood – The state of being fully awakened.

Caodong – Chinese term for "Soto."

Chan – Chinese term which the Japanese pronounced as "Zen," meaning meditation.
Chanoyu – Ritual Japanese tea ceremony.
Dai- – A prefix meaning "great," as in Dai-kensho.
Daimyo – Japanese term roughly equivalent to "Lord."
Daisan – Private meeting between teacher and student, similar to dokusan or sanzen.
Dao – Formerly "Tao." The "way." The term originates in Daoism (Taoism) and refers to the fundamental nature of reality.
Daoism – The teaching regarding the nature of the Dao.
Daodejing – Formerly Tao Te Ching. The basic text of Daoism.
Denbo – In some schools of Rinzai Zen, the second of three stages in the transmission process, culminating in inka shomei.
Denkai – In some schools of Rinzai Zen, the first of three stages in the transmission process, culminating in inka shomei.
Dharma – A term with multiple meanings but generally referring to the teachings of Buddhism.
Dharma Heir – The heir of a Zen teacher whose understanding of the Dharma qualifies him/her to be a teacher as well.
Dharmakaya – In Mahayana Buddhism, one of the "three bodies [kaya]" of the Buddha. It is the realm of Emptiness from which all being arises and to which all being returns.
Dharma Transmission – see Transmission
Dhyana – Sanskrit term for "meditation," from which the Chinese term "chan" and the Japanese "zen" are derived.
-do – A suffix referring to a room or space dedicated to a specific activity or purpose. A zendo, for example, is area set aside for the practice of meditation (zen).
Dokusan – Private interview between student and teacher. Cf. Sanzen.
Dukkha – The first Noble Truth, the reality of suffering. One of the Three Characteristics of Existence, which see.
Eightfold Path – See "Four Noble Truths."
Emptiness (Sunyata) – A basic and easily misunderstood Buddhist concept about the nature of Reality. Essentially, emptiness refers to an intuition (rather than an intellectual understanding) of the fact that all things are empty of self-nature, i.e., are composed of a variety of elements which are in a constant state of flux and are interdependent with all other elements. The term may also refer to the formless—and yet creative—Void from which all things arise and to which they return.
Five Defilements – See Klesas.
Four Noble Truths – 1) All of existence is characterized by suffering [dukkha]; 2) Suffering is caused by craving; 3) Suffering can be

ameliorated by overcoming craving; 4) Craving can be overcome by following the Noble Eightfold path, which consists of right view, right intention, right speech, right action, right livelihood, right effort, right mindfulness, and right meditation.

Four Vows (or Bodhisattva Vows) – 1) To save (liberate) all beings; 2) to eliminate endless blind passions; 3) to pass innumerable Dharma Gates; 4) to achieve the great way of Buddha.

Fusu – A temple official in charge of administrative and financial matters.

Gassho – To bring the palms of the hands together, often accompanied by a bow. It is a sign of respect and reverence.

Go – A two person board game which originated in China about the 5th century BCE.

Gongan – Chinese term for koan.

Guanyin – See Kannon

Hara – The abdomen, especially when understood as a person's center.

Hua tou – see Wato

Heart Sutra – A short sutra on "emptiness" frequently chanted in Zen monasteries and temples.

Hinayana – "The Lesser Vehicle." A term used in Mahayana Buddhism to refer to earlier schools of Buddhism. Those schools prefer the term Theravada, The Way of the Elders.

Hondo – The main hall of a Japanese Temple. Cf. Buddha Hall.

Hungry Ghosts – "Pretas." Hungry Ghosts are images of the unquenchable appetites to which all persons are subject.

Ikebana – Flower arranging.

Inji – The attendant to an abbot or teacher.

Inka (inka shomei) – "Authorized seal proving attainment." Official transmission, especially in the Rinzai School. It is the recognition by a teacher that the student has completed training and is ready to teach independently.

Jataka Tales – Popular folk tales about the previous lives of the Buddha in various animal and human forms.

-ji – A suffix meaning "temple."

Jikijitsu – The monitor in charge of a zendo.

Jukai – Formally accepting the Precepts and becoming a Buddhist.

Kanji – Japanese adaptation of Chinese ideograms.

Kannon – "Guanyin" in Chinese. The female Bodhisattva of Compassion.

Karma – Literally, "action." The concept in Asian thought that actions have consequences. Popularly viewed as one's past actions, in this or previous lives, resulting in one's current situation.

Karuna – Compassion.

Katsu! – A tradition but meaningless shout, sometimes expressed as "Ho!"

Kendo – The Do (way) of the sword – Japanese swordsmanship.

Kensho – Seeing into one's True Nature. Enlightenment.

Kinhin – Walking meditation.

Klesas – The Five Defilements or Poisons: Ignorance, Attachment, Anger, Pride, and Envy.

Koan – (Gongan in Chinese. The plural of "koan" is "koan.") Usually an anecdote from the lives of the Zen masters of the past—primarily those in Tang Dynasty China—often expressed in the form of a question. The question or situation described becomes the focus of a Zen student's meditative practice and helps the student attain insight. While koan cannot be resolved through reasoning, an understanding of them can be achieved through intuition. Individual koan are referred to as "Cases," in the sense of legal precedences in jurisprudence.

Kyosaku – "The Encouragement Stick." A long stick flattened at one end, used by monitors during zazen to encourage (or wake up) meditators.

Li – In Daoism, the constantly new, non-repetitive, and creative patterns that arise in nature

Linji – The Chinese name of Rinzai.

Maha Prajna Paramita – The great wisdom that carries one to the other side.

Mahasattva – A particularly advanced Bodhisattva.

Mahayana – "The Greater Vehicle." The Buddhist schools which evolved from the earlier Theravada tradition, much as Protestantism evolved from Catholicism. Zen is a form of Mahayana Buddhism.

Maitreya – The Buddha of the future.

Makyo – Hallucinations to which meditators may be subject.

Mantra – A word, phrase, or short prayer which is repeated as a focus of meditation.

Maya – Illusion.

Metta – Loving-kindness.

Mettabhavana – Meditation on loving-kindness.

Middle Way – The Buddha's teaching, referring to a way of life mid-way between that of a householder and that of an ascetic.

Mondo (Wenda in Chinese) – A Zen dialogue.

Mu – "Wu" in Chinese. Meaning, "No, not, nothing." Usually refers to the opening koan in the Mumonkan: A student of the way asked Joshu in all seriousness, "Does a dog have Buddha-nature?" Joshu replied, "Mu!"

Muji – The koan "mu." See above.

Mumonkan – A classic koan collection, also known as The Gateless Gate.

Nirmanakaya – The body (kaya) of the Buddha as a physical individual who lived at a particular time in a particular place. See also "Dharmakaya."

Nirvana – In early Buddhism, the "blowing out" of the energy which seeks rebirth, achieved by overcoming desire and attaining arhatta.

Osho – Priest.

Ox-Herding Pictures – A series of ten illustrations portraying the stages of growth in Zen practice. The illustrations show a young man seeking, finding, and taming an ox.

Pali – The language in which most early Buddhist scriptures are composed.

Paramitas – The Six Perfections: generosity, ethical behavior, tolerance, diligence, concentration, and insight.

Parinirvana – Nirvana after death. Often refers to the death of the Buddha.

Prajna – Wisdom.

Prajna Paramita - "Perfection of Wisdom." In Mahayana Buddhism, the advanced teachings suitable only for those on the Bodhisattva path, in contrast to more general teachings such as the Four Noble Truths

Precepts – Ethical teachings Buddhists commit to abide by.

Rakusu – A bib-like garment representing the robe of the Buddha.

Realization – Realization of one's True Nature, and therefore realization of the True Nature of all of Being. Awakening.

Rinzai – The School of Zen practice derived from Linji Yixuan.

Rohatsu – The anniversary of the Buddha's enlightenment in December. The sesshin associated with this anniversary is considered the most daunting of the year.

Roshi – Literally, "Old Teacher." In North American Zen, it has come to mean a fully qualified Zen teacher.

Samadhi – The state of concentration or absorption.

Samsara – The repeated cycle of rebirth, life, and death.

Samu – Work period.

Samugi – Work clothes. Informal clothing worn by Zen monks.

-san – A Japanese suffix roughly equivalent to "Mr." or "Ms." It can also refer to a mountain, as in Tahoma-san.

Sanbo Zen (formerly Sanbo Kyodan) – Zen school combining elements of both the Rinzai and Soto traditions, derived from the teachings of Daiun Harada and Hakuun Yasutani.

Sangha – The community.

San matsu documents – Official documents of transmission, particularly in the Soto School of Zen.

Sanzen - Private interview between student and teacher. Cf. Dokusan.

Satori – Awakening, enlightenment.

Seiza – Traditional manner of sitting on one's heels in Japan.

Sensei – Teacher. In American Zen, usually implying less authority than a Roshi would have.

Sesshin – (The plural of "sesshin" is "sesshin.") A Zen retreat, traditionally seven days long.

Shika – In the Rinzai-ji system, the temple administrator. In other temple systems, the Guest Master.

Shikan Taza – Simple awareness as a meditation practice. In shikan taza, the meditator does not have a particular focus, such as the breath or a koan.

Shingon – A Buddhist sect brought to Japan from China by Kobo Daishi.

Shinto – Traditional pre- Buddhist Japanese religion.

Shodo – Calligraphy.

Shoji – In Japanese architecture, a window or door made of translucent paper stretched over a wooden frame.

Shoken – Taking individual vows with a single teacher.

Skhanda – The five aggregates or elements which make up a person. As enumerated in the Heart Sutra, these are: physical form, sensation, thought, impulse (choice), and consciousness.

Soto – The School of Zen descending from Sozan Honjaku and Tozan Ryokai.

Soto-shu – The administrative headquarters of the Soto Zen in Japan.

Sunyata – see emptiness

Susokkan – Breath meditation.

Sutra – In Buddhism, scriptural writings usually, but not always, attributed to the Buddha.

SZBA – Soto Zen Buddhist Association.

Taijitu – Traditional Chinese image of a light and dark tear drop shape forming a circle, representing the complimentary opposites of Yang and Yin.

Takuhatsu – Ritual begging.

Tan – A platform in a zendo on which meditators sit.

Tao – see Dao.

Taoism – see Daoism.

Tatami – A mat traditionally made of rice straw, twice as long as wide.

Tathagata – A title by which the Buddha referred to himself, meaning "The One Who Has Attained."

Teisho – A formal talk given by a Zen teacher.

Ten Ox-herding Pictures – see Ox-herding Pictures.

Tenzo – Temple cook.

Theravada – The preferred term referring to Buddhists in the Pali tradition.

Three Characteristics of Existence – Annica (impermanence), dukkha (suffering), anatta (no permanent self).

Three Gems – see Three Refuges

Three Refuges – Buddhists take "refuge" in the Buddha, the Dharma, and the Sangha.

Three Treasures – see Three Refuges.

Transmission – Formal recognition that an individual has completed their training and may become a teacher.

Tripitaka (The Three Baskets) – The canonical scriptures of Buddhism in three parts: (1) the Sutras (the recorded teachings of the Buddha); (2) the Abhidharma, a collection of commentaries on those sutras; and (3) the Vinaya (the rules governing monastic life).

Unsui – A postulant.

Upaya – Skillful means. The variety of techniques used by a teacher to assist a student to come to awakening.

Vedanta – Hindu philosophy.

Vipassana – Meditation techniques associated with Theravada Buddhism.

Void – see emptiness.

Wato (hua tou in Chinese)– A single word or image taken from a koan and used as a focus in meditation. "Mu" is a wato.

Wenda – See "mondo."

Wu – see Mu

Wu wei – A Daoist concept which can be translated as "non-action" or "non-interference," in the sense of an action that comes about without intent, without effort.

Yang and Yin – Yang and Yin are the traditional complimentary opposites in Chinese thought. Yang is masculine, light, dry, warm, and active; yin is feminine, dark, moist, cool, and passive. Yang is also considered positive and yin negative, although these are neutral terms in Daoist thought. The essential quality of Yang and Yin is that they arise simultaneously and interdependently.

Zabuton – The mat on which a meditation cushion (zafu) is placed.

Zafu – "Buddha" (fu) "seat" (za). A meditation cushion.

Zazen – (zuo chan in Chinese) Seated (za) meditation (zen).

Zen – Literally, "meditation." Zen Buddhism is the meditation school of Buddhism.

Zendo – The training area (do) in which students practice meditation (zen).

Zenji – A teacher of the Dharma.

Zuo Chan – See "zazen."

About the Author

Rick McDaniel taught at the University of New Brunswick and Saint Thomas University before starting a 27 year career in International Development and Fair Trade. He is the creator of the YMCA Peace Medallion.

A long time Zen practitioner, he is the author of *Zen Masters of China: The First Step East*, *Zen Masters of Japan: The Second Step East*, *The Third Step East: Zen Masters of America*, *Cypress Trees in the Garden: The Second Generation of Zen Teaching in America*, and *Catholicism and Zen*.

He can be reached at rickmcdaniel@bellaliant.net.

www.ingramcontent.com/pod-product-compliance
Lightning Source LLC
Chambersburg PA
CBHW021753230426
43669CB00006B/63